Young Sidney Hook

YOUNG
Sidney Hook

MARXIST AND PRAGMATIST

CHRISTOPHER PHELPS

CORNELL UNIVERSITY PRESS ITHACA AND LONDON

Library of Congress Cataloging-in-Publication Data

Phelps, Christopher, b. 1965
Young Sidney Hook : Marxist and pragmatist /
Christopher Phelps.
   p.   cm.
Includes bibliographical references and index.
ISBN 0-8014-3328-2 (alk. paper)
1. Hook, Sidney, 1902–1989.   I. Title.
B945.H684P48   1997
335.4—dc21   97-23738

Cloth printing
10 9 8 7 6 5 4 3 2 1

FOR

MARGARET DORSEY PHELPS

AND IN MEMORY OF

CHARLES DEXTER PHELPS, M.D.

(1937–1985)

He found the works of Sidney Hook sublime,
And planned to read Karl Marx when he had time.
　　　　　　　　　　　　—Granville Hicks, 1938

Contents

Acknowledgments

The writing of a biography may be less social than some forms of human production, but it is social nonetheless. My debts begin with several mentors who expanded my sense of the possibility of the past and guided me through the various incarnations of this biography. At Reed College, among many fine teachers, Ray Kierstead, Richard Fox, Julia Liss, and, above all, Casey Blake inspired me to take up cultural and intellectual history. At the University of Oregon, Howard Brick pointed me in the direction of Sidney Hook and, after I had warmed to the topic, provided me with valuable insight, criticism, and encouragement at every stage. Blake and Brick were exemplary teachers and advisers, and I continue to learn a great deal from each. At the University of Rochester, Robert Westbrook, Daniel Borus, and the late Christopher Lasch, whom I admired, further deepened and challenged my understanding of twentieth-century American intellectual history. My courses and conversations with Westbrook, along with his exacting and astute (if hieroglyphic) marginal notes, were particularly crucial to refining my thinking on American pragmatism.

Reconstructing Hook's life would have been far more difficult without the aid of those who shared their personal memories with me. His widow, the late Ann Hook, and his two sons, John B. Hook and Ernest B. Hook, were very gracious. Ernie Hook not only read the entire manuscript but spent virtually an entire day on the phone, giving me his reactions and advice without the slightest gesture toward censorship. Against the many horror stories of families thwarting the efforts of biographers, the Hook family stands as shining counterexample, especially since my political assessment of Sidney Hook is not shared by them, in the main.

Others who by various connections knew Sidney Hook between the 1920s and 1950s were very helpful and forthcoming, among them Daniel Bell, Theodore Draper, Sender Garlin, Albert Glotzer, Corliss Lamont, Freddy Paine, Meyer Schapiro, Morris U. Schappes, Diana Trilling, David Weiss, and B. J. Widick. In the case of a controversialist like Hook, the cooperation of such personal witnesses cannot be taken for granted. On several occasions I found my inquiries declined, often because of the suspicion or presumption that a biographer will automatically grind axes for his subject. The experience has convinced me that no biographer of Sidney Hook will satisfy every reader, though I hope through the exercise of rigorous, independent judgment to have repaid those who trusted me with their memories and perceptions. They have, no matter what, my gratitude.

Many who did not know Hook personally but lived in political proximity to him gave me assistance on various historical points. Survivors of the revolutionary anti-Stalinist socialist groups of the 1930s, including the American Workers Party and the Trotskyist movement, helped me to understand that experience: Alexander Buchman, Leon Goodman, Morris Lewitt, Ted Selander, and Mark Sharron. Herbert Aptheker, Dorothy Healey, and A. B. Magil, all Communists in the 1930s, answered my questions. Minor queries on the American Communist Party were answered expertly by historians Maurice Isserman and Harvey Klehr.

The principal research for this work lay in Hook's many published writings, for which Barbara Levine's *Sidney Hook: A Checklist of Writings* (1989) was indispensable. Hook's correspondence is scattered far and wide; a complete list of repositories consulted appears in the appendix. The most important collection by far is the Sidney Hook Papers at the Hoover Institution on War, Revolution, and Peace at Stanford University, where 185 boxes of Hook's personal papers and effects have been immaculately organized and catalogued in the superb register compiled by archivists Dale Reed and Rebecca Mead (1991). Many archivists assisted me, but Reed's help with a steady stream of requests over the years merits a special note. Grants from the University of Oregon Department of History, the Graduate School of the University of Oregon, and the Dexter Perkins Fund of the Department of History at the University of Rochester made my research possible. Above all, the generosity of my mother and father permitted me to reach the people who knew Hook as well as the archives that hold material on him. For all that my parents gave and continue to give me, including a love of learning and commitment to the public sphere, I dedicate this book to them.

In addition to Howard Brick and Robert Westbrook, the following people read the manuscript in whole or in part: Casey Blake, Daniel Borus, Joseph Fracchia, Jack Maddex, Jeffrey Ostler, Daniel Pope, and Alan Wald. Wald and I have had countless sharp, and therefore extremely useful, disagreements about the history of the intellectual left. He generously shared with me his substantial, thorough correspondence with Hook, now to be included in the Hook Papers at the Hoover Institution for use by other scholars. Because I began my research after Hook's death, I am indebted to S. A. Longstaff, Howard Brick, and Theodore Draper for permitting me to see the notes they took during interviews they conducted with Hook for their own research. I imposed upon Joseph Fracchia and Celia Applegate to translate from German, Michael Donnelly from Russian. Sally Hollier helped with a last-minute scramble for photographs. Peter Agree, my editor at Cornell, wisely paired the manuscript with Robert Cummings and Gregory Sumner, readers whose astute criticism proved immensely useful in the process of revision.

One area of agreement between pragmatism and Marxism, as the young Sidney Hook realized, is their mutual conviction that theory has little value without some connection to lived experience. This book is no exception. The understandings of socialism and democracy expressed in these pages owe much to my friends and comrades. In Solidarity and on the editorial board of *Against the Current*, especially, my politics have been tried, tested, refined, refuted—and in the end enhanced immeasurably. I am confident that the issues addressed by this biography are not of antiquarian interest, that they have a direct and practical import which will become apparent when popular power and social justice are again placed on the stage of history by egalitarian movements from below.

Last but always first, Carol Hollier accompanied me across the continent and back, assisted me in my research, and made it all worthwhile. With her by my side, I have written history under circumstances of my choosing. Serendipitously, our daughter Emma Eleanor arrived as this manuscript was making its way across the copyeditor's desk. Nothing adequately expresses the happy revolution Emma has brought to our lives, turning everything upside down, sometimes literally, and reaffirming my hope and wonder at the untold possibilities of the new.

CHRISTOPHER PHELPS

Eugene, Oregon

Abbreviations

Only the most frequently cited names and collections are abbreviated. A complete list of collections consulted appears in the appendix.

COLLECTIONS

Dewey Papers	John Dewey Papers, Southern Illinois University at Carbondale, Morris Library, Special Collections
Hook Papers	Sidney Hook Papers, Hoover Institution, Stanford University, Palo Alto, California
Hook-Dewey Collection	Sidney Hook Collection of John Dewey, Southern Illinois University at Carbondale, Special Collections
Wald Collection	Private Collection of Professor Alan Wald, Department of English Language and Literature, University of Michigan, Ann Arbor

NAMES

JD	John Dewey
SH	Sidney Hook

Young Sidney Hook

Introduction

At noon on May 23, 1985, the philosopher Sidney Hook attended a luncheon at the White House, where he dined with, among others, Jacques Yves Cousteau, the deep sea explorer; Air Force General E. "Chuck" Yeager, the first man to break the sound barrier; entertainers Jimmy Stewart and Frank Sinatra; and former UN Ambassador Jeane Kirkpatrick. All were there to receive the Medal of Freedom, America's highest civilian medal of honor. "My guess," offered President Ronald Reagan as he presented the awards, "is that probably as long as this nation lasts, your descendants will speak with pride of the day you attended a White House ceremony and received this, the Medal of Freedom. And 50 years from now, a century from now, historians will know your names and your achievements. You have left humanity a legacy."[1]

What is the legacy of Sidney Hook? To most observers, including Reagan, Hook's life was significant because of his tireless crusade from the 1940s through the 1980s against communism. The Medal of Freedom Citation that Reagan presented to Hook heralded the philosopher as "one

---

[1] Lisa McCormack, "America's Heroes Receive Their Due," *Washington Times*, 24 May 1985, 1B, 3B; Michael Deaver to SH, 26 March 1985 (Hook Papers, box 1). We may hope that those historians of the future will be more accurate than the Reagan administration, which misspelled Hook's first name as "Sydney" on his Medal of Freedom Citation (Hook Papers, box 1).

of the first to warn the intellectual world of its moral obligations and personal stake in the struggle between freedom and totalitarianism." Although to his last day Hook called himself a socialist, his relentless anti-communism had won him a respectful audience on the right. Few conservatives had any qualms about reconciling Hook's claim to socialism with their admiration for him. Conservatives found it easy to "simply shrug off" Hook's socialism "as a personal, forgivable idiosyncrasy," wrote Hook's friend Irving Kristol, arguably the founder of neoconservativism. One young right-winger told Kristol that Hook was "the best kind of socialist: an anti-socialist socialist." That was the view of the dean of the intellectual right, William F. Buckley Jr. "On my television program, he insisted he was still a Socialist," wrote Buckley in a memorial tribute to Hook, "but he agreed that dogmatic socialism was still unappealing. On the other hand, if you take from socialism its dogma, you are left merely with this or that form of the welfare state, and by such standards Ronald Reagan is also a Socialist."[2]

During the Reagan years, indeed, Hook sometimes appeared to approach the status of crown philosopher. In addition to his receipt of the Medal of Freedom, he was chosen to deliver the Thomas Jefferson Lecture of the National Endowment for the Humanities in 1984, and he joined the Committee for the Free World, a hawkish intellectual brigade led by Midge Decter in support of Reagan's revived Cold War in Europe and Central America. Hook spent the Reagan years as a senior research fellow at one of the country's two top conservative think tanks, the Hoover Institution on War, Revolution, and Peace in Stanford, California, where his files grew thick with complimentary letters from such high-ranking Reagan officials as William Bennett, Pat Buchanan, Jeane J. Kirkpatrick, Lynne Cheney, and Edwin Meese, as well as foreign policy hawks Henry Kissinger and Zbigniew Brzezinski. Ronald Reagan himself sent warm greetings for Hook's eightieth birthday party in 1982 and a holiday card in 1984.[3]

In 1964, however, Hook had written that a philosopher should be "the critical conscience, not the poet laureate, of the status quo." True to his

[2] Medal of Freedom Citation; Irving Kristol, "Life with Sidney: A Memoir," in *Sidney Hook: Philosopher of Democracy and Humanism,* ed. Paul Kurtz (Buffalo, N.Y.: Prometheus, 1983), 31; William F. Buckley Jr., "Fond Remembrances of Sidney Hook," *New York Daily News,* 23 July 1989.

[3] On Jefferson lecture: Stanford News Release, 13 July 1989 (Hook Papers, box 3). On Committee for the Free World: Jerry W. Sanders, *Peddlers of Crisis: The Committee on the Present Danger and the Politics of Containment* (Boston: South End, 1983), 305. Letters in Hook Papers: William Bennett to SH, 8 December 1982 (box 6); Pat Buchanan to SH, 28 September and 9 March 1985 (box 7); Jeane J. Kirkpatrick, 14 March 1983 (box 17); Lynne Cheney to SH, 24 April 1989 (box 9); Edwin Meese to SH, 31 July 1981 and 29 October 1981 (box 21); Henry Kissinger to SH, 13 April 1987 (box 17); Zbigniew Brzezinski to SH, 14 January 1981 and 17 November 1984 (box 7); Ronald Reagan to SH, 28 October 1982 and n.d. 1984 (box 24).

word, Hook did criticize the Reagan presidency, although not from a position where one might expect to find a socialist. Reagan, Hook alleged, was guilty of an "irresolute" foreign policy against Communist aggression—making him one of the few critics to have found Ronald Reagan soft on Communism. Privately, he worried that Reagan was a "nice soft-hearted fellow who won't be intelligent in a crisis." Fundamentalist Christians in Reagan's New Right coalition were disquieted by Hook's avowed secular humanism and his advocacy of the right to voluntary suicide for terminally ill patients, but Hook, for his part, aimed his real fire at the left. In a pattern established by his writings on academic freedom and Communism in the 1950s and his criticisms of the student New Left in the 1960s, Hook became a brigadier general in the academic culture wars of the 1970s and 1980s, condemning university affirmative action programs as "quotas" and objecting to multicultural reform of the core humanities curriculum at Stanford and elsewhere. Consequently, the National Association of Scholars—a largely conservative faculty organization—now honors outstanding figures in its battle against "political correctness" with an annual Sidney Hook Award.[4]

This book seeks to understand and recover the legacy of a much younger and very different Sidney Hook. Although it provides an explanation for the genesis of Hook's subsequent anti-communism, it leaves to other biographers the job of fully reconstructing and interpreting the Sidney Hook of the McCarthy period, the 1960s, and the Reagan era. The young Hook cannot be wholly separated from the old, of course, especially given the way his life has been interpreted. Most retrospective analyses of the young Hook are driven by a teleological fixation upon his later politics, whatever one chooses to call them—Cold War liberal, right-wing social democrat, or neoconservative—and the literature on Hook is sharply divided along partisan lines according to authors' opinions of his later views.[5]

[4]   SH to J. Michael Bailey, 22 July 1988 (Hook Papers, box 6). See also Hook, "How Today's Thinkers Serve Society," *National Observer*, 20 July 1964; and Hook, *Out of Step* (New York: Harper & Row, 1987), 598.

[5]   Hook himself never accepted the term "neoconservative"; he preferred to be known as a Cold War liberal and social democrat. See Paul Kurtz, "An Interview with Sidney Hook at Eighty," *Free Inquiry* 2 (Fall 1982): 4–10; Paul Berman, "The Last True Marxist Is a Neoconservative," *Voice Literary Supplement*, March 1984, 1, 10–14; and Sidney Hook, *The Social Democratic Prospect* (New York: Social Democrats, USA, 1976). Hook's postwar voting record is one gauge of the difficulty of pidgeonholing his politics. In 1952 he would have voted for Stevenson had he thought it would make any difference but instead cast his ballot for Darlington Hoopes, the Socialist Party candidate. In 1964 Hook voted for the Socialist Labor Party in protest; in 1968 he voted for Hubert Humphrey; in 1972 he cast the first Republican ballot of his life for Richard Nixon as a "lesser evil" than George McGovern. In 1976 he abstained, but in 1980 and 1984 he voted for Ronald Reagan. See Hook, "An Open Letter to George McGovern," 20 September 1972 (Socialist Party of America Papers, 1919–1976 Addendum, Microfiliming Corporation of America, Glen Rock, NJ, 1977, Reel 2), and SH to J.

Those who shared Hook's trajectory or were for other reasons sympathetic to the older Hook have treated his earlier radicalism somewhat sentimentally, as the romantic dream of a principled young man, carried over in his harmless residual self-description as a socialist. Correspondingly, they have seen his later anti-communism as the product of maturation and realism. The two *Festschriften* in honor of Hook—both edited by humanist philosopher Paul Kurtz, who presented them to Hook on the occasion of his sixty-fifth and eightieth birthdays—are replete with examples of this approach, which has often been conducted with little more sophistication than the old joke that a twenty-year-old who is not radical has no heart, while a forty-year-old who is not conservative has no brains. Serviceable as humor, that cliché hardly suffices for historical analysis. When applied to Hook, it has more often than not resulted in a caricature of his early Marxism.[6]

Others friendly to Hook in later years have, paradoxically, offered a completely different interpretation of his trajectory. Rather than positing that Hook moved from innocence to wisdom, these writers reject emphatically the idea that Hook changed at all. Instead, they maintain, throughout his life Hook displayed an admirable consistency in his methods, principles, and integrity. Philosopher Nicholas Capaldi, for example, writes that despite the seeming contrast between Hook's endorsement of the Communist ticket in 1932 and his move to the Hoover Institution in 1973, the idea that he changed in the years between is "a collective concoction of all those individuals who at one time or another found themselves in the same trench" with him but later found themselves his political opponents. Rather, Capaldi claims, Hook "is one of the few who has consistently adhered to the cause of liberation, and it is his critics who are guilty of a false consciousness."[7]

Michael Bailey, 22 July 1988 (Hook Papers, box 6); Hoopes and Reagan information from interview with Ernest Hook, 10 August 1996. The only socialist organization that Hook joined after the American Workers Party of the 1930s was Social Democrats, USA, which is depicted in one recent account as a "small, aging, hawkish, anti–New Left" group; see Tim Wohlforth, "Trotskyism," in *Encyclopedia of the American Left*, ed. Mary Jo Buhle, Paul Buhle, and Dan Georgakas (Urbana: University of Illinois Press, 1992), 784.
[6] The most sophisticated example of the idealistic-radical versus matured-philosopher approach is Lewis Feuer, "From Ideology to Philosophy: Sidney Hook's Writings on Marxism," in *Sidney Hook and the Contemporary World: Essays on the Pragmatic Intelligence*, ed. Paul Kurtz (New York: John Day, 1968), 35–53. See also Kurtz, *Sidney Hook: Philosopher of Democracy and Humanism*. The disappointing blandness and uncritical adulation of these collections stands in contrast to the spiciness of the philosopher they intend to honor, as was nicely expressed by philosopher Robert Paul Wolff in his review of the first: "Happy Birthday, Sidney Hook! Sorry There's Nothing to Fight About," *New York Times Book Review*, 24 November 1968, 60.
[7] Nicholas Capaldi, "Sidney Hook: A Personal Portrait," in Kurtz, *Sidney Hook: Philosopher of Democracy and Humanism*, 18.

Hook himself saw his career as that of a consistent iconoclast in pursuit of freedom. In a 1971 holiday card to his old friend James Rorty, whom he had first encountered in their mutual support of the 1932 Communist campaign, Hook wrote, "I am still fighting for what we believe—out of step as usual." In his 1987 autobiography, which he titled *Out of Step,* Hook maintained that throughout his career his method had always been scientific and democratic, although he pleaded guilty to having made errors in its application along the way, necessitating revision in practice. He eschewed dissent for its own sake but insisted that despite the Medal of Freedom and other signs of establishment approval, his commitment to scientific method guaranteed his independence. Even this nonconformist posture was enough to discomfit some of his celebrators. The review by Edward Shils of Hook's biography in the *American Scholar,* for example, was entitled "More at Home Than Out of Step."[8]

There is cause for skepticism about Hook's claim to consistency of spirit, though, for in his later period he only reluctantly consented to the republication of his book *From Hegel to Marx* (1936), and he never allowed republication of *Towards the Understanding of Karl Marx: A Revolutionary Interpretation* (1933), the book that established his reputation as the foremost American scholar of Marx. Late in life, Hook contemplated drafting another version of the 1933 book to incorporate his subsequent understandings, but he had not produced such a revision when he died of congestive heart failure at the age of eighty-six in 1989. Changes would surely have begun with the subtitle. In contrast to the first edition, Hook's new book would have opposed the revolutionary elements of Marx's thought, since over the years Hook's own common ground with Marx had shrunk to near invisibility. In the late 1940s he parted from the term "Marxist" as a self-description and spent his later years as an acid critic of Marxism. One senior research fellow at Stanford recounted that Hook even on his deathbed sat him down to discuss "the problem of Marxist academic intellectuals and their debasement of university curricula with massive infusions of Marxism and Third-Worldism."[9]

If confusion prevails among neoconservatives about how to understand Hook's development, many on the left have fared little better. The typical assumption of radical historians has been to presume that Hook's earlier radicalism must have contained some fundamental ideological flaw that led him to back the Cold War and, later, to make common cause with Reagan. Just beneath the surface of some such critiques has lurked the tire-

[8] SH to James Rorty, 16 December 1971 (James Rorty Papers, University of Oregon); Edward Shils, "More at Home Than Out of Step," *American Scholar* 56 (Autumn 1987): 577–86.
[9] Stanford News Release, 13 July 1989 (Hook Papers, box 3); Arnold Beichman, "Never Too Frail to Fight for Freedom of Democratic Ideas," *Washington Times,* 17 July 1989.

some canard that systematic criticism of existing Communist regimes leads inevitably to capitulation to capitalism. Michael Nash has claimed that the anti-Stalinism of Hook in the 1930s, along with that of V. F. Calverton and others in the American Workers Party milieu, set the stage for the Cold War witch-hunts. Michael Parenti, likewise, wrote as recently as 1990 that anti-Stalinism is simply a stance taken "by persons on the left who don't want to sound like Joe McCarthy and must therefore disguise their redbaiting."[10]

The trajectory of Sidney Hook, indeed, seems to confirm every suspicion of those who would find anti-Stalinism automatically antiradical. Yet this biography argues that Hook's early revolutionary anti-Stalinism had a character quite distinct in principle from his later Cold War liberalism, despite subsequent obfuscations by his friends and critics alike. These findings corroborate in greater detail what Julius Jacobson, editor of *New Politics*, has written regarding the New York intellectuals: "It was not anti-Stalinism that proved to be sufficient cause for that capitulation to the West; the causal link between what they were and what they became was their abandonment of an independent socialist perspective."[11]

The identification of anti-Stalinism with capriciousness has, naturally, been on the wane since 1989, and it is not the primary left-wing explanation offered for Hook's course. More radical historians have argued that the corruption of Hook's Marxism was due to his adherence to the philosophy of pragmatism, in particular to the intellectual influence of his Columbia University mentor John Dewey, the most important pragmatist of the twentieth century. Pragmatism, they argue, is inherently bourgeois,

[10]   Michael Nash, "Schism on the Left: The Anti-Communism of V. F. Calverton and His *Modern Quarterly*," *Science & Society* 54 (Winter 1980–81): 437–52; Michael Parenti, review of *Anti-Communism*, ed. Judith Joel and Gerald Erikson, *Science & Society* 54 (Spring 1990): 104. This spurious line of thought has a long history. Several generations of official publicists in the Soviet Union and Eastern Europe labored to show that opposition to bureaucratic rule was the same as opposing socialism, generally by identifying revolutionary critics of Stalinism with fascism, imperialism, and war-mongering. This slander dates back to the Moscow show trials of the 1930s and their American defenders. Mike Gold, a crude but influential American Communist writer of the 1930s, claimed in 1937 that the Marxism of anti-Stalinist intellectuals was merely a mask to obscure their function of drawing other radicals into rapprochement with bourgeois society: "Tory authors would not be effective for this, only Trotzkyite authors, renegades who have learned the left phraseology, are effective": Gold, *The Hollow Men* (New York: International, 1941), 73.
[11]   Julius Jacobson, "Reflections on Fascism and Communism," *Socialist Perspectives*, ed. Phyllis Jacobson and Julius Jacobson (Princeton: Karz-Cohl, 1983), 144. Alan Wald writes, to similar effect, that "it was not the anti-Stalinism *per se* that was responsible for the metamorphosis of these intellectuals into neo-conservatives but a host of social and historical factors, which put an end to their socialist perspective": Wald, "The New York Intellectuals in Retreat," in Jacobson and Jacobson, *Socialist Perspectives*, 167. For an earlier account in the same vein, see George Novack, "Radical Intellectuals in the 1930s," *International Socialist Review* 29 (March–April 1968): 21–34.

and when it got the better of Hook, he abandoned Marxism. In the most recent of the few attempts to chronicle the history of American Marxism, for example, Paul Buhle writes that as Hook left Marxism behind in the late 1930s, he "returned to his own pragmatist origins, holding that Marxist doctrines had no objective content. . . . Hook's subsequent move to the right evolved out of the inner consistency of this pragmatism."[12]

Here is a familiar assumption: Marxism and pragmatism, like oil and water, cannot mix. In generous moments Marxists have called pragmatism the American version of petty-bourgeois liberalism; in spiteful ones, a fig leaf for imperialism. That Marxists have lacked subtlety in this engagement does not make them any more negligent than their liberal opponents, who have equally debased pragmatism in the course of battling Marxism. Borrowing the terminology of pragmatism to forge a celebratory American identity, liberal historians, journalists, and politicians at midcentury often saluted John Dewey as "America's philosopher." Subsequently, pragmatism's key words acquired popular connotations that were often exactly the opposite of what Dewey meant by them. "Instrumentalism" now frequently implies technocratic efficiency and not, as in Dewey's writings, the careful scrutiny of ends and means through moral and social reason. "Science" often suggests certainty and elitism rather than what it meant for Dewey: an experimental, fallible process of inquiry pursued democratically by an educated public. Even "pragmatism" itself in everyday parlance connotes crass opportunism rather than intelligent action, anti-intellectualism instead of a variety of philosophical investigation. With this tortuous legacy of distortion, it is no wonder that most Marxists see in pragmatism the ideology of capitalism, or that pragmatists can imagine nothing less pragmatic than Marxism. Widespread skepticism about the very idea of a "pragmatist Marxism" reinforces a tendency to perceive Hook's early project as doomed from the outset.[13]

[12]   Paul Buhle, *Marxism in the USA* (New York: Verso, 1987), 166–67.
[13]   For the case that pragmatism is petty-bourgeois, which rests upon its historical association with political liberalism and middle-class reform currents, see George Novack, *Pragmatism versus Marxism* (New York: Pathfinder, 1975). For the argument that it is the ideological expression of monopoly capital and imperialism, which draws upon Dewey's pro-war stance during World War I and his criticism of the Soviet Union, see Maurice Cornforth, *In Defense of Philosophy: Against Positivism and Pragmatism* (London: Lawrence & Wisehart, 1950); Harry K. Wells, *Pragmatism: Philosophy of Imperialism* (New York: International, 1954); and J.S., "Against Pragmatism," *The Communist* 2 (Summer–Fall 1978): 3–60. A facile dismissal of pragmatism is also made in Shlomo Avineri, *The Social and Political Thought of Karl Marx* (Cambridge: Cambridge University Press, 1968), 74–75. Each of these three strands counterposes Marxism and pragmatism from a particular left-wing perspective—Trotskyist, Stalinist, and social democratic, respectively. There have from time to time been more sympathetic treatments of pragmatism from within Trotskyism and social democracy, at least; see, e.g., James Kloppenberg, *Uncertain Victory: Social Democracy and Progressivism in European and American Thought, 1870–1920* (New York: Oxford University Press, 1986). For a neopragmatist call for

Recent scholarship, however, has brought about a renaissance of Deweyan pragmatism that should give us pause. Historian Robert Westbrook's definitive biography, *John Dewey and American Democracy* (1991), maintains that a radical conception of democracy was the guiding thread of Dewey's thought. At the same time revolutionary Marxists are considering with greater seriousness than ever before how to underscore the continuity of classical liberal values—including democracy and individual political freedoms—within Marxism so as to resist the bureaucratic tyranny that has characterized most existing "socialisms." Taken together, the new dialogues on pragmatism and democracy on the one hand and socialism and democracy on the other present a refreshing opportunity to reconsider the early Sidney Hook. They render inadequate the standard interpretations—the radical one that pragmatism led Hook astray, as well as the conservative one that Hook abandoned Marxist "ideology" for pragmatist philosophy. Each of these longstanding assessments *presumes* that Marxism and pragmatism are incompatible, thereby foreclosing Hook's early standpoint before it has been examined and missing the important questions: How did Hook get to Marxism in the first place? How did he come not simply to endorse Marxism but to write especially brilliant works of Marxist philosophy? What made his Marxism distinctive?[14]

There has been almost no systematic exploration of Hook's early thought, despite the vital topics it addressed: epistemology, dialectics, history, materialism, science, morality, and democracy. From the mid-1920s through the 1930s Hook argued that pragmatism and Marxism were, properly understood, each necessary to the other's fulfillment. In contrast to the widespread assumption that his was a quixotic pursuit, this book takes that philosophical project seriously. If Deweyan pragmatism is considered as a form of democratic radicalism rather than conventional liberalism, then one may see that it had a place in Hook's trajectory quite different from that usually ascribed to it. Long before it had a chance to corrupt his Marxism or lead him astray, pragmatism helped him arrive at the particular *type* of Marxism that he espoused, one opposed not only to

---

radical intellectuals to dispense with Marxism and socialism, see Richard Rorty, "The Intellectuals at the End of Socialism," *Yale Review* 80 (April 1992): 1–16.

[14] On pragmatism and democracy, see Robert Westbrook, *John Dewey and American Democracy* (Ithaca: Cornell University Press, 1991); Casey Blake, *Beloved Community: The Cultural Criticism of Randolph Bourne, Van Wyck Brooks, Waldo Frank, and Lewis Mumford* (Chapel Hill: University of North Carolina Press, 1990), 86–93. From a considerable body of work on Marxism, liberalism, and democracy, one useful recent exchange is Harry Brighouse, "Socialism, Justice, and Individual Rights," and Milton Fisk, "Is Democracy Enough?" *Against the Current* 5 (November–December 1990): 16–33, 33–37; and Ernest Mandel, "Socialism and Individual Rights," *Against the Current* 6 (May–June 1991): 41–42.

capitalism but also to the philosophical determinism and political bureaucracy of both Stalinism and social democracy. Pragmatism, that is, was significant in Hook's early thought for a previously unrecognized reason: it imbued him with an appreciation of democracy, flexibility, and action, a disposition that enabled him to break through ossified varieties of Marxism and deliver one of the most substantial contributions to Marxist philosophy in American history. Where appropriate, I do not shrink from identifying internal contradictions that help to explain shortcomings in Hook's thought. I do not, however, deny categorically or in advance the plausibility of a pragmatist Marxism.

This intellectual biography reaches toward an understanding of the early Marxism of Sidney Hook. Against the thesis that his Marxism was an immature outlook abandoned with the onset of wisdom, it maintains that his early thought was a sophisticated, fruitful formulation of democratic revolutionary theory. Against the claim that he maintained a strict continuity of liberal iconoclasm, it argues that a profound transformation in the final years of the 1930s divides the early Hook from the later Hook. It finds tragic his failure to maintain his revolutionary perspective as the American left entered its period of great crisis on the eve of the Second World War—but not deplorable in the simplistic and highly moralistic way in which it has often been cast. Finally, in contrast to the notion that pragmatism and Marxism are automatically incompatible, this biography seeks a serious and critical examination of the pragmatist and Marxist basis for Hook's early thought. In each respect, this book is a challenge to all who have been led by a teleological fixation upon Hook's subsequent anti-communism to treat his early thought dismissively. At the same time, it seeks a better explanation for Hook's later transformation than existing accounts offer.

All this requires treating the early Hook *historically*, recognizing that his formal thought existed within society, absent of any pretense of standing apart from it. His theoretical allegiances demanded worldly engagement and relevance, since both pragmatism and Marxism emphasize purposive action. Furthermore, Hook was by nature feisty, argumentative and persistent. For a philosopher, he was rarely drawn to the calm waters of contemplation. His life was punctuated by strenuous engagements of ferocious intensity, lending his personality an insistent and urgent character that often intimidated those around him. "He was too logical, I often felt," recalled the writer Matthew Josephson, who was allied politically with Hook in the early 1930s, "and he was so quick in argument that he answered opponents without waiting to hear them out." Hook never lost his reputation as a fearsome debater and relentless logician, no matter what his politics.

As he once told his son, he did not take much pleasure from "technical philosophy or academic exegesis"; what he really enjoyed was "a good fight."[15]

Hook's philosophical thought, therefore, cannot be understood apart from the people with whom he fought—alongside and against—and the issues over which he fought. These include his personal and intellectual relationships with his philosophical mentors, Morris Cohen and John Dewey; his formal political associations with the Communist Party and the American Workers Party; his consecutive sympathies for Communism, Trotskyism, and social democracy; his editorial attachment and literary contributions to key magazines such as the *Modern Quarterly, Marxist Quarterly,* and *Partisan Review;* his assessments of such historical events as the rise of Hitler to power in Germany, the Moscow trials in the Soviet Union, and the Second World War; and the social, political, and economic conditions of the United States in the 1930s, with their attendant possibilities and constraints. Only with an understanding of this total environment can one undertake an analysis of Hook's thought and the causes of his eventual transformation, thereby making it possible to assess whether the pragmatist Marxism of the early Sidney Hook is worthy of salvage from the proverbial dustbin of history.[16]

In 1994 William Phillips, lifelong editor of *Partisan Review,* the flagship periodical of the New York intellectuals, made a startling charge regarding academic disdain for his old political mentor, Sidney Hook. Hook's writings on Marx and Marxism, Phillips asserted, have been deliberately ignored by younger scholars. Echoing conservative charges of a "New McCarthyism" of the left on campuses, Phillips declared Hook "the victim of an ideological blacklist" that reflects a lingering Stalinism in academia: "Could it be that the old Stalinist branding of Hook as pariah has spread almost unconsciously through the entire field of Marxist writings and general philosophic studies? Could the fact that he was an influential anticommunist have led to his excommunication? Could there be a Stalinist unconscious in the cultural underground?"[17]

---

[15] Matthew Josephson, *Infidel in the Temple: A Memoir of the 1930s* (New York: Knopf, 1967); "Eulogy by Ernest Benjamin Hook," Service of Remembrance for Sidney Hook, Stanford University, 18 July 1989 (Hook Papers, box 3).
[16] This method of the history of ideas follows the lead of the young Hook himself, who wrote, "The full import of a doctrine is not to be sought only in the formal analysis of isolated texts. It is to be derived from a consideration of these texts in relation to the positions and views they oppose." A "complete treatment" in Marxist fashion, he continued, would also include "an account of the industrial transformations, the political mass movements, as well as the cultural developments of his age": Hook, *Towards the Understanding of Karl Marx: A Revolutionary Interpretation* (New York: John Day, 1933), 65, 67.
[17] William Phillips, "The Ideological Blacklist," *Partisan Review* 62 (1994): 7–8.

The allegation that Hook's writings have been subjected to a neo-Stalinist "boycott," although not the most fantastic claim to be made by a partisan in the culture wars, is impressively inflated. If Hook has been neglected by contemporary Marxists, the reasons are less fantastic. Most obviously, Hook was not a Marxist for the last fifty years of his life. His early writings can be hard to obtain. His first and most important book on Marx, *Towards the Understanding of Karl Marx* (1933), is a rare find in secondhand shops. Criticism of Hook's later politics, moreover, hardly comes from Stalinist circles alone. Phillips need look no further than one of the last essays by his *Partisan Review* coeditor Philip Rahv, who during the Vietnam War branded Hook a prime example of those "political philistines . . . who at opportune moments still choose to call themselves socialists but who in practice support and defend the American capitalist drive for world hegemony."[18]

Hook is, in any case, far from ignored. Almost as Phillips's editorial hit the bookstores, Columbia University Press released a new edition of Hook's 1936 classic, *From Hegel to Marx*. The prominent African American intellectual Cornel West has cited the early Hook as a strong influence on his own pragmatism and left socialism. Historian Russell Jacoby provides a brief, careful assessment of Hook's career in *The Last Intellectuals* (1987). Hook is the subject of entries in *The Biographical Dictionary of the American Left* (1986), *The Encyclopedia of the American Left* (1992), and *A Companion to American Thought* (1995). John P. Diggins, in *The Rise and Fall of the American Left* (1992), places such an emphasis on Hook's early philosophical polemics that he bestows upon Hook's break with the American Communist Party in 1933 a provocative (and undoubtedly overstated) significance: "America became a country with a communist party without a leading Marxist philosopher. The American party lost the battle for cultural hegemony without knowing it."[19]

[18] Philip Rahv, "What and Where Is the New Left?" (1972), in *Essays on Literature and Politics, 1932–1972*, ed. Arabel J. Porter and Andrew Dvosin (Boston: Houghton Mifflin, 1978), 353 n. "The favorite trick of such types," Rahv continued, "is to substitute the word 'democracy' for the word 'capitalism' when writing or talking about the American system. In this way they make it appear that any opponent of capitalism is *ipso facto* an enemy of democracy."
[19] John Patrick Diggins, *The Rise and Fall of the American Left* (New York: Norton, 1992), 160. Diggins devoted so much space to Hook's debates with Max Eastman that when Maurice Isserman reviewed the book ("Left Out," *New York Times Book Review*, 8 March 1992, 9), he expressed dismay that Diggins spent "five pages on the philosopher Sidney Hook but never mentions so important a labor leader as Harry Bridges." See Cornel West, *The Ethical Dimensions of Marxist Thought* (New York: Monthly Review, 1991), xxi; Cornel West, *The American Evasion of Philosophy: A Genealogy of Pragmatism* (Madison: University of Wisconsin Press, 1989), 114–24; Russell Jacoby, *The Last Intellectuals* (New York: Basic, 1987), 103–6; Jeff Beneke, "Hook, Sidney," in *Biographical Dictionary of the American Left*, ed. Bernard K. Johnpoll and Harvey Klehr (New York: Greenwood, 1986); Steven Best, "Hook, Sidney," in *Encyclopedia of the American Left*; Robert Westbrook, "Hook, Sidney," in *A Companion to American Thought*, ed.

Phillips's charge, indeed, runs against the more common line of thought these days about the New York intellectuals: that even if not another line is written on them, we know their story. The circle of writers, critics, scholars, and editors who in the 1930s came together in common cause against Stalinism and were, by the postwar period, known collectively as "the New York intellectuals" is extraordinarily well chronicled. The number of books by and about this cohort—Dwight Macdonald, Mary McCarthy, William Phillips, Philip Rahv, Harold Rosenberg, Meyer Schapiro, Delmore Schwartz, Diana Trilling, Lionel Trilling, and Edmund Wilson, among others—has grown so great that the stack itself has become an object of attention. Ellen Schrecker refers to the "vast and ever-growing literature by and about the New York intellectuals"; Paul Buhle writes that the New York intellectuals' path to "acceptance of post–World War II warfare-welfare capitalism" is a "sort of scholarly cottage industry"; and Christopher Hitchens speaks of "a groaning shelf-full of reminiscence, self-reference and the multiple glossings of clique-think."[20]

Do we really need a biography of yet another New York intellectual? In a word, yes. The outpouring of work by and about Sidney Hook's political and intellectual companions has given us much knowledge of his milieu but surprisingly little about him. Phillips's fantasies of Stalinist suppression are wildly exaggerated, but he justly brings to our attention the need for a more comprehensive examination of Hook's early thought. This biography, the first of Sidney Hook, aspires to give satisfaction both to William Phillips and to any remaining skeptics on the left who doubt that Hook's early politics and philosophy are worth their time. The many acknowledgments of the theoretical richness and historical importance of his early work stand in sharp contrast to the inadequate, fleeting, and often mistaken, misleading, or glib references to him in existing memoirs and histories of the New York intellectuals. Hook's own massive memoir, *Out of Step* (1987), specifically disavowed any intention of explaining his philosophical development. That account of his many political engagements, punctuated by his opinions on twentieth-century history, features a number of invaluable personal recollections. But since he unavoidably viewed the past through the prism of his later years and often made small but significant errors in dates and other details, his memoir must be weighed carefully against other records. Of the many historical studies of Hook's

Richard Wightman Fox and James T. Kloppenberg (Oxford: Blackwell, 1995), 312–13; The most insightful review of Hook's autobiography also recognizes the importance of his early radicalism: Robert Westbrook, "Stream of Contentiousness," *Nation* 224 (30 May 1987): 726–30.
[20]   Ellen Schrecker, *No Ivory Tower* (New York: Oxford University Press, 1986), 25; Paul Buhle, *History and the New Left* (Philadelphia: Temple University Press, 1990), 7; Christopher Hitchens, *For the Sake of Argument* (London: Verso, 1993), 206.

circle, Alan Wald's *The New York Intellectuals* (1987), is superior in its treatment of Hook before 1940. Wald provides the most detailed biographical information about the early Hook and is most aware of the significance of his period of revolutionary socialism following his break with Communism. Since Wald's objective was an inclusive history of the anti-Stalinist intellectual left, however, his attention to Hook could not exceed a few condensed, if perceptive, pages.[21] Without indulging in what Freud once called "the narcissism of small differences," I should specify that although Wald's narrative framework and mine are largely compatible, we part ways over certain crucial aspects of interpretation, especially the merit of pragmatism, toward which Wald, like most Marxists, is opposed.

When called upon to describe those he had known, Hook often replied with consternation that it would take a novelist to do them justice. He himself inspired at least one fictional portrait in *Sam Holman* (1983), a novel that his old friend James T. Farrell—best known for the fictional trilogy *Studs Lonigan* (1932–35)—completed just before his death in 1979. A re-creation of the world of the New York intellectual left in the 1930s, *Sam Holman* is based closely upon the life of Herbert Solow, thinly disguised by a reversal of initials. Sidney Hook likewise appears as the minor character Henry Smart, a New York University philosophy professor who lives in Brooklyn and plays an indispensable behind-the-scenes role in helping Leon Trotsky's followers merge with other socialist groups. When the protagonist attends the first party held by Smart and his wife at their new apartment in Brooklyn, with many academics in attendance, he gets drunk and marvels at Smart's tolerant handling of a bright young student who is in the process of succumbing to infantile leftism. Smart is admirable not just for his patience toward any student who shows signs of promise but for his keen intelligence and honesty. Smart, Holman avers, is "not the kind of man to say something unless he meant it."[22]

[21] Hook, *Out of Step;* Alan Wald, *The New York Intellectuals: The Rise and Decline of the Anti-Stalinist Left from the 1930s to the 1980s* (Chapel Hill: University of North Carolina Press, 1987).
[22] James T. Farrell, *Sam Holman* (Buffalo, N.Y.: Prometheus, 1983), 183–99. Another novel based upon the 1930s New York intellectual left is Isidor Schneider's *The Judas Time* (New York: Dial, 1946), a bitter portrait of the anti-Stalinist "renegades" by a Communist loyalist. Schneider's wife was a secretary for the League of Professionals for Foster and Ford, in which Hook took part, so he may have met Hook. One of Schneider's fictional apostates from Communism, Professor Virgil Ayre, does make a stray remark that sounds as if it might have been lifted from Hook: "I have come to the conclusion that the Communist Party has no more relation to Communism than the Christian sects have to Christianity" (156). In no other way, though, does the character of Ayre or any of the other characters fit Hook's career or type; their neuroses and pathologies are too extreme. On Hook's desire for a novelist as biographer, made in reference to Muste, Rorty, and Freeman, see SH to A. J. Muste, n.d. (Hook Papers); and SH to Alan Wald, 22 April 1985 and 12 July 1986 (Wald Collection).

That hardly exhausts the literary possibility of the young Hook. Images readily spring to mind of Hook arguing volubly, sharply, emphatically, cigarillo in hand. But acquaintances often contrasted Hook's awesome, devastating capacities as a polemicist with his amiable social presence. "He seemed pleasant, very pleasant, certainly not arrogant in his manner," says Sender Garlin, who as a young radical considered himself privileged to be invited to the apartment of Joseph Freeman for discussions with Hook, V. F. Calverton, and others in the early 1930s. "He seemed friendly, democratic in his manner. His writing is arrogant. He was the sort of guy who didn't suffer fools gladly, that is. He apparently knew his business." Norman Podhoretz too has remarked upon Hook's "normally abrasive manner in debate—a manner which gave no hint of how kindly a man he could be in personal relations."[23]

Ours is a time in which biography is too often confused with exposure. Although some biographies do manage to achieve a speculative interior psychology worthy of the novel, this one may not claim such distinction. Sidney Hook, public intellectual, was a private man. He left very little record of the desires, anxieties, and emotions that occupy even the most philosophical of minds in everyday life. Such inner sentiments, in any event, do not appear to have much potency as explanations for the development of his politics or philosophy. Hook's scrappy intellectual disposition, for example, was evident in his earliest school essays and dotted every plateau of his development; it does not, therefore, account for any of his *specific* shifts in thinking. Accordingly, this biography's emphasis is intellectual and political more than personal and psychological. Though it does illuminate Hook's personal relations with his family and friends to the fullest extent the record permits, its subject is necessarily, above all else, Hook's formal thought in its most systematic exposition.

A note on terminology: Following the lead of the anti-Stalinist left itself, I use the term "Communist" with a capital C to refer to the people, parties, and ideas affiliated with the official Communist movement, which in the 1930s had its gravitational center in Stalin's Soviet Union. The word "communist" without a capital letter refers to those who saw themselves as revolutionaries seeking to overthrow capitalism and establish a classless society but who were not necessarily associated with the Communist Party—who were in fact often opposed to it. Similarly, "Socialist" refers to the ideas and members of the official Socialist Party, whereas "socialist" implies a commitment to socialist aims not necessarily tied to any particular organi-

---

[23] Interview with Sender Garlin, 9 May 1992; Norman Podhoretz, *Breaking Ranks: A Political Memoir* (New York: Harper & Row, 1979), 179.

zation. These terms are not without their own complications, granted, but the distinctions between them are not semantic. Many anti-Stalinist radicals in the 1930s considered official Communism the *antithesis* of Marxism, a travesty rather than the embodiment of communist principles. Anti-Communism to them did not at all entail anti-communism. Indeed, they believed opposition to Communism essential to the fight for genuine communism—a society premised upon egalitarian and participatory norms. Many socialists, likewise, were critical of the Socialist Party for its reformist politics. For a period in the mid-1930s, such distinctions were crucial to the thought of Sidney Hook.

CHAPTER ONE

Revolution and Philosophy, 1902–30

By the beginning of the 1930s, when he gained a reputation for his dialectical skills and formidable knowledge of Marx, Sidney Hook had become perfectly comfortable with the role of socialist philosopher. Confident of the value of a dual commitment to intellectual life and political action, he understood that practice to be in keeping with the tradition exemplified by Marx himself: the fearless polemicist who drafted *The Communist Manifesto;* the gifted historian who published *The Eighteeenth Brumaire;* the prodigious researcher who wrote *Capital;* the leader and organizer of international associations of revolutionary workers. That such a combined form of scholarly and political life—both philosophical and revolutionary—was possible, however, was not at all self-evident to Hook in his adolescent and collegiate years. Only with time was he able to imagine it possible to connect his professional commitment to philosophy with an openly socialist politics.

Until the middle of the 1920s Hook's commitment to revolutionary action and passion for philosophy acted as countervailing forces and ambitions, pulling him first one way, then the other. In high school, he opposed American intervention in the World War, unsettling school officials who viewed him as a troublemaking young "Bolshevik." At college, however, Hook retreated for a time from political activism, affected by the conser-

vatism of the period and enticed by a conception of philosophy which rested upon contemplative disengagement from worldly concerns. Only through a series of influences—including firsthand exposure to the pragmatism of John Dewey, personal links to the Communist Party, an epic debate with Max Eastman, and extensive research into the intellectual origins of Marxism—did Hook finally become confident by the end of the 1920s that he could harmonize his socialist convictions with his scholarship, his philosophical inclinations with his revolutionary aspirations.

Philosophy and Revolution in Tension, 1902–23

When Saul Hook entered the world on December 20, 1902, he was the fourth child born to immigrants from Central Europe who had met and married in the United States. Isaac Hook, thirty-one, was from Moravia, a former province of Bohemia, then of Austria, and then of Czechoslovakia. Jenny Halpern Hook, four years younger than her husband, had arrived at age sixteen from Galicia, a province of southwestern Poland controlled for much of the nineteenth century by the Hapsburg empire. The surname Hook was probably adapted from Czech. By the late nineteenth century, when the Hooks separately left Europe behind, both Moravia and Galicia were experiencing a mass emigration of Jews as anti-Semitic restrictions mounted. In Europe, Isaac Hook had worked the land, but upon arriving in New York City, where agriculture was at best a marginal occupation, he became a tailor. He worked such long hours that he would arrive home exhausted, sometimes falling asleep over dinner, to the amusement of his children. Jenny—whose high cheekbones and black hair made her very attractive, her daughter-in-law Ann would later recall—was a witty, warm, temperamental woman who worked all day caring for the children and household. She had a passion for romantic novels, however, and often became so engrossed in her reading that she burned the family supper.[1]

When he was enrolled in school at the age of five, Saul became Sidney at his mother's instigation. She may, her grandson Ernest Hook speculates, have come across that name in a novel she was reading at the time; in any case, Sidney Hook lived by that name for the rest of his life, with little confusion. The boy had two sisters, Lillian and Selma, and a brother, Herbert. (David, the first Hook child, died while still a toddler from an accident resulting in severe burns.) Brooklyn's Williamsburg district at the time was one of the worst slums in New York. The Hooks lived first on Bushwick Avenue and then Locust Street, occupying gaslit railroad flats in vermin-infested tenements and sharing bathrooms with others in their building. The family was forced to endure the seasonal periods of slack in the needle trades, sometimes going for three months without income. The only source of heat in the winter was a single coal stove in the kitchen.[2]

In elementary school, Sidney and his friends formed a Jewish street gang and engaged in fistfights with Irish and Italian boys, perhaps steeling the young Hook for later rounds as an intellectual pugilist. He found his teachers and the curriculum at Public School 145 stultifying, but he compensated by making frequent visits to corner branches of the public library. By the age of eight he already needed spectacles to correct myopia and a squint that he had developed from reading in dim light during the evening. He was thrilled by American history and historical fiction, and he had patriotic fantasies of commanding battleships, winning the presidency, and becoming a general. He quickly acquired a grandiose and precocious vocabulary.

Many writers, noting the heavily Jewish composition of the New York anti-Stalinist left, have located the political and cultural predilections of the New York intellectuals—modernist, Marxist, cosmopolitan—in their ethnicity. Since all sectors of American radicalism in the twentieth century, from anarchism to Communism, have had Jewish adherents in proportions far beyond the percentage of Jews in the general populace, attempts

---

[1] Interview with Ann Hook, 28 August 1993; birth certificate for Saul Hook, 21 January 3 (Hook Papers, box 3); Ernest Hook to author, 19 April 1992; interview with Ernest Hook, 10 August 1996; interview with John B. Hook, 23 August 1993; marriage certificate for Sidney Hook and Carrie Katz, 17 March 1924 (City Clerk of New York, Brooklyn Office). This section draws intermittently from Hook's autobiography, *Out of Step* (New York: Harper & Row, 1987), from which only direct quotations are cited.
[2] Interview with Ernest Hook, 10 August 1996. Sidney Hook outlived all his siblings (Ernest Hook to author, 19 April 1992).

to credit ethnicity for the special radical sensibility of the New York intellectuals are dubious. That many of the New York ensemble, including Dwight Macdonald, F. W. Dupee, and Edmund Wilson, were not Jewish further complicates things. The interpretation that Jewishness was the defining attribute of the New York circle ultimately forces its defenders to resort to pirouettes such as Irving Howe's deftly evasive remark that "by birth or osmosis," all were Jews.[3]

Especially when compared with Howe, or Alfred Kazin, Sidney Hook was never especially preoccupied with his ethnicity or the New York Jewish experience (not in his writings, at least).[4] He consciously rejected Judaic belief and practice at a very early age. Even as an adolescent he viewed Talmudic scholarship as mystical scholasticism, rejecting it as a viable release for his intellectual interests. Hook initially refused the bar mitzvah, only capitulating in the end to save his father and mother from the stigma of community disapproval. From this experience he discovered that he had no conventional religious faith, and he remained militantly secular for the rest of his life.[5]

It might be said, however, that lack of faith is the definitive problem of the modern Jewish intellectual. Howe contends, too, that the Jewishness particular to the New York intellectuals was shaped by their standing as "the first group of Jewish writers to come out of the immigrant milieu who did not define themselves through a relationship, nostalgic or hostile, to memories of Jewishness." But these qualities obviously diminish the force of *Jewishness* as a defining factor in the thought of even those New York intellectuals who were Jews. Because of the origins of his parents, moreover, Hook was given to the German rather than the Yiddish phrase. He

3 Irving Howe, "The New York Intellectuals," in *Decline of the New* (New York: Harcourt, Brace & World, 1970), 212. The strongest case for Jewishness as the defining thread of the New York intellectual experience is Alexander Bloom, *Prodigal Sons: The New York Intellectuals and Their World* (New York: Oxford University Press, 1986).
4 The chief notable exception, Hook's "Promise without Dogma: A Social Philosophy for Jews," *Menorah Journal* 25 (October–Dcember 1937): 273–88, proves the rule. The article was not a celebration or even exploration of Jewishness but a strategic guide to fighting anti-Semitism, which Hook argued required socialist politics, not merely the anti-fascist politics of the Popular Front. A social philosophy suitable for Jews, he declared, must recognize cultural diversity, protect religious freedom, be democratic, assure economic security, and guarantee intellectual freedom. The Soviet Union had failed to provide these, and the New Deal, too, had to be surpassed. In short, Hook's "social philosophy for Jews" was democratic socialism, the social philosophy appropriate to the rest of humanity, as well.
5 Diana Trilling, in *The Beginning of the Journey* (New York: Harcourt Brace, 1993), 182, recalled that Hook once told her he had converted his orthodox father to atheism when he was only ten or eleven. But if this were so, Hook's own recollection about his bar mitzvah would make no sense: Hook's father would have had no reason to be upset by his reluctance to participate in the bar mitzvah, nor would the rite of passage have been the occasion for his recognition of his faithlessness. On the bar mitzvah, see Hook, *Convictions* (New York: Prometheus, 1990), 16–17.

never displayed the intense personal sensitivity to issues of assimilation, tradition, and alienation that propelled even irreligious writers such as Howe to the study and interpretation of their culture and heritage.[6]

Exposure to socialism came from beyond the family flat for the young Hook. His father, like many European immigrants thrust suddenly into a bewildering urban world, adopted fairly conventional political beliefs. In 1912, the heyday of the Socialist Party, when Socialist presidential candidate Eugene V. Debs received a higher percentage of the national vote than he or any other revolutionary socialist candidate achieved before or since, Isaac Hook supported Republican William Howard Taft on the grounds that he advocated a tariff that would benefit the needle trades. But as war loomed in Europe, the ethnic enclaves of the Williamsburg section of Brooklyn experienced a new wave of radicalism. Russian immigrants, remembering the czarist regime bitterly, tended to be skeptical of a war to make the world safe for democracy in which Russia was an ally. German immigrants, for their own reasons of background and ancestry, saw no reason for the United States to enter into a war against their homeland. Irish immigrants, too, were deeply suspicious of British war aims. Around this time Hook made a friend whose father, a skilled metalworker, often made sarcastic jokes at the expense of the rich. Soon Hook began to read socialist writings. By the age of thirteen he considered himself a socialist, and before long he was reading the Socialist newspapers avidly and had begun to delve into the writings of Karl Marx. He especially loved the fiction of socialist Jack London, whose novel *Martin Eden* (1909), the story of a working-class autodidact in San Francisco who becomes an ardent admirer of Herbert Spencer, whetted Hook's interest in philosophy.[7]

In February 1916 Hook enrolled at the scholastically rigorous Boys High School, where his political adamance repeatedly landed him in hot water with teachers and administrators. Sender Garlin, a classmate in 1916 when both were fourteen years old, remembers Hook, his Adam's apple sticking out, arguing with right-wing classmates about capitalism. "How about poverty?" Hook would exclaim, pressing his point mercilessly. "How about misery? How about prostitution?" His adolescent dialectical skills, combined with his anti-war convictions, did not endear him to his stiff, formal teachers. One of them attempted to get Hook expelled by alleging that he

---

6 Howe, "The New York Intellectuals," 215.
7 Jack London, *Martin Eden* (New York: Regent Press, 1909). The protagonist is immensely impressed by two disputatious proletarian philosophers: "The books were alive in these men. They talked with fire and enthusiasm, the intellectual stimulant stirring them as he had seen drink and anger stir other men. What he heard was no longer the philosophy of the dry, printed word, written by half-mythical demigods like Kant and Spencer. It was living philosophy, with warm, red blood, incarnated in these two men till its very features worked with excitement" (313).

had refused to sing "The Star-Spangled Banner" during a school assembly, though Hook denied the charge. In several separate incidents Hook was told by teachers to leave the room: once when he defended the conspirator Catiline against the Roman statesman Cicero; and once when his essay on the assigned topic "Love of Country" held that patriotism was a ploy of hypocrites and exploiters to stir an unsuspecting proletariat to war, making love of country "detrimental and derogatory to the progress and advancement of civilization."[8]

In 1917 Hook was a campaign volunteer and soapbox speaker for the Socialist candidate for mayor of New York, Morris Hillquit. President Woodrow Wilson's push for American entry into the World War was a formative moment for Hook, who like most of the left opposed the war on revolutionary internationalist grounds, arguing that only a decisive working-class victory resulting in the abolition of capitalism could produce a lasting peace. In 1919, his senior year, Hook and several other radical students formed the Red and Black Party, a name that referred to school colors but also gave rise to fears of socialism and anarchism in the administrative corridors at Boys High. Meeting in the school's basement lunchroom and, occasionally, at the Brooklyn Socialist Party headquarters on Tompkins Avenue, the rebels drew up a program calling for representative student government and an aid fund for needy students—mild reforms already in place in some other New York City schools. In the election to the largely symbolic student activities board, the Red and Black Party slate did surprisingly well. Hook, given the nickname "Brainy" in its campaign literature, ran for president of the board and won a majority of the senior class vote, but the more easily intimidated younger classes sent the radical slate down to defeat by voting disproportionately for the superpatriotic Active Allies slate. The margin was narrow, as Hook got a total of 608 votes and the Active Allies candidate 821. The election attracted sensational attention from the Brooklyn daily press, which branded the Red and Black Party "Bolshevik" and raised the spectre of reds overrunning the schools. Boys High officials, braced by the newspapers' charges, took action: Hook and his comrades were blocked from Arista, the school's honor society, solely on the basis of their activities in the Red and Black Party. In retaliation, Hook wrote a letter that was published anonymously in the Socialist Party's *New York Call*, exposing the undemocratic practices of administrators. The *Call* published several successive articles, all of which kept their author's identity secret. Bravado characteristic of the fresh initiate to radicalism ran through the youthful missives. "Capitalism must in-

[8] Interview with Sender Garlin, 9 May 1992; Hook, *Academic Freedom and Academic Anarchy* (New York: Delta, 1971), 46–47; Hook, "Love of Country," 7 February 1917 (Hook Papers, box 38, folder 17).

deed be on its last legs," Hook proclaimed, "if it is convulsed with fear when school boys voice their demands for the amelioration of conditions vitally affecting them."[9]

During his City College years, 1919 to 1923, Hook kept his radical beliefs alive, but his activist orientation was gradually supplanted by a newfound engagement with scholarly philosophy. He had become interested in philosophy through the socialist movement—not through the rigid scholasticism of Boys High—so it was ironic that enhanced interest in philosophical scholarship would cause an ebb in his political activity. Initially, though, his activism continued unabated. City College during Hook's undergraduate years was not yet the legendary hotbed of socialist politics that it would become during the Depression years when Stalinists and Trotskyists would hold down their own cafeteria alcoves, but the thoroughly urban, largely immigrant, and predominantly working-class character of its students did leave room for a small campus left to operate, even in a period of deepening national reaction. As a freshman in 1919, Hook helped to organize a Social Problems Club, a group of socialist, communist, and syndicalist students who met, usually in secret, to share their excitement about developments in Russia, where the dual revolution of 1917 had replaced one of Europe's monarchical powers with the first lasting revolutionary socialist government in history. Hook was part of the club's dominant Communist tendency, led by a few older students, above all by one named George Siskind. Although the Social Problems Club had no perceptible contact with the national Communist movement, it considered itself Communist and collectively discussed V. I. Lenin's *State and Revolution* (1917). Even as the Red Scare heated up, Hook stayed the course. He passed out pamphlets on behalf of Upton Sinclair when it was announced that a City College journalism professor was going to give a talk denouncing Sinclair's piercing indictment of the American press in *Brass Check* (1919). On May Day 1921 Hook and his friend Sam Chovenson went to pick up some literature at the city headquarters of the Industrial Workers of the World and were apprehended in a surprise police raid, but the pair managed to escape by dashing out a rear door. The next year, when British philosopher Bertrand Russell (a thinker greatly admired by the undergraduate Hook) returned from a trip to the Soviet Union and reversed his previous endorsement of Bolshevism on the grounds that it was a threat to the heritage of Western civilization, a disappointed Hook sent him a letter

[9] Red and Black Party Program; "'Bolsheviks' Lose Boys' High Election," Brooklyn newspaper clipping; and "Boys' High Also Has Inquisition on Radicalism," *New York Call*, n.d. (all in Hook Papers, box 2); "Boys' High School Students Persecuted as 'Bolsheviki' for Daring to Seek Reform," *New York Call*, 15 March 1919; Hook, *Out of Step*, 17–38.

suggesting that the inevitable wars of capitalism were far more destructive of art and beauty than any social revolution could be.[10]

For the most part, however, traditional philosophical concerns came to absorb Hook's attention. City College was an intellectual hothouse, featuring a quality education for poor students, lack of "school spirit" in the conformist sense, and an openness to Jewish students unmatched elsewhere in higher education in a decade of rising xenophobia and anti-Semitism. A toll was undoubtedly exacted on Hook's political activism by his time-consuming jobs as a salesman at the City College Book Store and a hat checker at the Broadway Dance Casino in Brooklyn. But the academic environment of City College and the inspiration of his powerful mentor Morris Cohen were paramount in luring him from activism to scholarship.

Hook was not free from censorious treatment even at City College. He was driven from one government class for defending the rhetorical abilities of John C. Calhoun over those of Daniel Webster. "Young man!" the instructor thundered. "When you're not preaching sedition, you are preaching secession!" But Morris Cohen, one of only a few Jewish professors at an institution where the student body was overwhelmingly Jewish, was a paragon of independent thought. He left an indelible impression on his students, who remembered his mode of presentation more often than they adhered to his ideas. Literary critic Irving Howe once described a course with Cohen as "an experience of salutary terror." In the lecture hall Cohen would issue a question and then pounce on his students' answers, cutting them apart with even more precise questions. His hope was to deliver a sense of the grandeur and seriousness of unresolved issues, and he thought of himself as a "logical disinfectant," stimulating an appreciation for dissent and scrubbing out poorly formulated, one-sided ideas. Hook made some of his best friends at City College, including Ernest Nagel—a modest, quiet, extraordinarily intelligent student who would accompany Hook to graduate school in philosophy at Columbia and remain a friend for life, even though, as a lifelong liberal, he never took to Marxism. The friends began reading Cohen's published work outside of class so as to anticipate his line of questioning, which spared them from being called upon in the classroom but not from the professor's withering scrutiny in private sessions. Although Hook would later come to consider Cohen's educational method unnecessarily cruel, Cohen was the first of his teachers and professors to win Hook's deep respect. His own subsequent renown for

[10] SH to Alan Wald, 15 September, 1984 (Wald Collection); SH to Bertrand Russell, 12 July 1922 (Hook Papers, box 25).

skilled intellectual contentiousness surely owed something to his training under Cohen.[11]

Like others, Hook was impressed by Cohen's cleverness and agility. Daniel Bell recalled that a student once asked Cohen to prove to him why he should study logic. "How will you know it is a good proof?" Cohen replied. In his writings, Cohen advanced a "principle of polarity," which held that the world was composed of opposites requiring each in order to exist. Ideal and real, universal and particular, actual and possible, objective and subjective: each element represented a partial, incomplete solution to the problem at hand; a desirable outcome would permit neither one victory. Cohen was at odds with Hegel and Dewey, whose philosophies would inform Hook's subsequent writings. Against Hegel, whose idealism posited that history was the unfolding of an idea, Cohen defended the naturalist position that thought interacts with a strictly physical external world. Against pragmatism, which contends that knowledge is created by humanity, subject to revision, and never fully descriptive of nature, Cohen posited the ontological existence of an innate logical order from which principles of human reason are deduced. Only constant logic, Cohen insisted, makes it possible for the mind to understand contingent matter.[12]

Inspired by Cohen to pursue philosophy with intellectual rigor, Hook shelved activism for study. His grades in some subjects, particularly physics and chemistry, were poor, but he received several commendations for his efforts in philosophy, including the Ward Medal of Logic, presented to him after his success in Cohen's course "Logic and Scientific Method." A precocious undergraduate, he wrote letters to a number of leading philosophers of the day, from whom he received brief replies on technical points related chiefly to scientific method. Hook must have adopted Cohen's philosophical perspective rapidly, for by 1920 he had already written a somewhat convoluted paper that purported to refute pragmatism from a realist point of view.[13]

[11]   Hook would dedicate his first book, *The Metaphysics of Pragmatism* (Chicago: Open Court, 1927), to Ernest Nagel "in affection and esteem." See also Hook, *Academic Freedom and Academic Anarchy*, 48; Irving Howe, *A Margin of Hope* (New York: Harcourt, Brace Jovanovich, 1982), 62; Hook, *Out of Step*, 42–44, 53–68.
[12]   Daniel Bell to SH, 30 June 1986 (Hook Papers, box 6). For a full treatment of Cohen's world view, see David Hollinger, *Morris R. Cohen and the Scientific Ideal* (Cambridge: MIT Press, 1975).
[13]   Transcript of Record for Sidney Hook, City College of New York (Hook Papers, box 1); "The Pragmatic Conception of Truth," 1920 (Hook Papers, box 38, folder 19). Hook's replies from philosophers, all in Hook Papers: C. D. Broad to SH, 20 November 1922 (box 7); John Burnet to SH, 26 March 1923 and 9 August 1925 (box 8, folder 4); Norman Campbell to SH, n.d. 1922 (Hook Papers, Box 8); S. J. Chapman to SH, 9 February 1923 (box 9); Robert H. Lowie to SH, 18 December 1921, 3 December 1922, 25 September 1922 (box 19); and G. E. Moore to SH, 19 December 1922 (box 21).

Hook retained sympathy for Communism but found activism incompatible with scholarship. The bifurcation was reflected intellectually in his two debut articles, which were published in the philosophical journal *Open Court*. Appearing in 1922, when Hook was still an undergraduate, "The Philosophy of Non-Resistance" argued for revolution and against Tolstoyan pacifism. The philosophy of love and nonresistance, Hook wrote, was appropriate only to some circumstances: "The danger to society arises when the pragmatic criterion is not retained, when those modes of conduct which are adapted to specific situations are reified above the dialectical flow of natural and social forces." References to a pragmatic criterion, dialectical flow, and reification might seem the seedbed for a pragmatist Marxism, but Hook's second article revealed that the terms did not reflect a lasting synthesis. He had originally written "A Philosophical Dialogue" for Harry Overstreet, the head of City College's philosophy department and a Dewey enthusiast. Overstreet was amiable, but his intellect was insufficiently sharp to impress Hook and his friends. Hook's paper imitated the form of a Platonic dialogue. An imaginary Pragmaticus argues with a companion, Universalus, that philosophy should move from contemplation to practice. Universalus replies, "Were philosophy to readjust itself to your eloquent plea that it devote its energies primarily to the solution of pressing social and moral problems, then philosophy would no longer be philosophy but a phase of social science." In the end, Universalus emerges victorious and has the final say: a vague assertion that abstract thought can be removed from temporal concerns and yet offer intrinsic rewards.[14]

John Dewey might have had no disagreement with the views Hook attributed to Universalus, but the young Hook clearly considered them a refutation of pragmatism. By counterposing contemplation to experience, Hook had in his writing, as in his life, made philosophy and politics divergent. His first article argued adamantly for the politics of forceful revolution, summoning to his defense philosophical arguments against quietism and supernaturalism. His second piece insisted that philosophy had a special obligation to remain aloof from worldly concerns. Hook thus simultaneously proposed a politics of revolution and a philosophy of disengagement. "My first impression was that your philosophy was a method to be summed up best in the term deductive logic," a friend wrote him in confusion after reading the two articles. "Then I thought you were a rationalist, then an idealist and now abacadabra—I give up." The incongruity was unlikely to endure.[15]

14 Hook, "The Philosophy of Non-Resistance," *Open Court* 36 (January 1922): 5; Hook, "A Philosophical Dialogue," *Open Court* 36 (October 1922): 624.
15 J. Pargot to SH, 30 July 1924 (Hook Papers, box 23).

Although Hook would not reconcile his politics and philosophy for several years, he did move toward a more harmonious arrangement in the middle of the 1920s, when he shifted his philosophical allegiance from Morris Cohen to John Dewey. Hook graduated from City College with a degree in social sciences in February 1923 and was accepted for the Ph.D. program at Columbia University, which he planned to enter in the fall. That summer he taught elementary school at Public School 43 in Brooklyn, where he was assigned a class of undisciplined, overgrown sixth-graders who had been held back. Throughout his years at Columbia, Hook taught elementary school in Williamsburg during the day, and night classes in English to working adults at the Seward Park Evening School. Only in his last year at Columbia, when he received a tuition scholarship, was he able to drop the daytime teaching job. Because his demanding schedule left only late afternoons free for attending lectures, Hook at first took philosophy courses mainly from W. P. Montague, F. J. E. Woodbridge, and Irwin Edman. As soon as he could, however, he enrolled in courses taught by John Dewey, one of the foremost intellectuals, let alone philosophers, in America.

Dewey's pragmatism had its roots in late nineteenth-century American philosophy, especially the writings of Charles Sanders Peirce and William James. Beliefs are rules for action, the pragmatist theory of inquiry argues, and thinking is the production of habits for action. Our conception of an object, pragmatists maintain, is determined by our understanding of its potential effects. The coherence of any idea, therefore, is insufficient to judge the idea's veracity or "warranted assertibility" (the substitute term for truth that Dewey came to prefer because of its less absolutist connotations). Ideas must be verifiable in experience. Dewey, in fact, called pragmatism "experimentalism." This extension of basic scientific method into the realm of social and moral life he distinguished from preceding empiricisms by its emphasis upon creative thought in the generation of knowledge. Pragmatists contend that people are not mere creatures of physical or spiritual forces. Humans anticipate, aim toward, and thereby shape—to one degree or another—future outcomes. Since consequences cannot always be foreseen, pragmatism requires that all propositions be treated as hypothetical, fallible, and provisional. At the same time, classical pragmatists refuse to condone cynicism, skepticism, and nihilism; they strive to enhance self-critical intelligence and expand democracy.[16]

---

[16] Readers familiar only with the neopragmatism of philosopher Richard Rorty and others influenced by the linguistic turn may be surprised by this anatomy of classical pragmatism (or "paleo-pragmatism," as Robert Westbrook has dubbed it). The contemporary pragmatist

Hook had first read Dewey's writings when they were assigned by Harry Overstreet at City College. He had been impressed by the similarity between Dewey's historical method in *Reconstruction in Philosophy* (1920) and Marx's historical materialism. In *Reconstruction,* Dewey traced the origins of philosophy—especially the dualistic tendency to pit concepts against each other as stark opposites, such as mind and matter—to the initial division of labor, when religion, myth, and historical memory came into conflict with and separated from technical knowledge. The conceit of philosophy, Dewey argued, was to try to resolve this contradiction by pursuing higher purposes and ultimate ends, allegedly timeless and supernatural, while denying the very real connection between philosophy and social development. "When it is acknowledged," he wrote, "that under disguise of dealing with ultimate reality, philosophy has been occupied with the precious values embedded in social traditions, that it has sprung from a clash of social ends and from a conflict of inherited institutions with incompatible contemporary tendencies, it will be seen that the task of future philosophy is to clarify men's ideas as to the social and moral strifes of their own day. Its aim is to become so far as is humanly possible an organ for dealing with these conflicts."[17]

Reconstruction in Philosophy contained all the key elements of Deweyan pragmatism: the inseparability of knowledge from action; the testing of ideas in meliorative practice; the replacement of absolute universality and certainty with fallibility and provisional truth; the value of education; and the requirement of democracy for the all-rounded growth of individuals and social life. Dewey also refuted common misunderstandings of his ideas. He wrote, for example, that pragmatism "does not mean the lowering in dignity of philosophy from a lofty plain to one of gross utilitarianism. It signifies that the prime function of philosophy is that of rationalizing the *pos-*

boom, which reaches well beyond philosophy into literary criticism, feminism, legal theory, and critical social theory, often takes forms influenced by poststructuralism and postmodernism. These forms differ in important ways from the Deweyan intellectual milieu in which Hook, as a second-generation pragmatist, formed his views. The literature on pragmatism is immense, but for useful historical overviews, see David A. Hollinger, "The Problem of Pragmatism in American History," in *In the American Province* (Bloomington: Indiana University Press, 1985), 23–43; Cornel West, *The American Evasion of Philosophy: A Genealogy of Pragmatism* (Madison: University of Wisconsin Press, 1989); Richard J. Bernstein, "The Resurgence of Pragmatism," *Social Research* 59 (Winter 1992): 813–40; and James T. Kloppenberg, "Pragmatism: An Old Name for Some New Ways of Thinking?" *Journal of American History* 83 (June 1996): 100–138. One recent distillation of criticisms of pragmatism is John Patrick Diggins, *The Promise of Pragmatism* (Chicago: University of Chicago Press, 1994), which gave rise to replies by James Hoopes, James T. Kloppenberg, and Robert Westbrook, printed with a rejoinder by Diggins, in the *Intellectual History Newsletter* 17 (1995): 3–30.

17   John Dewey, *Reconstruction in Philosophy* (New York: Henry Holt, 1920), 26. On Overstreet, see Hook, *Out of Step,* 82.

sibilities of experience, especially collective human experience." Rather than dispense with morality, wrote Dewey, pragmatism would rescue morality from formalism by connecting it to actual life, with democracy as both the means and end of practice.[18]

Though impressed by Dewey's social approach to intellectual history, Hook remained under Cohen's sway. He was especially unpersuaded by Dewey's theory of logic. In *Reconstruction in Philosophy* Dewey argued that logic is an account of the procedure of thought, the means of intentional reconstruction of experience, and thus neither simply empirical nor simply normative but both. Hook, following Cohen, saw logic instead as an immutable and fixed source of human reason. At Columbia, Hook would periodically interrupt the famous philosopher in the middle of his lectures to challenge him from the standpoint of Cohen. "It was only at the end of the year," Hook later recalled, "when I sat down to write a definite refutation of pragmatism, that I discovered to my astonishment, as I developed my argument, that I was coming out in the wrong place. Instead of refuting Dewey's views, I was *confirming* them!" Hook's adoption of pragmatism was an intellectual, not a personal, conversion. Though congenial, Dewey lacked Cohen's charisma and was monotonous and dry at the lectern. But Hook decided that Cohen had misunderstood Dewey. For Dewey, "practical" was synonymous with "experimental," not "useful." Cohen's failure to perceive this basic distinction, Hook decided, had led him to the false impression that Dewey was arguing against the possibility of abstract thought. By early 1926 Hook had become a pragmatist.[19]

He was also an outstanding student. Art historian Meyer Schapiro, then a brilliant undergraduate who was permitted to enroll in Columbia graduate courses, vividly recalled Hook's precocious behavior toward one of their professors in a seminar on the philosophy of science: "Sidney was always challenging him in the class, and it caused a lot of feeling, because his way of challenging the professor was rather graceless. But he made very good points. When this professor referred to some old philosopher, trying to quote him, Sidney would correct him. This happened a few times, and some of the students felt annoyed by Sidney's interventions, but his points were always interesting and well-taken." Hook won the respect of the entire department at Columbia, as he had at City College. He and Dewey es-

18   Dewey, *Reconstruction in Philosophy*, 122.
19   "I came to see," Hook wrote in *Pragmatism and the Tragic Sense of Life* (New York: Basic, 1974), 113, "that Cohen had little original vision and that he was primarily an excellent judicial critic rather than an interpretive one. When Cohen got through criticizing almost any great contemporary thinker, one asked oneself: How could any philosopher be such an ass as to believe such stuff? The truth was that most of the time he didn't." See also Dewey, *Reconstruction in Philosophy*, 132–35. Hook, *Out of Step*, 84; Harry Overstreet to SH, 24 February 1926 (Hook-Dewey Collection, box 1, folder 2).

tablished an especially loyal and close friendship that would extend, almost without antagonism, until the latter's death in 1952. Dewey treated Hook as an intellectual colleague, consulting with him on philosophical questions, sending him drafts of his books to read and criticize. Hook's devotion to Dewey, in turn, extended beyond the intellectual. When Dewey's wife died in the summer of 1927, Hook wrote to his mentor, "Let me assure you that there is at least one person, the warmth of whose affection for you is more 'filial' than professional—who considers it an honor and delight to be of help to you in any way and at any time." Dewey, meanwhile, had a superlative admiration for his pupil, writing in a formal evaluation that Hook's "range of information in the history of thought . . . was as broad, accurate, digested and lucidly expressed as that of any student I have ever seen examined." In a private 1927 letter to the social psychologist George Herbert Mead, Dewey wrote, "I almost feel I am ready to quit, as he has not only got the point but sees many implications I hadn't."[20]

Hook's dissertation, written under Dewey, was published as a book in 1927. *The Metaphysics of Pragmatism* was a mischievous title that Hook selected, he admitted, with "malice prepense." (Significantly, the phrase "malice prepense" was used first by Dewey in a similar context, to describe his historical account of absolute Being.) Metaphysics, the study of the nature of things, usually indicates a search for absolute reality and a claim to totalizing knowledge about the sciences. Pragmatism, by contrast, emphasizes flux and change, forsaking philosophy's traditional pursuit of timeless truth. How, then, could there be a "metaphysics of pragmatism"? Pragmatism, Hook maintained, rules out only a certain *type* of metaphysics. Insofar as it presumes to have a method, he asserted, pragmatism must necessarily refer to a theory of existence and, hence, to a metaphysics.[21]

By that, Hook took metaphysics to mean something more watery than it often does, enabling him to situate pragmatism within the classical philosophical tradition while defending Dewey against Cohen's detractions. Dewey's foreword to *The Metaphysics of Pragmatism* praised the volume be-

[20] Interview with Meyer Schapiro, 25 October 1993; SH to JD, 15 July 1927 (Dewey Papers, box 8, folder 1); JD, evaluation of SH, 4 February 1927 (Hook Papers, box 174); Dewey to Mead quoted in Barbara Levine, *Sidney Hook: A Checklist of Writings* (Carbondale: Southern Illinois University Press, 1989), vii. For Dewey's early technical consultation with Hook, see JD to SH, 27 May, 21 June, 8 June, and 30 June 1927 (Hook-Dewey Collection, box 1, folder 2); and SH to JD, 9 June 1928 (Dewey Papers). Further glowing reports on Hook, all in Hook Papers, include John Coss to SH, 13 August 1924; Irwin Edman to Committee on Scholarships, Columbia University, n.d.; Adam Leroy Jones, 3 May 1926 (box 1); Harry Overstreet to Columbia Committee on Fellowship, 24 February 1926 (box 23); H. A. Overstreet, 11 February 1925 (box 1); Morris Cohen to Columbia Committee on Scholarships, 9 February 1925 (box 9).
[21] Hook, *The Metaphysics of Pragmatism*, 6. For "malice prepense," see Dewey, *Reconstruction in Philosophy*, 24.

cause "more than anything on its subject with which I am acquainted, it expresses an equilibrium which is constantly and deliberately sustained between that newer movement which goes by the name of pragmatism and instrumentalism and essential portions of classical thought." In an indirect challege to Cohen, Hook argued on behalf of the principle of inference, which holds that guiding principles are not intuited but are instead habits of thought that have through practice over time become accepted. Logic, therefore, was historical and experimental. As Hook wrote, "The intelligibility of any deductive system or even of a solitary definition demands at some point an *objective* signification." *The Metaphysics of Pragmatism* conveyed other Deweyan theses that would become staples of Hook's thought: that "copy-book" epistemologies, which consider knowledge a mirror of reality, fail to account for the mind's active participation in creating understanding; that instrumentalism, purposive reasoning, cannot be separated from social and moral judgment; that understanding the limitation of possibilities leads to the liberation of possibilities; and that social reform and revolution require not blind revolt against abuses but resolute, intelligent action guided by social theory.[22]

This new theoretical emphasis on action, democracy, and the testing of ideas through inquiry was an important opening for the reconciliation of Hook's philosophical interest with his radical politics. Yet in *The Metaphysics of Pragmatism* Hook remained bound to such classifications of traditional metaphysics as categories, epistemology, determination, and freedom. His tendency to cloud such topics in a thick fog of jargon reflected a lingering desire that philosophy stand above the world and an affection for the special vocabulary of a profession that was on its way to becoming an isolated preserve of the technically trained. Except for a few flashes of humor that prefigured his mature polemical adroitness, the prose of *The Metaphysics of Pragmatism* was ponderous. This was not a merely stylistic matter but part of a greater weakness, for even as Hook endorsed purposive action in theory, his conception of philosophy remained removed from the world. He did not emulate the historical approach to philosophy that he had admired in Dewey, and his brief references to Marx and Engels, though uncommon for an academic dissertation of the day, were incidental to the book's major themes.

[22] Dewey, "An Introductory Word," in Hook, *The Metaphysics of Pragmatism*, 3; Hook, *The Metaphysics of Pragmatism*, 75. In his review of the book, *Mind* 37 (April 1928): 242, the British pragmatist F. C. S. Schiller accused Hook of misrepresenting metaphysics and of trying to combine Cohen and Dewey, but Hook clearly specified the broad meaning he imparted to metaphysics. The work is better understood as a break with Cohen on the question of logic, although Hook preserved Cohen's naturalist critique of idealism.

In addition to transferring his fealty to pragmatism, during his last year at Columbia Hook had begun to move, hesitantly, toward socialist activism again. In his first significant public protest since his high school days, he helped to organize a picket on the steps of Low Library against the execution of Sacco and Vanzetti, the Italian immigrant anarchists accused of murder in Massachusetts, whose fate became a cause célèbre among liberals and radicals. He also teamed with David Kvitko—a Russian-born Columbia student and Communist who had been an official in the Amalgamated Clothing Workers of America—to translate *Materialism and Empirio-Criticism,* the principal philosophical work of the Bolshevik leader V. I. Lenin, into English. Kvitko had translated Lenin's book from the Russian at the request of Alexander Trachtenberg at International Publishers, the Communist publishing house, and Hook used the published German translation to improve upon Kvitko's crude rendering. The product of their collaboration appeared in 1927.[23]

Throughout the period, despite his hectic teaching schedule and new-found devotion to academic philosophy, Hook preserved a perceptible thread of connection to the Communist Party. In the 1920s such a connection was a rarity for a graduate student and young instructor. As the heady days of the early Soviet revolution passed, the revolutionaries who launched the American Communist movement in 1919 found the political climate stifling. Police and vigilante repression, the business offensive against labor, and conservative political hegemony combined to discourage radical organizing in the 1920s. Hook was among the few young intellectuals to stick it out through radicalism's dog days, but conflicting accounts make it difficult to reconstruct the precise nature of his involvement. In later years, whether out of embarrassment or for fear of implicating family and friends, he was circumspect about the details of his relationship to Communism in the 1920s and early 1930s, and the anecdotes he told, which reflected poorly on the Party, did not help to illuminate his period of collaboration.

Was Hook ever a member of the Communist Party? In 1952 Joseph Freeman, a leading Communist cultural figure of the 1930s who had by then left the Party, asserted in an unpublished reminiscent letter that Hook had been a "card-carrying Party member" in the 1920s. Likewise, the entry on Hook in *The Encyclopedia of the American Left* (1990) claims that "during the early 1930s, Hook was a member of the Communist Party." But

[23] Hook, *Out of Step*, 88, 122–23; Theodore Draper, interview with Sidney Hook, 17 May 1957 (Theodore Draper Papers, Emory University, box 13).

Hook emphatically denied ever having been a member, and all reliable evidence supports his claim. Theodore Draper, Sender Garlin, Albert Glotzer, Corliss Lamont, A. B. Magil, John McDonald, and Felix Morrow, who knew Hook in the 1930s and represent a tremendous range of political opinion in both their early and later lives, do not believe Hook was ever a Communist Party member. The Communist Party U.S.A. has no record that he was ever on its membership roles. The warranted conclusion is that Hook was never a member of the Communist Party.[24]

That he was not a dues-paying or card-carrying member of the Party should not, however, obscure Hook's very close relationship to the Communist movement from the early 1920s until 1933. Lack of membership did not necessarily signify political distance and should not obscure the fact that Hook was squarely within the Communist periphery. Party leaders frequently advised sympathetic intellectuals to retain independence so as to preserve their credibility; even publicly declared Communist intellectuals frequently abstained from participation in Party units. As one

[24] Joseph Freeman to Floyd Dell, 14 April 1952 (Hook Papers, box 133, file 6); Steven Best, "Hook, Sidney," in *Encyclopedia of the American Left*, ed. Mary Jo Buhle, Paul Buhle, and Dan Georgakas (Urbana: University of Illinois Press, 1992), 332–33. Freeman's account should not be ruled out, some might say, since in 1952 he was free from any factional ties and also closer to the events than was Hook in the early 1980s when he denied Freeman's version. Then again, Freeman may have had some bitterness toward Hook in 1952, since in his letter he maintains that the young Hook would never have been able to hold his job at NYU in the early 1930s if the later Hook had been around keeping Communists out of the university. The 1952 letter, more revealingly, is mistaken in several ways. Freeman asserts that Hook spent two years at the Marx-Engels Institute in the Soviet Union, when in fact Hook only spent one summer in Moscow after a single year in Germany. Freeman states that Hook married Carrie Katz prior to 1921–22 and claims she was his secretary at the *Liberator;* but Hook and Katz married in 1924. Furthermore, Freeman engages in baseless speculation by suggesting that Hook's trip to the Soviet Union was paid for by Party or Soviet funds, whereas in fact, the Guggenheim Foundation covered Hook's expenses. At best, therefore, since Freeman had only a passing familiarity with Hook's career, there is no reason to trust his account. Hook repeatedly denied Freeman's claim about his Party membership in the 1920s: see SH to Alan Wald, 15 September and 26 November 1984, 19 April and 22 April 1985 (Wald Collection). There is absolutely no doubt, in any case, about his status in the early 1930s. In 1978, in fact, he considered filing a lawsuit against the *New York Times* until it printed his denial of the assertion in a *Times* obituary for Matthew Josephson that Hook had been a Party member in the early 1930s. See SH to George Palmer, 20 March 1978, and SH to James Burnham, 22 March 1978 (James Burnham Papers, Hoover Institution, box 3, folder 3); and SH to Alan Wald, 25 August 1984 (Wald Collection). The testimonies of those close to Hook at the time, or involved on the left and in a position to know, constitute a compelling preponderance of informed opinion against the assertion that Hook was a dues-paying Communist: Theodore Draper to author, 30 January 1992; interview with Sender Garlin, 9 May 1992; Albert Glotzer to author, 12 December 1991, 5 and 25 January 1992; Corliss Lamont to author, 11 December 1991; A. B. Magil to author, 24 February and 8 March 1992; John McDonald to Alan Wald, 6 August 1985, and Felix Morrow to Alan Wald, 10 October 1984 (Wald Collection); Audrey Cline, National Organization Department of the CPUSA, to author, 15 May 1992.

1930s radical put it, if Hook wasn't a member of the Communist Party, he was a "dues cheater."[25]

The most important bond between Hook and Communism was personal. On March 17, 1924, at the age of twenty-one, he was married in a civil ceremony to Carrie Katz, twenty-two, daughter of Hyman and Sylvia Shrager Katz of 927 DeKalb Avenue, on a block adjacent to that of Hook's parents' residence in Brooklyn. Carrie's parents, like Hook's mother, were Galician-born Jews who had emigrated to New York. A high school graduate who never went to college, Carrie was a charter member of the Communist Party and belonged to the William Z. Foster faction. (Heavily trade unionist in composition, the Foster faction at mid-decade was out of favor with the Comintern but would ascend to control at Stalin's directive by 1929.) Most remember Carrie Hook as a kind and likable woman. Late in life, Hook himself recalled her as politically naive, "sweet, gentle, shy and soft-spoken," a vegetarian on moral grounds who had quit a career as a social worker because of her acute sensitivity to human pain and suffering. Although she was a stenographer and for a brief period a telephone operator for the *Daily Worker*, she was chiefly a rank-and-filer who had virtually no influence in the Party. As a 1930 letter to Hook from his City College friend Sam Chovenson, referring to himself and Carrie, put it, "While we may be Communists—that does not mean we are of the politician type."[26]

[25] Interview with B. J. Widick, 23 March 1992.
[26] Interview with Ann Hook, 30 August 1993; Sam Chovenson to SH, 26 March 1930 (Hook Papers, box 9); marriage certificate for Sidney Hook and Carrie Katz Hook, 17 March 1924 (City Clerk of New York, Brooklyn Office). One account would contradict the foregoing interpretation of Carrie Katz Hook. Felix Morrow, a friend of Hook's who in the early 1930s joined the Communist Party and then the anti-Stalinist left, insisted in later correspondence that Carrie Katz Hook was a domineering wife and an insider on the Ninth Floor, the top floor of the Party's national headquarters, perhaps as a secretary to Party leader Earl Browder. Morrow's account was compounded by Joseph Freeman's claim in 1952 that she had worked as his secretary for *The Liberator*, a radical magazine, in 1921–22. Hook's denial of these claims is substantiated by Communist cultural figure A. B. Magil, who joined the Party in 1927 and became a Party staffer in 1929. Magil recalls that Carrie was a Party member but denies that she worked at Party headquarters. Although he knew Freeman personally, Magil never heard him say that she worked for him at the *Liberator*. It may be that Freeman was confused about a job Katz had after her separation from Hook. Sender Garlin, longtime writer for the *Daily Worker*, recalls that Katz handled the switchboard for the *Daily Worker* for a brief time in the 1930s. Felix Morrow to Alan Wald, 10 October 1984 (Wald Collection); Alan Wald to author, 5 May 1991; Freeman to Floyd Dell, 14 April 1984 (Wald Collection and Hook Papers); SH to Alan Wald, 15 September and 26 November 1984 and 4 February 1985 (Wald Collection); A. B. Magil to author, 8 March 1992; interview with Sender Garlin, 9 May 1992. As part of a general policy of skipping the details of his private life, Hook did not mention his first wife by name in *Out of Step*, but he was perfectly willing to speculate about the influence of wives upon other men, even to the point of drafting a prolegomenon to a theory of spousal politics: "Over the years I have observed that, if a woman got politics or religion, within a year or so either the husband or lover became infected with the same ideological virus, or the relationship was dissolved" (134). By his own rule of thumb, there-

The connection to the Communist Party that his marriage gave Hook meant, at the very least, that the Party's internal affairs cannot have eluded him. His wife's comrades were his friends, and the Party's internal documents and press would have been brought into the home regularly. Carrie and Sidney lived together throughout the 1920s, and she accompanied him in 1928 and 1929 to Germany and the Soviet Union. On September 30, 1930, she gave birth to their child John Bertrand Hook (named, most likely, after Dewey and Russell). The end of their marriage in the early 1930s seems to have been due to personal incompatibility as much as political difference. In Europe, Sidney was content to go to the archives and read every day, while Carrie wanted to explore the city streets and experience the people and places. "She was more humanitarian, more feeling, more interested in people," recalls their son, "whereas he was more interested in the intellectual side and the books." By 1933 the couple had separated, but Sidney still dedicated his book *Towards the Understanding of Karl Marx* (1933) to *"C.K.H., in friendship."* The estranged couple remained friendly until Hook's increasingly bitter split with the Party caused their remaining ties to dissolve.[27]

In the autumn of 1927 Hook became an instructor at New York University, where he was hired by the chairman of the philosophy department, Philip Wheelwright and where he would eventually teach for forty successive years. Yet from the outset, even with the intellectual sponsorship of Dewey, the most important philosopher of the day, Hook's appointment was precarious. All faculty positions were uncertain in the era before regularized tenure, and openness about Marxist politics carried great risk for a young faculty member. At NYU's Washington Square College, furthermore, Hook was the first Jew known to teach in any department. Nonetheless, he continued to exhibit the commitment to activism that he had renewed in his last year at Columbia; for example, he founded a Social Problems Club, as he had at City College.[28] Perhaps he enhanced his courage by not at first considering himself bound permanently to NYU. In the fall of 1927 and throughout 1928 he explored the possibility of a job

fore, Hook's marriage ought to have had great consequence for his political thought. Elsewhere, he wrote about the importance of Alger Hiss's wife Priscilla to understanding the contested espionage case. Hook's personal associations should not be exempt from the same sort of historical analysis, providing of course that the strictest standards of evidence are met. See Dick Burress to SH, 27 June 1988, and SH to Dick Burress, n.d. (Hook Papers, box 8).

[27] Certificate of Birth for John Bertrand Hook, 30 September 1930 (Hook Papers, Box 3); interview with John B. Hook, 23 Aug. 1993.

[28] Sam Gordon, who first established contact with the City College Social Problems Club in 1927–28, called it "more or less, but not entirely, a sort of transmission belt for the YCL (Young Communist League)." See Gordon's contribution to *James P. Cannon as We Knew Him*, ed. Les Evans (New York: Pathfinder, 1976), 53.

at the University of Chicago, but it never materialized, despite the initial interest and excitement of the Chicago philosophy department.[29]

Just as Hook's endorsement of pragmatism in *The Metaphysics of Pragmatism* and his renewed political activism signaled an apparent joining of revolutionary socialism with philosophical scholarship, so in his writing Hook began to argue that pragmatism and Marxism, properly understood, complement each other. He had been reading widely in Marxist philosophy, from the original works of Marx and Engels to such highly theoretical continental works as *History and Class Consciousness* (1923) by the Hungarian Marxist Georg Lukács—a book that Hook read in German more than four decades before it was translated into English with the renewal of Marxist scholarship in the 1960s. Hook favored Lukács's emphasis on Marx's theory of *praxis*, or transformative activity, but to his mind Lukács had placed Marx in an overly Hegelian light.[30]

The sophistication of Hook's studies was in full evidence in "The Philosophy of Dialectical Materialism," his first major assessment of Marxism, which was published in early 1928 in the *Journal of Philosophy*, a leading professional journal edited by one of Hook's Columbia professors, F. J. E. Woodbridge. In two installments, Hook's article outlined the changing meaning of materialism in the developing thought of Marx and Engels and then examined Lenin's *Materialism and Empirio-Criticism*. The first section in particular, though it reflected the unfinished and still uneven thought of its author, was one of the best expositions of Marxist philosophy to appear in the United States during the 1920s.

Prevailing ignorance about the ideas of Engels and Marx among American philosophers, Hook observed, was ironic, for the two founders of modern communism had held philosophy indispensable to the proletariat and the proletariat crucial to philosophy. As Engels wrote, "The working-class movement is the heir of classical German philosophy." Mocking "peace-loving university professors" who saw dialectical materialism as "an unholy alliance of French atheistic materialism and an errant speculative idealism," Hook maintained that Marxism should instead be understood as "the living union of philosophy and life, of the thought we profess and

[29] The professor Hook would have replaced, James Tufts, recovered from an illness with unexpected speed, so the position never opened. It is possible, though not verifiable, that anti-Semitism accounted for Chicago's about-face. See A. W. Moore to SH, 17 October and 28 May 1928, 10 March 1929 (Hook Papers, box 21); Philip Wheelwright to SH, 19 August and 17 October 1928 (Hook Papers, box 30); JD to SH, 4 January 29 (Hook-Dewey Collection, box 1, folder 2); SH to Philip Wheelwright, 28 January 1928, 26 March 1929 (Hook Papers, box 30); Hook, *Out of Step*, 210.
[30] Hook confirmed that he had read Lukács before his trip to Germany—SH to Alan Wald, 14 April 1985 (Wald Collection)—presumably in preparation for writing "The Philosophy of Dialectical Materialism," pts. 1 and 2, *Journal of Philosophy* 25 (1 and 15 March 1928).

the activities we pursue," a union that Marx himself had recognized only in the course of intellectual and social struggle. After an initial attraction to Hegelian idealism, Marx subscribed to Ludwig Feuerbach's materialism. But because Feuerbach "held to a crude correspondence theory of truth which logically deprived thought of any *initiating* power," Hook explained, Marx was compelled to write *The German Ideology* (1845), a critique of post-Hegelian philosophy, especially Feuerbach's.[31]

The dialectical materialism of *The German Ideology*, according to Hook, was distinct from prior materialisms in three ways: it did not subscribe to mechanism, the idea that physical matter is the source of ideas; it was historical rather than static, doing justice to change and time; and it understood that "human social activity is historically conditioned by economic development" and class struggle. Marx emphasized the importance of objective conditions but disavowed fatalism of any sort, despite the confusion of some of his interpreters. Citing Marx's theses on Feuerbach, with their emphasis on human praxis, Hook argued that "like scientific pragmatism which came long after him," Marx was simultaneously "struggling against two opposed tendencies—sensationalistic empiricism and absolute idealism." Marx's theses on Feuerbach, Hook concluded, were "a striking anticipation of the *instrumentalist* theory of knowledge."[32]

In the second installment Hook criticized Lenin's *Materialism and Empirio-Criticism*, the very work he had helped to translate. He began with the admission that Lenin's book was "peppered with opprobrious epithets and will turn the stomach of any one who is unacquainted with the controversial literature of Marxism." Indeed, stated Hook, next to Lenin all prior polemicists were "mere stammerers," despite a tradition stretching back even further than Marx and Engels. Although severity was not a mere indulgence for Lenin, who wrote in extremely difficult conditions on a subject that he believed had direct bearing on the vital prospects of the revolution to which he had devoted his life, Hook nevertheless took Lenin to task for "unconscionable" distortions of opponents' arguments and, more fundamentally, for his impoverished epistemology. Knowledge, wrote Hook, does not simply "reflect" reality. Any account of knowledge must recognize the role of the human mind in its creative generation: "To understand that knowledge is an affair of getting ideas and not of receiving impressions is to escape the fatuity of the correspondence theory of truth and make the existence of knowledge and the action implied in its attainment intelligible." Lenin, Hook argued, failed to distinguish between realism and materialism—between an experiential theory of knowledge

[31]Hook, "The Philosophy of Dialectical Materialism," pt. 1, 113, 114, 117. *The German Ideology*, from which Hook quoted, had only just been published in German in 1926.
[32] Hook, "The Philosophy of Dialectical Materialism," pt. 1, 122, 119, 118.

and the monistic theory of "stuff" that Marx had transcended in his writings on Feuerbach.[33]

In order to avoid such oversights, Hook alleged, "dialectical materialism must take its cues from the scientific pragmatism of Dewey." Lenin's error, Hook posited, had been an overly literal appropriation of Engels, who in some isolated statements tended toward a monistic and determinist epistemology that was not consistent with the rest of his writing. Hook did not disavow Engels, for he argued that such statements should be viewed against Engels's work as a whole. "Despite some unhappy phrases of Engels, both he and Marx stand committed to a belief in 'causal reciprocity' and not to univocal causal determination of matter or things in history." Hook was so critical of dialectical materialism in his concluding passages, however, that he appeared on the verge of declaring Marxism itself guilty of "methodological monism"—a dogmatic reduction of all historic events to economic development. Marxism's monistic proclivities, in Hook's opinion, derived from the mistaken conflation of Engels's assertion that in *some* cases changes of the mode of production were decisive causes of cultural transvaluations with the idea that economics can account for *all* cases of cultural change. Hook appeared, therefore, to distinguish Marxism from monism. In his final paragraph, however, he contended that the "living protagonists" of dialectical materialism "are false to the spirit and promise of their own doctrine"—a stern judgment, apparently directed against the mainstream of Russian Marxism, which at the same time suggested that dialectical materialism had promise if it could be cleansed of accumulated error.[34]

A residual intellectual conflict between philosophy and politics had in this fashion left its mark on Hook's thought in "The Philosophy of Dialectical Materialism." His analysis of Lenin was particularly ambiguous. Though a rigorous critic of Lenin's epistemology, Hook at the outset of his essay had argued that "the Russian Revolution of November, 1917, was due in part to Lenin's belief that Marxism must be interpreted as a voluntaristic humanism rather than as the teleological fatalism embraced by Social-Democrats everywhere else."[35] In this respect he gave Lenin credit for saving, not debasing, Marxism, but he offered no means of joining his potentially contradictory judgments about Lenin and Lenin's fidelity to Marx. Was Lenin a determinist or a voluntarist? A vulgar materialist or a creative advocate of action? Hook's article, though an exceptionally lucid account of the development of Marx's epistemology, was vague if not inconsistent in its overall judgment of dialectical materialism and the rela-

[33] Ibid., pt. 2, 141, 142, 146, 152.
[34] Ibid., pt. 1, 124.
[35] Ibid., pt. 1, 114.

tionship of Leninism to Marxism. It also left the precise relationship of pragmatism to Marxism unclear. In some passages Marxism appeared to be an anticipation of pragmatism; in others pragmatism appeared a necessary corrective to Marxism.

Against Max Eastman, 1927–28

It was in the course of an extended debate with Max Eastman—one conducted in the context of Hook's reinvigorated socialist activism and continuing association with John Dewey—that Hook began to wriggle his way free from this tangle and argue more decisively that Marxism and pragmatism required each other in order to realize their respective promise. Like other major intellectual syntheses, Hook's pragmatist Marxism had a long period of gestation. Its inception lay in his moment of surprise when he discovered as an undergraduate that Dewey's *Reconstruction in Philosophy* was reminiscent of Marx. But since Hook had in the intervening years evinced ambivalence about both Marxism and pragmatism—first by disputing Dewey from the perspective of Cohen, then by rejecting Lenin's epistemology and calling dialectical materialism into question on pragmatist grounds—one should be cautious about conflating Hook's initial *interest* in both philosophies with his subsequent elaboration of their basic *affinity*. Only in the course of his debate with Eastman did he shelve his residual doubts about the doctrines' compatibility and defend at length their symbiotic potential.

Max Eastman, twenty years Hook's senior, presented an important challenge, for he was the only other prominent student of Dewey to have become a revolutionary socialist. After studying under Dewey in the first decade of the century, serving as his teaching assistant in a course on logic at Columbia, and writing a dissertation on Plato with him, Eastman in 1912 took the helm of *The Masses*. Under his editorship the magazine became an exuberant voice of the literary left, printing poetry, journalism, and essays by John Reed, Upton Sinclair, and Emma Goldman alongside cartoons and drawings by Robert Minor and Art Young. Eastman edited the magazine until it was suppressed during the World War for its anti-war stance. Eastman traveled to the Soviet Union in 1922–24, warning of bureaucratic degeneration there in *Since Lenin Died* (1925). He was the first American to establish ties with the Bolshevik leader Leon Trotsky, whose massive *History of the Russian Revolution* he would translate in the early 1930s. The archetypal Greenwich Village radical, Eastman was an enthusiast of both anarchy and science, combining a bohemian flair for free love with an admiration for social engineering, and a passion for freedom of thought in art and writing with an opposition to literary modernism.

A peculiar interpretation of Eastman's debate with Hook has gained ascendancy: the typical sketch portrays Eastman as the independent thinker trying to break free of a left orthodoxy represented by Hook. Their respective political associations in early 1928 probably account for this interpretation. Hook was politically close to the Communist Party, despite his epistemological doubts; Eastman was collaborating in literary matters with Trotsky, to the irritation of the Communist leadership, which would later that year expel all of Trotsky's supporters from its ranks. Without a doubt, Eastman was eclectic. As he grew ever more critical of the Stalin regime in the Soviet Union, he began, in contrast to Trotsky, to reject central elements of Marx's thought, including his dialectical method, which Eastman considered a mystical abstraction. He still considered himself a Marxist, but he treated dialectics as an inessential and contradictory aspect of Marx's work. He also argued, even more curiously, that Marx's ideas were best understood as an anticipation of Sigmund Freud's psychoanalysis, that "ideology" meant the same thing to Marx as "rationalization" and "sublimation" to Freud—an unusual premise that brought condemnation from Bertram D. Wolfe in the Party's theoretical journal, *The Communist*. The prevailing interpretation of the Hook-Eastman debate, therefore, is not wrong to emphasize Eastman's idiosyncrasy. It does tend to miss that Hook was a budding heretic in his own right. Though aligned with the Party, he was in no respect a parrot. Nor was he a dogmatist. Hook defended Marx on the basis of his experimental and flexible method, not as an oracle of immutable truth. It was Eastman who sought prove Marx dogmatic and to attribute doctrinaire qualities to Hook. The debate is best understood, therefore, as a struggle over the meaning of Marx between two creative revolutionary socialists, neither of whom had sacrificed his intellect to dogma.[36]

[36]Standard accounts also miss the sequential character of the debate, which took place in several distinct episodes over a period of years. The source of the tendency to see Eastman as the victim of Hook's doctrinal orthodoxy is Eastman himself in his "Excommunication and Exorcism as Critical Methods," *Modern Quarterly* 7 (May 1933): 210–13, and "A Master Magician," *Modern Quarterly* 7 (June 1933): 290–93, 307. See also Eastman, "Marx Anticipated Freud," *New Masses* 3 (July 1927): 11–12; and Eastman, *Love and Revolution: My Journey through an Epoch* (New York: Random House, 1964), 460–63, 498–500. Richard Pells is unusually accurate in stating that "both men regarded themselves as disciples of John Dewey; consequently each preferred a social philosophy that left considerable room for human innovation and experiment." Pells misleads, though, when he writes that the "point on which they could never agree was whether Marxism satisfied this desire"; Eastman, while idiosyncratic, was every bit the Marxist Hook was. The biographers of Eastman, for their part, tend to interpret the clash as his attempt to escape the orthodoxy Hook represented and to see Eastman as unduly persecuted by Hook. See Richard Pells, *Radical Visions and American Dreams* (New York: Harper & Row, 1973), 133; Milton Cantor, *Max Eastman* (New York: Twayne, 1970); John P. Diggins, "Exorcising Hegel: Max Eastman," in *Up from Communism: Conservative Odysseys in American Intellectual History* (New York: Harper & Row, 1975), 17–73; and William O'Neill, *The Last Romantic: A Life of Max Eastman* (New York: Oxford University Press, 1978).

In his book *Marx, Lenin, and the Science of Revolution* (1927), Eastman argued that dialectical philosophy was a residue of Prussian absolutism, responsible for the tendency of Marxists to treat politics as religion. When Eastman condensed this argument and published it in the *New Masses,* he drew a sharp rebuttal from Hook. Marxism, Hook replied forcefully in another journal, *Open Court,* is not a dogma; rather, it "appears in the main as a huge *judgment of practice* in Dewey's sense of the phrase and its truth or falsity (instrumental adequacy) is an experimental matter." Hook castigated Eastman for his related claim that Marx's ideas were an anticipation of Freudian psychoanalysis—an attempt, as Hook saw it, to saddle Marx with a speculative and unscientific doctrine antithetical to his actual method. Because Eastman confused historical materialism with a vulgar theory of self-interest, Hook alleged, he had misunderstood what Marx meant by "ideology" and conflated social theory with psychology:

> Historical materialism takes its point of departure from the objective existence of an economic class struggle. In the interests of the struggle, ideas and doctrines are used as *instruments* in bringing the issue to a successful completion. The anticipated efficacy and adequacy of these ideas in furthering class interests explain their *acceptance* and *use* but not necessarily their *genesis* or *origin.* No social factor can *wholly* explain the mechanics of individual creation. But only social factors can explain why once these ideas have seen the light, they have been *accepted.*

Thus, wrote Hook, Marxism "turns out to be a self-critical theory explaining its own acceptance on the basis of its own principles." Though he stated it with some qualification, Hook was arguing, in a set of propositions far less ambiguous than the comparable sentiments of his *Journal of Philosophy* series, that Marx's historical materialism and Dewey's experimental naturalism were practically identical.[37]

Eastman and Hook's discussion of Freud was crude in comparison to later theories relating psychoanalysis to historical materialism by such writers as Herbert Marcuse, Erich Fromm, Norman O. Brown, Wilhelm Reich, Juliet Mitchell, and Christopher Lasch. But Freud proved increasingly marginal to the Hook-Eastman debate, which rapidly concentrated on two issues: the validity of the dialectic, and the compatibility of Marx and Dewey. In his *Journal of Philosophy* article Hook accused Eastman of making "cheap gibes" against Marx in *Marx, Lenin, and the Science of Revolution* while mak-

37 Eastman, "Marx Anticipated Freud"; Hook, "Marx and Freud: Oil and Water," *Open Court* 41 (January 1928): 10–25. An exchange of letters preceded the publication of Hook's article, but nothing was expressed there that did not enter into print. See Eastman to SH, 12 September 1927 and n.d. (Hook Papers, box 39, folder 5).

ing the case for "the alleged inconsistency between Marx's theoretical conception of history and his practical political activity." Eastman, in a letter of protest, denied having made "a gibe of any kind against Marx in my book," adding tersely that he, in contrast to Hook, had called himself "a Marxist when it cost something more than academic prestige to do it." Somewhat contradictorily, Eastman proceeded to insist that Marx's theory and modern scientific method were inconsistent, requiring a purge of Hegelian metaphysics from Marx: "I have proved to the best of my ability that, in spite of his metaphysical system, which is flimsy and false, Marx laid down all the fundamental principles of the science which Lenin applied." Whether or not this constituted a "gibe," it did appear to confirm Hook's point that Eastman perceived a contradiction between Marx's philosophical theory and his revolutionary practice. In a parting shot, Eastman claimed that Hook's ideas on dialectical materialism had been stolen from him without attribution.[38]

Meanwhile, Hook unveiled a full-length review of Eastman's book in the *Modern Quarterly*, a freewheeling periodical edited by the literary radical V. F. Calverton. Born George Goetz in Baltimore, Calverton in the late 1920s was a close collaborator of the Communist Party. The *Modern Quarterly* was his independent vehicle, reflecting his ambition to achieve a radical synthesis all of the humanities and social sciences, including theories of sexuality, literature, philosophy, anthropology, and sociology. The *Modern Quarterly* (for a time in the mid-1930s rechristened The *Modern Monthly*) was an important venue for Hook's early writing and provided a place for Hook and Eastman to slug it out until, some years later, Calverton finally called a halt to the brawl.[39]

The opening line of Hook's review indicated the debate's already intemperate tone: "Max Eastman has bungled a great theme." Eastman, he complained, did not seem to understand that in "rejecting the metaphysics of Marxism he is thereby committing himself to a definite metaphysical position, although that position may be confused in his own mind." Nor did Eastman, Hook observed, position Marx against his opponents who sought to solve social problems through religion, philanthropy, invocations of "real consciousness," or utopian communities—efforts which, no matter how well-intentioned, Marx found *instrumentally* useless. The central aspect of Marx's philosophy was human activity, not a supernatural motor. Marx

[38] Hook, "The Philosophy of Dialectical Materialism," pt. 1, 123 n. 15; Max Eastman, Letter to the Editor, *Journal of Philosophy* 25 (16 August 1928): 475–76.
[39] On Calverton, see Paul Buhle, "Modern Quarterly/Modern Monthly," in *Encyclopedia of the American Left*, 482–83; Leonard Wilcox, *V. F. Calverton: Radical in the American Grain* (Philadelphia: Temple University Press, 1992); and, dissenting from Wilcox, Christopher Phelps, "Impresario of American Radicalism," *New Politics*, Winter 1994, 167–71.

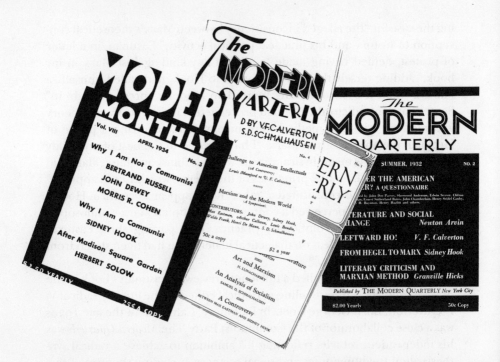

Issues of V. F. Calverton's periodical, with contributions by Hook, including debate with Max Eastman. Calverton's unilateral decision to title an article by Hook "Why I Am a Communist" put Hook's job at risk. (Montage by Christopher Phelps.)

sometimes stressed the limitations placed on action by historical conditions—not in order to assert a mechanical view of history but to throw cold water on those who believed that attaining socialism was merely a matter of exertion. To Marx, wrote Hook, human activity was *necessary* but not always *sufficient* for fundamental change. As for the dialectic, Hook challenged Eastman's presumption that it meant the same thing to Marx and Hegel. Concerning Hegel, he was largely in accord with Eastman. In 1926, when he had undertaken an intensive study of Hegel at Columbia under the tutelage of Vladimir Simkhovitch, Hook had written a paper concluding that the main line of Hegel's thought was directly connected to his political aim of consolidating the German nation under a unified, conservative Christian rule.[40] Against Eastman, however, Hook argued that Marx appropriated Hegel's philosophical *method* while breaking de-

[40] Later, Hook would recall Simkhovitch as "the Russian-American economic historian who fancied himself, in one of his phases, as the American Bernstein": Hook, *Revolution, Reform, and Social Justice: Studies in the Theory and Practice of Marxism* (New York: New York University Press, 1975), 4. See also Hook, "Some Political Motives in Hegel's Thought," and SH to V. G. Simkhovitch, 29 July 1926 (Hook Papers, box 38, folder 26).

finitively from his *politics.* Without actually referring to the famous passage from Marx's preface to *Capital,* Hook in effect argued that Marx had extracted from Hegel "the rational kernel within the mystical shell."[41] Hook also turned the tables on Eastman, suggesting playfully that Eastman's criticism of Lenin's epistemology, though warranted, was first expressed by Hegel, who after all had been the greatest critic of "immediate consciousness"—the idea that the mind simply copies reality. "As punishment," Hook joked, "Eastman ought to read Hegel's *Phänomenologie des Geistes.*" Finally, he reminded Eastman of pragmatism's own debt to Hegel: "The fluidity of thing and fact and the changing *context* of judgment represent the heart of the dialectic, and not the antiquated terms in which Hegel dressed up the idea. Mr. Eastman may be surprised to learn that the dialectic— modified to be sure—appears in the instrumentalist logic."[42]

In this manner, Hook removed dialectics from all attempts to reduce it to Prussian absolutism, and at the same time reconciled dialectical materialism with Deweyan naturalism to his own satisfaction. Eastman, however, was far from quitting, and his snappy rejoinder pressed Hook to prove his point. His real disagreement with Hook, he wrote, was whether Marx had a "thorough-going instrumental view of human intelligence, and believed in the degree of indeterminism, etc., implied by such a view." Their great difference on this matter, Eastman maintained, had been obscured by such distortions as Hook's allegation that Eastman regarded Marx's dialectic as "the confused expression of a queer German," a characterization that Eastman labeled "moral and intellectual libel." He claimed that in their private correspondence Hook had confessed that he had been working on "a study of Marxism as a practical judgment," and Eastman further conjectured, in a repetition of his accusation of theft, that "the publication of my book must have been a keen disappointment to him."[43]

Tongue in cheek, Hook apologized to readers of The *Modern Quarterly* for writing that Eastman considered Marx's dialectic "queer." After all, he recalled, Eastman had suggested that Marx contradicted himself because his political activism clashed with his theoretical "fatalism," and Eastman also claimed that "animistic religion" was the essence of Marx's dialectic. "I should have used a *stronger* expression," quipped Hook. He disputed Eastman's contention that the debate was simply over Marx and instrumentalism by positing that the argument had always been multilayered:

41 Karl Marx, *Capital* (New York: Vintage, 1977), 103.
42 Hook, "Marxism, Metaphysics and Modern Science," review of *Marx, Lenin, and the Science of Revolution* by Max Eastman, *Modern Quarterly* 4 (May–August 1928): 388–94.
43 Max Eastman, "As to Sidney Hook's Morals," *Modern Quarterly* 5 (November 1928–February 1929): 85–87. No correspondence of the type he refers to survives, in either the Sidney Hook Papers or the Max Eastman Papers.

As against Eastman I have maintained (1) that Marx's apparent inconsistencies were matters of relative emphasis at *different* times and against *different* opponents; (2) that Marx, far from being a fatalist, who believed in the inevitability of human activity, underscored human purposes, ... asserting however that they are objectively conditioned; (3) that the existence of a dialectical in nature is implied in all thinking in which time enters and that this involes neither animism nor mysticism; and (4) that the confusion between the *motive* behind thinking and the *purpose* in thinking (which is a question of logical relevance) makes all psychoanalysis foreign both to the ideas of Marx and modern instrumental pragmatism.

The suggestion that he had been motivated by jealousy drew a pointed response from Hook: "If our arguments were the same there might be some psychological plausibility in such a statement despite its logical irrelevance. But since, as he admits, our views on Marx are worlds apart, is it not more plausible that I should welcome an opportunity to show how false his position was?" Eastman's book had indeed caught his eye, given his prior interest in Marx and Dewey, Hook acknowledged—but because he found Eastman's theses *irritating*, not because they were similar to his own views.[44]

Although it would resume with a vengeance about five years later, the Hook-Eastman debate was momentarily spent. Eastman revealed in his memoirs that he fell into a period of dark depression at the time, caused by several factors including Hook's articles, which may account for his withdrawal from the engagement over *Marx, Lenin and the Science of Revolution.* "Suffice it to say," Eastman wrote, "that no such bitter pain of humiliation was ever caused to me, before or since, by a critic of one of my books."[45] The debate had a different significance in Hook's development. It demonstrated that he, like Lenin, was no "mere stammerer" when it came to polemic. But more important, Hook was forced by Eastman's wholesale rejection of dialectics to affirm Marx's dialectical method unequivocally and to draw out its affinities with Deweyan pragmatism. He was approaching a full-scale elaboration of his pragmatist Marxism.

European Travels and Fellow Traveling, 1928–29

"We were living through one of the most critical periods in American history," James Rorty would later recall of the late 1920s, a period when he, like Hook, was an independent radical in proximity to the Communist Party. "Behind us was a war and a revolution which had already es-

---

[44] Hook, "As to Max Eastman's Mentality," *Modern Quarterly* 5 (November 1928–February 1929): 88–89.
[45] Eastman, *Love and Revolution*, 499.

tablished international communism as an enduring, conquering force. Ahead of us was the collapse, in a major depression of the American economy, of the American culture, the American way of life."[46] In 1928 and 1929 Hook traveled for scholarly purposes to Germany and the Soviet Union, where he witnessed fascism and revolution firsthand. Upon returning home he witnessed the crash in U.S. financial markets and the onset of the Great Depression. Combined with his extensive European researches into Marx and post-Hegelian German philosophy, these world-significant events deepened his revolutionary convictions and strengthened his commitment to Marxism.

On July 1, 1928, Hook and his wife sailed for Germany, sponsored by a Guggenheim Fellowship to conduct research for a year in post-Hegelian philosophy. Hook passed his time on the boat reading, playing cards, and eating heartily; he experienced no seasickness. In Germany they lived in Munich, where Hook gained access to the library and lectures at Ludwig-Maximilians-Universität-München. German philosophy in the Weimar period was captivated with the phenomenology of Edmund Husserl, Martin Heidegger, and Karl Jaspers. Hook was impressed by the showmanship of German professors and by the interest of the average German student in philosophy, but he had little patience with the jargon and pomposity of German philosophical discourse. "What mattered if no one could define his terms," he wrote soon afterward. "The talk was grand and loud and everyone felt that it was important." Hook established contact with a small Social Democratic student group—which he found marginal and ineffective—and attended right-wing meetings, attracted innocently by the word "socialism" on the National Socialist fliers he had seen. Although signs prohibited Jews from attending Nazi events, Hook passed without question— probably, he later speculated, because of his American appearance.[47]

In August the Hooks traveled to Vienna, where they intercepted Dewey for a moment on his return from a tour of schools in the Soviet Union. Hook wrote to his father that he had visited an ancient synagogue and a cemetery where some of their ancestors were buried, and he informed his parents that Vienna was the "reddest" city he had yet seen: "Here I am in the most beloved city of Europe. I feel like a bloated millionaire in comparison to the poverty stricken masses here." That did not prevent him from appreciating Vienna's more opulent features: "I've visited the king's

[46] James Rorty, "It Has Happened Here," unpublished memoir, version 1, n.d., chap. 10, p. 3 (James Rorty Papers, University of Oregon).
[47] SH to Eileen Hood, 27 March 1928 (V. F. Calverton Papers, New York Public Library, Hook Correspondence); SH to Isaac Hook, n.d. 1928 (Hook Papers, box 3); Hook, "A Personal Impression of Contemporary German Philosophy," *Journal of Philosophy* 27 (13 March 1930): 142. On Nazi meetings, see Hook, *Out of Step*, 103.

castles, dined in his wine cellar, worked in his library—have done all but slept in his bed." In October the Hooks moved to Berlin, where they settled in for serious study and tried to take in some of the city's rich cultural offerings. "Berlin," Hook wrote to his parents, "is a cleaner and more intelligent New York."[48]

Hook found German politics exhilarating. On a postcard to his brother Herbert he wrote that "politics is to the daily reading fare of the German what sport is to the American. That's why the atmosphere here is more invigorating!" He witnessed street clashes between young Social Democrats and Communists, a consequence of the sectarian Comintern doctrine that Social Democracy was "social fascism," a threat worse than Nazism because it led the working class away from the proper course. In spring 1928 the Nazis had received more than a million votes, and in September 1930 they would poll 6.5 million, yet every leftist Hook met in late 1928 and early 1929 was convinced that the Nazi threat was ephemeral. In his 1987 autobiography Hook recalls that he was bothered by the failure of the Social Democrats, who led the government, to pursue reform vigorously and to put a stop to illegal fascist paramilitary activity. His ambivalence toward the warring wings of socialism, he maintained, left him an outsider as well as a foreigner: "My interest in Marxist theory remained strong, but every Communist group I ever met or came in contact with was suspicious of me because of my 'heresies.'" But this recollection is imperfect. Hook's argument with the Social Democrats in the 1920s was that a reformist strategy was inadequate to the task, no matter how vigorously pursued. His curious attraction to pragmatism may have been known to German leftists, but since he published no criticism of the KPD, the German Communist Party, until four or five years later, he was most likely a critical supporter of the KPD with philosophical and political reservations. Hook's ties to the American Communist Party, after all, were still strong. He and Carrie were visited in Berlin by Alexander Trachtenberg, the head of International Publishers, and they met weekly with a couple they had known in New York as Party members and who were then living in Berlin (as part of a Soviet espionage network, Hook later alleged).[49]

In Europe, Hook's knowledge of the Marxist theoretical tradition expanded considerably. His Guggenheim grant subsidized research into German philosophical debates of the 1840s, when a young circle of thinkers

[48]   Corliss Lamont to SH in Berlin, 25 August 1928 (Hook Papers, box 3); JD to SH, 28 August 1928 (Hook-Dewey Collection, box 1, folder 2); SH to Herbert Hook, 25 August 1928, SH to Charlotte Hook, 6 and 15 September 1928, and SH to Isaac Hook, 9 September 1928 (Hook Papers, box 3).
[49]   SH to Herbert Hook, 13 October 1928 (Hook Papers, box 3); Hook, *Out of Step*, 94–115; SH to Alan Wald, 15 September 1985 (Wald Collection). On the Nazi vote, see Irving Howe and Lewis Coser, *The American Communist Party* (New York: Praeger, 1962), 185.

gave Hegelian philosophy new life in pursuit of such Enlightenment aims as freedom of religion, free speech, and universal suffrage. The young Marx was first an associate and then a strong critic of this set of figures, who came to be known as the Young Hegelians. In retracing this legacy, Hook became versed in how Marxism emerged from classical German idealism. He also paid a visit to Edward Bernstein, founder of the "revisionist" strain of reformism within German Social Democracy, which called upon social-ists to discard all talk of revolution and work for incremental social im-provements. Bernstein told Hook that he considered socialism a child of the Enlightenment and believed there was Bolshevism in Marx, statements that cheered the revolutionary Hook, to whom they gave evidence of the bourgeois heart of reformism. Finally, and significantly, Hook attended lec-tures by Karl Korsch, a dissident Marxist and former Communist delegate who had been reprimanded by Bolshevik leader Grigori Zinoviev in 1924 at the Fifth World Congress of the Comintern for supposed theoretical de-viations and expelled from the KPD in 1926. Korsch had written devastat-ing philosophical refutations of the determinism and fatalism of the Second and Third Internationals. His emphasis on the role of action in Marxism encouraged Hook to persist in his budding effort to combine pragmatism and Marxism.[50]

On December 12, 1928, Hook described Berlin as "cozy and Christ-maslike" in a card to his parents, and on December 20 he celebrated his twenty-sixth birthday. But the long winter took its toll on his spirits. In Feb-ruary he relayed news of "beastly cold"; in March he wrote to his mother, "We have been having the loveliest spring weather to compensate for the last month's bitter frost. Berlin is getting monotonous, though"; in late April, "The trees are still bare and stand like frosty sentinels waiting to be warmed into life." To escape, he departed for travels on the Rhine. He found Heidelberg "really the first German town to live up to expectations. Pretty blossoms, pretty faces, beery students with sword scarred cheeks!" Students sang beneath his window in the evening. Returning by way of Frankfurt for a Kant conference, he was soon back in Berlin, whence he departed for Soviet Russia in early June, financed by an extension of his Guggenheim grant and enticed by an invitation from David Riazanov, di-rector of the Marx-Engels Institute.[51]

Hook was among the first Western scholars to gain access to the Soviet

[50] Hook first recounted the Bernstein incident in *Towards the Understanding of Karl Marx: A Revolutionary Interpretation* (New York: John Day, 1933), 43 n. 5; he expanded it much later in *Out of Step*, 113–14. See Karl Korsch, *Marxism and Philosophy*, ed. Fred Halliday (New York: Monthly Review, 1970); and Karl Korsch, *Three Essays on Marxism*, ed. Paul Breines (New York: Monthly Review, 1971).

[51] SH to Charlotte Hook, 12 December 1928, 14 February, 21 March, 23 April, 10 and 21 May 1929, and 3 June 1929 (Hook Papers, box 3).

Union's holdings of original material by Marx, Engels, and the Young Hegelians. Housed in a former palace, the Marx-Engels Institute was the foremost library in the world on the subject, containing an impressive collection of unpublished and untranslated letters and manuscripts, gathered largely through the assiduous labors of Riazanov. Hook would later recount that he was received by the staff of the institute as a "bourgeois philosopher," to his chagrin. The chilly attitude, if his impression was accurate, may have been a reaction to his criticism of Lenin in the *Journal of Philosophy*. A fellow City College philosophy graduate, Joseph Ratner, had warned Hook before his trip, "Be sure not to let any good Communist in Europe know how un-heroically you treat Lenin in your current articles. The Communist may not like it." But time may have exaggerated Hook's perception that he was slighted at the Marx-Engels Institute, because all evidence suggests he was warmly received in Communist circles. He was met at the Moscow station by David Kvitko, the man who had been his partner in translating Lenin's *Materialism and Empirio-Criticism*. His housing was arranged by another American Communist Party acquaintance who had moved to Moscow and married a Chinese Communist official. Immediately after he returned to the United States, moreover, Riazanov himself wrote him to declare, "On my part I expect your work will be a valuable contribution to the investigation of philosophic history preceding Marx and trust soon to have the pleasure of reading the result of your studies."[52]

Although he spent the bulk of his fourteen weeks in Moscow studying at the institute, Hook did see something of the new Soviet society beyond its walls. He was impressed with the achievements of Communism, concluding that the dire reports in the Western press about starvation were greatly exaggerated. "Food is plentiful but the prices are steep," he wrote his family upon his arrival. "The cultural level and the political morale, however, are unique in quality and intensity." Even after several weeks in Soviet Russia, Hook could barely contain his enthusiasm:

[52] Hook, *Out of Step*, 116–31; Joseph Ratner to SH, 19 March 1928 (Hook Papers, box 24); David Riazanov to SH, 3 June, 19 July, and 21 September 1930 (Hook Papers, box 20). Riazanov also informed Hook that a Dr. E. Czobel wished to tell him that he had been pleased to assist Hook during his Moscow stay. A short time later, when Riazanov was considering a visit to New York, he asked Hook for advice, further indication that Hook was regarded as a colleague by the institute's staff. Riazanov (1870–1938), author of *Karl Marx and Friedrich Engels* (New York: International Publishers, 1927), directed the Marx-Engels Institute from its founding in 1920 and oversaw the first attempt to publish a complete edition of Marx's writings, the *Marx-Engels Gesamtausgabe (MEGA);* twelve volumes were issued before Stalin dismissed Riazanov, who eventually perished in the purges. For further information on Riazanov, see Georg Lukács, *Record of a Life* (London: Verso, 1983), 179–80; and Dirk J. Struik, introduction to the 1973 edition of *Karl Marx and Friedrich Engels* (New York: Monthly Review), 3–10.

This is Moscow—bizarre and gorgeous—a city of startling contrasts—carrying ugly scars of the past and seeds of the future. Food is mean and clothes are rather shabby—but every brick, every road, every machine is a symbol of the new spirit. I have seen no Potemkin village. Just mingling with the people has enabled me to tap veins of enthusiasm that run deep under the surface of things. And just think of it! A country in which the red flag is a national banner and the *Internationale* the national anthem.

He later avowed that he had begun to see a darker side to Soviet society while he was there: in summer 1929 Stalin's campaign against the Left and Right Oppositions was at a high pitch, and Hook claimed to have been unsettled by indications of political repression. Even before his trip to the Soviet Union, he contended in 1985, he had been moved by the public suicide note that Sovict revolutionist Adolph Joffe had written to Trotsky. In the note, published in *Inprecorr,* the Comintern journal, a despairing Joffe had told Trotsky that "politically, you were always right, . . . now more right than ever," but that lacking "Lenin's unbending will, his unwillingness to yield," Trotsky had too often compromised without warrant. Joffe's forlorn observations about the course of the revolution did not, however, stem Hook's expressions of enthusiasm in 1929. No apprehension or ambivalence about the USSR is evident in his postcards to his parents from Moscow.[53]

In September, Hook returned to New York by boat after meeting Dewey momentarily in Frankfurt and making sightseeing stops in Amsterdam, London, and Paris. When he resumed his instructorship at Washington Square College of New York University, which paid merely $2,400 for the 1929–30 academic year, his Marxist commitment had been reinvigorated by his firsthand knowledge of the rising threat of fascism in Germany, extensive research in post-Hegelian philosophy, and the opportunity to witness life in the Soviet Union. The unprecedented stock market crash that autumn, moreover, appeared to confirm Marx's analysis of the tendency of capitalist economies to enter periodic crises of overproduction.[54]

That year, Hook offered a course in dialectical materialism, the first ever taught on Marxism in the NYU philosophy department. He also began to lecture before socialist audiences and at the artists' and writers' colony Yad-

[53] Moscow notes: SH to Charlotte Hook, 10 and 24 June 1929 (Hook Papers, box 3). On Joffe: SH to Alan Wald, 15 September 1985 (Wald Collection); Leon Trotsky, *My Life* (New York: Pathfinder, 1970), 537.
[54] JD to SH, 10 May 1929 (Hook-Dewey Collection, box 1, folder 2); SH to Charlotte Hook, 22, 23, and 30 August 1929, and SH to Selma Blair, 22 August 1929 (Hook Papers, box 3). On NYC pay, see Philip Wheelwright to SH, 19 August 1928 (Hook Papers, box 30).

Children swimming in fountain, Washington Square Park, mid-1930s. Hook taught at NYU's Washington Square campus for more than forty years. (Courtesy New York University Archives, Bobst Library.)

do in Saratoga, New York. In the summer of 1930 he taught a course at Columbia University. This round of teaching and speaking engagements provided the first opportunity for many young radicals in New York to study Marxist ideas systematically. Historian Theodore Draper, for example, heard about the NYU class on Marxism from a cousin, and when he audited it with the instructor's permission, he found Hook a "powerful teacher." Hook was an inspiration for many other young leftists as well. Sender Garlin, who was present at a 1930 symposium on popular culture attended by Hook and the chair of a John Reed Club meeting at which Hook spoke in the early 1930s, recalls: "He was a lowly instructor, which is a glorified term for an academic sharecropper. An instructor at NYU in 1930 wasn't big stuff—academically, I mean. But he had very impressive credentials as a young scholar: not only a favorite student of John Dewey, but extensively educated in Germany. There were very few academics who not only admitted but were *proud* of the fact that they were Marxist scholars." Indeed, when Hook began to publish widely on issues of Marxism and philosophy in the first years of the 1930s, he was almost certainly the only openly Marxist academic philosopher in the United States.[55]

The Communist Party remained at the center of Hook's politics. Though he was never technically a member, throughout the 1920s and first years of the 1930s he was clearly acting in solidarity with the Party. His participation in the Communist faction of the City College Social Problems Club in 1919–20, his marriage to Carrie Katz in 1924, his collaboration with David Kvitko in translating Lenin's *Materialism and Empirio-Criticism* for International Publishers in 1927, his formation of a second Social Problems Club at NYU in 1927, his visits in Berlin with American Communists, his invitation to the Marx-Engels Institute by David Riazanov, and his association in Moscow with American Communists all demonstrate a consistently close and friendly relationship with the Communist movement, despite a momentary withdrawal from political activism during his student days at City College. When he returned to the United States on the eve of a new decade, Hook returned to this organizational association *and* his scholarship—to both activism and philosophy.

[55] Theodore Draper to author, 11 January 1992; interview with Sender Garlin, 9 May 1992. On Columbia: John Coss to SH, 4 November 1929 and 4 February 1930 (Hook Papers, box 10). Yaddo: Irwin Edman to SH, 31 January 1931 (Hook Papers, box 11); V. F. Calverton to SH, n.d. (Hook Papers, box 8). Course on Marxism: SH to Philip Wheelwright, 28 January 1929 (Hook Papers, box 30).

CHAPTER TWO

Communism and Pragmatism, 1930–33

When Hook returned to New York City from his European travels in the middle of 1929, he was confident, after a decade of experimentation, that radical political engagement and philosophical investigation could be combined successfully. Yet in the opening years of the 1930s he faced a new set of problems as a revolutionary scholar. The epochal crisis that brought global capitalism to its knees created new opportunities and audiences for Marxist ideas, but Hook was called upon to defend and articulate the theoretical compatibility of pragmatism and Marxism against a variety of detractors. Furthermore, he was forced to define more precisely than before his relationship to the Communist Party, the organization that had until then appeared to him the most viable instrument for socialist revolution in the United States.

An important dimension of Hook's project upon his return to the United States from the Soviet Union was to imbue Marxism with a sensibility attuned to American conditions and to win it a legitimate place in American intellectual culture. Not only did he approach Marx by way of pragmatism, the principal American contribution to philosophy, but his rising reputation as the foremost Marx scholar in the United States gave him a unique chance to help explicate and popularize Marx's ideas before a broad public. He translated a number of original writings by Marx and Engels into English, spoke frequently at colleges and other institutions, and wrote a series of articles on topics related to historical materialism for political periodicals, philosophical journals, and the *Encyclopaedia of the Social Sciences*. The quickening pulse of radical activity and Hook's connection to the American Communist Party gave this theoretical work a feeling of great practical significance. "I felt," he recalled in his memoir, "somewhat like Paul bringing the glad news of salvation to the spiritually hungry Gentiles."[1]

In a more strictly professional capacity as well, Hook returned from Europe an authority on German thought. Despite complaints of "chronic poor health," his philosophical output in the first years of the new decade was tremendous. In 1930 and 1931 he wrote biographical entries for the *Encyclopaedia of the Social Sciences* on a series of post-Hegelian philosophers, including the Young Hegelian Bruno Bauer, the mechanistic materialist Ludwig Büchner, and the autodidact socialist philosopher Joseph Dietzgen. He reviewed a spate of books on Hegel for prestigious philosophical journals and wrote several articles on Edmund Husserl's phenomenology, which he praised for its critique of sensationalist epistemology but criticized for its transcendentalism. In an apparent effort to bridge the gulf that now yawned between him and Morris Cohen, Hook wrote a tribute to his erstwhile mentor in the *New Republic*. Their philosophical rupture was irreparable, however. Within a year they squared off at the Eastern Division of the American Philosophical Association on the very question that had led initially to their estrangement, with Cohen defending the existence of intuitive logic and Hook insisting on the experimental naturalism characteristic of instrumentalism. Soon afterward, Hook published a lengthy critique of Cohen's *Reason and Nature,* a book which Cohen intended as a challenge to Dewey's *Experience and Nature*. Hook's philosophical interests were also sustained throughout the decade by his participation in the regular discussions of an ad hoc club of veterans of the Columbia graduate program—including Meyer Schapiro, Philip Wiener, and Ernest Nagel—who gathered every few weeks to hear one another's papers. The club met faithfully for fifteen years, until it finally broke apart over irreconcilable

[1] Hook, *Out of Step* (New York: Harper & Row, 1987), 135. For the translations, see "Kant and Political Liberalism," by Karl Marx, trans. SH, *Modern Monthly* 7 (July 1933): 352–54; "On Hegel's 'Concrete Universal'," by Karl Marx, trans. SH, *Modern Monthly* 7 (September 1933): 496–97; "Appendix: Four Letters on Historical Materialism by Frederick Engels," trans. SH, in *Towards the Understanding of Karl Marx* (New York: John Day, 1933), 323–42. The first was from *The German Ideology,* the second from *The Holy Family;* all three were from texts never before translated into English. For a typical speaking engagement, see Hampshire County Progressive Club Forum Program, 1932–33 (Hook Papers, box 40, folder 28).

conflicts between admirers of the logical positivist Rudolf Carnap and the rest of the group.[2]

Hook's newly acquired knowledge of German philosophy and Marxism complemented his pragmatism, which was itself taking on an increasingly radical character. Throughout the early 1930s he maintained that Deweyan pragmatism, with its commitment to democracy and unfettered scientific inquiry, required for its fulfillment a socialist society, achievable only through revolution. The label "pragmatist Marxism" might therefore serve as an apt designation of Hook's thought in the 1930s. It distinguishes his thought from other Marxian doctrines of the day, especially the cumbersome textual exegeses emanating from Stalin's Soviet Union, and it captures Hook's dual philosophical project of the 1930s: his examination of Marxist intellectual history through a pragmatist lens, and his efforts to persuade his mentor, John Dewey, that revolutionary politics followed logically from his democratic social thought. Yet the term is potentially misleading. To the young Hook the phrase "pragmatist Marxism" would have been largely redundant, and he never paired the words in such a way. To him there was no clear place where pragmatism began and Marxism left off. Indeed, in the early 1930s—in contrast to the late 1920s—he did not so much as mention Dewey's name in a single one of his major writings on Marx, not even in *Towards the Understanding of Karl Marx* (1933), the work most often cited as the centerpiece of Hook's Deweyan Marxism. Still, his Marxism in the early 1930s was, incontestably, bound up with his pragmatism. In contrast to official Communism, which in countless primers treated Marxism as an accumulated body of absolutely certain truths reaching its pinnacle in the work of Lenin and Stalin and requiring adherence by the letter, Hook considered Marxism a *method of action* to be tested—and,

2   Philosophical discussions: interview with Meyer Schapiro, 25 October 1993. Poor health: SH to Will Herberg, 15 August 1931 (Hook Papers, box 15); and Philip Wheelwright to SH, 18 October 1931 (Hook Papers, box 30). Hook contributed "Bauer, Bruno," "Büchner, Ludwig," "Dietzgen, Joseph," "Engels, Friedrich," and "Feuerbach, Ludwig Andreas" to *Encyclopaedia of the Social Sciences*, ed. E. R. A. Seligman (New York: Macmillan, 1930–31). On Hegel, see Hook, review of *Hegels Staatside* by Julius Löwenstein, *Journal of Philosophy* 26 (12 September 1929): 526–30; Hook, review of *Hegel und die Hegelsche Schule* by Willy Moog, *Journal of Philosophy* 28 (27 August 1931): 497–500; Hook, "The Contemporary Significance of Hegel's Philosophy," *Philosophical Review* 41 (May 1932): 237–60; Hook, review of *Phenomenology of Mind* by Hegel, *Journal of Philosophy* 29 (23 June 1932). On Husserl, see Hook, "Husserl's Phenomenological Idealism," review of *Formale und Transzendentale Logik* by Edmund Husserl, *Journal of Philosophy* 27 (3 July 1930): 365–80; and Hook, Review of *Ideas* by Edmund Husserl, *Symposium* 2 (October 1931): 531–40. On Cohen, see Hook, "The Philosophy of Morris R. Cohen," *New Republic* 63 (23 July 1930): 278–81; Ernest Nagel, "The Thirtieth Annual Meeting of the Eastern Division of the American Philosophy Association," *Journal of American Philosophy* 28 (1931): 88–98; Hook, "Reason and Nature: The Metaphysics of Scientific Method," review of *Reason and Nature* by Morris R. Cohen, *Journal of Philosophy* 29 (7 January 1932): 5–24.

if necessary, reconsidered—in the course of revolutionary practice. In this manner, a pragmatist sensibility permeated his Marxism, whether or not that influence was explicitly stated or fully elaborated.

Early Considerations on Dewey and Marx

One of Hook's central aims in the early 1930s was the defense and extrapolation of Dewey's thought from a revolutionary standpoint. In 1930, for instance, Hook published a critical review of *Contemporary American Philosophy,* a showcase anthology edited by George Adams and one of Hook's Columbia professors, W. P. Montague, and meant to illustrate the diversity of methods and concerns among philosophers. Hook's review took the philosophical discipline to task for its almost exclusive concentration on religion and epistemology, its corresponding removal from public life, its narrow provincialism, and its ignorance of Marx and class struggle: "There is little sympathy and less interest in the pressing problems of social philosophy or in the philosophy of politics, law and education. . . . Dewey, of course, is the most conspicuous exception to these generalizations." Hook faulted his fellow philosophers for their failure to incorporate the insights generated by pragmatism. Even though pragmatism had gained a reputation as "the typical American philosophy," he wrote, various transcendental metaphysics continued to dominate the discipline, leaving pragmatism's "deeper implications . . . yet to be understood."[3]

Even this relatively straightforward defense of Dewey revealed that Hook's studies in Marxism had deeply influenced his understanding of what pragmatism meant and what was important about it. In contrast to the often highly abstract quality of *The Metaphysics of Pragmatism,* published only three years before, Hook's review of *Contemporary American Philosophy* voiced impatience with technical discussions of the nature and possibility of knowledge. Such debates, he implied, were unresolvable byproducts of philosophy's arrogant desire to reign supreme in an age of specialization and science. Pragmatism for Hook had thus become, first and foremost, a philosophy of social action. This shift in emphasis also shaped his emergent style. Although he persisted in his claim that pragmatism was a metaphysics, Hook's prose was far less abstruse and jargon-ridden than it had been in *The Metaphysics of Pragmatism.*

Hook's celebration of pragmatism in the early 1930s was not mere apologetics, for he also called upon pragmatists to draw out what he con-

---

[3] Hook, "Contemporary American Philosophy," review of *Contemporary American Philosophy,* ed. George Adams and William Pepperell Montague, *New Republic* 63 (16 July 1930): 237–40.

sidered the logical social conclusion of their philosophy. In so doing, he implicitly acknowledged for the first time a potential point of contradiction between Marx and himself, on the one hand, and Dewey on the other. Though an enthusiast of Dewey's epistemology (or, more precisely, of Dewey's disposal of the epistemology industry), Hook naturally took exception to his teacher's politics of middle-class reform. That Dewey was a reformist, however, did not place him as far from the revolutionary Hook as one might imagine. Unlike many a reformist, Dewey was to Hook's mind authentically radical, deeply democratic and egalitarian in outlook, a seeker of the end of class society. "The objective precondition of the complete and free use of the method of intelligence," he quoted from Dewey, "is a society in which class interests that recoil from social experimentation are abolished. It is incompatible with every social and political philosophy and activity and with every economic system which accepts the class organization and vested class interest of present society."[4]

Throughout his life, from the Civil War to the Cold War, Dewey wrote very little on Marxism and appears never to have read Marx with the depth and care that he devoted to many other major thinkers. But he was sometimes sympathetic to revolutionary socialism in a fashion that has not been appreciated by Marxists who would treat his views as unadulterated petty-bourgeois ideology. In 1928, for example, when he traveled to the Soviet Union to tour its educational facilities, he wrote to Hook from Moscow with evident excitement:

It is immensely stimulating intellectually to live in a country that has a definite philosophy of life—I feel that the theory is important more as a set of symbols functions in a practical movement, than as the essential thing, & that the mutual outcome may be something quite different from the symbolic formulations—Anyway from my own standpoint I have been misled by taking theory too seriously, & not knowing what is going on in life—a genuine & significant rebirth of culture perhaps the greatest the world has ever seen.

Upon his return, Dewey's enthusiasm for the Soviet experiment was unabated. "The Russian educational situation is enough to convert one to the idea that only in a society based upon the cooperative principle can the ideals of educational reformers be adequately carried into operation," he wrote in the *New Republic.* Though his appreciation of Soviet education, combined with his admission that pacifism might be insufficient to the task of social transformation, gave him more in common with revolutionary so-

---

[4] Quoted in Hook, "Education and Politics," review of *The Educational Frontier,* ed. William Kilpatrick, *New Republic* 75 (24 May 1933): 49.

cialism than is usually recognized, it is equally true that Dewey stopped short of calling for a socialist revolution in the United States, and that his emphasis on democratic education and progressive reform as the primary methods of social change differed markedly from Marx's contention that a revolutionary movement of the working class and its allies would be the decisive lever of social change in the epoch of capital.[5]

Because Hook saw great theoretical and methodological affinities between Marxism and pragmatism, these *strategic* differences between Marx and Dewey constituted a gnawing dilemma for him. The most frequent criticism of Hook's early intellectual project is the claim that he suppressed those differences, reading Marx into Dewey and Dewey into Marx. In the entry "Philosophy" in *The Encyclopedia of the American Left* (1992), for example, Steven Best, Paul Buhle, and Douglas Kellner write, "Hook tried to subsume Marxism into Deweyan pragmatism, before rejecting it altogether in the 1940s." Philosopher Nicholas Lobkowicz, in *Theory and Practice* (1969), likewise refers to "Hook's attempt to identify the Father of Communism as a precursor of Dewey and thus indirectly of himself." From an opposite political vantage but with precisely the same effect, Edward Shils writes, "Hook did not try to make Dewey into a Marxist; he tried, rather, . . . to discover a fundamental Deweyan instrumentalism in the thought of Karl Marx."[6]

The claim that Hook's Marx was merely Dewey recast presumes that Hook had no significant differences with Dewey during the 1930s. But Hook knew full well that Marxism could not be satisfactorily "subsumed" within Deweyan pragmatism, and he never viewed Marx as a mere "precursor" of Dewey. He did resist the presumption of many pragmatists and Marxists that the choice was a stark one—Marx *or* Dewey. Yet throughout the early 1930s he pressed Dewey from a Marxist standpoint to follow through on the revolutionary implications of his writings. Hook contended that the vision of radical democracy implicit in Dewey's conception of science, in which the results of inquiry were to be scrutinized and tested

---

[5] JD to SH, 25 July 1928 (Hook-Dewey Collection, box 1, folder 2); *John Dewey: The Later Works*, vol. 3 (1927–28), ed. Jo Ann Boydston (Carbondale: Southern Illinois University Press, 1981), 232–33.

[6] Edward Shils, "More at Home than Out of Step," *American Scholar* 56 (Autumn 1987): 577–86, refers specifically to *Towards the Understanding of Karl Marx*, though the book contains not a single reference to Dewey. Shils is correct if he simply means that Hook did not try to call Dewey's writings Marxist, but his formulation is misleading if taken literally, for Hook did try to make Dewey into a Marxist, or at least to persuade him to adopt a revolutionary perspective—though through personal reasoning, not sophistry or misleading attribution. See also Steven Best, Paul Buhle, and Douglas Kellner, "Philosophy," in *Encyclopedia of the American Left*, ed. Mary Jo Buhle, Paul Buhle, and Dan Georgakas (Urbana: University of Illinois Press, 1992), 576; Nicholas Lobkowicz, *Theory and Practice* (Notre Dame: University of Notre Dame Press, 1967), 409–10.

by the whole of the educated and interested public, necessitated a social revolution. Social experimentation, to take place unfettered, would require the abolition of class rule and its hierarchy of private gain over public interest. Dewey himself drew a similar conclusion when he wrote to Hook in 1932:

> It has just dawned on me why I have never been able to understand the basis of many criticisms. I have always thought of the method in its social applications in contrast with the methods which history shows to have governed social action and which still do. In consequence it always seemed to be too obvious to need emphasis that its implications in its bearing upon existing social institutions was revolutionary—In my opinion in the long run it is the most revolutionary proposition ever made. It doesn't imply "evolution" in the sense of gradual imperceptible graded changes out of the present but a profound social mutation.

Hook sought to take that understanding one step further. "The only quarrel one can have with him," he wrote of Dewey in the *New Republic* in 1931, "is his failure to appreciate the instrumental value of *class struggle* rather than class collaboration in effecting the transition from Corporate America to Collective America." If pragmatism were truly open and experimental, Hook argued, then it would not close its eyes to existing class struggles or to the historically demonstrated inability of subordinate classes to win political power except through social and economic revolution. For Dewey's philosophy to achieve its full flowering, for his aim of a cooperative society to be achieved, Hook argued, pragmatists would have to recognize the need to prosecute the class struggle "more widely and vigorously and intelligently."[7]

Although Dewey never became a Marxist, he was favorably impressed with Hook's writings on Marxism. "I think your statement that the important point is how Marx should be interpreted, not what he 'really meant,' is a good key note for your discussion of him," he wrote to Hook in 1929. Apparently aware of the influence he had had upon Hook's style of Marxism, Dewey added, "It saves you from the charge of apologetically reading into Marx newer ideas." Still, he professed unfamiliarity with Marx's thought. After Hook sent him an article that would later be incorporated into *Towards the Understanding of Karl Marx*, Dewey excused the brevity of his comments with the disclaimer, "As I have told you before my first hand knowledge of Marx does not enable me to make a judgment of any intel-

[7] JD to SH, 9 December 1932 (Hook-Dewey Collection, box 1, folder 2); Hook, "John Dewey and His Critics," *New Republic* 67 (3 June 1931): 74; Hook, "Education and Politics," 50.

ligence." Dewey did express hope that Hook's treatment would help to "compose quarrels that are merely wastes of good energy," but in that very hope he revealed an impatience with the complexities of Marxist philosophy that had seized the attention of his favorite pupil.[8]

Dissenting within Communism, 1930–32

For a host of reasons—admiration for the Soviet experiment, disillusionment with capitalism, opposition to fascism, fear of impending war—many people, intellectuals included, decided to join the American Communist Party in the 1930s. Often they would quit after a time, frequently denouncing Marxism along with Communism. Hook loosely fits this model, but his trajectory should be distinguished in several respects from the standard "God that failed" story. Hook was inspired by Bolshevism very early, at the time of the October Revolution in 1917, and he remained sympathetic to Communism throughout the 1920s, when few intellectuals were. He collaborated openly with the Party in the early 1930s without actually joining it, but he broke with it in 1933, before most intellectuals had even considered affiliating with it. In rejecting the Communist Party, furthermore, Hook attacked it not from a liberal or conservative position but from the standpoint of revolutionary Marxism, the very perspective that the Party claimed to represent. Finally, the features that attracted intellectuals to it in the 1930s—its claim to Marx, its connection to the Soviet experiment, its role in the global struggle against fascism—were the very points at which Hook found the Communist Party wanting.[9]

Most left-wing activity in New York City revolved around the Communist Party. Although Hook was not a Party member, he joined the Teachers Union of the City of New York (Local 5 of the American Federation of Teachers, in which the Party was highly active) and moved among a growing body of intellectuals in New York who argued that the social and economic crisis could be overcome only through the establishment a society free from exploitation and oppression. Some, like Hook, were longtime revolutionaries of one stripe or another. Others were drawn to left-wing politics only in the course of the Depression, and Hook's argumentative skills influenced many to join the left. James Burnham was attracted to Marxism in 1931 after he read a manuscript titled "Towards the Under-

---

[8] JD to SH, 12 February 1929 and 9 October 1931 (Hook-Dewey Collection, box 1, folder 2). "Compose," in keeping with Dewey's often curious style, here means something like "transcend" or "bring to a harmonious conclusion."

[9] Several of these points borrow from Alan Wald, *The New York Intellectuals: The Rise and Decline of the Anti-Stalinist Left from the 1930s to the 1980s* (Chapel Hill: University of North Carolina Press, 1987), 5. For the interpretation-setting standard on ex-Communist apostates, see Richard Crossman, ed., *The God That Failed* (1949; New York: Harper, 1963).

standing of Karl Marx" that Hook submitted to the *Symposium,* which Burnham edited. Hook had the same effect on others in the summer of 1931 when he spent several months in residence at Yaddo, the mansion in Saratoga, New York, which provided a retreat for gifted writers and musicians. Also present were Malcolm Cowley and Max Lerner, already moving leftward; composer Marc Blitzstein; Catherine Bauer, a disciple and lover of Lewis Mumford; and Lionel and Diana Trilling, then unknown young literary intellectuals. By the end of the summer, Hook had converted the Trillings and Bauer to Communism, in part by persuading them of the virtues of the Soviet Union.[10]

Radical intellectuals—journalists, artists, poets, novelists, critics, editors, scholars—in New York were grouped loosely around various literary and political magazines. Although several journals were explicitly under the aegis of the Communist Party—its theoretical organ, *The Communist,* and the literary *New Masses*—most of the newly radicalized magazines were unaffiliated with any organization. They included V. F. Calverton's iconoclastic *Modern Quarterly,* to which Hook's contributions dated back to his clash with Eastman; the *New Republic* and *The Nation,* liberal journals of opinion whose editors were being pushed in ever more radical directions by the social calamity; the *Menorah Journal,* an innovative Jewish publication edited by Elliott Cohen; and *The Symposium,* a more philosophical periodical edited by Philip Wheelwright and James Burnham, colleagues of Hook at NYU. Calverton had since the late 1920s been friendly to the Communist Party, despite some moments of tension, and was involved in several collaborative projects with Hook. Once they contemplated trying to get Dewey to consent to publication of a book of his essays, and in 1930 and 1931 Hook attended meetings every Thursday evening at Calverton's book-lined apartment on Morton Street in Greenwich Village to plan a collection of left-wing writings tentatively titled *America at the Crossroads.* Other regulars included Joseph Freeman, Scott Nearing, and Granville Hicks. Although the symposium never materialized, Hook was committed to the plan while it lasted. Lubricated by Calverton's liquor, the meetings gave rise to impassioned debate. One night in April 1930 Hook got into a hot argument over the politics of culture with Mike Gold, the crusty Communist writer. The row lasted until three in the morning, at which point Gold took on fellow literary radical Joshua Kunitz—who kept the battle going

<hr/>

[10] Teachers Union, Local 5 AFT, membership card (Hook Papers, box 3); Diana Trilling, "The Beginning of the Journey," *Partisan Review* 60 (1993): 348–65 (her recollection that this "new revolutionary faith" of Hook's involved "bowing to historical necessity," however, does not correspond to his well-established skepticism about any fatalistic declarations of historical inevitability); on Burnham, see Hook, *Out of Step,* 533.

until dawn. On other nights at Calverton's salon Hook met world-class intellectual celebrities Bertrand Russell, Harold Laski, and Alexander Goldenwieser.[11]

Hook's association with the Communist Party was a delicate balancing act in the first years of the 1930s. He expressed sympathy for Communism in a more concerted and public manner than before, but at the same time he began to experiment with a position of intellectual independence and to establish relations with other currents of Marxism, especially Trotskyism. Hook meant no disloyalty. In the fashion of Morris Cohen, he saw himself as a "logical disinfectant" for the Communist movement, helping to expose and scrub out poorly formulated ideas. But his timing was not the best. The American Communist Party had become monolithic in the late 1920s following several splits, all while Hook was out of the country. In October 1928 leaders James P. Cannon, Martin Abern, Max Shachtman, and their supporters were expelled from the Party after Cannon returned from a meeting of the Communist International and began quietly to distribute the critical response of Leon Trotsky to the Comintern's draft program. In May 1929 the titular leader of the Communist Party, Jay Lovestone—who was popular with the ranks but had the misfortune of being an associate of Nikolai Bukharin's within the Comintern—was removed from power in accord with Stalin's wishes. The immediate result of this fragmentation of American Communism was the creation of small groups under the leadership of Cannon and Lovestone, informally referred to as the Left Opposition and Right Opposition. Each clamored for readmission, to no avail. For those remaining within the Party, the expulsions indicated a new level of intolerance on the part of the leadership and Comintern for criticism and differences within the ranks.[12]

[11] SH to V. F. Calverton, n.d. and 28 August 1931 (V. F. Calverton Papers, New York Public Library Hook Coorespondence); Daniel Aaron, *Writers on the Left* (New York: Oxford University Press, 1977), 244–45; Sender Garlin, interview with author, 10 May 1992; Leonard Wilcox, *V. F. Calverton: Radical in the American Grain* (Philadelphia: Temple University Press, 1992), 127; Draper interview with Hook, 17 May 1957 (Theodore Draper Papers, Emory University, box 13).

[12] The Cannon group supported Trotsky's Left Opposition in the Soviet Union; it began publishing *The Militant* immediately after the expulsion, formed the Communist League of America, and eventually participated in the establishment of the Fourth International. The Lovestone group participated in the International Communist Opposition and was first known as the Communist Party (Majority Group) and then, more realistically, as the Communist Party (Opposition). It published *Revolutionary Age* from 1929 to 1932 and then *Workers' Age* until 1941, at which time the organization dissolved. The purging of the Right and Left Oppositions from the Communist movement in every country was the means by which Stalin and the bureaucracy he orchestrated were able to consolidate power, eliminating potential rivals and discrediting competing strategies; see Julius Jacobson, "The Communist Past—Myth and Reality," *New Politics* 18 (Winter 1995): 125–67.

Despite this ominous bureaucratic consolidation, Hook tried to endorse the politics of the Communist Party while retaining intellectual independence. From his perspective, this disposition presumed an ultimate loyalty and fidelity to Communism; as he expressed it at the time, he believed that Communism "demands not less criticism but more, for it must contend not only against misrepresentations of its enemies but against the nearsightedness of its friends." That nearsightedness was brought home to Hook on more than one occasion. In 1932, as his friend V. F. Calverton began to be routinely denounced in the Communist press for real and imagined deviations, Hook spoke at a convocation of the John Reed Clubs to discuss the 1931 resolution of the Comintern's International Committee of Revolutionary Writers criticizing the *New Masses*. The other invited speaker, Joseph Freeman, had been friendly to him. But, Hook reported to Calverton,

> in the discussion from the floor which revolved for the most part around my critical remarks on super-orthodoxy I was criticized for being intellectual, intelligent, setting myself up over the party, and writing for Calverton and the *Modern Monthly*. One nut referred to me as "that arch-enemy of the working class who has made critical remarks on Mr. [*sic!*] Lenin." I made a plea for printing stuff even if it was deviatory (in the minds of editors) and said that the trouble with the Modern Quarterly was not that it printed deviations but that it did not *correct* them. (I had in mind Briffault's last two squibs.)

Hook could put this incident in humorous perspective because Freeman, in his closing remarks, had again been friendly, and the writer Josephine Herbst told him afterward that many revolutionary intellectuals were disgusted with the way the John Reed Clubs had been conducted. Still, the evening portended conflicts to come.[13]

In print, Hook criticized mainly the philosophical and historical offerings of individual Communists, not the Party's policies or organization. In early 1932, for example, he reviewed a history of Russia from International Publishers, calling it the "most scholarly" work of Russian history available and "the dullest." He faulted its author, Soviet historian M. N. Pokrovsky, for failing to recognize that the materialist conception of history regards the mode of production as "the decisive, but not exclusive factor in social change," and thereby for ignoring the social effects of ideas: "True, ideology and literature are social effects. But they are social causes of other effects." After these stern reservations, Hook concluded that Pokrovsky

---

[13] SH to Calverton, 19 September 1932 (Calverton Papers). Robert Briffault (1876–1948) was, in works such as *Breakdown* (1932), a rather crude sociological writer.

might improve his history "not by abandoning his historical method and philosophy but by applying it with more subtlety and caution."[14]

While expressing support for the Communist Party, Hook for the first time began to study dissenting versions of communism, especially the ideas of Leon Trotsky. Hook's first real encounter with an admirer of Trotsky came in 1929 when Felix Morrow, an NYU graduate who had audited one of Hook's classes, introduced him to Herbert Solow, a journalist. Morrow, four years younger than Hook, and Solow, roughly his age, were both writers for the *Menorah Journal*. Influenced by the writings of philosopher Horace Kallen on cultural pluralism, the *Menorah* writers were concerned with problems of Jewish ethnicity and culture. Their cosmopolitan ideals, combined with resistance to assimilation, provided a bridge to revolutionary internationalism, leading them to Marxism in the early 1930s under the editorship of Elliott Cohen. The catalyst for the group's evolution was the onset of the Great Depression, in conjunction with a conflict with the magazine's directors over Zionism. Unlike the *Menorah* group, Hook had never been animated in his writing by issues of Jewish identity. His appreciation of cultural diversity was derived from Dewey more than Kallen. He took his Jewishness more or less for granted, and he was an irreligious naturalist. Still, he found attractive new allies among the *Menorah* writers. He and Solow, a brilliant Columbia graduate who was the *Menorah* group's strongest critic of Zionism, lived close to each other in Brooklyn and became good friends, united by their shared sympathies for the Communist Party. When Solow began to admire Trotsky's ideas, he encouraged Hook to adopt them, as well.[15]

As the literary historian Alan Wald has argued, many radical intellectuals in the early 1930s who were in search of an authentic revolutionary Marxism and dismayed by the Communist Party's sectarian practice, fear of criticism, ossified Marxism, and authoritarian organization found Trotsky's example inspiring. Trotsky, exiled from the Soviet Union in 1929, was a towering, historic figure who for a variety of reasons commanded respect among New York's revolutionary intellectuals: a Jew who had shaken loose the chains of religion, a Russian thinker with global knowledge and insight, a clever wit and brilliant stylist with gifts not merely literary, the former leader of the Petrograd Soviet and the Red Army, and a persecuted dissenter who battled valiantly and tragically to save his ideas and socialism from bureaucratic travesty. For revolutionary communist intellectuals,

[14] Hook, "Half-Baked Communism," review of *Breakdown: The Collapse of Traditional Civilization* by Robert Briffault, *Nation*, 8 June 1932, 655; Hook, "Pictures of the Past," review of *History of Russia* by M. N. Pokrovsky, *Saturday Review* 8 (30 April 1932): 100.
[15] Elliott Cohen, an accomplished editor, quit the *Menorah Journal* in October 1931, taking Solow and Morrow with him. After the World War II, Cohen would establish *Commentary*, a journal of Jewish politics and culture. For an excellent treatment of the *Menorah Journal*, see Wald, *The New York Intellectuals*, pt 1. For this paragraph see also Hook, *Out of Step*, 179–83.

Leon Trotsky was proof that it was possible to combine theory and practice in the service of human emancipation.[16]

Hook was "sympathetic to the Trotskyists" before 1933, as he admitted decades later. Maintaining that he never accepted the "entire Trotskyist line" in the early 1930s, he allowed that he had shared political beliefs with Solow and other Trotskyists, and that he admired Trotsky's gifts and deplored his exile and plight. To be sure, Hook never joined the Communist League of America, the Trotskyist political organization in the United States between 1929 and 1934, but to act on "the entire Trotskyist line" in the early 1930s did not require membership in the CLA. Despite the Communist Party's 1928 expulsion of Cannon, Shachtman, and many others sympathetic to Trotsky, the lines of division were not yet absolute between the CP and the CLA. CLA members at the time considered themselves Communists who had been illegitimately denied their organizational rights; while opposing the Communist Party's *political* policies, *organizationally* they demanded reinstatment to full membership. Indeed, the main aim of the CLA was to win over the Communist ranks to the goal of unity. By critically supporting the Party, therefore, Hook was about as close to following the Trotskyist line as anyone got in 1931. As he explained in a 1974 letter, he found the Trotskyists more inviting than the Lovestoneites or Stalinists in the early 1930s because the Trotskyists "seemed more sincere, open to argument, and were being persecuted."[17]

Even though Hook was not a member of the Trotskyist organization, his position between 1931 and early 1933 is best understood as that of a sympathizer of Trotskyism working within the Communist Party milieu. Hook openly agreed with Trotsky in February 1932, when he reviewed the first volume of Trotsky's *History of the Russian Revolution,* which had just been translated into English by Max Eastman. In addition to expounding favorably upon Trotsky's theory of why a socialist revolution had been possible in Russia, despite the initial pontifications of Mensheviks, Bolsheviks, and German Social Democrats on the need for a long period of capitalist development, Hook explicitly refuted the idea that Trotsky stood in contradiction to Lenin, a distortion already gaining ground within Stalinist circles. The hesistancy of Trotsky to join the Bolsheviks until July 1917 "in no way detracts from his greatness," Hook wrote, observing that Lenin held Trotsky in highest confidence. Approvingly, he noted the place of Lenin as "the hero of Trotsky's book."[18]

[16] Wald, *The New York Intellectuals,* 74, 91.
[17] Hook, *Out of Step,* 183; Hook to Wald, 1 August 1974 (Wald Collection).
[18] Leon Trotsky, "Help Is Needed Immediately!" (Hook Papers, box 167); Hook, "An Epic of Revolution," review of *The History of the Russian Revolution,* vol. 1, by Leon Trotsky, *Saturday Review 8* (27 February 1932): 549–51.

In August 1932 Hook's friend Herbert Solow visited the Soviet Union, returning secretly by way of Prinkipo, Turkey, in order to meet Trotsky. Only Hook and Elliott Cohen were informed of the trip, presumably because Solow did not want to burn his bridges to the Communist Party. From Istanbul, Solow wrote Hook that he had been shocked by conditions in the USSR, and that upon meeting Trotsky for the first time he was "neither conquered nor conqueror." In a longer, more detailed missive to Hook from the Orient Express, Solow wrote that Trotsky had "an amused glint in his eye when he asked me about you," because Trotsky had already put the very same question to his translator, Eastman, who was still smarting from his scrap with Hook four years before. Trotsky "has of course no sympathy for E's philosophic nonsense," Solow assured Hook. He had been interested to hear that Hook took a favorable view of Lenin's *What Is to Be Done?* but he reminded Solow that the work had been severely criticized—even by Lenin himself, who referred to it as a "product of its time." When Solow spoke of the great enthusiasm among many radical intellectuals in New York for his *History of the Russian Revolution,* Trotsky urged that Solow and his allies read the Left Opposition's criticism of Comintern policy toward the Chinese revolution in 1927 and other drier political matters to test the extent of their commitment.[19]

While displaying an unusual openness to Trotsky and his followers, Hook entered into more reserved, though friendly, relations with representatives of other socialist tendencies. He corresponded and met with Will Herberg, a leading intellectual in the Lovestone group. Hook warned Herberg that his criticisms of the "would-be objective sociology of the vulgar Marxists" applied as much to Nikolai Bukharin, darling of the Right Opposition, as to Karl Kautsky or Rudolf Hilferding. Herberg, for his part, said that he had been studying Hook's work carefully with the "not altogether benevolent purpose" of writing a critique of it from the express viewpoint of orthodox Marxism. "By 'orthodox Marxism' I certainly do NOT mean the somewhat crude 'mechanical Marxism' of Bukharin when he deals with philosophical questions," Herberg specified. Despite Hook's differences with the Communist Party (Opposition), as the Lovestone group was formally known, he was treated favorably in its press, which credited him with "a keen mind and a clear style." Hook was also admired by Socialist Party leader Norman Thomas, in spite of

[19] Corroboration of Solow's report is found in Eastman's own recollection that when he visited Trotsky in 1932, Trotsky's face became red in the course of an argument about the dialectic: Max Eastman, *Great Companions* (New York: Farrar, Straus & Cudahy, 1959), 155. See also Herbert Solow to SH, 14 and 10 August 1932 (Hook Papers, box 28); and Leon Trotsky, "A Discussion with Herbert Solow," in *Writings of Leon Trotsky, Supplement (1929–33),* ed. Dorothea Breitman and Frank Lovell (New York: Pathfinder, 1979).

their political differences. When Hook sent Thomas copies of his articles on Marx, Thomas replied, "I am almost persuaded that you are right in your judgment of what was central in Marx. This does not make me a thoroughgoing Marxist but it does give me on the whole a better and more sympathetic view than orthodox Marxism of any of the schools which you criticize."[20]

For the most part, however, Hook worked to build support for a critical Marxism within the domain of the Communist Party. He gave Felix Morrow, who in the early 1930s was writing regularly for the *Daily Worker* and the *New Masses,* advice about how to improve those publications, and in 1931 and 1932 he led a failed effort to bring together the various tendencies within the Communist intellectual milieu around a new publication. Hook and a group of Communist sympathizers—including Morrow, Solow, and Corliss Lamont, who as a philosophy student at Columbia had grown sympathetic to Communism while befriending Hook—proposed a new magazine to be called the *American Radical: A Journal of Revolutionary Criticism.* The journal's primary purpose, as outlined in a prospectus drafted by Hook and amended by Lamont, was to promote a mass labor party, "Socialistic or Communistic in principles if not in name, and capable of applying these principles with pragmatic flexibility in every phase of the class struggle." The problem with existing revolutionary journals, argued the prospectus, was that their "appeal is to the initiated and to the immediate circle of party sympathizers, not to the thousands of intelligent minds and courageous spirits whose interest in the cause of working class emancipation, already emotionally awakened, needs critical guidance." The magazine would be oriented toward the Communist Party but would have formal independence and would invite participation from all left currents. The group proposed that Hook be its editor, with the understanding that he would have complete freedom and responsibility for editorial policy. The project dissipated, however, despite exploratory attempts at fund-raising in 1931 and again in 1932. The Communist Party was suspicious of its independence; other socialists and labor radicals, such as A. J. Muste and J. B. S. Hardman of the Conference for Progressive Labor Action (CPLA), objected to its apparent subservience to the CP. "The type of magazine which seems to me is needed at present would not, if I had my way, make itself, and so obviously, a subordinate publication of the Communist Party," wrote Hardman to Hook in November 1931. Although the journal never got off the ground, the project did create a bond between Hook and Muste, who complimented Hook on his writings on Marx and invited him

20 SH to Will Herberg, 15 August 1931 (Hook Papers, box 15); J.C.W., untitled review of *Modern Quarterly,* for Winter 1930–31, *Revolutionary Age,* 7 February 1931, 4; Norman Thomas to SH, 7 August 1931 (Hook Papers, box 28).

to the 1931 CPLA conference to discuss "whether another working-class party is necessary in the United States."[21]

Despite his attempt to show his theoretical mettle and offer his intellectual services to the Party, Hook was increasingly treated with suspicion in Communist circles, especially because of his unusual philosophical standpoint. Few of his orthodox Communist acquaintances from the 1920s were comfortable with his pragmatism as it developed. "I should advise you to jettison Dewey's instrumentalism," one friend, Joseph Tauber, wrote him in 1928. "An adherent of the class struggle has a right to discriminate against certain stuff as contraband." In 1931 his old friend Sam Chovenson wrote, "Your salvation will probably come when you throw overboard Dewey as you have done with Cohen." Worried about the potential liberal influence of Dewey upon Hook, Chovenson expressed concern that "you might commit a grave error in your youth, which error will then be ingrained in you through experience, with the result that the revolutionary movement will have lost a very capable supporter and have gained a sturdy opponent. . . . The communist movement is in dire need of such like you."[22]

Suspicion of Dewey and pragmatism was rife in pro-Communist circles during the early 1930s. The views of Tauber and Chovenson correspond, for example, to a 1932 attack on pragmatism by Emmanuel Kanter, coeditor of a self-declared journal of "Marxism Leninism Stalinism." Instrumentalism, according to Kanter, was a "philosophy based on the professional middle-class," a form of radical subjectivism measuring truth by "effects that make us happy," in contrast to Marxism's claim of an objective world "prior to and outside our experience." Hook's attempt to bring the two doctrines into harmony made him positively dangerous: "Dr. Hook, who is well-versed in both Marxism and Instrumentalism, is one of the most dangerous neo-revisionists in America. Dewey is less harmful in this respect because he is almost completely ignorant of Marxism. Max Eastman is altogether harmless because he is ignorant of both Marxism and Instrumentalism." There is no evidence that Hook ever saw Kanter's attack (to which he would never have been able to reply, since Kanter's ob-

---

[21] The proposed journal is mentioned in neither Hook's biography nor any book on the New York intellectuals. In a 1957 interview with Draper (Theodore Draper Papers, Emory University, box 13), Hook said that the reason the magazine never got off the ground was Lamont's failure to fund it, but he may have been confusing it with the *Marxist Quarterly* of 1937, which did fold when Lamont withdrew his money. "Prospectus of 'The American Radical,'" n.d. (Hook Papers, box 18); Corliss Lamont to SH, 30 June and 21 August 1931, 11 July 1932 (Hook Papers, box 18); Corliss Lamont to author, 11 December 1991; Herbert Solow to SH, 14 August 1932 (Hook Papers, box 28); Felix Morrow to SH, 28 June 1931, 29 August 1932 (Hook Papers, box 21); J. B. S. Hardman to SH, 17 November 1931, 2 March 1932 (Hook Papers, box 14); and A. J. Muste to SH, 25 and 29 August 1931 (Hook Papers, box 17).

[22] Joseph Tauber to SH, 5 November 1928 (Hook Papers, box 28); Sam Chovenson to SH, n.d. (1930–31?) and 17 February 1931 (Hook Papers, box 9).

scure publication died immediately), but it is instructive in its manifestation of the common prejudice against pragmatism in Stalinist circles.[23]

Many of his friends urged Hook not to let philosophical differences de-
ter him from cooperation with the Communist Party. In July 1932 Celia
Kuhn, who had relocated to Pittsburgh to organize for Worker's International Relief, wrote to Hook, "Just before I left New York I spoke to [Earl]
Browder about you and he told me there's lots of work that has to be done
and if you are really sincere in your desire to help, it was up to you to take
the initiative. I agree with him. You know sufficiently about the movement
not to need any special attention." In a subsequent letter, Kuhn, whose activism Hook was helping to fund, unburdened herself of her frustrations
and impatience with philosophy in hard times:

> How can one spend time in reflections about such abstractions as truth,
> knowledge, values when presented with a group of hungry men, when faced
> with a group looking to you for daily guidance and direction. It is easy to say
> that one should strike a balance and perhaps one can even quote Lenin on
> the subject, but it is a problem nevertheless. And as for ultimate values, I've
> forgotten how to speak or feel about such things. Personality? Individuality?
> This is not a period in which one can develop personality. It is not a question
> of what is best for a personality but rather a question of what is best for the
> masses, the movements. . . . Later, under communism, we can speak of per-
> sonality, of ultimate values; yes, later when we have no classes, when antago-
> nisms caused by class society will be wiped out, then we will speak of the
> development of individuality for it is only then that development can pro-
> ceed unhampered.

Kuhn urged Hook to overcome his hesitancy about the sectarianism of
Communist-directed organizations by taking his criticisms to the highest
level of the Party and related groups, where he might receive answers more
satisfactory than those of the unreflective and unimaginative faithful at the
bottom. She also characterized Hook's disagreements with the Party as being about "non-essentials" and urged him to submit to Party discipline even

---

[23] Emmanuel Kanter, "Dewey vs. Marx," *Marxist Quarterly* 1 (Summer 1932): 37–53. Kanter, a shadowy figure, was the author of *The Amazons* (1926) and *The Evolution of War* (1927).
His *Marxist Quarterly* lasted only one issue (and is not to be confused with the more impressive 1937 journal of that name). He was probably not a member of the Communist Party,
which even in its Stalinist phase laid claim to Marxism and Leninism but almost never to
"Stalinism" as such. That Kanter's books were both published by the socialist firm Charles H.
Kerr suggests an association with the Proletarian Party—which broke away from the early
Communist movement and led an independent, parallel existence for decades, taking charge
of Kerr in the late 1920s—but his name does not appear in any existing accounts of the Proletarian Party.

though not a member: "You must eventually take a definite side and perhaps take the leadership in some organization."[24]

Felix Morrow, too, who had secretly joined the Communist Party in 1931 and accepted a traveling job to report on Depression conditions around the country for the *Daily Worker* and the *New Masses,* advised Hook in the summer of 1932 to patch things up with the Party. Morrow did not suggest, as had some of Hook's more doctrinaire Party acquaintances, that he disavow pragmatism, but he did recommend that Hook show his loyalty to the Party. "If you are a Communist and know you must build on what we have," he said, "you too will go well out of your way to demonstrate that your dissatisfaction with Lenin's epistemology is not going to interfere with your working for the movement." Morrow recalled that David Kvitko had once advised Hook not to join the Party because he would have more influence on it as an outsider "but I can't feel that advice is right," he warned. "I'm not suggesting that you join the Party for years, but you simply must make your peace with the Party."[25]

The Communist Campaign of 1932

In the fall of 1932 Hook tried to make political peace with the Party, perhaps in conscious accord with Morrow's advice. In September a group of writers and intellectuals, including Hook, released a statement endorsing the Communist ticket in the national election: for president, William Z. Foster, a former steel union leader; for vice-president, James W. Ford, the first African American to be nominated for national office by any party in the twentieth century. In addition to Hook's personal acquaintances such as Elliott Cohen and Felix Morrow, the fifty-three signators included many well-known intellectuals, most of them not Party members themselves: novelists Sherwood Anderson, John Dos Passos, and Theodore Dreiser; writers Waldo Frank and Matthew Josephson; literary critics Newton Arvin, Malcolm Cowley, Granville Hicks, and Edmund Wilson; art historian Meyer Schapiro; economist Lewis Corey; African American writers Langston Hughes, Countee Cullen, and Eugene Gordon; dramatist Sidney Howard; humorist Kyle Crichton; and journalists James Rorty and Lincoln Steffens.

Hook also modified his critical stance toward Communism by writing several pieces harmonious with official positions. He even submitted an article on education to *Soviet Russia Today,* the magazine of the Friends of So-

[24]   Celia Kuhn to SH, 25 July 1932 and 1 August 1932 (Hook Papers, box 18). Hook's replies do not survive.
[25]   Felix Morrow to SH, 29 August 1932 (Hook Papers, box 21); Wald, *New York Intellectuals,* 47–49.

Campaign poster for the 1932 Communist ticket, which Hook endorsed. (Courtesy Tamiment Institute Library / Robert F. Wagner Labor Archives, New York University.)

viet Russia, but it was rejected as overly highbrow. "Sad days!" Hook lamented, reporting the rejection to V. F. Calverton, who had come under Party attack for perceived heresies. "I guess they don't read *Capital* anymore. The only people I know who are studying Marx these days are out of the party. Those inside don't have to. Not because they once did—no, because they have *il lumine naturale*." In September, Hook reviewed a series of books on the USSR for *The Nation* under the title, "Myth, Fact, and Poetry of Soviet Russia." He wryly observed that Waldemar Gurian's *Bolshevism,* a critique of Communism from the perspective of Catholicism, showed that Bolshevism was evidently not a religion—not in the eyes of the religious, at least. He praised Joseph Freeman's book *The Soviet Worker* as a superior guide to contemporary Russian theory and practice. He credited Waldo Frank with capturing poetically the spiritual culture of contemporary Russian life in his *Dawn in Russia* but faulted his "mystical idealism" and crass rejection of dialectical materialism. It could not have been lost on the Communist Party that Freeman, a Party intellectual, was the clear favorite in Hook's trilogy, despite some trifling suggestions about how Freeman might better present statistics. Nor could the Party object to the treatment of its views as "fact" in contrast to the inferior alternatives of "myth" and "poetry."[26]

Philosophically, Hook demonstrated his loyalty to revolutionary communism by moving to clear up the impression left by his 1928 articles on dialectical materialism in the *Journal of Philosophy,* which many had interpreted to mean that he found little of value in Lenin's philosophy. In a September review for the *American Journal of Sociology* of a new edition of Lenin's famous book *What Is to Be Done?* (1902), Hook appreciatively recapitulated Lenin's critique of fatalism and his famous refutation of "economism"—the notion that workers will come to class consciousness automatically through shop-floor demands for higher wages and better conditions. Hook found in the history of the reception of *What Is to Be Done?* a transparent personal resonance:

> It is interesting to note that this brochure earned for Lenin the honorable epithet of "heretic" from his more orthodox Marxist brethren. Because he stressed the causal efficacy of class-*consciousness* in accelerating social change, he was called an idealist. Because he taught the necessity of agitation "among all classes of the population" he was accused of concealed reformism, of trying to undermine the proletarian base of the party. And because he sought to convert the Social-Democratic party into a centralized, militant organization he was dubbed a conspiratorial Blanquist.

[26] A. A. Heller, editor of *Soviet Russia Today,* to SH, 29 August 1932 (Hook Papers, box 15); SH to V. F. Calverton, n.d. (Hook Correspondence, Calverton Papers); Hook, "Myth, Fact, and Poetry of Soviet Russia," *The Nation,* 14 September 1932, 237–38.

This historical portrait, from which dissenting, "heretical" communists like Hook could take comfort, gave Lenin a flavor different from that of the stale hagiography increasingly preferred by the Comintern. Hook minced no words in declaring Lenin's decisiveness about the renewal of Marxism after the betrayal of German social democracy: "From a set of case-hardened and petrified dogmas about social evolution, Marxism was transformed back to its original expression as a flexible method of revolutionary practice." In 1932, unlike 1928, there could be no doubt that Hook was a Leninist in politics. If he retained his criticism of Lenin's epistemology, he did not feel compelled to make note of it.[27]

More intellectuals—and more prominent ones, including John Dewey, Heywood Broun, Van Wyck Brooks, W. E. B. Du Bois, and the editors of the *New Republic*—endorsed Socialist candidate Norman Thomas that autumn. But the announcement by fifty-three leading intellectuals that they were supporting the Communist ticket was a sensational public indication of the sharp leftward turn of intellectuals as a result of the Great Depression. In October 1932 the pro-Communist group organized formally as the League of Professional Groups for Foster and Ford and was provided an office in the same building as Communist Party headquarters. It quickly found a staff secretary in James Rorty, a poet, reporter, and onetime editor of the *New Masses*. He was recruited for the job by Elliott Cohen, who had by that time left the *Menorah Journal* to manage the National Committee for the Defense of Political Prisoners, a Party-sponsored civil liberties outfit that had emerged from efforts to defend the miners' struggles in Harlan County, Kentucky. League members commissioned a subgroup to draft a statement of intent, and the result of their efforts, a thirty-page pamphlet called *Culture and the Crisis,* was published in October 1932. Its appeal to technical and professional workers to throw off the constrictions and degradations imposed upon their work by capitalism owed much to the example of Thorstein Veblen, though it transposed Veblen's radical concern for technical strata into Marxism. "As responsible intellectual workers," proclaimed the preface, "we have aligned ourselves with the frankly revolutionary Communist Party, the party of the workers."[28]

Hook had helped draft the initial version of the pamphlet in collaboration with James Rorty, Lewis Corey, Malcolm Cowley, and Matthew Josephson, but he did not have much influence on its final contents. "I had written

[27]   Hook, Review of *What Is to Be Done?* by V. I. Lenin, *American Journal of Sociology* 38 (September 1932): 315–17.
[28]   League of Professional Groups for Foster and Ford, *Culture and the Crisis: An Open Letter to the Writers, Artists, Teachers, Physicians, Engineers, Scientists, and Other Professional Workers of America* (New York: Workers Library, 1932), 3.

eloquently about workers' democracy and about communism as a fulfillment of the liberal ideals of Western civilization," he later recalled, "but all
this was deleted by the invisible hands that saw the manuscript through the
press." No passage in the pamphlet—save perhaps the assertion that the
Party "does not sit back in sectarian blindness waiting for Communism to
come by gentle inevitability in the distant future"—reads as if Hook had
had a hand in it. Apart from some graceful passages in its introduction and
a supple analysis of the capitalist crisis almost certainly written by Lewis
Corey, *Culture and the Crisis* repeated all of the standard Communist political positions of the day, including the call for an autonomous "Black Belt"
and the tendentious labeling of the Socialist Party as "the third party of capitalism," a party "of mere reformism which builds up state capitalism, and
thus strengthens the capitalist state and potential Fascism."[29]

Despite the Party's heavy-handed approach in editing *Culture and the Crisis*, Hook and other league members were highly visible, enthusiastic backers of the Foster-Ford ticket. The League of Professional Groups for Foster
and Ford distributed 40,000 copies of *Culture and the Crisis* and held a number of rallies, including one attended by several thousand people at Coop-
er Union. Hook, the only professional philosopher and the most
prominent academic to have signed the pamphlet, was in Rorty's judgment
"perhaps our most distinguished and certainly our most politically sophisticated member." Although he did not have tenure at NYU—he was a mere
instructor from 1927 until 1932, and after that he was promoted only to
an assistant professorship—Hook chaired a meeting at which William Z.
Foster spoke before students at NYU, a gutsy act of conviction given his precarious status. Hook went even further than most of the signers of *Culture
and the Crisis* by endorsing William Patterson, the Communist candidate

[29] Hook definitely helped to write the pamphlet, because a surviving letter from Malcolm
Cowley to SH, 20 October 1933 (Hook Papers, box 40, folder 13), alludes to his involvement.
Otherwise, its authorship is not certain, and various memoirs by the drafters vary widely.
Hook named himself, Corey, Cowley, Rorty, Josephson, and "one or two others" as the writ-
ers of *Culture and the Crisis*. Lewis Corey named himself and Hook. James Rorty named himself, Corey, Cowley, Josephson, and Solow. Matthew Josephson named only himself, Cowley,
and Rorty. Malcolm Cowley named himself, Corey, Josephson, and a few anonymous others.
Two or more of these recollections, therefore, confirm five names: Corey, Cowley, Hook,
Josephson, and Rorty. Others may have been involved to a lesser extent. All accounts complain that the pamphlet suffered at the hands of anonymous Party editors. In a minor dis-
crepancy, Josephson claimed that the statement was written in his rural farmhouse, whereas
Cowley said it was drafted in the back of someone's brownstone; possibly they were recalling
the writing of separate segments by different subgroups. See *Culture and the Crisis*, 23, 20;
Hook, *Out of Step*, 185; Theodore Draper, interview with Mrs. Lewis Corey, 11 February 1954
(Draper Papers, box 3, folder 44); Rorty, "It Has Happened Here," unpublished memoir, version 1, chap. 11, p. 8 (James Rorty Papers, University of Oregon); Matthew Josephson, *Infi-
del in the Temple* (New York: Knopf, 1967), 152–53; Malcolm Cowley, *The Dreams of the Golden
Mountains* (New York: Viking, 1980), 113–15.

for mayor of New York. Privately, however, he retained his criticisms of the Communist Party, as Matthew Josephson discovered when Hook presided over a New York campaign rally sponsored by the league on October 13, 1932, and attended by about 800 people. Hook introduced Josephson as the first speaker. As they walked home together later that night, Hook at one point in their conversation burst into a tirade against the Party's "stupid leadership."[30]

The Fragmentation of Left Intellectuals, 1932–33

The 1932 presidential election was a debacle for the Communist Party, in part because the simultaneous heart attack and nervous breakdown suffered by Foster on the campaign trail in early September effectively removed him from the race (though not from the ballot), and also because there was a likely undertabulation of the Communist vote in many parts of the country, but primarily because the Communist Party failed to generate any significant enthusiasm for its candidates and program. Especially embarassing was the far more impressive showing of Norman Thomas. The Socialist Party, chief competitor of the CP on the left, had been subjected to excoriation and derision in the Communist press, but Thomas won eight times the votes that Foster did. Despite the setback, the pro-Foster intellectuals wished to continue their political project. On November 21, 1932, the League of Professional Groups for Foster and Ford reconstituted itself as the League of Professional Groups in order to preserve a link between radical intellectuals and the Communist Party. Almost immediately, however, it split wide open. The differing affiliations of the revolutionary intellectuals—some strict independents, some Communists or close fellow travelers, others favorable to Cannon and Trotsky, still others partial to Lovestone and Bukharin—came into explosive conflict as the varying camps of dissidents tried to open up debate over aspects of the Party's program. The various factions had united around the presidential campaign, but once that conjunctural basis for unity passed, their differences resurfaced with a vengeance. At the same time, the Communist Party lost its immediate incentive to cultivate an alliance with the left-leaning intellectuals, and its tolerance even for mild criticism declined. Hook, adrift in these turbulent eddies, was simultaneously drawn away from the Communist Party

---

[30] Hook, *Out of Step*, 184–85, wrote that he had been initially skeptical of Josephson's recollection, but concluded that it must have been accurate. See also Edward P. Johanningsmeier, *Forging American Communism: The Life of William Z. Foster* (Princeton: Princeton University Press, 1994); Harvey Klehr, *The Heyday of American Communism* (New York: Basic, 1984), 81; Rorty, "It Has Happened Here," chap. 11, p. 11; Hook, *Out of Step*, 149; Josephson, *Infidel in the Temple*, 163; Cowley, *The Dreams of the Golden Mountains*, 116.

by his personal association with the Trotskyist and independent left and propelled away from it by the clumsy attempt of Party officialdom to bring him into line on doctrinal matters. The result was his permanent estrangement from the Communist Party.[31]

In the winter months of 1932–33, while Herbert Hoover sat as a lame-duck president and the Depression reached its nadir, conflict wracked the League of Professional Groups. Its new executive board was dominated by Communists and their close associates, although Felix Morrow, who was covertly sympathetic to Trotskyism, sat on it. The league defined the purpose of its new program as "to propagandize and activize the professions, to engage in communist activity on the cultural front, to provide technical aid to the Communist Party and its mass organizations." In actuality, however, the group was so preoccupied with internal struggle that it was ineffectual. When Hook and Morrow in early 1933 tried to recruit Morris U. Schappes to the league, the young left-wing intellectual resisted on the grounds that the group didn't seem to amount to much more than a collection of names on a letterhead and had not stimulated concerted cultural work. "As it is organized it doesn't do anything except telegraph in protest, or march in Wall Street, or sponsor meetings at which its delegates literarily describe the Hunger March as seen by a New Englander like Cowley," wrote Schappes. "All of which is useful, but I don't think I have the time and money for another organization without a definite group program."[32]

Tensions were exacerbated as perceptions grew that the Party was attempting to control the league's activities from the top. Corey, for example, was commissioned to write a pamphlet for the league, but after he turned it in, Party officials claimed to have lost it. In addition to such suspicious events, which smacked of subterfuge, the group was divided internally by vigorous debates over aspects of Communist policy. Disputes arose over the Party's program of "self-determination for the Black Belt" and its policy of dual unions, strategies that many dissidents considered to be absurd under American conditions, and mechanical, because they set communists apart from—if not against—mass movements.[33]

The chief debate within the league, however, centered on the main line of Comintern policy, which since 1928 had rested on the apocalyptic

[31] Foster's failure in the race coincided with his eclipse as leader of the Party by Earl Browder. See Johanningsmeier, *Forging American Communism;* and Cowley, *The Dream of the Golden Mountains,* 113.

[32] Klehr, *The Heyday of American Communism,* 82; Morris U. Schappes to SH, 6 February 1933 (Hook Papers, box 2). Schappes shortly thereafter joined the Communist Party; later he was imprisoned as a result of the Rapp-Coudert investigation of New York schools; after 1945 he founded the magazine *Jewish Currents:* Morris U. Schappes to author, 25 February and 23 March 1992.

[33] Klehr, *The Heyday of American Communism,* 428 n. 31.

premise that capitalism had entered a "Third Period" of final crisis and imminent collapse. Since this Third Period was to bring decisive and ultimate struggle between the working class and the ruling class, the first task of Communists was to discredit and displace all false leaders who would disorient and mislead the working class at a critical time by inviting it down the disastrous path of reformist compromise. Correspondingly, the Communists branded the Socialist Party "social-fascist" and considered it the third bourgeois party. This line of thought, bizarre in the United States, was positively tragic in Germany, where the Social Democratic government, shaken by the global economic crisis, was threatened by a rising fascist movement. Hook had already grasped the likely consequences of Third Period hyperbole in 1928, when he witnessed mass brawls between Communist and Socialist youth in the streets of Berlin, each wing of socialism oblivious to the growth of Nazism. But like others, he had repressed his criticism of the theory of social fascism. He agreed with the intransigent opposition to capitalism promoted by the Communists and concurred that social democracy was impotent in the face of capitalist crisis; he comforted himself with the belief that if the Nazis ever really threatened to take power the Communists would be forced to set aside their differences with the Social Democrats. Throughout the fall of 1932, however, the phenomenal growth of Nazi power in Germany did not prompt any shift in Communist strategy. In January 1933 Hitler became chancellor of Germany; in March he seized dictatorial power. Hook realized that his hope that the Communists would unite with Social Democrats to fight the Nazis had been illusory, and along with other dissenters he became an outspoken critic of the Third Period. The time he had spent in Germany having made the issue even more poignant, he was part of a tendency in the league arguing for a united front of all working-class organizations to supplant Third Period sectarianism.

In the winter of 1932–33 the league held a public lecture series under the heading "The Culture and the Crisis" at Chaffard's French Restaurant on Seventh Avenue near 23rd Street. The restaurant offered the group a big upstairs banquet room free of charge, providing enough people bought dinner beforehand. No matter what the topic of the evening, each meeting would end with a heated exchange over the theory of social fascism. The dissident intellectuals' estimation of Trotsky had risen dramatically since his prediction of disaster in Germany had come true, and they clashed with the Communist intellectuals (such as Joseph Pass and Joseph Freeman) and their fellow-traveling allies (including Malcolm Cowley and Kyle Crichton) over topics ranging from the Comintern's responsibility for the 1927 defeat of the Chinese revolution to the appropriateness of Third Period strategy to American conditions. Hook was in the thick of the spirited battles. Once he stood up to criticize dual unionism, only to be met with a disdainful riposte from Cowley: "Who are *you* to disagree with William Foster on trade unionism?" On another occasion, in the course of a raucous debate that erupted after he lectured on philosophy, Hook turned to the crowd of hecklers, raised his glass in a mock toast, and proclaimed, "I give you the hemlock!" His ironic inverted reference to Socrates brought the house down.[34]

Hook was more cautious on paper than in person. In April 1933, even as his rift with the Communist Party widened, he participated in a *New Masses* symposium on fascism along with many other independent intellectuals, among them James Rorty, Granville Hicks, and Waldo Frank. Hook's brief contribution subscribed to the Communist analysis of Nazism. Hitler, he wrote, "is not merely an individual; he is the incarnation of a principle, a system, which seeks to bolster up the hegemony of finance-capital with properly administered doses of blood and iron." That assertion contrasted with Trotsky's subtler thesis that Hitler's movement was based in the small shopkeepers and salaried workers of the petty bourgeoisie, who had to struggle before they managed to compel finance capital to back open dictatorship. Hook did stress, however, the need for "*united action* of all workers, farmers and intellectuals," and he called upon intellectuals to aid in "the *united front* now in process of crystallization *of all working-class organizations.*" Hook did not blame the Third Period strategy or the Communists for Hitler's ascension, but his italics underscored the urgency of abandoning sectarian shibboleths.[35]

In May 1933, Hook for the first time criticized the Comintern doctrine of social fascism and presented a more sophisticated explanation for fascism's appeal. In "Why the German Student Is Fascist," which he published in *Student Outlook* (the monthly organ of the League for Industrial Democracy's Intercollegiate Student Council, a Socialist youth group), he outlined the factors contributing to the popularity of Nazism among German youth: the grip of nationalism and tradition on the mind of the German student after the war, the vengeance of frustrated imperial ambition, the diminished opportunity for civil service careers with the onset of austerity, and the demagogic appeal of the Nazis' "radical" critique of bourgeois democracy as a drag upon further economic expansion. He also argued that the Social Democrats, when in power, had helped to pave the way for

[34] On the restaurant meeting, see Malcolm Cowley, *The Dream of the Golden Mountains*, 123, 126; Wald, *The New York Intellectuals*, 58. The Foster remark is quoted in Hook, *Out of Step*, 187–88; the Socrates reference in John McDonald to Alan Wald, 6 August 1985 (Hook Papers, box 133).

[35] Hook, untitled contribution to "Against the Fascist Terror," *New Masses* 8 (April 1933): 12–13. For Leon Trotsky's prescient writings on Nazism, see his *The Struggle against Fascism in Germany*, ed. George Breitman and Merry Maisel (New York: Pathfinder, 1971).

Nazism by their assertions that the German republic had the potential to resolve within its parliamentary order the antagonism of capital and labor—a doctrine later appropriated by fascism in its own state ideology. He maintained that they should have opened the university to working-class students and refused to countenance persecution of liberal and radical professors by right-wing students. Although the Social Democrats thus received the brunt of Hook's criticism, he found both Socialists and Communists guilty of the "tactical errors . . . especially from 1929 to 1932" that had permitted the Nazi takeover. He repeated the assertion of his *New Masses* article that the tide of fascism was forcing Communists and Socialists together in common cause, adding that "in many universities they are fighting shoulder to shoulder for survival against the furious attacks of the reactionaries." But Hook also observed, more realistically, that "this last-hour union, carried out in the teeth of the official policies of the Socialist and Communist parties, is too late."[36]

Towards the Understanding of Karl Marx, 1933

As his conflicts with the dominant forces of the Communist movement mounted, Hook put the finishing touches on *Towards the Understanding of Karl Marx: A Revolutionary Interpretation,* a masterful examination that even today remains one of the most compelling guides to Marx's thought. The book took germinal form in Hook's writings of the late 1920s and was, in finished form, his greatest accomplishment of the early 1930s.[37] Its release, timed to commemorate the fiftieth anniversary of Marx's death, coincided with the "bank holiday" declared by President Franklin Delano Roosevelt in March 1933, a date that seemed to mark the nadir of capitalism's basic financial institutions.[38]

The premise of the work was that Marxism "is not an armchair philosophy of retrospection, but a philosophy of social action; more specifically, *a theory of social revolution.*" Since Marx's death that understanding, Hook argued, had been buried beneath an accumulation of interpretations to the

[36] Hook, "Why the German Student is Fascist," *Student Outlook* 1 (May 1933): 4–6.
[37] The book's essential ideas were partially present as early as Hook's *Journal of Philosophy* series on dialectical materialism in 1927. He published an outline argument for it in *Modern Quarterly* in 1930, expanded it in a series of lectures delivered in 1930–31 at the New School for Social Research, and published several advance chapters in small magazines during the early 1930s.
[38] There is little dispute that *Towards the Understanding of Karl Marx: A Revolutionary Interpretation* (New York: John Day, 1933) ranks among the most important works of Marxist philosophy in American history, but one petty irritation warrants a footnote: it would be hard to find a book whose title has been so often rendered incorrectly, even by expert scholars on Hook, as *Toward the Understanding of Karl Marx, Towards an Understanding of Karl Marx,* or some other inexact approximation.

contrary. Hence, the first and more powerful half of *Towards the Understanding of Karl Marx* was devoted not to an explication of Marx but to a critical history of his interpreters. The eclipse of the active element in Marxist theory was mainly due, Hook held, to the rise of reformist Social Democracy in nineteenth-century Germany, a phenomenon that he explained by historical factors: economically, Germany rose to imperialist stature, permitting state insurance and rising wages for skilled workers, and encouraging nationalism and conservative trade unionism; politically, the combined influence of Bismarckian repression and subsequent liberalization caused timidity among leading socialists, a penchant for restrained language, and a desire to maintain electoral respectability. The two wings of German Social Democracy—the "orthodoxy" of Karl Kautsky and Rudolf Hilferding, which held Marxism an objective science of social development proving the inevitability of socialism, and the "revisionism" of Edward Bernstein, who argued for abandoning talk of revolution altogether and declaring the party an association of democratic social reform—were in Hook's judgment equally illegitimate claims to the tradition of Marx: "Instead of dialectical materialism, the German socialists became sensationalist and mechanical, ignoring *praxis*."[39]

Marxist orthodoxy between 1895 and 1917, Hook wrote, was "not only fatal to honest thinking; it involved the abandonment of the revolutionary standpoint which was central to Marx's life and thought." This criticism of Marxism's ossification within German Social Democracy and the falsity of its claim to uphold Marx's method was consistent with Georg Lukács's essays in *History and Class Consciousness* (1923), especially "What Is Orthodox Marxism?" But Hook was even closer to Karl Korsch, whose *Marxism and Philosophy?* (1923) declined to compete for the mantle of "orthodoxy," renouncing the very impulse to orthodoxy as dogmatic and religious. Hook gave rather grudging credit to Lukács for linking "Marx up—unfortunately much too closely—with the stream of classical German philosophy." Korsch had confirmed the "practical-historical axis of Marx's thought," Hook wrote, though he had underestimated "the difficulties in treating the formal aspect of Marx's thought from this point of view."[40]

---

[39] Hook, *Towards the Understanding of Karl Marx*, 9, 33. The latter quotation illustrates why Paul Buhle, *Marxism in the USA* (London: Verso, 1987), 166–67, is mistaken to interpret the book as a critique of dialectical materialism. Only much later did Hook treat dialectical materialism as metaphysical dogma; in this work he considered it the correct term for Marx's philosophical standpoint. Of course, like his earlier article on the subject, the book emphasizes the *dialectical*, or active and historical, nature of Marx's materialism. He meant nothing religious, mystical, or dogmatic by it. Perhaps Buhle meant to counterpose the book to Stalinism, but since Hook never explicitly criticizes the Communist Party or its official philosophy anywhere in this work, even that interpretation would have to be heavily qualified.

[40] Hook, *Towards the Understanding of Karl Marx*, ix, xii.

Reformists seemed on the surest footing in their claims of orthodoxy—that is, an accurate representation of Marx—when citing certain phrases from Engels, Marx's lifelong collaborator. But even Engels, Hook maintained, was not what German Social Democracy had made him out to be. In a series of late-life letters that Hook translated into English for the first time and appended to his book, Engels warned against fetishism of legality and crude economic determinism. The "orthodoxy" of Social Democracy, Hook concluded, was in reality based upon a highly selective reading of Engels.[41]

One contemporaneous challenge to Second International reformism came from French syndicalist Georges Sorel, who was appalled by parliamentary co-optation in France and trade union conservatism in Germany. Sorel, wrote Hook, repudiated the reformist fetishism of pacifism and celebrated direct mass action but fell prey to irrationalism and anti-intellectualism with a cult of "myth" that forsook rational politics. Marxism's real line of preservation lay elsewhere, in the theory and activism of Polish-German revolutionary Rosa Luxemburg and Russian Bolshevik leader V. I. Lenin. Both Luxemburg and Lenin had criticized social democratic reformism, pressed for working-class self-emancipation, repudiated economism, and advocated that the seizure of political power be the aim of the socialist movement. Whereas the German Social Democrats voted for war bonds, Luxemburg and Lenin argued for class struggle to defeat imperialism and war. Thus, as the leaders of the Second International proudly proclaimed their Marxist "orthodoxy," Luxemburg and Lenin and their sundry "deviations" had shown a greater fidelity to the revolutionary method of Marx and Engels.

[41] A common criticism of *Towards the Understanding of Karl Marx* is its supposed bias against Engels, whom, critics allege, Hook blamed for supplying the scriptural justification for economic determinism in Marxism. The objection is inexplicable. It is true that Hook criticized Engels in places—he also criticized Marx and Lenin—but he summoned Engels as an authority just as often, and he *criticized* those Marxists who cited Engels to justify their economic determinism and fatalism. The letters translated by Hook and appended to the book were meant to demonstrate Engels's flexibility and *opposition* to economic determinism. The allegation that Hook maligned Engels is not merely mistaken; it misleads, because Hook's interpretation of Engels was situated strategically within his central project of rescuing both Marx and Engels from their doctrinal usurpation by the Second International. It is ironic that Hook's attempt to refute a one-sided reading of Engels has been met by a similar reading of Hook. Those who have faulted the early Hook, especially in *Towards the Understanding of Karl Marx*, for a supposed anti-Engels bias include Max Eastman, *The Last Stand of Dialectical Materialism: A Study of Sidney Hook's Marxism* (New York: Polemic, 1934); Cristiano Camporesi, "The Marxism of Sidney Hook," *Telos* 12 (Summer 1972): 115–27; Wald, *The New York Intellectuals*, 125–26; Buhle, *Marxism in the USA*, 166; and George Novack, *Polemics in Marxist Philosophy* (New York: Pathfinder, 1978), 109. For favorable references to Engels by Hook, see *Towards the Understanding of Karl Marx*, 30–33, 117, 129, 139, 153–54, 172, 179–80, 182–83; for critical reference to Marx and Lenin, whose assertions that revolution in the United States might come about peacefully struck Hook as untenable, see 290–93.

Still, neither Luxemburg nor Lenin—the heroes of Hook's book—passed without criticism. On the famous point of dispute between the two over forms of socialist organization, Hook came down on Lenin's side, judging tight discipline appropriate to Russia's repressive conditions. Hook also dissented from Luxemburg on national liberation, challenging her theory that accumulation crisis would inexorably require imperialism's collapse at its core. As for Lenin, Hook resurrected his epistemological objections to the mechanical materialism of *Materialism and Empirio-Criticism*. In contrast to "The Philosophy of Dialectical Materialism," however, this work was appreciative of Lenin's general intellectual contributions, especially the emphasis upon revolutionary practice in *What Is to Be Done?* In that call to action, Hook maintained, lay Lenin's "true philosophy," that which he actually had to follow in order to bring about the Soviet revolution. Hook went so far as to praise Lenin as the only accurate interpreter of Marx.[42]

Mistaken interpretations of Marx, Hook argued, depended upon the extraction of his statements from their polemical context. Only a historical reading, one that positioned Marx in relation to the doctrines he sought to refute, would reveal his method. What seemed wildly contradictory in Marx—here incitement to voluntary action, there an emphasis on unalterable economic causality—became "the application of the same principles and purposes to different historical situations," if grasped contextually. Another frequent mistake, Hook wrote, was to seek in Marx's writings an absolute law or pure science: "Social science is class science; and what Marx means by science is not what is meant by the word today, but *criticism based upon the observable tendencies of social development.*" Because revolutionary commitment infused all of Marx's theory, the search for an objective Marxist science outside of class struggle would end in frustration or distortion.[43]

At the core of Marx's thinking was his dialectical method, which, Hook asserted, had a number of exceptional characteristics: a historical and materialist basis, unlike Hegel's idealist abstraction; an insistence on cultural interconnectedness without any single explanatory principle; an admission of the interrelation of cause and effect, so that consciousness was not simply effect and the external world not merely cause; and the realization that social change occurs through a combination of social conditions, felt needs, and action. Although Marx carried over from Hegel the dialectical understanding that change involves unity through preservation, difference in destruction, and qualitative novelty, he did not, according to Hook,

[42] Hook, *Towards the Understanding of Karl Marx*, 62–64.
[43] Ibid., 67, 69.

take dialectics to mean an abstract triadic model capable of mechanical application to any social process. Marx merely took from idealism the insight that knowledge is active and that sensations are social, not just biological impressions on passive subjects. The significance of Marx's method was not in its abstract character, as so many mistakenly supposed, but in its practical implications. Proper dialectical understanding, Hook explained, illuminates the path between and beyond reform and utopia. Reformers try to mediate irreconcilables, utopians to suppress cultural and economic continuities. Each meets with futility. Revolutionary socialism, by contrast, pursues sweeping social transformation while simultaneously proposing to build from what exists. Marxism draws upon the visionary qualities of utopianism as well as the practicality of the reform impulse, while refusing either to draw up fixed blueprints of the new social order or to capitulate to contemporary political situations. "Marxism," Hook concluded, "is neither a science nor a myth, but a realistic method of social action."[44]

Towards the Understanding of Karl Marx received a wide audience and high praise from reviewers. In *The Nation* the independent radical Benjamin Stolberg pronounced the book "the most significant contribution to Marxism which has as yet appeared in America" and fairly gushed that "it is thrilling to behold such intellectual courage in a university teacher." In the *New Republic* the British scholar of politics Harold J. Laski called it "the most stimulating introduction" to Marx "so far written in English." Along with the praise, though, came a telling line of criticism: although Dewey's name did not appear once in the entire text of *Towards the Understanding of Karl Marx,* both Laski and Stolberg faulted Hook for attempting to imprint Dewey into Marx. "By using . . . characteristically pragmatic terms in all their technical implications," wrote Stolberg, "Dr. Hook persuades himself that Marx was a sort of left-wing, revolutionary Dewey. The truth is that both the Marxian epistemology and its psychology are the exact opposite. . . . Marxian 'instrumentalism' has none of the worship of empiricism of the pragmatists. It is calculated to advance revolutionary tactics *within* a strictly a priori social logic. It learns from means only when they are conceived to serve its ends, while pragmatism is the idolatry of endless means. Pragmatism, indeed, is the most sophisticated expression of the planlessness of modern capitalism."[45]

Stolberg was correct about the pragmatist bent of *Towards the Understanding of Karl Marx,* but in reproducing the left's conventional biases against pragmatism he failed to engage Hook. He omitted, for example,

[44] Ibid., 114.
[45] Harold J. Laski, "Introduction to Marx," *The New Republic* 75 (28 June 1933): 186–87; Benjamin Stolberg, "The Americanization of Karl Marx," *The Nation* 136 (12 April 1933): 414–15.

Hook's pragmatist reading of Marx's theses on Feuerbach, which Hook astutely took to mean that "any problem which cannot be solved by some actual or possible practice may be dismissed as no genuine problem at all." By locating pragmatism within capitalism, Stolberg could not admit to the possibility of the revolutionary socialist pragmatism conceived by Hook. "The task of the revolutionary philosopher," Hook had written, "is to bring social classes to an awareness of what it is they are doing and of the historical conditions of their activity." Although Stolberg had substituted intellectual prejudice for argument, *The Nation*'s review was representative of the fate Hook's project would so often meet on the left despite widespread recognition of his lucidity and scholarship.[46]

Communist leaders did not temper their criticism, as had Stolberg, with appreciation of Hook's achievement. Their vitriol was disproportionate. *Towards the Understanding of Karl Marx* did not once polemicize against the Marxism of the Comintern or express any qualms about developments in the Soviet Union since 1917.[47] And Hook's salute to Lenin and the Third International as the rescuers of Marx from reformism had certainly not escaped the book's reviewers: "To Dr. Hook," wrote Stolberg, "it is Lenin who is the greatest Marxian revolutionary, not merely tactically but also dialectically."[48] Nonetheless, *Towards the Understanding of Karl Marx* provoked severe Communist misgivings, for Hook endorsed a form of dialectical materialism incompatible with that doctrine as it was coming to be defined by the Party. Communist theoreticians were increasingly treating Marxism as an infallible science capable of revealing absolute historical laws, presenting the dialectic as a tripartite formula of thesis-antithesis-sythesis, and treating culture as a secondary sphere fundamentally determined by an economic base.[49] By challenging Communism to abandon such narrow formulations, by arguing that this sort of philosophical dogma had nothing in common with Marx, by criticizing Russian masters such as Georgi Plekhanov and Nikolai Bukharin for their monistic simplification, by expressing debt to the heretics Lukács and Korsch, Hook had not merely pushed philosophical boundaries. He had overstepped them.

---

[46]   Hook, *Towards the Understanding of Karl Marx*, 76, 185.
[47]   On the contrary, Hook hailed the Soviet Union's "progressive elimination of national, cultural and racial hostilities among its heterogenous peoples," which he said had been done by "voluntary participation in a socialist economy" and "not by suppressing national units or indigenous cultures" (*Towards the Understanding of Karl Marx*, 247), an estimation that he would in not too long a time come to reconsider.
[48]   Stolberg, "The Americanization of Karl Marx," 414.
[49]   For a sampling of Stalinist philosophy from the 1930s, all attempting to codify dialectical materialism into a fixed system, see V. Adoratsky, *Dialectical Materialism* (New York: International, 1934); Howard Selsam, *What Is Philosophy? A Marxist Introduction* (New York: International, 1938); David Guest, *A Textbook of Dialectical Materialism* (New York: International, 1939).

Breaking with Communism, 1932–33

Had Hook's sole difference with the Communist Party been its Third Period program, he might have been able to sustain a relationship of critical sympathy, for soon after the German disaster the Party began to advocate a "united front from below"—a stunted form of the united front in which Party members tried to persuade rank-and-file Socialists to join them in common action while still denouncing Socialist leaders in emphatic terms. The Comintern's sectarianism and contribution to the Nazi seizure of power, however, formed only one issue in Hook's rupture with the American Communist Party; a sustained attack on his writings immediately after the 1932 election was more important. Although *Towards the Understanding of Karl Marx* had not yet appeared in print, Hook had completed the manuscript and had since 1930 been publishing articles enunciating its themes. When vilification of Hook erupted in the Party press just prior to the publication of the book, it was clear that the Party was preparing in advance for its appearance.

Late in 1932 Hook received a telephone call from Joseph Freeman, inviting him to a meeting with top Communist officials to discuss his views on Marxism. Rumors had been circulating that the Party wanted to recruit Hook, perhaps because of his status as an authority on Marx, perhaps in order to utilize his connections as the means to win Dewey over. But when Hook reached the ninth floor of Party headquarters on East 13th Street, he found that the meeting had quite a different purpose. He was directed to a table at which sat the Party's highest leaders, including Earl Browder, Clarence Hathaway, James Ford, Alexander Trachtenberg, Sam Don, Avram Landy, Joseph Pass, Joseph Freeman, Robert Minor, and V. J. Jerome. Browder requested a summary of his forthcoming book, and Hook delivered it. Then Sam Don—a graduate of the Lenin School in Moscow who served for years on the staff of the *Daily Worker*—claimed that Hook's arguments for the primacy of historical process rather than physical matter were idealist and cited a number of passages from Engels to prove it. Hook responded that because revolutionaries seek to create a new society different from existing reality, the mirror theory of consciousness was inadequate; a copybook theory of knowledge could not account for anticipation, let alone imagination. The dispute, which lasted over an hour, also touched upon Hook's disparagement of universal laws of social development, his views on dialectics, and his doubt that Marx meant the "inevitability" of communism to be taken literally. Trachtenberg, Freeman, and Browder appeared to Hook to be fairly receptive to his reasoning except on the question of the dialectic, which he interpreted simply as the element of conscious activity in human action and did not see as extending to nature itself. Browder asked Hook how he then differed from Max Eastman, a figure scorned by the Party in part for his own renunciations of the dialectical theory of nature. Hook recounted his severe criticisms of Eastman's attack on dialectics and conception of revolution as social engineering. Party leaders also appeared discomfited by Hook's assertion of the relative autonomy of politics and philosophy. Hook explained his view that since dialectical materialism or any other metaphysical position did not necessarily entail any specific set of social beliefs, one could be a communist or socialist and not a dialectical materialist, or a materialist without espousing socialism. After the meeting ended, with Hook having answered each criticism leveled against his work, he and Browder retired for a cup of coffee to a cafeteria on University Place, where Browder complained to Hook about the chaos caused to the Party in 1929 by the departure of the Lovestone group.[50]

Although Hook had answered his opponents, he had not dissuaded them. He did not know that his most persistent antagonist during the meeting, Sam Don, was at that time a critic of Browder's conciliatory gestures toward "bourgeois intellectuals." Former *Daily Worker* correspondent Sender Garlin describes Don as a "literal-minded kind of fundamentalist," and Don proved true to that reputation in his volley against Hook in a *Daily Worker* article on December 14, 1932; he castigated Hook and even upbraided the Party's theoretical magazine, *The Communist,* for having not yet attacked Hook's "scholastic and absolute revisionism." This scorcher made Hook the first intellectual supporter of Foster and Ford to come under Party fire. The January 1933 issue of *The Communist,* as if in answer to Don's cue, unveiled a condemnation of Hook by V. J. Jerome, "Unmasking an American Revisionist of Marxism." Although he had clearly sided with Don during the ninth-floor meeting, Jerome, who had audited a course of Hook's at NYU in 1930–31, had refrained from saying much in the course of the debate. His article was crude and tendentious; he ignored Hook's admiration for Marx and Lenin and repeated criticisms of the social democratic views of Bernstein, Kautsky, and Hilferding, baselessly imputing to Hook the view that "not in Marx, not in Lenin, nowhere *except in German revisionism* can Hook find the true Marxism!" Jerome accused Hook of being "a willful distorter and falsifier of Marxism," and maintained that his "pluralistic hypotheses are a return from scientific militant materialism to reactionary idealist experientialism." He dismissed Hook's polemics

---

[50] This reconstruction is drawn from Hook, *Out of Step,* 158–65. His account of the meeting cannot be verified, but his recollection of the conversation's subjects corresponds to the issues at stake in the subsequent published debate, as well as to philosophical positions he expressed in *Towards the Understanding of Karl Marx.* On rumors that the Party sought Hook as a member, see John McDonald to Alan Wald, 6 August 1985 (Hook Papers, box 133).

against Max Eastman as quarrels within the same bourgeois family, and linked both Hook and Eastman by their association with Dewey, whom he described ad hominem as "this American bourgeois in cap and gown" and "a blatant supporter of the social-fascist presidential candidate, Norman Thomas!" The fact that Hook, in contrast to Dewey, had thrown his public support behind the Communist slate was conveniently suppressed. Jerome blustered that "with Hook the speaker for the proletarian platform has come Hook the ideologist of the platform for the bourgeoisie, Hook the carrier of the specific philosophy of the American bourgeoisie dressed in phrases of Marxism." In a final triumph of Third Period logic, Jerome proclaimed that "despite his objective position among the intellectuals uniting toward the revolutionary movement, Hook is subjectively a force pulling away from it."[51]

Radical intellectuals were unimpressed. Not even those who were themselves critical of Hook's pragmatism found Jerome's approach productive. Rather than stigmatizing Hook, Jerome's hatchet job reinforced the convictions of many who were already finding the Communist Party's theoretical and political approach hapless. J. B. S. Hardman, editor of the trade union publication *The Advance*, wrote to Hook, "If the job had not been done so clumsily and to a considerable degree dishonestly, I should not like to take exception to it, for the 'revision' is there. The trouble with professional and labeled Marxians is that they neither know Marx nor care to know him; if anybody isn't going about the matter religiously he is their enemy entirely. They only feel safe in an atmosphere of faith. Then they know how to exact it and how to break it."[52]

Jerome's blast failed to satisfy even those intellectuals who remained dedicated Communists. *New Masses* editor Granville Hicks wrote to Hook that "it ought to be possible to criticize a man's ideas without calling him a social-fascist," and went on to confess, "Personally I cannot accept your instrumentalism, and I should have welcomed an intelligent analysis of it. But Jerome's article is practically worthless."[53] Even at the late date of Sep-

---

[51] Sam Don in *Daily Worker*, 14 December 1932, 4, quoted in Klehr, *The Heyday of American Communism*, 83, 428 n. 34; information on Don (born Sam Donchin) drawn from A. B. Magil to author, 8 March 1992, and interview with Sender Garlin, 9 May 1992; Jerome article: V. J. Jerome, "Unmasking an American Revisionist of Marxism," *The Communist*, January 1933, 50–82.

[52] J. B. S. Hardman to SH, 17 January 1933 (Hook Papers, box 2).

[53] Granville Hicks to SH, 25 January 1933 (Hook Papers, box 2). Within a few more years Hicks himself would take a shot at Hook. At the height of the Popular Front he published a bit of humorous doggerel in the *New Masses;* his "Revolution in Bohemia" (1938), concerns Halstead Weeks, a dilettante who flirts with revolution, only to go over to the anti-Stalinist left and then withdraw from politics completely: "He found the works of Sidney Hook sublime / And planned to read Karl Marx when he had time." See *Granville Hicks in the New Masses*, ed. Jack Alan Robbins (Port Washington, N.Y.: Kennikat Press, 1974), 314.

tember 1933, Smith College professor Newton Arvin wrote Hook that he had greatly enjoyed *Towards the Understanding of Karl Marx:* "I don't know what the official Party attitude toward it is (though I suppose it is unfavorable), but if you are still proscribed as a heretic, I fear that I am one, too, for I haven't succeeded in seeing anything that, in my ignorance perhaps, strikes me as wrong with it."[54]

The smear campaign against Hook did not abate, however; in January 1933 the *Daily Worker* unleashed a wave of invective. One article described approvingly the disruption by hecklers of a teachers' meeting at which Hook and his old City College professor Harry Overstreet spoke. In another polemic, H. M. Wicks—a "master of vituperation," as former Communist Sender Garlin recalls—purported to explain "how Hook serves capitalists." After calling him a "shallow vulgarizer," "muddled pretender," and "philosophic hack," Wicks alleged that Hook had been privately telling "those who will listen that no one in the Communist Party, U.S.A. or in the Communist Party of the Soviet Union knows the first thing about philosophy."[55]

In February and March *The Communist* published Hook's reply to Jerome, which he had previously shared with Arvin, Hicks, and Corliss Lamont.[56] The move was highly unusual for a journal devoted to laying down uniformly correct positions, since it admitted implicitly the value of exchange over fundamental differences within Marxism. Rather than simply producing Hook's reply, however, *The Communist* printed it within a two-part article by Party leader Earl Browder, alternating long passages from Hook's response with Browder's point-by-point rebuttal. Browder criticized Jerome and Wicks for the clumsy manner in which they had carried out their attacks, but he came down in their favor on the general charge that Hook had "an understanding of Marxism in conflict with that of the Communist Party and the Communist International." Hook began his rebuttal to Jerome with quotations from Marx, Lenin, even Stalin (this was the first and only time that Hook would summon Stalin as a positive authority in defense of a position) meant to demonstrate that each of them had rejected dogmatism. He rightly accused Jerome of "intellectual dis-

[54]   Newton Arvin to SH, 8 September 1933 (Hook Papers, box 5).
[55]   M. B. Schnapper, "Teachers Expose, Discomfit Sidney Hook and Overstreet," *Daily Worker*, 25 January 1933; H. M. Wicks, "Revolutionary Theory Applied to Present-Day Problems," *Daily Worker*, 10 January 1933; interview with Sender Garlin, 9 May 1992. Harry Wicks (1889–1957), a member of the CP 1922–38, was expelled after it was discovered that he had been working as an undercover agent for a private company, raising the distinct possibility that his attack on Hook was a deliberate exacerbation of tensions by a provocateur. See Harvey Klehr, "Wicks, Harry," in *Biographical Dictionary of the American Left*, ed. Bernard K. Johnpoll and Harvey Klehr (New York: Greenwood, 1986), 414–15.
[56]   Granville Hicks to SH, 25 January 1933 (Hook Papers, box 2).

honesty" for misrepresenting his position and called for a "creative Marxism" rather than one based upon sacred texts. "The teachings of Marx, Engels and Lenin are the most valuable truths we have.... But they themselves have urged that any movement which refuses to learn *new* things in *new* situations—to submit all principles to the test of experience and action—is doomed to sectarianism and futile failure." Browder, however, accused Hook of arrogance in presuming that he, and not the Communist Parties of the world, understood Marxism properly. Hook's philosophy, Browder concluded, was idealist, so that "while it puts on a brave revolutionary face as emphasizing action, more action, [it] achieves the opposite result in reality by laying the foundation for confusion and disruption."[57]

Before that exchange Hook had harbored hopes that Browder would come to his defense, though in a letter to Will Herberg he lamented "illiterate party bureaucrats like Jerome and Don and Wicks, [who] attempt to settle things merely by quotation." With the mutilation of his reply to Jerome in *The Communist* and Browder's refutation, it was clear that Hook could expect no redemption from on high. "What a piece of work," wrote Herberg. "Are you satisfied now that you can expect nothing from Browder? Browder not only endorses all of Jerome's lies and outright forgeries but even 'blames' Jerome for not going far enough: 'Jerome's crime in this respect is serious because he thereby detracted slightly from the full force of his attack against Hook's revisionism.' In my opinion, Browder's article is even more ignorant and even more indecent, if that is possible, than Jerome's." Morris U. Schappes concurred: "Well, Browder is as bad as Jerome, and he doesn't seem able to learn from your demonstration of Jerome's blunders."[58] By late spring 1933 Hook and the Communist Party were completely estranged. Hook's philosophical convictions ran too deep to permit him to capitulate to Party authority, as Browder insisted. Precisely because he remained a communist and revolutionary Marxist, Hook was unable to submit to the authoritarian and monolithic form of discipline that had been demanded from him by the Party.

The onslaught against Hook's Marxism by Party officials had only lent

---

57   Earl Browder, "The Revisionism of Sidney Hook," *The Communist*, February 1933, 135, 145, and March 1933, 289, 299. The Browder condemnations were given added weight when they were reproduced in Earl Browder, *Communism in the United States* (New York: International, 1935), 316–33. Immediately after these articles were published, according to Hook in *Out of Step* (166–73), Browder invited him to a private evening meeting and attempted to recruit him to espionage. There is no corroborating evidence for this story, and though within the realm of possibility, the tale seems logically implausible. Why would the Party try to recruit for top-secret spying someone whom it no longer trusted?

58   Will Herberg to SH, 7 February and 26 March 1933 (Hook Papers, box 15); Morris U. Schappes to SH, 6 February 1933 (Hook Papers, box 2).

urgency to a differentiation long in the making. Hook's pragmatism had given to his Marxism a methodological emphasis upon provisional truth rather than absolute certainty, scientific inquiry over doctrinaire fidelity, flux and change over fixity and determinism, and the potential of human action over fatalism. Although Hook did not deny the importance of theoretical works and historical conditioning, he sought to restore the active and subjective component of Marxism against the hardened Marxism propounded by the Second International. Though occasionally critical of official Communism, he had been a dedicated fellow traveler and political supporter of the Party. His criticisms derived not from a hostility to communism as a principle and social goal but from the perception that official Communism was straying from its stated aim and classical theory. He had sought to refute the copy-book materialism of Lenin's *Materialism and Empirio-Criticism* but only so as to make sense of the revolutionary activism of the Lenin of *What Is to Be Done?* Now, it appeared, Lenin and the rest of the revolutionary tradition required rescue from the Communists. Intellectual historian Morton White wrote that John Dewey had led a "revolt against formalism" in philosophy; Hook helped to initiate a revolt against formalism within American Marxism.[59] The formalists—typified by Jerome, Wicks, Don, and Browder—temporarily crushed his revolt, but unwittingly they had driven Hook to revolution.

[59] Morton White, *Social Thought in America* (New York: Viking, 1952).

CHAPTER THREE

Marxism, Democracy, Science, 1933–36

During the cold winter months of early 1933, many intellectuals in New York City once attracted to the Communist Party entered into its opposition from the left. Like Hook's, their dissatisfaction grew out of the Nazi triumph, which shattered hopes for the Comintern as a bulwark against fascism. Confidence was not restored as members of the League of Professional Groups met with arrogant, injudicious treatment at the hands of Party officials. James Rorty, for example, though the league's secretary, was not even apprised in advance of V. J. Jerome's blistering denunciation of Hook in *The Communist*. Astounded by that screed, Rorty rose from his desk and headed upstairs to ask Browder why Hook had come in for so vicious an attack: "Again I puffed up the stairs to the Ninth Floor. Was the Party trying to liquidate our best member? This time Browder wouldn't even talk to me. Instead I was told to see a minor member of the hierarchy whom I had never met before and whose name I have now forgotten. Sorry, he said, without appearing to be at all sorry. Jerome's review was right out of the horse's mouth. That was the Party line and if Hook was offside, so much the worse for Hook." By early summer, irritated by such cavalier bureaucratic maneuvering, Rorty had quit his post. As the league dissolved, a number of promising projects began to founder. The year before, Hook had been asked to write a preface on Marxism and a chapter on philosophy for a volume of Marxist essays that Granville Hicks proposed to edit, a successor to the Calverton-initiated *America at the Crossroads*. By March 1933, however, the contributors to the Hicks project, most of whom were cross-listed on the roster of the league, were so badly divided about the meaning and purposes of Marxism that this projected anthology too had to be abandoned.[1]

With the league's collapse, the writers and artists who had come together in revolutionary unity during the 1932 campaign went their separate ways. Many remained within the orbit of the Communist Party, though no organization analogous to the League of Professional Groups would exist for them until two years later, when the League of American Writers was created. Despite the official attacks, intellectuals in the Communist milieu were not uniformly hostile to Hook's works. In April 1932, for example, Newton Arvin invited him to a meeting to share his expertise on "the philosophic aspects of Marxism." But the camps were becoming more fixed as Stalinism became a dividing line on the left. Other members of the league, including Hook's comrades Herbert Solow and Felix Morrow, were drawn to the Communist League of America (CLA), which shared the politics of Leon Trotsky and was led by James P. Cannon and Max Shachtman. Another swath of league veterans—including Hook, Rorty, Calverton, and Edmund Wilson, among others—affiliated with a band of militant labor activists led by A. J. Muste, who in late 1933 issued a call for an entirely new revolutionary organization, the American Workers Party (AWP). Lionel Abel is thus correct to recall that the view "advanced by Sidney Hook during the early thirties" was that "one could be a Marxist without being a Communist," but his accompanying sentence misleads: "Hook was asserting that it was possible to think along Marxist lines without joining any particular group, or assuming responsibility for any group's actions." In fact, in the early and middle 1930s, Hook believed socialist organization a necessary condition for the unification of Marxist theory and practice. His move away from the arena of the Communist Party was accomplished through a *deeper* commitment to socialist organization, not its renunciation, for he actually joined and helped lead the American Workers Party, taking part more seriously than he ever had with the Communist Party.[2]

The AWP's distance from related efforts on the left, especially the CLA, should not be exaggerated. From 1933 to 1936 Hook was basically sympathetic to Leon Trotsky's politics, if not his philosophy, and consistently acted in solidarity with the American Trotskyists. Like almost every mem-

[1] James Rorty, "It Has Happened Here," unpublished memoirs, version 1, chap. 11, p. 12 (James Rorty Papers, University of Oregon); Harvey Klehr, *The Heyday of American Communism* (New York: Basic, 1984), 79–80.
[2] Newton Arvin to SH, 12 April 1932 (Hook Papers, box 5); Lionel Abel, *The Intellectual Follies: A Memoir of the Literary Venture in New York and Paris* (New York: Norton, 1984), 121.

ber of the AWP, Hook was a persistent critic of the organizational structure and theoretical perspective of the Communist Party. AWP members, however, did not always share Trotsky's basic political analysis and terminology, as did Hook for the most part when explaining the degeneration of the Russian Revolution into Stalinism. Few endorsed Trotsky's initiative for a Fourth International to supplant the Comintern, as did Hook. Organizationally, Hook was never a Trotskyist; he never joined the CLA or its successor organizations, such as the Socialist Workers Party. But from Hook's vantage point in 1933, the differences between the AWP and the CLA were not matters of principle: the groups were in common cause rather than competition. While creating and building the AWP, Hook acted with the express purpose of strengthening the whole of the revolutionary anti-Stalinist left. Even before the new group was formally constituted as a party in 1934, he initiated discussions between the respective leaders of the soon-to-be AWP and the already established CLA, negotiations that explored the possibility of uniting the two groups.

In addition to the practical political task of strengthening the democratic revolutionary socialist movement, Hook undertook extensive theoretical labors in the mid-1930s. Following the success of *Towards the Understanding of Karl Marx,* his continued excavation of the origins of Marxism culminated in *From Hegel to Marx* (1936). Hook's philosophy developed in increasingly self-conscious opposition to the petrified Marxism of Communist intellectuals who propounded what he considered dogmatism in method, authoritarianism in politics, and foolhardiness in tactics. But Hook's Marxism, seasoned by pragmatism, faced its real test between 1933 and 1936 from quarters other than the Communist Party and its supporters, whose response was predictable, formulaic, and unconstructive. The more significant interrogators of Hook's ideas in the mid-1930s were Leon Trotsky, Max Eastman, John Dewey, Bertrand Russell, and Morris Cohen. The task of responding to the varied challenges of this formidable array of thinkers honed Hook's perspective. He was forced to provide better answers to the crucial questions that had been raised implicitly in his earlier writings: Is Marxism anything more than a method of revolution? What is the proper form of democracy within a socialist revolution? Is Marxism a science and, if so, what type of science?

Trotsky, Marxism, and Method, 1933

As his alliance with the Communist Party came unglued in the spring of 1933, Hook was at liberty to explore the possibility of establishing friendly relations with Leon Trotsky, the leading international exponent of dissident Marxism. Hook's initial knowledge of Trotsky and

favorable remarks about certain of Trotsky's views had been merely introductory and indirect, and even that brief form of interaction had been in-
terrupted by the Communist campaign in the election of 1932. But after
Earl Browder's denunciation in *The Communist* made it clear that Hook
could no longer hold to his philosophical convictions and continue to col-
laborate with the Communist Party, he leaped at the chance to enter into
more direct cooperation and communication with Trotsky.

His first opportunity came when he was paid a visit by B. J. Field, a member of the Communist League of America trained in economics, statistics,
and linguistics, who later that year would lead a major strike of hotel workers in New York City. Field asked Hook to serve as treasurer of the American Committee of the Commission for Help to the Imprisoned and
Deported Bolsheviks (Left Opposition), an international effort chaired by
Trotksy. An open letter written and signed by Trotsky—"Help is Needed
Immediately!"—was printed in *The Militant* of March 6, 1933, above
Hook's name and address, to which readers were encouraged to send do-
nations. Trotsky's plea referred to the persecuted Left Oppositionists as
"the vanguard of the October Revolution" and claimed that repression
confirmed "the correctness of the criticism and the warnings of the Left
Opposition." Those political judgments extended far beyond the simple
humanitarian reasons that Hook later claimed were his only reason for permitting the use of his name. Hook obtained the permission of novelist
John Dos Passos to use his name as well to help the deported and imprisoned Left Oppositionists, although Dos Passos specified that any funds so
raised were to be used for relief only and warned Hook that he deplored
the factional rows in the Communist movement as detrimental to the
prospects of revolution. That did not prevent Hook from deriving pleasure
from the Dos Passos coup. "When that news breaks—won't some people
growl?" he gloated to V. F. Calverton, who also was on the committee, along
with Diego Rivera and Herman Simpson.[3]

On March 21, 1933, Hook posted a letter addressed to "Comrade Trotsky," in which he complained that the American Communist Party "is woe-
fully ignorant of the writings of Marx, attempts to settle all theoretical

[3] In his autobiography, *Out of Step* (New York: Harper & Row, 1987), 179–83, Hook incorrectly states that he aided the American Committee for the Commission for Help to the Imprisoned and Deported Bolsheviks (Left Opposition) in 1931. For later claims of
humanitarian, rather than political, motives, see SH to Alan Wald, 28 December 1978 (Wald
Collection). See also Leon Trotsky, "Help Is Needed Immediately!" undated handbill (Hook
Papers, box 167); "Help Is Needed Immediately!" in *Writings of Leon Trotsky, 1932–33* (New
York: Pathfinder, 1972), 121–23; on B. J. Field, James P. Cannon, *The History of American Trotskyism* (1944; New York: Pathfinder, 1972), 126–35; John Dos Passos to SH, n.d. (Hook Pa-
pers, box 132, File 13); SH to V. F. Calverton, n.d. (V. F. Calverton Papers, New York Public
Library, Hook Correspondence).

issues by decree, regards all questions whether they concern *natur-dialektik* or proper united-front policy as 'axioms which cannot be submitted to discussion,' and propagates the most mechanical and fatalistic conception of Marxism imaginable." Whereas fatalism had traditionally served social democrats as an excuse for quietism and conciliation, Hook explained, the American Communists now had created their own brand of fatalism to mask the catastrophic consequences of their adventurism and "infantile leftism." Despite three years of severe crisis, wrote Hook, the CP had attracted just 10,000 members across the nation; the police force of New York City alone numbered 30,000. Any radical who dared to dissent sharply from a given Communist position, Hook explained, was greeted with charges of "Trotskyism, semi-Trotskyism, tainted by Trotskyism, tendencies towards Trotskyism." To give Trotsky the flavor of his own theoretical views, Hook enclosed one of his articles from *The Nation*, "Marxism: Dogma or Method?" and promised to send a copy of *Towards the Understanding of Karl Marx*.[4]

A brief exchange ensued, and in slightly revised form the letters were reproduced in the correspondence column of *The Nation* on July 5, 1933, most likely at Hook's initiative. Since Trotsky had not found the time to read *Towards the Understanding of Karl Marx*, he focused exclusively on "Marxism: Dogma or Method?" Hook had taken the fiftieth anniversary of Marx's death as an appropriate occasion to recapitulate his essential interpretation of Marx, especially his insistence that monistic theories of economic causation could not properly be derived from Marx's writings. Trotsky responded that the choice presented in Hook's title did not adequately express the full range of options. "Marxism is not a dogma," Trotsky concurred. "But it is not *only* a method, it is also a doctrine." In English the term "doctrine" suggests "doctrinaire" or "indoctrination" and is therefore barely distinguishable from dogma, but Trotsky meant merely that the dialectical method, at least in its application by Marx, established a theory of capitalist economy and a theory of history, each of which should be considered a science insofar as it was an established body of tested propositions expressed in theoretical form. Trotsky therefore sought to correct Hook's closing sentence that Marxism is "neither a dogma, myth nor objective science, but a realistic method of class action." If Marxism was "realistic," Trotsky replied, then it had to be "based upon the true knowledge of the objective—in that case social—processes; the knowledge of the objective is a science." Indeed, concluded Trotsky, Marxist policy was "realistic insofar as it is based upon Marxism *as a science*."[5]

[4] SH to Leon Trotsky, 21 March 1933 (Leon Trotsky Papers, Harvard University).
[5] Leon Trotsky to SH, 11 April 1933 (Leon Trotsky Papers, Harvard University); "Trotzky and Sidney Hook," *The Nation* 137 (5 July 1933): 18–19.

Trotsky's argument that Marxism was a method of understanding social reality *as well as* a method of forging revolution pointed to a weakness in Hook's prior formulations. Hook tended to associate and even identify the deterministic and fatalistic implications of some forms of Marxism, particularly the forms propounded by German social democracy and by the degenerated Comintern, with the claim that Marxism had arrived at a purely scientific understanding of the material processes of social reality. Yet in his response—more demure in his private correspondence with Trotsky than in his published rejoinder in *The Nation*—Hook suggested that Trotsky might have been confused by the English expressions he had used in "Marxism: Dogma or Method?" His denial that Marxism was an "objective science" on the order of the natural sciences, Hook explained, was not meant to deny that "Marxism is a *scientific* method (in theory and practice) of achieving the social revolution." But he persisted in arguing that Marxist theory was inseparable from revolutionary activity, a point, he assured Trotsky, raised not out of "barren scholasticism" but rather to illuminate "the *class* character of Marxism and the direct orientation of its doctrines upon revolutionary activity in behalf of the proletariat." The distinction was important, he argued, because some, such as Rudolf Hilferding, had suggested that one could be a Marxist without fighting for communism, and others, such as Max Eastman, had claimed that Marxism was an objective science of engineering that stood above historical and class conditioning. "I think my position coincides with yours wherever you address yourself to concrete analysis," Hook told Trotsky. "I take exception to some of your theoretical formulations especially when you speak of the 'natural laws' of social revolution without distinguishing between the 'natural laws' of the physical sciences and those of the social." Although Hook would sometimes counterpose objective science to Marxism on other occasions, the clarification prompted by Trotsky formed the essence of Hook's thinking about the relationship between Marxism and science, a problem that he would reconsider within a year.

Trotsky shared with Hook a conviction about Marxism's imperative to conscious action. "It is important to remember that Marxism both interprets the world and teaches how to change it," Trotsky wrote in an open letter to American intellectuals published in early 1933, a deliberate appeal to the rapidly scattering supporters of the League of Professionals for Foster and Ford. "The will is the moving element in the domain of knowledge, too. If Marxism loses its will to transform political reality, it loses the ability to understand it." That Hook had theoretical differences with Trotsky in 1933 ought not to obscure their considerable political agreement. In an April 1933 review of the second and third volumes of Trotsky's *History of the Russian Revolution*, Hook was even more fulsome in his praise than he had been in his review of the first. He expressed admiration for Trotsky's extraordinary stylistic gifts and praised his contention that the Soviet revolution of October 1917 was justified. Trotsky, he wrote, had demonstrated admirably the "character of the Bolshevik party as a whole which, despite the waverings of some of its leaders, mustered sufficient intelligence, flexibility and will to action to insure a practically bloodless triumph." Hook did part ways with Trotsky's contention that the revolution was "inevitable," an assumption that he believed was contradicted by Trotsky's repeated illustrations of the decisive political interventions made at opportune times by the Bolsheviks, which Hook took as proof of the importance of subjective action in creating the Russian Revolution. Yet Hook made the bold judgment that "Trotsky is indisputably the most brilliant Marxist in the world today—a Marxist in blood, temperament, and concrete logic." By the standards of the Communist Party, as Hook knew perfectly well, such appreciation was tantamount to treason.[6]

Eastman Revisited, 1933

A second challenge to Hook's Marxism, also revolving around conceptions of Marxism and science, came in 1933 when Max Eastman unexpectedly revived their old dispute. By all appearances, the acrimonious debate had run its course in 1928–29. Both Hook and Eastman had participated in a symposium titled "Marxism and Social Change" in the Winter 1930–31 issue of *Modern Quarterly*, but their articles were independent contributions. Eastman's return to the fray came when he published in the *New York Herald Tribune* a review of *Towards the Understanding of Karl Marx* bearing the biting subtitle, "Sidney Hook's Day-dream of What Marx Might Have Said Had He Been a Pupil of John Dewey." Eastman complimented Hook for his clear and graceful style, but he objected to the equation of dialectical materialism with scientific pragmatism as a distortion of Marx's ideas "beyond recognition." The premise of Eastman's assault was familiar: that the dialectical method in Marx, no matter how many coats of scientific gloss Hook might apply to it, was mystical and obfuscatory.[7]

Shortly thereafter, in a two-part series for the *Modern Quarterly*, Eastman

---

[6] Leon Trotsky, "On the Revolutionary Intellectuals," *Modern Quarterly* 7 (March 1933): 83; Hook, "Russia in Solution," review of *History of the Russian Revolution*, vols. 2 and 3, by Leon Trotsky, *Saturday Review*, 8 April 1933, 521–22.

[7] Max Eastman, "An Interpretation of Marx," review of *Towards the Understanding of Karl Marx* by Sidney Hook, *New York Herald Tribune*, 16 April 1933, 6. In *Out of Step*, 139, Hook makes three minor errors in recounting this incident: he recalls the phrase as "What Karl Marx Would Have Thought Had He Been a Student of John Dewey"; he calls this the title rather than the subtitle; and he remembers it as a review of *From Hegel to Marx* (1936) instead of *Towards the Understanding of Karl Marx* (1933).

portrayed himself as the victim of doctrinal orthodoxy on all sides. In the first part he castigated those, including the Communist Party and Trotsky, who had hurled such epithets as "vulgar" and "petty bourgeois" at him. The second part, "A Master Magician," expressed Eastman's belief that Hook was aiding the relentless orthodox suppression of his work. This querulous polemic, revealing that the old wounds inflicted by Hook had never healed, was suspect, especially since Hook, in his April 8 review of Trotsky's *History of the Russian Revolution,* had gone out of his way to pay Eastman compliments of the highest order for the service he had provided with his translation. After recycling his weak charge that Hook had stolen from his arguments for the *Journal of Philosophy* article of 1928, Eastman introduced a fresh point of dispute. Despite their mutual background as students of Dewey, Eastman now claimed, only *he* had demonstrated a willingness to criticize pragmatism "from the standpoint of scientific skepticism." Even as a student of Dewey, wrote Eastman, he had suggested irreverently that if pragmatists really believed their talk about testing ideas in action, they ought to give up their seats in philosophy. This disposition, he concluded, explained his differences with Hook:

> What I want to do with Marxism, then, is to recognize its purposive charac-
> ter, distinguish its definitions of fact from its aim and method of procedure,
> and so put an end to the endlessly proliferating fog-colonies of cant and wish-
> fulfillment thinking in an age of science, and still worse in the name of sci-
> ence. Sidney Hook refuses to have Marxism restated in this scientific, and
> therefore philosophically skeptical, manner. He insists that Marxism remain
> a philosophy, but thinks to identify this philosophy substantially with "the
> metaphysics of pragmatism" in which he believes.

So it was that the Eastman-Hook debate came at last, five years after it began, to concentrate on the point that had, perhaps, been most important
all along: the meaning of pragmatism and its compatibility with Marxism.[8]

Hook replied via a review of the new Modern Library edition of Marx's writings, edited and introduced by Eastman. Refreshingly, Hook supported Eastman against critics in both the Socialist and Communist Parties who had voiced "shrill abuse and denunciation instead of critical analysis." Eastman's interpretation of Marx had some merit, Hook noted, such as its em-
phasis on Marx's revolutionary activism. His mistakes deserved serious response rather than hyperbolic accusations of "counter-revolution." With that common ground established, Hook turned to the defense of his own

---

[8] Max Eastman, "Excommunication and Exorcism as Critical Methods," *Modern Quarterly* 7 (May 1933): 210–13; Eastman, "A Master Magician," *Modern Quarterly* 7 (June 1933): 292.

turf. To Eastman's familiar contention that Marx propounded an economic determinism in contradiction to his political activism, Hook responded:

> The problem is to account for the conditioning character of the economic milieu, and the active character of class consciousness which transforms a determinate probability into an historic necessity. What philosophy is more adequate to resolve the problem than dialectical materialism—not in its vulgar form as expressed in the ignorant and insolent pretentiousness of the self-styled "orthodox" who do not even know the meanings of the words they use—but as it is to be found in a fresh, critical study of the writings of Marx?

A further fault, Hook added, was that Eastman's concept of a "science of revolution" had deeply elitist implications: "If Marxism is the science of revolution does not this suggest an unhealthy perception of the relationship between the scientists of revolution—the professional revolutionists—and the working class?" In a manner clearly influenced by Dewey's radical interpretation of science as a universally understandable and popularly applicable method of inquiry, Hook wrote, "The engineering conception of Marxism blurs the distinction—unfortunately not very sharply drawn in the minds of many who call themselves communists—between the 'dictatorship over the proletariat' and the 'dictatorship of the proletariat.' In its theory the engineer fascism of technocracy similarly speaks of the dictatorship over the masses. . . . Marxists know that without democratic control from a mass base, no group can set itself up as dictator and rule in the interest of all." The legacy of pragmatism was at stake as much as the meaning of Marx. Eastman presumed himself to be within the pragmatic tradition, arguing for action and science, and also a ruthless skeptic on all points of doctrine. Hook claimed that, to the contrary, Eastman was neither pragmatic nor skeptical but technocratic, putting more faith in an elitist version of science and engineering than in a democratic process of inquiry and revolution from below.[9]

A further elaboration of these points might have yielded important results, but no sooner had the debate been rejoined than it collapsed altogether in a hopeless tangle of recriminations that filled both parties with feelings of futility. Apart from Eastman's weak reply that the danger of a dictatorship over the proletariat would diminish "if the relation between professional revolutionists and the proletariat is stated as it actually exists

9   Hook, review of *Karl Marx's Capital and Other Writings*, ed. Max Eastman, *Modern Quarterly* 7 (May 1933): 248–50. For further remarks by Hook on technocratic planning, see "The Philosophical Implications of Economic Planning," in *Planned Society: Yesterday, Today, Tomorrow*, ed. Findlay MacKenzie (New York: Prentice-Hall, 1937), 663–77.

and not as demanded by an optimistic philosophy of the universe," there was no further genuine engagement between Hook and Eastman over the "science of revolution." Both had become dejected, each despairing of the possibility of changing the other's mind or accomplishing anything worthwhile through further polemic. Eastman expressed hope that "this unending jabber of conflicting opinion stops" and worried that *Modern Quarterly* editor V. F. Calverton would be "overburdened by the doings of Dewey's bright boys." Hook, for his part, wrote, "It will be clear to anyone who has read my original review of Max Eastman's *Marx and Lenin,* his reply, my rejoinder, and now—after about five years—his counter-rejoinder, that further controversy with him would be fruitless." In private correspondence to Calverton, Eastman described Hook as a "contemptible and dishonest pup," whose "shifty-mindedness irritates me beyond words." Since only innuendo remained, Calverton, expressing regret that Hook and Eastman had become "personal enemies and vent their spleen in public to the obscene enjoyment of the bourgeois world," called an end to the unseemly spat.[10]

Perhaps the shower of fireworks accompanying each article had done more to attract interest to the Hook-Eastman dispute than the merits of the philosophical exchange itself, but the clash acquired a reputation as one of the great intellectual fracases of the early 1930s. In 1934 Eastman challenged Hook to a public debate over the issues in their literary dispute and attempted to recruit Dewey to preside as moderator. But Dewey declined: "Your idea is an ingenious and intriguing one. But the trouble is I don't know enough Marx to go into the scheme and I don't see the least probability of my getting the time to acquire the needed knowledge. When I talk with you I incline to think you must be right, and the same—in reverse—when I talk to Sidney. This is doubtless a deplorable confession but there it is." Trotskyist leader Max Shachtman jokingly proposed that the Eastman-Hook confrontation be billed the "Debate of the Colossi." In the end nothing came of the idea because, as Calverton reported to Eastman, "Hook demands some kind of apology as to your initial aspersions as to his purpose and character before he will consent to debate with you."[11]

[10] Max Eastman, Letter to the Editor, *Modern Quarterly* 7 (June 1933): 320; Eastman, "Man and History," *Modern Quarterly* 7 (July 1933): 350; Hook, "A Note from Sidney Hook," *Modern Quarterly* 7 (July 1933): 350; Max Eastman to V. F. Calverton, 11 July and 24 August 1933 (V. F. Calverton Papers, New York Public Library, Eastman Correspondence); V. F. Calverton, "To Max Eastman and Sidney Hook," *Modern Quarterly* 7 (August 1933): 511.

[11] The dispute was revisited single-handedly by Eastman in a privately printed pamphlet rehashing his case, *The Last Stand of Dialectic Materialism: A Study of Sidney Hook's Marxism* (New York: Polemic, 1934), about which William L. O'Neill writes, "Almost no one appears to have read it"; *The Last Romantic: A Life of Max Eastman* (New York: Oxford, 1978), 145. The episode also made reappearances in Eastman's *Marxism: Is It Science?* (New York: Norton, 1940) and

Most who witnessed the published joust as it was played out across the field of little magazines believed that Hook had bested Eastman. Literary critic Alfred Kazin, for example, wrote in his memoir of the 1930s:

> Eastman, almost twenty years older than Hook and over the years distracted from the strict practice of philosophy by poetry, Freudianism, travel, friendship and other pleasures of sense, did not argue as well as Hook. No one ever did. When it came to close argument, Hook was unbeatable; one saw that he could not imagine himself defeated in argument. The concentration of all his intellectual forces upon the point of issue was overwhelming, the proofs of inconsistency on the part of his opponents were unanswerable; to watch Hook in argument was to watch him moving in for the kill.

More important than sealing Hook's reputation as a fearsome debater, the five-year conflict served as a testing ground for Hook's pragmatist Marxism. Against Eastman's conflation of Marx and Freud, Hook had argued that Marxism privileged social analysis over the psychoanalysis of personal behavior. Against Eastman's assertion that the Hegelian dialectic imparted to Marx a religious dogmatism, Hook argued that dialectical materialism and experimental naturalism were mutually complementary and, properly understood, helped to guard against sclerosis in thought. Finally, against Eastman's "science of revolution," Hook upheld democratic inquiry and rejected elitist conceptions of revolutionary leadership.[12]

The Challenge of Liberalism, 1934

Trotsky and Eastman, whatever their differences with Hook and each other, were considerably alike in world view. Both were revolutionary socialists opposed to the ideology and organization of the Stalin bureaucracy and its global proxies. Hook's quarrels with Eastman and Trotsky, that is to say, were within the family. A challenge of a very different kind confronted Hook just as his debate with Eastman waned, a challenge from outside the revolutionary household. In early 1934 when he helped his friend Calverton put together a package of articles for the April issue of

---

Hook's *Out of Step*. After it left the pages of *Modern Quarterly*, however, the debate lost its edge and interest. On the proposed Hook-Eastman public debate, see Eastman to Max Shachtman, 19 January 1934, and Shachtman to Eastman, 12 February 1934 (Max Eastman Papers, Indiana University); V. F. Calverton to Eastman, 18 November 1933 (V. F. Calverton Papers, New York Public Library, Eastman Correspondence); and Dewey's response in Max Eastman, *Great Companies* (New York: Farrar, Straus & Cudahy, 1959), 284–85.
[12]   Alfred Kazin, *Starting Out in the Thirties* (1962; Ithaca: Cornell University Press, 1989), 71–72.

the *Modern Monthly* (as Calverton's *Modern Quarterly* was rechristened that year). Bertrand Russell, John Dewey, and Morris Cohen all contributed essays on the subject "Why I Am Not a Communist." Hook knew each philosopher well: Dewey and Cohen, his mentors, participated only because Hook asked them to contribute; Russell, the eminent British philosopher, had asked Calverton in 1933 to pass on his compliments to Hook for his achievement in *Towards the Understanding of Karl Marx*. Hook's response to the essays of these eminent philosophers constituted his most concerted attempt yet to defend revolutionary socialism against liberal reformism.[13]

Russell, Dewey, and Cohen had taken "Why I Am Not a Communist" to mean, for the most part, "Why I Will Not Join the Communist Party." They recognized the distinction, as Dewey put it, "between communism with a small *c*, and Communism, official Communism, spelt with a capital letter." Their collective critique of Communism, therefore, did not pose any direct difficulties for Hook's Marxism. Russell even specified outright that he meant for his indictment to apply solely to the Third International, which he faulted for tolerating restrictions on intellectual liberty and for excusing the dictatorship of a small minority. If there was a common thread to their arguments, though, it was their philosophical objection to what they perceived to be communism's disregard for liberal values, a critique that appeared implictly applicable to any Marxist viewpoint. Dewey, for example, passed well beyond a critique of the Communists' lack of elementary honesty and disregard for fair play to criticize the very philosophy of communism as monistic. Historical materialism, he alleged, contained at its core the mistaken idea that society must pass through a fixed set of stages. Cohen employed his principle of polarity to contend that communism and individualism represented partial, incomplete truths: "No one ever wished to make everything communal property. Nor does anyone in his senses believe that any individual will ever with impunity be permitted to use his 'property' in an anti-social way when the rest of the community is aroused thereby." Despite their assertions to the contrary, thus, a good many of the arguments of Russell, Dewey, and Cohen constituted a challenge not merely to the Communist Party but to Marxism itself.[14]

In Hook's judgment, the critique of official Communism mounted by the three philosophers suffered from a severe defect: it lacked a realistic alternative program and could point to no clear path of action. Class col-

[13] The articles were all reproduced, among others, in *The Meaning of Marx*, ed. Sidney Hook (New York: Farrar & Rinehart, 1934). For Hook's role in organizing the discussion, see V. F. Calverton to SH, 25 April 1934 (V. F. Calverton Papers, New York Public Library, Hook Correspondence).

[14] Morris Cohen, "Why I Am Not a Communist," in Hook, *The Meaning of Marx*, 99.

laboration, their implicit approach, was not a viable option, for history had demonstrated that it would not result in security, democracy, or peace: "To profess a love for democracy in the abstract and not be willing to fight to give it concrete content, to take the rules of political democracy in a profit society—rules which are so flexible that they enable a Mussolini and Hitler to come to power—as the *fixed* limits within which to struggle for a truly human society, is to give a lease in perpetuity to the capitalist dictatorship upon the lives of the people." Marxists, by contrast, made no fetish of legality. Although they had no qualms about putting the electoral forms of bourgeois society to use, they understood that class domination makes genuine, full democracy impossible. They did not celebrate violence, but they criticized pacifism because it prevented crucial preparations for the defense of revolutionary gains should violent counterrevolution necessitate meeting force with force. Marxists likewise rejected putsches and coups d'état as routes to power, since such actions were not *social* revolutions that empowered the majority of working people. Marxism in this manner transcended the political impasse of liberalism. The Marxist method, Hook underscored, was for a majoritarian revolution of the workers and their allies to abolish all class distinctions.[15]

The central tenets of the liberal tradition appealed to Hook, but he objected to Cohen's argument that communism was necessarily a partial truth, opposed to liberal values. Hook identified two meanings of liberalism: the social and economic philosophy of laissez faire, and the values associated with free inquiry. These two meanings of the term, Hook posited, had been complementary during the initial period of bourgeois ascension, when the condition of free trade had made free inquiry possible to an extent greater than that afforded by any prior social system; by the twentieth century, however, the bourgeoisie was wracked by crises and found free inquiry dispensable, as the fascist states in Europe demonstrated most vividly. Capitalism had become an impediment to the liberal values of free thought, inquiry, freedom, and discussion. Hook acknowledged freely, on the other hand, that sometimes illiberal means (namely, violence) had to be employed. Fascism had proved that not "all matters can be settled by free discussion," he wrote: "The lessons of Italy and Germany must still be learned by the spokesmen of liberalism. During the transitional period the denial of liberties is directed, in theory at any rate, only against those whose activities are such as would restore the old order and therewith destroy the new freedom and liberties which the social revolution has won. The restrictions last so long as the class enemy exists, and only against the enemy on relevant political matters." As with much Marxist theory of its day, this

[15] Hook, "Communism without Dogmas," in *The Meaning of Marx*, 106.

passage blurred two phases: the emergency period of civil war and the longer transition to socialism. Despite this flaw, which caused him to leave many democratic protections inadequately specified, Hook was adamant that even in the "transitional period" Marxism would be distinguished from fascism by its refusal to use any and all means to take power: "Communists would not martyrize an entire people as the fascists have done, they would not countenance wholesale massacres of innocent victims, they would not pound and torture women in order to achieve power." The failure of Communist Parties to live up to this ethical injunction was evidence of their departure from Marxism.[16]

The rise of fascism in Italy and Germany and the looming threat of another global imperialist war were to Hook the most compelling justifications of revolutionary socialism. He rejected the theory—which Dewey, for one, had suggested in his contribution to the symposium—that fascism and communism were the same. Fascism, Hook wrote, was on the contrary a graphic demonstration of the need for socialist transformation: "Fascism, it must be remembered, is not a new social system but capitalism, *gleichgeschaltet* and armed to the teeth, compelled by the logic of a super-rationalized profit system and a frenzied religion of nationalism, to prepare for bigger and better wars." Rather than a "superficial political form," Hook emphasized, fascism was an outgrowth of the most basic tendencies within imperialism, a consolidation of capitalist rule carried out in the guise of a psychological reaction against the disorienting and disastrous consequences of capitalist production. The best way to combat fascism, therefore, was not by defending bourgeois democracy but by building a movement toward socialist revolution. Against Dewey's worry that revolutionary activity would only invite a fascist crackdown in America, Hook replied that such a potential merely warranted a more vigorous struggle. "Certainly I know that this would be Professor Dewey's answer if one were to tell him that agitation against lynching was adding fuel to the fire of southern Negro prejudice," he remarked archly.[17]

Critics who suggest that, even at the apex of his anti-Stalinist independent Marxism, Hook displayed softness toward Dewey's middle-class reformism have never come to terms with this central tenet of his mid-1930s thought. Reformism, he held, was not a pragmatic strategy, whether for the pursuit of reform or the liberation of the working class, since it compro-

[16] Ibid., 113–14: "I know from personal experience the infinite capacity of the Communist press to invent, distort, and slander, in short, to drag the name of communism down to the level of the bourgeois gutter press. But this is no part of the philosophy of communism, no communist party ever came to power by such practices, and the emergence of a mass revolutionary movement will sweep into the discard all who engage in such practices."
[17] Ibid., 115–116.

mised with the very social system it proposed to transcend. As Hook wrote in 1935,

> Dewey is more alive than his colleagues to the presence of classes and their struggles, but he is inclined to underestimate their significance and to regard class conflicts as only one of numerous other forms of social conflict capable of being settled by the same technique of collaboration and compromise by which other problems are solved. He carries over the optimism of the reform period in which he grew up and consequently does not see the limits which class conflicts place upon "experimental activity" in social affairs. Classes do not experiment to determine what the consequences of their own non-existence will be. As a result, Dewey's educational philosophy, in which his thought culminates and which obviously demands as a pre-condition the existence of a classless society before it can even be tried, remains an abstract ideal more honored in textbooks than life.[18]

This crucial difference with Dewey over class and politics was never obscured by Hook at his revolutionary pinnacle, despite his concurrence with Dewey in matters of philosophy and method.

Communism without Dogmas, 1934

Russell, Dewey, and Cohen had each sought to defend democracy and liberal values from fascism and Communism while working toward a more egalitarian society within the political framework of the existing state. In upholding Marxism against that liberal prescription, wrote the literary critic Edmund Wilson, Hook had provided "the best Marxist answer to liberals that I have seen." In the second part of his essay Hook turned to a related task: defending Marxism from the degradations of official Communism. "Communism without Dogmas" was his first sustained appraisal of official Communism since his break with the Party. Whereas Russell, Dewey, and Cohen had repudiated Communism for its illiberal traits, Hook concentrated on its violations of the principles of revolutionary communism as found "in the writings of Marx and Engels, and in the economic and political works of Lenin and Trotsky." By this careful phrasing, Hook sidestepped momentarily his publicly expressed *philosophical* reservations about Lenin's epistemology and Trotsky's historical teleology, enabling him to marshal their Bolshevik stature, place them within the economic and political legacy of classical Marxism, and turn their teachings with full force upon a Communist Party that claimed to be faithful to the heritage of October 1917.[19]

[18] Hook, "Our Philosophers," *Current History* 41 (March 1935): 703.
[19] Edmund Wilson to V. F. Calverton, 3 May 1934 (V. F. Calverton Papers, New York Public Library, Hook Correspondence); Hook, "Communism without Dogmas," 101.

But when he received his copy of the *Modern Monthly* in April, Hook discovered to his dismay that Calverton, exercising editorial license, had retitled the article "Why I Am a Communist." Hook *was* a communist, and he had referred to himself throughout the piece as one. But given the public association of that term with the Communist Party, and given that Russell, Dewey, and Cohen had expressly aimed their fire primarily at Communism, Calverton's move was certain to create the false impression that Hook was a defender of the official Communist movement. Hook's rejoinder would better have been called "Why I Am a Marxist." The real bone of contention, after all, was Marxism, not communism. As Hook noted, even Russell, Dewey, and Cohen "may, on the basis of their social writings, be regarded as communists of a sort, since they subscribe to the ideal of a classless society. But they are clearly not Marxists." In any case, the title Hook had given his piece before turning it over to Calverton, "Communism without Dogmas," described his position better.[20]

The first dogma of official Communism that Hook assailed was its faith in the inevitability of communism. No proof could be offered for the inevitability of proletarian revolution, and Marx's statements along such lines had been read far too literally; they should instead be understood as "either dramatic, revolutionary prophecy or a prediction on the basis of certain psychological assumptions whose truth and invariance are by no means self-evident." These remarks may now seem mundane, but they went against the grain in an era when socialists of all stripes tended to think that History was on their side. To abandon that grandiose assumption, Hook insisted, did *not* entail a denial of social causation; it did require Marxists to realize that the outcome of social revolution could not be deduced from the analysis of economic data. Revolutions depend upon human exertion, Hook observed, and that requires intelligence and courage, factors that do not spring automatically from capitalist crisis.[21]

In *Towards the Understanding of Karl Marx* and elsewhere, he had made similar arguments. But there and in his closely related arguments against Lenin's sensationalist epistemology, Hook had sometimes claimed that belief in the inexorability of socialism would result in quietism—that it would encourage socialists to sit back and let History do their work for them. In "Communism without Dogmas" Hook subtly altered this line of criticism. Belief in the inevitability of communism need not paralyze socialists, he

[20] When the essay was reprinted in *The Meaning of Marx*, Hook's original title was restored. Hook was also irritated with Calverton over the shortage of copies: "I need not conceal from you my feeling that the April issue was abominably handled. Certainly the demand should easily have been anticipated, what with all your years of editorial experience": SH to V. F. Calverton, 23 April 1934 (V. F. Calverton Papers, New York Public Library, Hook Correspondence). See also: Hook, "Communism without Dogmas," 102; Hook, *Out of Step*, 205.
[21] Hook, "Communism without Dogmas," 120.

now acknowledged; indeed, it might swell them with supreme confidence and make them fight with intransigent vigor. It did mean, however, that their activity would be "unintelligible and unintelligent," because "it denies that there are *genuine* alternatives of action—something which its propaganda assumes."[22]

If a variety of approaches and tactics are acknowledged, understood, and studied, Hook explained, then actions may be undertaken with the fullest possible understanding of the assumptions that undergird them. Belief in the inevitability of communism, however, mandated a uniform and apparently necessary path—with three damaging consequences. First, the doctrine of inevitability strengthened belief that the working class "spontaneously" generates political class consciousness, leading to an overestimation of the readiness for revolutionary activity on the part of the working class, "a mistaking of restiveness for radicalism, a tendency to read into the masses the perfervid psychological intensity of an isolated political group which thinks that because it *calls* itself a vanguard it has thereby created a mass army behind it." Second, the doctrine of inevitability had encouraged the mechanical application of the Russian model to all Communist Parties, regardless of the peculiarities of national cultures and conditions, because of the presumption that the first working-class group to come to power showed the way to the universal future. "Precedents of tactics which originally flowed from a special historical situation," Hook noted, "are converted into precedents of principle." Finally, Hook observed, the doctrine that all of history is rushing toward communism had led to the preposterous, disastrous notion that fascism was but a step on the certain road to communism—even a positive boon because it removed the obstacle of social democracy.[23]

Next, Hook attacked the dogma that communists must be dialectical materialists and that dialectical materialists must be communists. He restated his conviction that dialectical materialism could be "described in the technical idiom of contemporary Anglo-American philosophy as experimental, evolutionary naturalism," but he lamented the term's transformation into a concept more religious than naturalist in the clutches of official Communism. László Rudas, a Hungarian philosopher in residence at the Marx-Engels-Lenin Institute, for example, had gone so far as to state that only members of the Communist Party properly understood dialectical materialism, at the same time maintaining that only with the guidance of di-

---

[22]   The weakness in his criticism of the doctrine of inexorability on grounds that it bred quietism had first been brought to Hook's attention by Meyer Schapiro two years before; see Schapiro to SH, 3 February 1932 (Hook Papers, box 40, folder 13); Hook, "Communism without Dogmas," 121.

[23]   Hook, "Communism without Dogmas," 122, 123.

alectical materialism could a scientific judgment be made. Rudas, Hook noted, had arrived at the flagrantly foolish proposition that only Communist Party members were capable of scientific judgment. Against the Party's tendency to assert a class view or party line in every branch of science and art, Hook argued that no *particular* evolutionary biological theory or theory of physics could be deduced from historical materialism; its truth had to be settled experimentally. Any scientific theory, so long as it was naturalist, was theoretically compatible with historical materialism. Any suggestion to the contrary, Hook wrote, was nothing less than "sentimental theology." He was quick to add, however, that this flawed propensity of official Communism did not trace to Marx, despite Max Eastman's allegations in his sundry broadsides against dialectics. The dogma of "orthodox" dialectical materialism was in Hook's judgment as far removed from Marx as the mystical, supernatural idealism of Hegel.[24]

The assumption that the state would "wither away" of its own accord under communism, Hook next argued, like the doctrine of communism's inevitability, neglected the need for collective vigilance and action. Certain conditions were required before the state would recede, especially the organization of workers' councils with power controlled by working people themselves from the bottom up. Hook warned that suppression of proletarian democracy would result in "a degenerate workers' state in which the most important decisions are made by an uncontrollable bureaucracy," and that if the Communist Party ruled over the workers' councils without full freedom of discussion and deliberation, the result would be "a workers' state but not a workers' democracy." This carried noticeable traces of Trotsky, especially the thesis that such gains of the Soviet "workers' state" as nationalized property and planned economy had been distorted, but not wiped out, by bureaucratic revolution from above. The state, Hook wrote, would never wither away until "the democratic institutions of the workers' state are permitted to function and expand," an end unachievable except through "untiring activity to make the proletarian dictatorship, not only in its *property form,* but in its *political functioning,* a proletarian democracy." This precision about the need for a non-coercive relationship of party to class and stipulations for vigilance against sacrifice of democratic norms during the construction of socialism were clearly informed by Trotskyist theory—but also went beyond what many Trotskyists were prepared to specify in the mid-1930s. Hook's modification of Trotskyist themes was further demonstrated in his proposal that the slogan "workers' democracy" be raised as a substitute for "dictatorship of the proletariat," a term Trotsky thought more scientifically precise. The word "dictatorship,"

[24]   Ibid., 126, 136.

Hook argued, lent itself to confusion and had been used all too often to justify bureaucratic tyranny *over* the proletariat. This he clearly meant as a theoretical development within anti-Stalinist Marxism, not as a heretical departure. Hook's variation from Trotsky came, tellingly, wrapped in Trotsky's concepts and language. The "dictatorship of the Communist Party bureaucracy," Hook argued, is "a foreign excrescence upon the structure of the workers' state, as well as upon the communist party."[25]

The final dogma of official Communism subjected to Hook's scrutiny was that of a monolithic proletariat hostile to all manifestations of individuality. A repressive "proletcult" of collective conformity, Hook wrote, is antithetical to Marxism, which "seeks to provide the material guarantee of security without which the free development of individuality or personality is an empty or impossible ideal." In fact, he stressed, "the *free development of personality remains its ideal;* difference, uniqueness, independence and creative originality are intrinsic values to be fostered and strengthened; and indeed one of the strongest arguments against capitalism is that it prevents these values from flourishing for all but a few."[26]

Through this set of negations, Hook provided the philosophical counterpart to his earlier political conclusion that official Communism was so ensnared in a web of dogmas, so bound to archaic norms of authority, that further attempts to reshape it were useless. "In fact," Hook wrote at the beginning of his reply to Dewey, Cohen, and Russell, "it seems to me that just as Marx and Engels in 1848 called themselves communists to set themselves off from bourgeois socialists who had debased the term socialism, so it may soon become necessary to find another name for communism to differentiate it from the Communist Party which has corrupted the meaning of the term by its mistaken theories and tragically sectarian tactics." This was not the "disillusion" of the ex-Communist who disavowed the socialist ideal as a dangerous pipe dream. Hook still held that "only communism can save the world from its social evils," defining it as "a form of social organization in which the associated producers democratically control the production and distribution of goods." Hook's dismay over the new meanings that Stalinism had attached to the word "communist" did not lead him to relinquish the term, for no substitute could evoke a radically egalitarian society so pointedly. "The only valid criticism of the Communist Party," he wrote, "is that it is not communist enough." One could only conclude, he wrote, that "the time has come to build a new organization which will represent in philosophy and action the genuine ideals of communism."[27]

[25] Ibid., 139–41.
[26] Ibid., 142.
[27] Ibid., 102, 144, 101, 118.

The American Workers Party, 1934

Hook's declaration of the need for a new communist organization was neither abstract nor utopian, for he had in mind a very specific body: the American Workers Party. The AWP was a new political project led by longtime labor radical A. J. Muste, a respected figure on the independent left. Early in his career, Muste had been a Protestant minister, but being forced to resign during the First World War because of his pacifism prompted him to turn to labor organizing. In 1919 he helped to lead a three-month textile strike in Lawrence, Massachusetts, and he subsequently became director of the Brookwood Labor College, an innovative educational institution for workers and labor organizers located in New York state. In May 1929 he and his associates launched the Conference for Progressive Labor Action (CPLA) as a political vehicle to advocate industrial unionism, the creation of a labor party, unemployment benefits, and the five-day work week within the labor movement. When Muste encouraged Hook in the fall of 1933 to take part in the founding of a new revolutionary party, the invitation did not come out of the blue. As early as 1931 he had expressed admiration for Hook's interpretation of Marx. "Your view of Marx is the one on which I have for a good while agreed," Muste wrote, "although I have never felt that I was a sufficiently erudite scholar in Marx or in the literature of Marxism to be sure that this interpretation was the only possible one." One of Muste's close associates, J. B. S. Hardman, had in 1932 invited Hook to join the pool of writers for the CPLA's newly launched paper, *Labor Action*. These prior seeds bore fruit early in 1933, when Hook's estrangement from the Communist Party coincided with Muste's efforts to turn the CPLA into a new revolutionary socialist party independent of both the Communists and the Socialists.[28]

On the surface, at least, Hook's participation in the AWP appeared to indicate a certain distance from Trotskyism, since he had chosen to join with Muste rather than the Left Opposition, which had established its own organization, the Communist League of America (CLA). Trotsky himself, upon hearing of the dissolution of the League of Professional Groups, anticipated in a private communication to his American followers that "differences and discussions" would likely emerge with

[28] A. J. Muste to SH, 25 August 1931 (Hook Papers, box 17); J. B. S. Hardman to SH, 2 March 1932 (Hook Papers, box 14). On Muste, see A. J. Muste, "Sketches for an Autobiography," in *The Essays of A. J. Muste*, ed. Nat Hentoff (Indianapolis: Bobbs-Merrill, 1967), 1–174; Jo Ann Robinson, *Abraham Went Out: A Biography of A. J. Muste* (Philadelphia: Temple University Press, 1981); Nat Hentoff, *Peace Agitator: The Story of A. J. Muste* (New York: A. J. Muste Memorial Institute, 1982); Maurice Isserman, *If I Had a Hammer: The Death of the Old Left and the Birth of the New Left* (New York: Basic, 1987), 125–69; Jon Bloom, "Muste, A. J.," in *The Encyclopedia of the American Left*, ed. Mary Jo Buhle, Paul Buhle, and Dan Georgakas (Urbana: University of Illinois Press, 1992), 499–500.

Hook.[29] But those differences were not as great as they might seem. Hook's friend Felix Morrow, along with George Novack, had in early 1933 joined the CLA, and his friend Herbert Solow was a close Trotskyist sympathizer who would join the CLA in 1934. Hook's involvement in the AWP, moreover, was revealed to be complementary to the CLA rather than opposed to it. Hook began immediately to push for unity with the Trotskyists.

The AWP, though small and short-lived, has not received the historical attention it deserves. Muste, as general secretary, brought with him the newspaper *Labor Action* and a core of militant labor activists grouped around the CPLA: J. B. S. Hardman, a former leader of the Jewish Federation in the old Socialist Party and editor of *The Advance,* the official newspaper of the Amalgamated Clothing Workers Union; Gerry Allard, head of the Illinois Progressive Mine Workers, a union that had fought both mine owners and AFL officials for the right to organize along industrial lines; Louis Budenz, a dynamic mass leader of important strikes in the 1920s; William Truax, Arnold Johnson, Anthony Ramuglia, and Elmer Cope, organizers of the CPLA-initiated Unemployment Leagues in Ohio and elsewhere in the Midwest, which had a greater combined membership than the rival, CP-initiated Unemployed Councils; African American intellectuals George Schuyler and Ernest Rice McKinney; and many talented women organizers, including Mary Ann Johnston, Aurelia Ricci Johnson, Irene Allard, Mary Truax, Esther Cope, and Margaret Rodgers Budenz. Along with Hook, a number of notable intellectuals—many of them survivors of the shipwrecked League of Professional Groups—decided to join the AWP: *Modern Monthly* editor V. F. Calverton, whose publication remained open to contributors from all corners of American radicalism, though it frequently published articles by Muste, Hook, and other AWP members;[30] journalist and poet James Rorty, the former league secretary; philosopher James Burnham; Columbia University history professor George Counts; and Ludwig Lore, a left-wing writer who had been expelled from the Communist Party on questionable grounds of "Trotskyism" at the early date of 1925.[31]

29 Leon Trotsky, "Intellectuals Regrouping" (13 April 1933), in *Writings of Leon Trotsky, Supplement (1929–33),* ed. George Breitman (New York: Pathfinder, 1979), 231.
30 In the mid-1930s the *Modern Monthly* came close to being a theoretical journal for the AWP, though it insisted upon editorial independence and also published writings of intellectuals affiliated with other parties and views. Haim Genizi is mistaken to characterize it as "an anti-Marxist journal" in these years, as is Michael Nash to equate its standpoint with the ideology of the Cold War witch-hunts: see Genizi, "Edmund Wilson and *The Modern Monthly,* 1934–35," *American Studies* 7 (1973): 301–19; Nash, "Schism on the Left: The Anti-Communism of V. F. Calverton and His *Modern Quarterly,*" *Science & Society* 54 (Winter 1980–81): 437–52.
31 Hook, *Out of Step,* 190–91; Margaret Rodgers Budenz to SH, 21 August 1987 (Hook Papers, box 7); "An Open Letter to American Intellectuals," *Modern Monthly* 8 (March 1934): 87–92; SH to Alan Wald, 1 August 1974 (Wald Collection); Albert Glotzer, "Ernest Rice Mc-

Many students and young people, radicalized by the long unemployment lines that awaited them after graduation, were recruited to the AWP, including S. L. Solon, who wrote a column on student politics for the *Modern Monthly*. Burnham and Hook, through their dynamic teaching at New York University, prompted many students, such as sisters Sylvia and Ruth Ageloff, to enroll in the AWP. The Ageloffs' sister Hilda, a labor activist, was first to join, but Sylvia and Ruth, who studied under Hook, were the ones who really entered the public spotlight. Ruth would serve as a secretary for the Dewey Commission's famous 1937 investigation into the charges against Trotsky. Sylvia would be unwittingly exploited by the GPU (Soviet secret police, forerunner of the KGB): she married Ramon Mercader, who, unknown to her, was a Stalinist agent and used his intimacy with her to gain access to Leon Trotsky's Mexican villa and assassinate him in 1940.[32]

This combination of workers, intellectuals, and youth meant that spirits were high when the Provisional Organizing Committee for the American Workers Party was formed in December 1933 at a meeting of about a hundred people. Technically, the POC was responsible for disseminating information and preparing for the national convention that would formally launch the new party in July 1934; in actuality, it acted as a leadership body with the assumption that the AWP was, for all practical purposes, an already existing organization. At Muste's request, Hook drafted the founding statement of principles for the new party, though in its final form it reflected the suggestions and approval of all POC leaders. The principal task of the statement was to establish the American Workers Party in contradistinction to the Socialist and Communist Parties. A new party of the left had to justify itself, of course, by showing that existing radical organizations were inadequate, misguided, or devoted in principle to different purposes. Against the Socialists, the statement drafted by Hook recapitulated the standard revolutionary criticism of social democracy. It avoided the Communists' Third Period vitriol, however, and put unusual onus upon the Socialist Party's labor policy: "Its adherence to pure and simple parliamentarism, its utter failure to see economic and political life in terms of an actual class struggle for power, its flirting with liberal elements and ten-

Kinney," *Biographical Dictionary of the American Left*, ed. Bernard K. Johnpoll and Harvey Klehr (New York: Greenwood, 1986). On the Unemployed Leagues, see Frances Fox Piven and Richard A. Cloward, *Regulating the Poor* (New York: Vintage, 1971), 105–8; Dianne Feeley, "In Unity There Is Strength: The Struggle of the Unemployed throughout the 1930s," unpublished paper, 1983.
[32] The Ageloff sisters, for whom these events were deeply traumatic, have refused all interviews since and declined to be interviewed for this biography. My information is drawn from conversation with Ruth Ageloff's son Eric Poulos, 12 September 1993, and Isaac Don Levine, *The Mind of an Assassin* (New York: Farrar, Straus & Cudahy, 1959).

dencies, its toleration of and often alliance with reactionary forces in the A.F. of L., its failure to battle vigorously against racketeering and allied evils in the unions, render it unfit for working class leadership in the present crisis." The Communist Party received equally incisive criticism. The statement decried its sectarian, disruptive activities in the unions and other mass movements, as well as its failure to establish credible leadership of the American working class—"despite the fact that it started out with tens of thousands of the most militant former Socialists in its ranks" and "despite the prestige which it had because of its connection with the USSR." The CP's internationalist outlook and revolutionary image were not what they seemed, for the form these took made the CP more responsive to Russian conditions than American: "Throughout its existence, the Party has thought and felt in terms of Russian and European rather than American working-class experience."[33]

The idea that American communists ought to respond primarily to American conditions was not original. It had been advised by Marx and Lenin in their letters to Americans, and it had for several years been put forward by the Right Opposition group led by Jay Lovestone, the Communist leader expelled from the Party in 1929 in part because of his belief in "American exceptionalism." The American Workers Party, nonetheless, stood out in the early 1930s by the degree of importance it placed upon the search for an American road to socialism. It minced no words about its socialist and revolutionary aims, but the titles of its major institutions—*Labor Action,* the Unemployed Leagues, the American Workers Party—indicated a sensibility to the American vernacular and a strategy aiming at mass appeal. The January 17, 1934, issue of *Labor Action* carried an editorial by Budenz which dubbed this ethos the "American approach," and at a February 1934 dinner on behalf of the fledgling party Hook proclaimed, "Of all the radical parties in the field, the AWP distinguished itself by its realistic approach to the American scene and to the fundamental problems of the conquest of political power within that scene." There was much truth in this self-congratulation. In addition to the virtue of sounding reasonable on paper, the "American approach" proved fairly successful in the field. Sizable branches, often joined or created by disaffected Communist Party members, were built in Toledo, Ohio; Charleston, West Virginia; Gulfport, Mississippi; and Allentown, Mount Carmel, and Dickson City, towns bordering on the anthracite coal region of Pennsylvania. Ted Selander, Sam Pollock, Art Preis, and other AWPers, mostly acting through the Unemployed Leagues, were the principal coordinators of a massive action against the Electric Autolite Company in Tole-

[33] "Why the New Party," *Labor Action,* 20 December 1933, 1, 2.

do, Ohio, in April and May 1934. The strike, supported by Toledo's central labor council and relying for its success on the political mobilization of unemployed workers who refused to scab, approached the dimensions of a general strike as ten thousand demonstrators massed on the picket line and won recognition for the union and a 5 percent wage increase. The AWP-led Toledo Autolite strike marked the beginning of the wave of industrial unionism in the auto industry that eventually culminated in the creation of the United Auto Workers.[34]

It would be an error, however, to characterize the AWP's "American approach" as patriotic. The new party was deeply internationalist. It consciously sought to act upon a proper understanding of the real desires and conditions of the American working class, but it made a deliberate effort to resist any trace of national chauvinism. The same issue of *Labor Action* that carried a summary of the AWP founding statement, for example, featured a lead editorial by Muste, "Labor Internationalism," which condemned the self-serving and shallow "internationalism" of the Comintern and called for a more principled form of international solidarity premised upon cooperation among autonomous workers' movements. On March 17, 1934, Hook, Muste, and Budenz spoke at an AWP-sponsored meeting to commemorate the anniversary of the Paris Commune. And in the July 15, 1934, issue of *Labor Action*, Muste again took up the theme of labor internationalism, deriding the "childish chauvinistic notion that American workers are better fighters than those of other nations." Yet he maintained that "the job of achieving the revolution in the U.S. is in a special sense the job of American workers." The organization's American focus and internationalist politics were complemented by its multiethnic and multiracial composition. Ludwig Lore, for example, had been born to Jewish parents in Germany, had become a prominent leader in the prewar Socialist Party as the editor of the *New Yorker Volkzeitung* and executive secretary of the German Socialist Federation. His influence brought several predominantly German unions in the New York bakery and foods trades within the AWP fold.[35]

That the AWP did not make a fetish of "native" American revolution was further illustrated by its willingness to consider merging with the Communist League of America—a group that owed its basic analyisis to the Left

[34] Louis Francis Budenz, "The 'American Approach'," *Labor Action*, 17 January 1934, 3; "Dinner Meet Reviews New Party Set-Up," *Labor Action*, 1 March 1934, 1, 2; Hook, *Out of Step*, 193; Art Preis, *Labor's Giant Step: Twenty Years of the CIO* (1964; New York: Pathfinder, 1978), 19–24.
[35] A. J. Muste, "Labor Internationalism," *Labor Action*, 20 December 1933, 3; Advertisement, "Paris Commune Anniversary," *Labor Action*, 15 March 1934, 2; A. J. Muste, "Building Labor Internationalism," *Labor Action*, 15 July 1934, 5; Paul Buhle, "Lore, Ludwig," and John Bloom, "American Workers Party," both in *Encyclopedia of the American Left*, 434–45, 32–33.

Opposition of the Soviet Union in the 1920s and that was, consequently, deeply concerned with the fate of the Russian Revolution. *The Militant,* the official newspaper of the CLA, published an open letter to the Provisional Organizing Committee of the AWP on January 27, 1934, pointing out that in September 1933, before the embryonic AWP had appeared, the CLA too had issued a call for a new revolutionary party. After years of attempting to gain readmission to the Communist movement in order to reform it, Trotsky and his global allies, including the CLA, had concluded from the catastrophe in Germany that the Comintern was incorrigible. Since further reform efforts seemed futile, Trotsky called upon revolutionary militants to renounce Stalin and his bureaucracy and begin to work toward the creation of a new Fourth International of working people. The CLA therefore proposed that the two groups explore the potential for unity.[36]

Negotiations began in February 1934, just two months after the AWP's Provisional Organizing Committee was launched. Hook, Muste, Hardman, Burnham, Budenz, and Calverton represented the AWP; Max Shachtman, Arne Swabeck, and Martin Abern negotiated for the CLA. *Labor Action* reported that the AWP team had pleaded with the Trotskyists to abandon the vestigial preoccupations of their formative period, when they had seemed to put more emphasis on the "negative task of attacking the line of the CP than the positive task of building an effective new party." The AWP team underscored that foremost in the work of any new organization should be the positive project of building socialist consciousness among American workers. Swabeck, in a March 1934 report to Trotsky on the negotiations, characterized the AWP group as "left centrist," a phrase that in the CLA lexicon designated an unstable formation between revolutionary socialism and social democracy. But Swabeck also reported that agreement had been reached on a critique of social reformism and Stalinism, indicating substantial potential for unity. Trotsky, in a reply from Europe, told Swabeck that any recommendation from so far away would be inappropriate, but "since you . . . have undertaken the fusion on your own initiative, we can from here extend our confidence to you to carry the matter through to its conclusion."[37]

[36] "Many Groups Discuss AWP Program," *Labor Action,* 15 March 1934, 4.

[37] Harvey Klehr and John Earl Haynes, who view Trotskyism and Stalinism as part of one continuum, are incorrect, therefore, to write that the CLA-AWP merger was a result of "following Trotsky's orders to his supporters around the world to seek coalitions with non-Communist leftists"; the merger was condoned by Trotsky after it was well underway; see Klehr and Earl Haynes, *The American Communist Movement: Storming Heaven Itself* (New York: Twayne, 1992), 91. See also "Many Groups Discuss AWP Program," 4; Trotsky exchange: Arne Swabeck, Secretary, to L. D. Trotsky, 9 March 1934, and Trotsky to Swabeck, 29 March 1934 (Socialist Workers Party Papers, State Historical Society of Wisconsin, reel 1, "Communist League of America 1932–34, Miscellaneous Materials").

Hook and Burnham were the most active AWP proponents of the merger. Burnham, the son of a Chicago railroad executive, had been educated at Princeton and Oxford and cut an aristocratic figure unusual for a revolutionary. He had been won to Marxism very early in the decade while a colleague of Hook's at NYU and would become a key leader of the Trotskyist movement in the late 1930s, popular especially among the youth. Together, he and Hook collaborated to achieve a fusion between the AWP and the CLA. In later recollections, Hook never explained satisfactorily why he devoted such enormous energy to the regroupment. Mainly he claimed that he had been misled by the Trotskyists, who, he alleged, had falsely assured him that they would embrace the phrase "workers' democracy" in place of "dictatorship of the proletariat." Likewise, Hook would suggest that his first use of the term "workers' democracy" at the end of 1933 marked the beginning of his opposition to Leninism. In *Out of Step*, for example, he argued that his use of the phrase in "Communism without Dogmas," the American Workers Party program, and other writings of the period was in direct opposition to "Leninist-Stalinist-Trotskyist" views of revolution. That the later Hook would recall his earlier thought in such a way is unsurprising, for by then he was persuaded that there was a straight, unbroken line of descent from Leninism to Stalinism and therefore no qualitative difference between them—or between Stalinism and Trotskyism. He tended to remember his political break with Communism in 1933 as the occasion for his ideological break from Leninism, though the two were actually several years apart.[38] In 1933 and 1934 Hook still saw vital and irreconcilable distinctions between Leninism and Stalinism, and for years after his break with Communism he defended the Russian Revolution. He regarded workers' democracy as perfectly consistent with Leninism. Like Trotsky, he viewed the rise of Stalinism as the manifestation of a bureaucratic counterrevolution that was radically discontinuous with Lenin's thought.[39]

[38] For examples of Hook's later tendency to see his own development as a direct passage from Communism to anti-Leninism, see Hook, *Out of Step*, 198; and SH to Paul Berman, 24 April 1973 (Hook Papers, box 112).

[39] A democratic interpretation of Leninism may seem counterintuitive to readers, especially in the United States, who are accustomed to think of Lenin as a dictator, his political theory of the proletarian vanguard as inherently elitist, and his revolutionary politics as sectarian. In Hook's time, however, many American radicals admired the Russian Revolution because of its original promise of a more expansive, workplace-centered democracy expressed through soviets (councils) of deputies elected freely by working people, peasants, and soldiers. To radicals like Hook, defending the original democratic promise of 1917 against later views of an authoritarian "Leninism" was extremely important, both out of fidelity to historical truth as they understood it, and in order to guard against the demoralizing political conclusion that working people were incapable of managing society themselves. In the 1930s, revolutionary socialists of Hook's persuasion fought a difficult, uphill struggle for this historical legacy against an improbable alliance of social democrats and bourgeois ideologues on the one

The "dictatorship of the proletariat," Hook argued, was a valid concept which, properly comprehended, meant "workers' democracy." With the advent of Stalinism, however, its meaning had been perverted to justify dictatorship *over* the proletariat. In a special May Day issue of *Labor Action* in 1934, Hook wrote that Marx, Engels, and Lenin had used the terms "workers' democracy" and "dictatorship of the proletariat" interchangeably, but that intervening events required revolutionary socialists to abandon "the linguistic fixations which obstruct clear thinking" so as to restore the proper meaning of "dictatorship of the proletariat" by replacing it entirely with "workers' democracy." Since Lenin's death, wrote Hook, the rule of the soviets had become improperly identified with the rule of the Communist Party, itself dominated by an unaccountable bureaucracy. But, he maintained, the proper organs of working-class democracy were soviets or workers' councils—"what De Leon called the industrial union," he added in a gesture to American revolutionary tradition (the former Columbia Professor Daniel De Leon led the Socialist Labor Party at the turn of the century; his writings, incidentally, were respected by Lenin). Hook remained a Leninist. He did not hold Lenin responsible for the dictatorship over the proletariat. He did not turn to the anarchist or Dutch ultra-left theories that councils could come spontaneously into being or operate without organic leadership or political organization. Hook's point, rather, was that any genuine communist party must acquire "leadership in the councils by virtue of the correctness of its line and not by choking off all other work-

---

hand and Stalinists on the other, all of whom—despite their difference over whether Leninism was deplorable or virtuous—agreed that Leninism was authoritarian and dogmatic. For the early prestige of the Russian Revolution among American liberals and radicals, see Daniel Mason and Jessica Smith, eds., *Lenin's Impact on the United States* (New York: New World Review, 1970); Philip S. Foner, ed., *The Bolshevik Revolution: Its Impact on American Radicals, Liberals, and Labor* (New York: International, 1967); and Christopher Lasch, *The American Liberals and the Russian Revolution* (New York: Columbia, 1962). For classic defenses of Lenin and the Bolsheviks, see John Reed, *Ten Days That Shook the World* (New York: Boni & Liveright, 1919); Georg Lukács, *Lenin: A Study on the Unity of His Thought* (1924; Cambridge: MIT Press, 1971); Leon Trotsky, *Lenin* (1924; Garden City, N.Y.: Garden City Books, 1959); Leon Trotsky, *The History of the Russian Revolution* (1930; New York: Monad, 1980); Victor Serge, *From Lenin to Stalin* (1937; New York: Monad, 1980); and C. L. R. James, *World Revolution, 1917–1936: The Rise and Fall of the Communist International* (1937; New Jersey: Humanities, 1993). The struggle of Lenin to prevent Stalin from taking power, demonstrating the discontinuity between their world views, is explored in Moshe Lewin, *Lenin's Last Struggle* (New York: Pantheon, 1968); and V. I. Lenin and Leon Trotsky, *Lenin's Fight against Stalinism*, ed. Russell Block (New York: Pathfinder, 1975). More recent scholarly works defending the Soviet revolution from a variety of critical perspectives are Samuel Farber, *Before Stalinism: The Rise and Fall of Soviet Democracy* (New York: Verso, 1990); Daniel H. Kaiser, ed., *The Workers' Revolution in Russia* (Cambridge: Cambridge University Press, 1987); Paul LeBlanc, *Lenin and the Revolutionary Party* (New Jersey: Humanities, 1990); Roy Medvedev, *On Socialist Democracy* (1972; London: Spokesman, 1977); and Roy Medvedev, *Leninism and Western Socialism* (New York: Verso, 1981).

ing-class elements that may be opposed to it." It was because many American workers rightly feared that "dictatorship of the proletariat" was nothing more than a smoke screen for the dictatorship of a party over the working class, and in turn of a bureaucracy over the party, that Hook called for a new term to describe the socialist society envisioned by Marx and Lenin. "If we remain true to the Marxist and Leninistic conception of the workers' state as a workers' democracy," he concluded, "and agitate in those terms, much greater headway in reorienting the masses toward revolutionary action can be made."[40]

Hook was committed to workers' democracy, in Lenin's original conception of it, seeking to restore proper meaning to the Marxist language that bureaucratic degeneration had corrupted. His later belief that in 1934 he had tried to persuade the Trotskyists to abandon their Leninism is, therefore, mistaken. His point of dissent from mainstream Trotskyism was over the *meaning* of Leninism, which he upheld. In good part the dissent was terminological and strategic, for the CLA, following Trotsky, refused to relinquish the term "dictatorship of the proletariat." Calling for freedom from "verbal symbols which no longer communicate their original meanings clearly," Hook reminded his comrades that the slogan animating the Russian masses in 1917 was not "the dictatorship of the proletariat" but "All Power to the Soviets!" In an important article—"On Workers' Democracy," published in the October 1934 *Modern Monthly*—Hook offered a criticism of greater substance. Relations of party and class, he held, were sometimes muddled by those such as CLA leader Max Shachtman who, with substantiation by quotation from Leon Trotsky, took the dictatorship of the party to be virtually identical to the dictatorship of the proletariat. Dictatorship by a workers' party, Hook argued, meant dictatorship over the masses of nonparty workers—including other radicals and independent communists—accomplished by force and repression. Force and repression, he countered, should be used only to enforce "the democratically arrived at decisions of the Soviets." Dictatorship of the party over the workers' councils would, no matter how honorable its intentions, make bureaucratic degeneration "practically inevitable." Again, this political criticism of Trotsky's followers and defense of political pluralism reflected a difference about how to *understand* Leninism, an argument within the fold. Citing an article by Lenin on soviet democracy, Hook

---

[40] Hook, "Marxism and Democracy: Some Notes on the Draft Program of the AWP," *Labor Action*, 1 May 1934, 5. Hook had, of course, made a similar argument in "Communism without Dogmas"; this general approach to the relationship between democracy and Marxism was the hallmark of his thought in this period. See also Hook, "On Workers' Democracy," *Modern Monthly* 8 (October 1934): 529–44; and Hook, "The Democratic and Dictatorial Aspects of Communism," *International Conciliation* 304 (December 1934): 452–64.

praised him for "skillfully" including "reference to both the dictatorial aspect of workers' democracy against the bourgeoisie" and "the educative (not dictatorial) role of the Communists within the Soviets."[41]

It does not appear, moreover, that Hook was misled at the time by the Trotskyists regarding their views about the interchangeability of the terms "workers' democracy" and "dictatorship of the proletariat." In September 1934 he received a letter from Chicago lawyer Albert Goldman, who would subsequently serve as Trotsky's attorney during the hearings of the Preliminary Commission of Inquiry in Mexico.[42] Goldman assured Hook that he, personally, was not a dogmatist. He professed his conviction not only that the word "communist" should be dropped from the united group's name but that given the term's utter debasement, it should be left to the Stalinists: "The task of getting American workers at this time to distinguish between 'good' and 'bad' communists is too colossal. I give up." Goldman was prepared to make other concessions in order to gain wider appeal and meet the "left socialists" halfway, but he found "workers' democracy" a rather loose phrase that did not necessarily have the same meaning as "dictatorship of the proletariat." Although he granted that a true dictatorship of the proletariat would require a workers' democracy, Goldman also ruminated that a reformist labor party, if elected, might plausibly claim to have ushered in a "workers' democracy," even if it did not act to defeat capital decisively or abolish exploitive relations of production. Furthermore, he voiced concern that the contraposition of workers' democracy to capitalist democracy might create illusions about the requirements of revolution: "Capitalist democracy is a concealed dictatorship. Workers' democracy is far more exclusive and openly dictatorial with reference to the capitalists than the capitalist democracy [is] with regard to the workers." Goldman closed, however, with acknowledgment of the importance of workers' democracy, party democracy, and political pluralism in a transitional proletarian state. He was even willing to forgo the phrase "dictatorship of the proletariat," but not without making the point that "there is danger connected with any substitute." Goldman's letter was a straightforward expression of an honest difference of opinion over terms of prole-

[41] Hook, "On Workers' Democracy." Originally an address presented at the University of Virginia on July 4, 1934, the paper was reproduced in a publication of the Carnegie Endowment for International Peace, paired with an article by Joseph Stalin; see Hook, "The Democratic and Dictatorial Aspects of Communism."

[42] Goldman's wife, not irrelevantly, was the sister of Lionel Abel, a young New York intellectual and Trotskyist who first met Hook around 1932 and was a friend of Hook and his second wife throughout the 1930s: interview with Lionel Abel, 14 November 1996. On Goldman, see Joseph Hansen, "The Militant," in *The American Radical Press, 1880–1960* (Westport: Greenwood, 1974), 1:326–36.

tarian rule. It indicated a sincere desire for a meeting of minds without papering over the lingering differences.[43]

To understand why Hook advocated the AWP-CLA merger, therefore, we must discard his own subsequent recollection that he was duped by the Trotskyists. Two additional reasons that he gave toward the end of his life are more plausible: he desired to withdraw from politics to philosophy, and he feared that the AWP, if left to its own devices, would be swallowed by the Communist Party.[44] Yet these do not suffice, either. Merger negotiations between the groups began just two months after the founding of the AWP, when Hook was probably not yet weary of his new political responsibilities; the desire to retreat from politics was more likely a contribution to Hook's *later* decision not to join the new, merged organization at the very end of 1934. The fear that the AWP would drift toward the Communist Party also appears mostly retrospective; long before Hook's involvement in the project, the entire bearing of the Muste circle was in conscious opposition to the Communist Party. The CP did win over some AWP leaders, but not until 1935, when the Comintern's announcement of the Popular Front led American Communists to begin to speak in terms reminiscent of the AWP's "American approach," despite great differences in political content.

Why, then, did Hook assist the merger? The overriding factor was his desire to see a unified revolutionary socialist movement capable of serious action and independent of official Communism. The purposes and programs of the AWP and CLA were more alike than not, and the groups would be larger and more concentrated if combined. Hook, moreover, was in virtually total agreement with Trotsky's call for a Fourth International to replace the Comintern. In the summer of 1934 Alex Stiller, an AWP member in Los Angeles, wrote to Hook to complain that the Party's draft program read like a manifesto written by Trotsky. Stiller asserted that the Third International was not "beyond all redemption" and suggested that the AWP focus on anticapitalism rather than anti-Stalinism. Hook replied that he concurred with Trotsky that "the CI is no longer revolutionary and cannot be reformed from within," and, reciting the standard Trotskyist litany, he reminded Stiller of the betrayals—Germany 1923, China 1927, Germany 1929–33—proving that Stalin had acted always in "consideration of the *immediate* needs of the Russian state and not the ultimate ones of the workingclass." Most of the AWP leadership, Hook informed Stiller, believed that fusion with the CLA was necessary for the sake of effective mass work and socialist unity, and they took Stiller's position to be essentially Lovestoneite.

[43]   Albert Goldman to SH, 31 August 1934 (Hook Papers, box 14); no response from Hook survives.
[44]   Hook, *Out of Step*, 202–3.

"I probably am the leftist of them all on the question of the 4th Int'l," Hook confessed, "or rather the call for one but I am not propagandizing for it and am prepared to wait until the Stalinists themselves drive them over to it."[45]

Hook was not, to be sure, in blanket agreement with Trotsky or the CLA. In his letters to Stiller he disagreed in passing with Trotsky's defense of the dictatorship of the party. In the course of the merger process, however, the dispute over the use of "dictatorship of the proletariat" versus "workers' democracy" did not emerge in the way Hook later recalled. In a memorandum prepared in late summer 1934 to summarize the negotiations, he reported to the AWP that the CLA had found the phrase "workers' democracy" too loose, allowing conflicting points of view to hide themselves. The AWP negotiating team had objected to the CLA's fixation on timeworn phrases like "dictatorship of the proletariat," when it should instead concern itself with their *meaning*, "more adequately and idiomatically expressed in the AWP program." The disagreement was thus not over the *content* of the ideas, as Hook sometimes would later maintained, but over the best manner of their *representation*. "Dictatorship of the proletariat," Hook argued in his 1934 memorandum, had just as many ambiguities and misleading associations as "workers' democracy," whereas the meaning given to "workers' democracy" by the AWP was perfectly clear with reference to its revolutionary character.[46]

But on the basis of that terminological dispute—in which Hook's proposed phrase "workers' democracy," though far more appealing in the American context, met with resistance—Hook developed an extensive criticism of what he considered a dogmatism in the CLA's leadership and approach. The Trotskyists, he wrote in his report, appeared to

imply that they had all the answers to the problems; that history fell into ready made patterns; that flexibility in analysis and action meant opportunism; that the overwhelming majority of the working class in America was intensely concerned with the issues which divided the Communist movement into a half dozen grouplets; that the subjective satisfaction of penning statements which were orthodox in line and phrase as judged by the revolutionary literature of the 19th century and selected writings of Lenin and Trotsky in the 20th, were more important than the objective consequences of isolation and sectarianism which resulted from trying to impose upon the

[45] SH to Allen Stiller, 25 July and 3 August 1934, and Allen Stiller to SH, 23 July and 20 August 1934 (Hook Papers, box 112).
[46] SH to Stiller, 26 July 1934 (Hook Papers, box 112); Hook, "Summary of Negotiations," in Memorandum to All POC Members, 30 August 1934 (Socialist Workers Party Papers, State Historical Society of Wisconsin, reel 1, "American Workers Party, 1934").

non-revolutionary working masses issues to which they were not yet awakened and phrases which they did not understand.

Despite the firmness of these criticisms, Hook came down decidedly in favor of unity with the CLA forces. In their joint recommendation, Hook and Burnham pointed to a number of possible dangers: that the AWP and CLA would remain separate factions and not fuse genuinely, that the CLA would continue to see itself as a faction of the Communist Party and not orient itself toward mass work or building the independent political party, and that energy would be wasted on endless debates on international issues. They nevertheless concluded that unity was necessary as a first step toward regroupment after a decade of divisions in the world revolutionary movement, and essential to the prospects for a new party, which neither small group alone could hope to construct. Furthermore, Hook and Burnham argued, some of the CLA's vices might instead be seen as virtues. For example, the Trotskyists' sectarian preoccupation with the Communist Party had resulted in an extensive training in revolutionary problems and theory. The CLA's outlook might be interpreted as a discipline militating against the more lax attitude of the AWP rather than a hidebound irrelevance. Taken in combination with the strengths of the AWP, these positive attributes of the CLA might give a united party greater potential than either organization had alone. Hook and Burnham, expressing conviction that the CLA was serious and sincere about unity, proposed that collaboration begin immediately with a united front, including joint publications.[47]

Hook and Burnham, Max Shachtman later recalled, were crucial to bringing off the merger: "Being what they were, they were much more interested in the sort of thing that preoccupied us—theoretical questions, programmatic precision, internationalism, an active struggle against Stalinism, a clear differentiation from reformism—in a word, things that were not quite uppermost in the minds of the traditional followers of Muste." Some sticking points remained with the Muste traditionalists, including the new group's name: because of their attachment to a special "American approach," many wanted to preserve the name American Workers Party. The CLA, however, thought it imperative to merge on transparently equal terms. Eventually, both groups agreed to a CLA proposal to call the new organization the Workers Party of the United States (WP-US). A second problem arose when a minority bloc against the merger hardened within the AWP leadership. Louis Budenz feared that the fresh start of the AWP

---

[47]   Hook, "Summary of Negotiations," and Hook and Burnham, "Analysis and Recommendations," in Memorandum to All POC Members, 30 August 1934.

was about to be lost in the "mumbo jumbo" of "radical ritualism." J. B. S. Hardman, in a more personal attack, accused Hook and Burnham of being Trotskyists. Hook responded at a special meeting of the AWP leadership in November 1934. That the merger did not preclude a continuation of the "American approach," argued Hook, was shown by the example of Minneapolis, where the CLA had led a massive, impressive citywide teamsters' strike in the spring of 1934 with precisely the same success that the AWP had achieved in the Toledo Auto-Lite strike. Against the charge that he was a Trotskyist agent, Hook retorted, "That I am sympathetic to the CLA's program is no secret; neither is it a secret that I have sharper differences with the CLA than has Hardman. His disagreements are based on personalities while mine revolve around the question of Workers' Democracy."[48]

In the end, the unity proposal won the approval of a majority of the AWP, including Muste, who occupied a crucial position in the American Workers Party as something of an "American Lenin." But unity took place at the cost of the minority's defection. Hardman merely dropped away, retiring from the left, but Johnson, Budenz, and Anthony Ramuglia quit rather than combine with the Trotskyists—and then went on to join the Communist Party. Apparently they became impressed with the CP's labor organizing and were persuaded by the Communist press, which condemned the AWP-CLA merger as an unholy alliance of Trotskyist "counter-revolutionaries" with Musteite "bourgeois nationalism." The Communist turn to a Popular Front in 1935, with superficial echoes of the AWP's "American approach," also made the CP more appealing to former AWP adherents than it had been in the Third Period. Johnson became a lifelong Communist leader, and Budenz was the *Daily Worker*'s labor editor for ten years before becoming a right-wing anti-Communist in 1946, having reconverted to his childhood Catholic faith. The split did not come as a shock, but the defection to the CP did, since it violated the entire political premise of the AWP as well as of the CPLA before it. An overwhelming majority of AWP members nonetheless supported the merger with the Trotskyists. Muste and other leaders were motivated by concern about their organization's static membership and chronic financial troubles, and the Toledo and Minneapolis strikes made the trade union militants in each group eager to unify. In the first two days of December 1934 a joint national con-

[48] This is further evidence that on the eve of the merger Hook was perfectly aware of his differences with the Trotskyists over the term "workers' democracy"; he advocated merger knowing that the differences had not been fully resolved. See "The Reminiscences of Max Shachtman," 1963 (Columbia University Oral History Research Office), 242; Budenz comments in Memorandum to All POC Members, 30 August 1934; and Hook's reponse in AWP Minutes, "Report of Special National POC Meeting Held in NYC November 6, 1934" (Max Shachtman Papers, box 6, folder 38, Tamiment Institute, New York University).

vention put the finishing touches on the establishment of the Workers Party of the United States. "Without Hook," avers Albert Glotzer, a Chicago Trotskyist in the 1930s, "I doubt that this unity would have taken place."[49]

Science, Religion, and Marxism, 1934–35

Notwithstanding the conventional prejudice against mixing politics and scholarship, immersion in the minutiae of party organization propelled Hook toward the resolution of several nagging ambiguities in his thought. In addition to sharpening his positions on socialist organization, liberalism, and democracy—with important implications for his thought well beyond the immediate factional issues at stake—his period of participation in the AWP leadership helped to clarify his views on science and Marxism. As early as *Towards the Understanding of Karl Marx*, in which he had argued that Marxism was not equivalent to natural science because of its necessarily partisan attachment to the class struggle, Hook had begun to spell out the relationship of Marxism to science. The issue acquired urgency in the debate with V. J. Jerome and Earl Browder which signaled Hook's excommunication from Communism, and it entered in subtle ways into all his important debates afterward: his correspondence with Trotsky regarding Marxism and method, his second encounter with Max Eastman over Marxism and pragmatism, and his defense of Marxism against Russell, Dewey, and Cohen. But in "The Philosophy of Technics in the U.S.S.R." and "The Mythology of Class Science," a pair of articles published in V. F. Calverton's pages early in 1934, Hook spelled out his views on natural science even more deliberately.

What, Hook asked, should be the place of experts, specialists, and technicians in helping to construct a socialist economy? How would it differ from their roles under capitalism? In bourgeois society, a "departmentalization of skill and its isolation from other phases of social activity" leads to a deadening of social understanding and awareness in "technicians"—a term Hook used broadly to designate professionals, specialists, and managers. Because they are familiar chiefly with what they do every day, he posited, technicians are prone to seek technical or technocratic solutions to social problems. They mistakenly presume that social troubles may be solved without politics if "approached in a purely scientific way without class bias or distorting passion." Since politics is inescapable, however, any

[49]   Albert Glotzer to author, 12 December 1991; SH to Paul Berman, 24 April 1973 (Hook Papers, box 112); Burnham to SH, 21 and 26 July 1934 (Hook Papers, box 112); Cannon, *The History of American Trotskyism*, 182, 188; Robinson, *Abraham Went Out*, 47; Louis Francis Budenz, *This Is My Story* (New York: McGraw-Hill, 1947); Interview with B. J. Widick, 23 March 1992 ("American Lenin").

merely technical solution is doomed to fail. From that failure springs the tendency of technicians, when frustrated, to develop a paradoxical hostility to technology, mechanical society, and scientific method and to advocate instead the authoritarian power of a new Caesar.[50]

This social-historical interpretation of technocracy and middle-class support for fascism extended the democratic criticisms of "social engineering" which Hook had first voiced in his debate with Max Eastman. He further elucidated the social basis of technical reason by contrasting technicians under capitalism with those in the Soviet Union. Although the USSR was not yet a socialist society, wrote Hook—again in a manner consistent with Trotsky's theory that the Soviet Union was a deformed but transitional state—it did represent a break from bourgeois norms. There the position of technicians was dramatically different because they produced and planned for a purpose rather than a market, which involved them necessarily in politics and social ethics and prevented them from developing a one-sided technical expertise in disregard of the wider implications of their work.

Hook repudiated, though, the notion that socialist society represents a complete break on all levels with all aspects of capitalist society, a view increasingly propounded by Communist practitioners of "dialectical materialism." Part of the problem, he argued, arose from the fallacy that Marx's call for the unity of theory and practice meant that from *every* theory *given* practices must follow. From this confusion came the assertion that each mode of production generates a set of scientific propositions tied to its class base, so that the science of the USSR was superior by virtue of being "proletarian science." That was nonsense. Since mathematicians in the Soviet Union and mathematicians elsewhere were exchanging conclusions, citing one another, and working on the same set of problems, one could only conclude that "at least some of the problems of pure science are studied because they arise out of the immanent development of the subject-matter of mathematical and physical inquiry."[51]

The theories generated by scientific inquiry, Hook further maintained, could not be understood simply by their social application. He circumscribed the topic with the aid of a pragmatist definition: "By a scientific theory is understood, of course, a set of propositions from which the experimentally observed data logically follows and which indicates what new experiment must be performed to test its relative truth or falsity." He also cautioned that he was referring solely to the natural sciences and mathematics, not the social sciences, which inescapably involved a politi-

---

[50] Hook, "The Philosophy of Technics in the U.S.S.R.," *Modern Monthly* 8 (February 1934): 31–36.
[51] Hook, "The Philosophy of Technics in the U.S.S.R.," 34.

cal point of view. Hook objected to any assertion of a class basis for science—a "proletarian physics," for example—on grounds that it opened the gate of plausibility to Nazi claims of a "national" German science. Many were already beginning to claim that fascism and communism were identical, and to Hook it was imperative that communists make every effort to preserve the differences between the two: "Unfortunately, some 'orthodox' Marxists and dialectical materialists have written about science and mathematics in a fashion which although quite distinct from the intent of the fascist argument, reproduces its logic. . . . They share the fascist assumption that theoretic science is not neutral to politics: they differ from the fascists in holding that it is proletarian politics and not bourgeois politics which represents the legitimate point of view from which the re-orientation of the sciences must be carried out." Claims for a "proletarian biology," Hook maintained, were dangerously similar to Nazi attempts to harness biology to racialism. He acknowledged that the social *acceptance* of scientific propositions was sometimes divided along class lines: Darwin's, evolutionary biology was opposed in ecclesiastical and conservative quarters but embraced by working-class movements. Nonetheless, Hook argued, the reception of evolutionism should not be conflated with the structure of Darwinian theory; a class interpretation and dissemination of a theory did not impart a class character to the theory itself. Furthermore, Hook observed, the social acceptance or rejection of a theory was not necessarily a function of class interest or world view. Einstein's theory of relativity, for example, had been opposed by some in Germany who considered it a plot of the Elders of Zion, by some intellectuals in France who considered it a mystical product of backward German culture, and by official "dialectical materialists" in Russia who called it reactionary and idealist.[52]

The ideological and social *origins* of a scientific theory were in Hook's opinion equally irrelevant to its veracity. Although Newton, Copernicus, and Pasteur were all deeply religious and regarded their theories as demonstrative proof of God, he noted, the truth of their scientific propositions was independent of their theological beliefs. Hook did not deny that dependence upon subsidies for research laboratories and expensive modern equipment colored the *interpretations* and *uses* of scientific findings, but the logical response to such distortions was not to adopt a "class" science but "to develop in every respect [the] true, objective, international and classless character" of the natural sciences and mathematics. "The argument addressed to the scientist," Hook insisted, "must show how capitalist society distorts his scientific activity and how a classless society would lib-

---

[52] Ibid., 35; Hook, "The Mythology of Class Science," *Modern Monthly* 8 (March 1934): 112–13.

erate it. The liberation of that activity would be accomplished by eliminating the closed doors, the duplications and the economic ambitions which hamper free research today."[53]

Hook's articles on science had made clear the fundamental distinction between social philosophies, such as Marxism, and the natural sciences and mathematics. But was Marxism itself a science? Since Marxism was ineluctably partisan, in what sense could it be called scientific? "Marxism and Religion," in the March 1935 issue of *Modern Monthly* further defined Marxism and science in Hook's thought. There he counterposed Marxism—a scientific, historical, and naturalistic method of social analysis and action—to the idealist, otherworldly, transcendental realm of religion. He reiterated his objections to any version of Marxism which claimed that socialism was inevitable simply by the operation of the "dialectical nature of things," a disposition that he characterized as fundamentally mystical. Properly understood, Marxism made sense of experience through truths determined by social adjudication. Personal vision, the touchstone of religious experience, was incapable of verification by others and therefore beyond the scope of science. Marxism was thus, unlike religion, *scientific*, but Hook argued that it was not itself a *science* in the strict sense of the term:

> To say that the method of Marxism is scientific does not mean that Marxism as the theory and practice of achieving the classless society is a *science*. Science as such is above classes and neutral to values. Its propositions of fact do not *uniquely* determine any values or ideals in behalf of which scientific knowledge is to be used. Consequently if the nature of Marxism were exhausted by the characterization of it as an objective science, it would be possible for a Marxist not to be a socialist, and even to be opposed to socialism. But the desire and will to achieve socialism is integral to Marxism. Marxism, then, since it expresses the ideals, aspirations and values of the working class in its struggle to abolish all classes—is something more than a science. It is a social philosophy, based upon science, whose judgments of value, checked and controlled as they may be at all points by knowledge and experience, ultimately express class *needs* and class *interests*.

If scientific practice was the elaboration of judgments that can be tested and confirmed by all others, then, according to Hook, many aspects of Marxist thought were scientific, particularly the tools and manner of social analysis distinct to Marxism—such as the theory of capitalist crises developed by Marx. As a politics of social transformation, however, Marxism en-

[53] Hook, "The Mythology of Class Science," 117.

tailed a commitment to the working class and oppressed groups which reflected values neither universally upheld in class society nor empirically
premised. Although this formulation opened up difficulties of its own,
Hook had at least cleared up the confusion that lingered from his exchange with Trotsky two years before, when he had implied that Marxism
was neither a science nor scientific.[54]

Withdrawal from Organization, 1935

Given his strenuous labors in bringing together the American
Workers Party and the Communist League of America, Hook's abstention
in 1935 from the new Workers Party of the United States came as a surprise
to virtually everyone. He was not alone in dropping away: Calverton, Rorty,
and several other AWP members decided for various reasons not to take
part in the new group, even though all (except for the handful won over
to the Communist Party) remained sympathetic to the WP-US. Rorty, for
example, withdrew for strategic reasons alone and proposed in a letter to
Muste to "take on a fellow traveler's role."[55] Muste himself would last just
a year in the Trotskyist movement. In the summer of 1936, while traveling
to Europe to visit Trotsky, he became profoundly fretful about signs of coming world war. After experiencing a religious epiphany while visiting a
cathedral, he reverted to the faith-based pacifism of his prewar ministeri-
al days, a turn that would eventually make him the elder statesman of the
fledgling antinuclear and anti-war movements of the 1950s and 1960s. Of
the figures who withdrew from socialist organization in 1935–36, only
Muste had been as important as Hook to the AWP and the merger process.
Since James Burnham went on to become a major Trotskyist theoretician
and leader who helped establish the Socialist Workers Party in 1938, Hook's
course is all the more curious.[56]

A series of factors apparently shaped his decision to remove himself from
membership and abstain from leadership in the WP-US early in 1935.

[54] Hook, "Marxism and Religion," *Modern Monthly* 9 (March 1935): 31.
[55] Rorty to Muste, n.d., and WP-US to Rorty, 1 February 1935 (James Rorty Papers, University of Oregon).
[56] The departure of Muste has created the impression that most of the AWP cadre dropped
away after the fusion. See, e.g., Jon Bloom, "American Workers Party." This view should be
offset by acknowledgment of the many important members who remained in the revolutionary movement throughout the 1930s and helped found the Socialist Workers Party in
1938, including Burnham, E. R. McKinney, Ted Selander, Ted Grant, Morris Chertov, Freddy Paine, Anne Chester, and Art Preis. Many, that is, adapted to Trotskyism for the remainder of the decade, at least, though many would be found in the Workers Party in the 1940s.
Even Albert Glotzer, who regrets the development, writes, "There was a considerable fusion
of the Trotskyist leadership with important members of the AWP leadership" (Glotzer to author, 25 January 1992).

Hook often maintained later that he backed away because he sought to give himself more time for theoretical pursuits. Even James P. Cannon, the top leader of American Trotskyism in the 1930s and 1940s, explained Hook's course in that way, though he put it more crudely: "Hook wanted the fusion in order to get the AWP off his hands and end his brief adventure in party politics. He wanted to retire to the side lines, the only place he has ever felt at home, and which he ought never to have left." But Hook and Cannon, each for his own reason, tended in their subsequent story-telling to exaggerate the extent of Hook's political withdrawal from the socialist movement in 1935 and his distance from the new organization. More likely, Hook simply decided that the consuming role of leadership in a socialist organization was not for him, despite his unwavering revolutionary conviction. B. J. Widick, a trade union activist and Muste loyalist in the 1930s, recalls that Hook's record as a leader was divided. Although he was recognized as the ablest Marxist theorist in America and a respected teacher who succeeded in recruiting a number of his students to the AWP, Widick remembers, the perception of many that Hook was conceited and abrasive made him less popular among socialist youth than Burnham. Yet Freddy Drake Paine, a waitress and factory worker in New York who came into the AWP with Muste from the CPLA, says that though Hook could be abrasive, she has fond memories of "kibbitzing" with him, whereas Burnham was "stiff-necked."[57]

Hook also had new family commitments to consider. In the early 1930s he and his first wife, Carrie, had drifted apart; they separated in 1933, and a divorce was arranged in Mexico (where divorce was convenient) in 1935. The breakup may not have been exclusively due to politics, though since Carrie remained an implacable Communist while Hook's anti-Stalinism was sharpening, the marriage would have been hard to sustain no matter how much love remained. In one late-life letter Hook wrote with a hint of bitterness that Carrie had "decided to stay married to the Communist Party in 1933."[58]

[57]   Cannon, *The History of American Trotskyism*, 178–79; interview with B. J. Widick, 23 March 1992; B. J. Widick to author, 21 November 1991; interview with Freddy Paine, 11 July 1996. Ann Hook recalled that her husband was never quite comfortable following a line, and was for that reason always a bit removed from organizational affairs (interview with Ann Hook, 30 August 1993). This may well have been typical of Hook's disposition by the time the two were married, though it does not square with the time he invested in the League of Professional Groups and the AWP leadership.

[58]   SH to Harry Slochower, 2 July 1983 (Harry Slochower Papers, Brooklyn College). Unfortunately, to the best of my knowledge, no pictures of Carrie Katz Hook from the 1920s or 1930s survive, not even in the possession of their son. After the divorce, she and her son moved to Mexico in 1936 (where they lived in Cuernevaca and Mexico City) and then to Los Angeles in 1937. She later married William Carroll, a veteran of the Spanish Civil War, whose various trades included printing and woodworking, but that marriage, too, ended in divorce.

In May 1935 Hook married again. Ann Zinkin, his new companion, was eight years younger than Sidney but, like him, had been raised in Brooklyn by Jewish parents. Her father, a metal-spinner later involved in the rag trade in Flatbush, was a Bundist and Socialist. In the 1920s the teenage Ann had been a flapper. Lionel Abel, who was involved briefly with Ann before she began to see Sidney and who remained friendly with them both across the 1930s, describes her as lively, attractive, and curious about life. Once, while visiting his place on 3rd Street in the Village, Ann caught sight of a magazine with a cover photo of Ernest Hemingway, who had just published *A Farewell to Arms* (1929). "That's the kind of man I love," she declared. "From that to Sidney Hook is quite a leap," Abel quips. Ann's impulses created more serious complications when, after she and Sidney became romantically involved, she began an affair with a now obscure figure, Herbert Abel (no relation to Lionel). Willing to forgive the dalliance, Sidney suggested that she go to Europe to decide what she wanted. In 1934 she spent six months in England and Italy and upon her return chose to make a life with him. Sidney, Lionel Abel believes, had "behaved extremely well."[59]

Ann and Sidney first met in one of his courses at New York University when he was only twenty-seven. "I wasn't such a *good* student," she recalled. "I was an enthusiastic student." In fact, Hook gave her a C in philosophy. He was nonetheless charmed by her vigor and candor, and she, fascinated by the world of ideas, loved their talks. "Let's have a debate," he would tell Ann. "You take a side, and I'll take the other." The couple attended parties together at the home of their friend Herbert Solow before they were married, and both were members of the American Workers Party. After their marriage in early 1935, the Hooks lived first on Barrow Street and then on Grove, in apartments near the Washington Square campus in Greenwich Village. Pursuing a lead supplied by Hook's friend Meyer Schapiro, they purchased a modest summer home on a dirt road near South Wardsboro, a speck of a village in rural Vermont near the Green Mountains. Within a year of their marriage, on March 23, 1936, Ann gave birth to a son, Ernest Benjamin Hook. When a second baby, Susan Ann Hook, was born on August 23, 1938, the family sought larger quarters and found an apartment in Brooklyn near Prospect Park, where they lived for many years.[60]

Carrie worked as a CIO staffer and in various secretarial jobs, including one at Stanford; she died on 27 August 1988. With minimal financial assistance from his father, John Bertrand Hook went to college and law school at Harvard and is now a lawyer in San Francisco (interview with John B. Hook, 23 August 1993).

[59] Interview with Lionel Abel, 14 November 1996; interview with Ann Hook, 30 August 1993; interview with Ernest Hook, 10 August 1996.

[60] Interview with Ann Hook, 30 August 1993; Ernest Hook to author, 19 April 1992; interview with Meyer Schapiro, 25 October 1993; interview with Ernest Hook, 10 August 1992.

Ann Zinkin, who became Hook's second wife, circa 1930. (Courtesy Ernest Hook.)

Under these changed personal circumstances, Hook may very well have grown more cautious and concerned about his job security. He was a popular teacher, voted "most stimulating professor" repeatedly by NYU students, but he had already had several close calls. During the presidential campaign of 1932 some speculated that he might be fired for his visible

Sidney Hook and Ann Zinkin Hook, circa 1940. (Courtesy Sidney Hook Collection, Hoover Institution Archives, Stanford University.)

activities on behalf of the Communist ticket. Early in 1934 he had again felt the chill winds of unemployment when Calverton published his reply to Dewey, Russell, and Cohen under the misleading title "Why I Am a Communist." Several bookshops near Washington Square College displayed the issue, with that inflammatory declaration emblazoned on the cover over Hook's name, in their windows. In December 1934 Hook had another close call when he and James Burnham were the target of front-page red-baiting in the *New York American*—owned by the notorious reactionary William Randolph Hearst—for their role as creators of the WP-US. Fortunately, at precisely that moment the Young Communist League chose to launch an attack against Hook. YCL spokesman Henry Martel, quoted in the NYU bulletin, called Hook "a slimy revolutionary and reptile of the worst type" (most likely an error of student journalism, since Martel surely meant *counter*-revolutionary) and, comparing Hook's opinions to those of Hearst, termed them both "advocates of fascism and enemies of the proletariat." The YCL's slander, ironically, served to reassure worried trustees and administrators that Hook was not the red menace he was reputed to be. Of the many tactical blunders made by the Communist Party in the 1930s, this one, inadvertently saving Sidney Hook's job, was surely among its all-time greats. Still, the publicity may have suggested to Hook the wisdom of a lower profile. He had been appointed departmental chair, making him a visible target, but he did not have tenure. In 1936 Lionel Trilling, a familiar acquaintance of Hook's, was told by Jacques Barzun that he would not be happy at Columbia as "a Jew, a Marxist and a Freudian." Two of these counts applied to Hook—indeed, he was ten times the Marxist in terms of publications. Trilling successfully fended off the dismissal, and NYU in any event was not Columbia, but the incident made a great impression upon other scholars in the small anti-Stalinist left in New York. Hook may not have felt vulnerable, given his self-confidence, but he may very well have grown more cautious as a result.[61]

No sharp political disagreement or absolute break was involved in Hook's withdrawal from organized socialism, however. As Ann Hook recalls, her husband was "sympathetic" to the newly formed group for several years afterward, though he was "torn in all directions" by his professional, familial, and political interests. For the next several years Hook was a political fellow traveler acting roughly, if not exactly, in concert with the Trotskyists and others who remained in revolutionary socialist organization. His first philosophical article of 1935, in fact, was published in *New International*, the Trotskyist theoretical journal.[62]

From Hegel to Marx, 1936

The elimination of organizational demands on his time freed Hook during 1935 to devote greater concentration to philosophy. The publication of Dewey's *Liberalism and Social Action* (1935) allowed Hook to reflect on the issues of liberalism and Marxism raised by the "Why I Am Not a Communist" debate of 1934. "As you know," he wrote to John Cham-

61 Hook claimed to have given personal counsel to Trilling during his time of trial at Columbia, though Diana Trilling denied it, and Lionel Trilling's diary, which is quite detailed about the affair in the entries reproduced by his widow in her memoir, mentions no such conversations; see Hook, *Out of Step*, 212–15; and Diana Trilling, *The Beginning of the Journey* (New York: Harcourt Brace, 1993): 266–67, 272–81. Evidence of Hook's excellent teaching ability is in Evelyn Labinski to SH, 27 October 1930 (Hook Papers, box 4); "Honor Einstein, F.D., La Guardia," *Bulletin* (NYU), 11 April 1938; and "Senior Notables Named in Album Poll," *Bulletin* (NYU), 20 March 1944, 4, which reports that Hook was voted "most stimulating professor, a title he has held for years." On Hearst attack and YCL blunder, see Hook, *Out of Step*, 205–6; "Two Extreme Radical Groups Merge Focus" and " 'College' Communism," *The New York American*, n.d. (Hook Papers, box 172); *W.S.C. Bulletin* (NYU), 15 February 1935, 1; SH to Albert Glotzer, 25 October 1984 (Hook Papers, box 14).
62 Interview with Ann Hook, 30 August 1993; Hook to Albert Glotzer, 25 October 1984 (Hook Papers, box 14); Hook, *Out of Step*, 205–6; Ernest Hook to author, 19 April 1992; Hook, "Marx's Criticism of 'True Socialism,'" *New International* 2 (January 1935): 13–16, also in *From Hegel to Marx: Studies in the Intellectual Development of Karl Marx* (1936; New York: Columbia University Press, 1994).

berlain, who had criticized *Liberalism and Social Action* in a review, "my own disagreements with Dewey on some things are considerable and I am not what you would call a 'softy' on questions of logical rigor, but I believe Dewey's book is the most remarkable piece of political writing of our generation." Socialist politics and liberal values, Hook explained, are perfectly commensurable:

> It seems to me that liberalism (as distinct from the economics of laissez-faire) represents a social, and in the last analysis, an ethical philosophy. It is a social philosophy with a varying content but relatively invariant form. Its fundamental values are respect for the intrinsic worth of personality, freedom of intellectual inquiry, intelligence, social democracy and what for lack of a better term might be called spiritual charity. There are conflicts between these values in concrete cases but this is true of every genuine ethical situation. The opposite of liberalism as a social philosophy is illiberalism whose values are exemplified to-day in Germany, Italy and in a lesser degree in Russia. Lest you regard it as anomalous that a Marxist come to the defence of liberalism in this sense, let me remind you that it was none other than Marx who proclaimed that "the proletariat regards its courage, self-confidence, independence and sense of personal dignity as more necessary than its daily bread." Socialism as an economic system simply extends the sphere within which liberalism as a social philosopy may operate.[63]

In addition to defending Dewey, Hook returned to his broader philosophical projects, especially his archaeological sifting through the writings of Marx and Hegel. Of the articles he published in 1935, three were slated for inclusion in a projected second book on Marx's thought, and much of his time that year was spent preparing the manuscript.[64]

On New Year's Day 1936, Hook finished *From Hegel to Marx: Studies in the Intellectual Development of Karl Marx,* greeted by virtually every review as a scholarly triumph and called by *The Economist* "far and away the best account of an obscure and important subject at present available in English."[65] *From Hegel to Marx* was indeed a remarkable achievement, compressing a decade of careful research and thought into a densely argued account of the way in which Marx came to develop his world view. Hook avoided the usual pitfall of those commentators who tended to explicate Hegel's turgid thought by replicating his difficult jargon, thereby compounding rather than dispelling confusion. He managed to explain

---

63 SH to John Chamberlain, 30 August 1935 (Hook Papers, box 8).
64 Hook told his son that the book came together during a summer spent at Yaddo: interview with Ernest Hook, 10 August 1996.
65 *The Economist* 124 (29 August 1936): 395.

Marx's relationship to Hegel without turning Marx into a Hegelian, as had Georg Lukács and many others.[66] In contrast to *Towards the Understanding of Karl Marx*, which directly challenged various interpretations of Marx by explaining how they evolved historically, *From Hegel to Marx* was a straightforward work of collective intellectual biography. Yet the two works on Marx shared a common method, for each sought to explain Marx's seemingly contradictory positions by situating them within the debates he had with others during his lifetime. Both books depicted the essential Marx as a revolutionary socialist devoted above all to transformative action.

From Hegel to Marx began with the germination of Hegelianism. Kant was the German analogue to the Enlightenment; Hegel at once continued and answered Kant's project. Like Kant, Hegel legitimated bourgeois society, but not on grounds of abstract reason or the rights of man, which were too likely to provoke and justify revolution. Hegel's defense of the emerging bourgeois world was based upon a developmental metaphysic that revealed a necessary and reasonable plan immanent in history itself. *From Hegel to Marx* placed Marx in emulation of and battle with each of the Young Hegelians—David Friedrich Strauss, Bruno Bauer, Arnold Ruge, Max Stirner, Moses Hess, and Ludwig Feuerbach—who in the 1840s applied Hegel's system to the task of social criticism. Although the Young Hegelians at first considered themselves faithful to Hegel, they reached conclusions which, in the end, drew them closer to the original revolutionary philosophy of the Enlightenment. They sought to criticize religion as irrational. Religion to them was not the unfolding of freedom and reason, as it was for Hegel; it comprised authority, tradition, and renunciation of self and was therefore a prop of the existing order, albeit a compensation to people in their individual struggles with the mysteries of life. In *Leben Jesu* (1835) David Friedrich Strauss created a scandal with his critique of Christian dogmas, demonstrating on internal grounds that the gospel accounts were completely contradictory and therefore logically implausible. Strauss remained religious, but he argued that the gospels ought to be understood as myth rather than history. Strauss was topped by Bruno Bauer, whose three-volume *Kritik der evangelischen Geschichte der Synoptiker* (1841–42) unveiled the even more dramatic contention not only that Christ was not divine but that he was not even historical.

It was against Bauer, Hook argued, that Marx first developed his critique of idealism. Though Bauer was an atheist and a celebrator of critical consciousness, he remained an absolute idealist on the plane of philosophy. Marx faulted Bauer for desiring to remain above the fray. Since Bauer

---

[66] Lukács, Hook noted, did "justice to the dialectical aspect of Marx's thought at the expense, alas, of Marx's *naturalism*" (*From Hegel to Marx*, 60).

sought a pure criticism uncompromised by involvement with the state, he would broach no alliance with the liberal bourgeoisie against the Prussian state. He even opposed the Jewish call for emancipatory rights because the action relied upon the state and entailed a concession to religion. To Marx, Bauer had it all backward, seeing religion as a mere excuse rather than the effect of social trauma. One cannot simply argue against religion, Marx maintained; its *roots* must be upended. The supposedly Jewish spirit of commerce was merely one aspect of a capitalist society and would be re-solved through social emancipation, not criticism. Finally, Bauer mistak-enly opposed working-class social demands as selfish, maintaining that the world could be revolutionized only through a transformation of people's souls and that only a philanthropic and ethical spirit would suffice. To this Marx rejoined that not solipsism but mass action expressed real human in-terest and behavior and was the only manner in which ideas took force. So it was that Marx arrived at the first element of historical materialism. His opposition to supernaturalism, wrote Hook, was due above all to his belief that it "produced either an irrational attitude toward social causation or a fatalistic resignation which paralysed action," but these criticisms did not prevent Marx from retaining an appreciation of the *activity* of human con-sciousness which owed much to his initial immersion in a philosophical idealism steeped in religiosity. [67]

Marx's polemics with regard to Ruge, Stirner, and Hess were in Hook's judgment equally consequential. Arnold Ruge, editor of a number of rad-ical bourgeois papers in the late 1830s and early 1840s, shared Marx's op-position to ideas celebrating withdrawal from the world but differed with Marx over liberal democracy. In atomized bourgeois society, Marx posit-ed, even a full extension of political enfranchisement would not bring about human emancipation, which required social equality. No political attack that sought to use the existing state to abolish inequality would suc-ceed on its own; a social revolution was required. Max Stirner's proto-an-archism proved even less congenial to Marx. Stirner argued that since egoism was a necessary and unavoidable part of every movement, people would become communists not because of some abstract ideal but because of an egoistic desire to become human. Marx took something from Stirn-er—chiefly his attacks on philanthropy as ineffectual sentimentalism—but also criticized him sharply for imagining a pure ego apart from society and for his petty-bourgeois inability to comprehend the *social* nature of pro-duction, which meant that nothing is the product of "one's own labor" alone.

Moses Hess and the "true" socialists were closer to Marx, in Hook's judg-

[67] Hook, *From Hegel to Marx,* 155.

ment, than any other radical German group of the 1840s. Hook discounted the attack by Marx and Engels on Hess in the *Communist Manifesto* (1848) as the result of a perplexing failure of communication, for Hess by then had changed his views to correspond with theirs, and he had, after all, recruited Engels to communism and wrote part of *The German Ideology* (1845). In the early 1840s Hess typified the diminishing enthusiasm among radical German intellectuals for the Prussian bourgeoisie as it failed to mount any opposition to the conservative bureaucracy. To indicate his opposition to bourgeois politics, Hess took from French radicals the label "socialist," but he severed its connection with the working-class movement. Socialism to him was an ethical abstraction, the perfect society, and he stood aside from class struggles in the belief that they represented particular interests. Hess rejected bourgeois liberalism in its every part and by so doing, Marx objected, contributed inadvertently to reaction, given the actual alternatives in Germany. "True socialists," as Hess and his followers called themselves, took ideas formulated in France, where workers were combating a bourgeoisie firmly in power since at least 1830, and mechanically applied them to Germany, where the bourgeoisie was going to be a necessary part of any movement against the semi-feudal Prussian regime. "It was not the fact that the 'true socialists' spoke in the name of morality which led Marx to oppose them," wrote Hook, "but the *nature* of the morality they professed—a morality which was timeless and placeless, that dealt in injunctions which were never specific, and which turned men's attention away from the determining social force of human behavior." Nor was Marx opposed to education as such, Hook emphasized, but only to education that obscured fundamental economic tendencies and filled the proletariat with utopian illusions.[68]

By this path, Hook had reached a position from which to unravel the riddle of Hegel and Marx. Quite obviously, Marx followed Hegel historically, but how was it that the great theorist of communist revolution and the official thinker of arch-conservative Prussia were connected philosophically? The ideas of Marx and Hegel, Hook acknowledged, were indeed opposed in myriad ways. Hegel was religious; Marx, an atheist. Hegel was a political accommodationist; Marx, a socialist revolutionary. Hegel considered the state a legal and ethical arbiter of justice; to Marx it was a product and instrument of class struggles. Philosophy was for Hegel retrospective evaluation; for Marx it was inseparable from social activity. Hegel built a systematic philosophical idealism premised upon absolute knowledge; Marx was a scientific naturalist for whom knowledge was neither delivered nor given but socially developed. For Hegel history was the

[68]   Ibid., 211.

autobiography of God; for Marx it was the collective pursuit of human ends.

Yet there were also continuities between Hegel and Marx. Each opposed the abstract ethical idealism of Jesus, Kant, and others, calling it utopian: "Because it endangered the stability of the state, Hegel stamped it as a revolutionary doctrine; because it hampered militant class activity, Marx condemned it as incipiently counter-revolutionary." Each opposed social atomism, refusing to dissociate the individual from the whole. Each contended that different aspects of society—education, religion, art, law—could not be isolated entirely, although they required distinction in analysis. For each, moreover, society was a whole, though they differed on the scope of that totality: "The notion of 'active totality' in Marx differs from the 'absolute whole perpetually renewing itself' in Hegel in that the Marxian totality is social and limited by other totalities, while the Hegelian totality is metaphysical and unlimited."[69]

Marx's dialectical method, often taken to establish his identity with Hegel, had been sorely misunderstood, Hook maintained. The importance of the triad in dialectics had been greatly inflated, for example: "It is not so much the number of phases a situation has which makes it dialectical but a specific relation of *opposition* between those phases which generates a succession of other phases." Unlike Hegel, Hook further argued, Marx meant to employ dialectical understanding in his analysis of the *social*, not natural, world. Social development, he asserted, was for Marx powered by conflict and opposition, which in their resolution established continuity through the denial of certain aspects and the preservation of others. In this sense alone, not some metaphysical process inherent in the nature of things, did Marx share Hegel's dialectical method.[70]

In two closing chapters on Ludwig Feuerbach, the last of the young German radicals to influence Marx's intellectual development, Hook gave further attention to Marx's method. Feuerbach, a leading critic of religion in the 1840s, had a profound effect upon Marx. He held that spiritual flights of fancy caused dehumanization and that sensory experience, not logic or reason, was the main criterion of experience. Although Feuerbach had often been portrayed as a vulgar materialist, Hook demonstrated that he was actually a critic of any claim that all intellectual activity could be explained in purely physical categories. Only *after* Marx's break from him did Feuerbach swallow a strictly physiological interpretation of being, coining the phrase "you are what you eat" and meaning it quite literally. The only men-

---

[69] Ibid., 47, 62. This statement might have been an implicit corrective to the rather sweeping treatment of totality by Lukács in *History and Class Consciousness* (1923). Certainly, along with Hook's comments on dialectics, it helps to distinguish their positions.

[70] Hook, *From Hegel to Marx*, 61.

tion of Dewey in the entire text of *From Hegel to Marx* came in connection with Feuerbach: Feuerbach at his best, Hook wrote, had upheld the idea that had inspired "humanistic movements from the days of Protagoras to those of Dewey," a vision forged with "reference to an undefined natural and social whole of which man is an organic part, and which without impinging on his individual freedom, lifts him to a consciousness of a common lot and destiny with other men."[71]

That Marx shared Feuerbach's naturalism and humanism between 1841 and 1844, argued Hook, was clear from *The Holy Family*. Only in the unpublished document that Marx left to the "gnawing of the mice," *The German Ideology* (1845–46), did he definitively break from Feuerbach, though still defending him against some of the objections of Bauer and Stirner. Marx, wrote Hook, was like Feuerbach in that he called for "a reconstruction of philosophy as a method of approaching the practical problems of men," regarded "human beings in their empirical contexts as the carriers of the cultural process," and explained "the false traditional conceptions of the world in terms of fetishistic expressions of activities unconsciously engaged in at different times and periods." The difference between them was that Marx retained the rational kernel of Hegel's dialectical method. He embraced Feuerbach's materialism as a corrective to idealism, but he also identified the chief defect of hitherto existing materialism: its neglect of human activity. Theory was significant, but not in the role assigned to it by the Young Hegelians or, before them, the entire tradition of continental philosophy: as a "higher," independent activity. Through *praxis,* wrote Hook, in a passage steeped in pragmatist sensibility, Marx reconceived both theory and practice: "A theory was a guide to action; practice, the specific activities which had to be carried out to test the thesis." Feuerbach's abstract call for communism, Marx had insisted, was nothing without connection to political organization. Pure criticism was impotent. The point was to *change,* not merely interpret, the world.[72]

Even today, *From Hegel to Marx* is important in its method of approach, for very few studies consider the mediating influence of the Young Hegelians of the 1830s and 1840s upon the young Marx; most jump straight from Hegel to Marx.[73] Hook translated lengthy passages of *The Holy Family* and *The German Ideology* into English for the first time and appended them to the book, as he had done with Engels's letters in *Towards the Understanding of Karl Marx*. Although *From Hegel to Marx* barely mentioned the "Economic and Philosophic Manuscripts of 1844," which had

---

71 Ibid., 254.
72 Ibid., 272, 281.
73 The chief exception is David McLellan, *The Young Hegelians and Karl Marx* (London: Macmillan, 1969).

been published in German a short time before, the book in all other respects was a striking anticipation of the "discovery" of the early Marx several decades later.[74]

Rather than distorting his understanding of Marx or deadening his revolutionary ardor, then, philosophical pragmatism combined with exhaustive research and rigorous standards of scholarship had enabled Hook to uncover and trace the development of Marx's early thinking in a fashion that would subsequently be confirmed by the community of scholars. *From Hegel to Marx* recovered the active, revolutionary, philosophical side of Marx's historical materialism in a decade that tended to favor productive forces and economic determinants over all other features of Marx's social theory. In Hook's life, the work takes on an additional significance, for *From Hegel to Marx* would prove to be his last full-length scholarly contribution as a revolutionary socialist, a final moment in his long period of commitment to radical philosophy and revolutionary political engagement.

[74] For a more extensive analysis of the book's reception and its place in the history of ideas, including a comparative treatment of Hook's approach and subsequent examinations of the young Marx, see Christopher Phelps, "Foreword to the Morningside Edition" in *From Hegel to Marx,* xi–xxx.

CHAPTER FOUR

Twilight of Revolution, 1936–38

As the shadows lengthened on the 1930s, Hook would reconsider and, eventually, repudiate the tenets of the revolutionary Marxism he had advocated and refined throughout his adult life. The decisive episode in dislodging him was the appalling spectacle of the Moscow trials in the late 1930s, but their effect was cumulative, not instantaneous. Initially, Hook held fast to his position that Stalin's regime was counterrevolutionary, that neither Marxism nor Bolshevism was responsible for the Soviet Union's bureaucratic degeneration, that the flagrant violation of liberal juridical norms on display in the Moscow courts between 1936 and 1938 were the antithesis of socialist revolution. He argued powerfully against a new batch of cries from liberals, conservatives, and radicals alike that the "amorality" of Marxism bore ultimate responsibility for Stalin's terror. Over time, however, the psychological and political tailspin of the New York anti-Stalinist left had its effect on him. In the face of repeated revelations about the magnitude of Stalin's atrocities, he began to revise, ever so slightly, his earlier assessment of the Russian Revolution and to test the thesis that Lenin, Trotsky, and other left-wing revolutionaries had after 1917 established a dictatorial, repressive political culture that eased Stalin's rise to power, even if their regime was not as terrible in scope as Stalin's. That reconsideration need not have ended in a retreat from revolutionary aims; it might even have resulted in a more sophisticated expression of Marxist views. But as Hook revisited a number of gnawing questions about Marxism and moral philosophy, he gradually revised his stance on the relationship of means to ends, signaling a retreat from militancy. By late 1938 he had gone so far as to embrace the view that Bolshevism, Stalinism, and fascism were all forms of "totalitarianism," a formidable modern despotism. Although this theory bore some relation to his earlier political ideas, it entailed at the same time the adoption of a new political perspective that introduced into his thinking many ideas he had long criticized.

At issue is not the word "totalitarian" itself, perfectly legitimate when used with limited scope to describe terroristic political states governed by single parties and ruled by dictators. The detour of socialist and liberal social theory in the late 1930s lay rather in elevating totalitarianism from a political *comparison* to the status of a central *category* capable of explaining the dynamics of societies ruled by such governments, blurring distinctions between them and within them. This specific theory of totalitarianism obliterated capitalism and class exploitation as the foremost concerns of socialist thought. Thus the activities of intellectuals like Hook started to revolve around an axis of totalitarianism versus democracy rather than capitalism versus socialism. Embrace of the doctrine of totalitarianism cast in this way marked Hook's transition from anti-Communism to anti-communism, dulling the edge of his democratic radicalism even as he spoke ever more ardently and abstractly of freedom and liberty. In the end, Hook no longer opposed Stalinism and capitalism equally on democratic and socialist grounds. He came to see capitalist democracy as an imperfect but worthy partner in the struggle against fascism and Communism, and criticism of capitalism consequently receded in his politics.[1]

Socialist Convergence, 1936

Hook had kept clear of membership in any socialist organization after steering the American Workers Party into the merger with the Trotskyists at the very end of 1934. He did not retreat into an exclusively professional life, however, for he remained politically engaged, especially in protesting the practices of the Communist Party from a revolutionary perspective. In January 1935 he challenged the playwright John Howard Law-

[1] For astute criticism of the equation of Communism and fascism under the doctrine of "totalitarianism" and its historical consequences for radicalism, see Howard Brick, *Daniel Bell and the Decline of Intellectual Radicalism* (Madison: University of Wisconsin Press, 1986), 30–36; and Julius Jacobson, "Reflections on Communism and Fascism," in *Socialist Perspectives,* ed. Phyllis Jacobson and Julius Jacobson (Princeton: Karz-Cohl, 1983), 119–54. For a defense of the theory, see Irving Howe, "The New York Intellectuals," in *Decline of the New* (New York: Harcourt, Brace & World, 1970), 228–29.

son to a debate over Lawson's public declaration that summary executions carried out in the Soviet Union were "necessary and admirable." But Lawson declined on the grounds that "your views are based upon a special interpretation of 'Marxism' which has no significance to the majority of the working class or the majority of sympathetic intellectuals, and an argument on the subject would therefore have only the most limited academic interest." In the summer of 1935 Hook wrote to Harry F. Ward, the national chairman of the American League against War and Fascism, a group closely associated with the Communist Party, to call upon the league to condemn the actions of CP members who had broken up meetings of other socialist organizations. Hook maintained that any group sincerely opposed to war and fascism should stand against terror of any sort exerted against working-class groups, and that a statement would be particularly powerful if it came from an association so closely allied with the CP. "My motive," Hook wrote, "is to bring hooliganism in the working-class movement to an end, and the simple premise of my addressing you as President of the American League is that you still believe—and are prepared to act upon—the ethical, political and social principles you have often and eloquently expressed." Ward, as one could have safely predicted, declined to take up the matter, ostensibly because he thought Hook's complaint more suitable for the American Civil Liberties Union.[2]

Throughout the mid-1930s Hook stayed sympathetic to the organization he had helped to create: the Workers Party of the United States. In his autobiography he stressed how far his feelings had been from "any organizational sympathy with the Trotskyists" in 1936, but that recollection was distorted. Although their philosophical dispute in 1933 showed that he did not treat Leon Trotsky with the idolatry of some of his American followers, Hook had also expressed admiration for Trotsky as the finest Marxist mind in the world, supported his aim of a Fourth International, and collaborated with his followers in the AWP-CLA merger. And even though Hook abstained from membership in the successive Trotskyist groups, had reservations about what he perceived as their dogmatic and sectarian tendencies, and did not attend their forums or functions, he was nevertheless part of a revolutionary anti-Stalinist intellectual milieu in New York for which Trotskyism was the political center. Intellectuals appreciative of the moral and political qualities of Trotsky were also attracted to the movement's connection to the working class and American revolutionary traditions. That link was personified in leaders such as James P. Cannon, who, though overly dependent on Trotsky for theoretical guidance, was a com-

[2] John Howard Lawson to SH, 22 January 1935 (Hook Papers, box 19); SH to Harry F. Ward, 18 August 1935, and Harry F. Ward to SH, 28 October 1935 (Hook Papers, box 5).

petent administrator with a shrewd strategic mind and venerable history as a Kansas-born Irish American organizer for the Industrial Workers of the World, and who had helped to establish the Communist and Trotskyist movements.[3]

Hook's consistent collaboration with the Trotskyists on political matters earned him their gratitude. In June 1935, for instance, he traveled to Cedar Crest College in Allentown, Pennsylvania, with his friend Felix Morrow, who by then was working on behalf of the Non-Partisan Labor Defense (NPLD), a nominally independent group closely associated with the WP-US. In Allentown, Hook spoke passionately before an audience of 250 on behalf of Winslow Haslett, a mathematics professor fired from Cedar Crest because of his labor activism. Hook deplored the incident as yet another case when "school officials, too stupid to understand the sanctity of free institutions, and too cowardly to defy influential red-baiters, fail[ed] to uphold traditional freedom of speech and opinion." He also lent the Trotskyists his skills in a capacity beyond civil libertarianism. In a January 1936 letter Cannon wrote that he was "very thankful" for Hook's "suggestions and advice," which he always found useful, and assured Hook of "our deep appreciation."[4]

Hook's philosophical forays against Communism, too, had been conducted in such a way as to place him very close to Trotsky's contention that dialectical materialism had been corrupted at the hands of Stalinism. Hook continued to argue from a perspective informed by pragmatism, with a corresponding emphasis upon provisional truth and action over absolutism, but he considered such tenets compatible with dialectical materialism. In a 1936 review of *Introduction to Dialectical Materialism* by August Thalheimer—a German Communist who, though expelled from the KPD

[3]   Hook, *Out of Step* (New York: Harper & Row, 1987), 224; interview with Mark Sharron, 28 August 1993; *James P. Cannon as We Knew Him*, by Thirty-Three Comrades, Friends, and Relatives (New York: Pathfinder, 1976).
[4]   Cannon's wording makes it clear that his thanks was for Hook's advice in general, not merely regarding the unspecified matter at hand: James P. Cannon to SH, 27 January 1936 (Hook Papers, box 132). Also pertinent is SH to V. F. Calverton, n.d. (V. F. Calverton Papers, New York Public Library, Hook Correspondence), most likely from 1935, in which Hook, after ribbing Calverton for being "in cahoots with the Japanese Emperor (cf. the Daily Worker, etc.)" and pillorying J. B. Matthews's candidacy for assemblyman on the New Jersey Democratic Party ticket ("such is the fate of all Stalinists—and reformists"), concludes: "The future belongs to the W.P.—don't you think?" The meaning is ambiguous. Hook may have been sincere, since the raison d'être of the WP-US was the kind of criticism of the Communist Party, Democratic Party, and reformists that he had just been conducting. But he may have been wryly pointing out the bleakness of the situation, since the WP-US was so small and beleaguered. It is impossible to prove either interpretation. On the Allentown free speech fight, see Winslow Haslett to SH, 8 June 1935 (Hook Papers, box 132); "Mass Meeting Raps Ouster of Teacher," *Philadelphia Record* (7 June 1935); "Prof Firing Stirs Mass Protests," *Philadelphia Post* (6 June 1935); "Voice Protest over Dismissal of Dr. Haslett," *Allentown Morning Call* (6 June 1935), 1, 16.

on political grounds, remained philosophically Stalinist—Hook called dialectical materialism "the great doctrinal mystery of Marxism," since it had "received more varied interpretation, in an extensive foreign literature, than any other aspect of Marx's thought." Rather than reject the concept, however, Hook argued that dialectical materialism in Thalheimer's hands was twisted, incorrectly, into monism and orthodoxy, as well as a "cosmic evolutionary optimism according to which the dialectical processes in nature and society make the realization of communism inevitable." The challenge was to recapture Marx's original meaning and to rescue it from the rigid orthodoxy that had replaced it: "Properly understood, dialectical materialism is a form of historical, experimental naturalism which stresses the role of human activity, under determined conditions, in transforming the social world. The fatal weakness of orthodox dialectical materialism is that although it recognizes the important, even if limited, function of human intelligence and activity in transforming the world, it stresses metaphysical dogmas according to which intelligence is either unnecessary or impossible."[5]

This political and ideological proximity to Trotskyism made Hook privy to the movement's most important undertaking. Beginning in June 1935, only half a year after the party's creation, WP-US leaders began to consult him about their hopes for bringing about a merger with the Socialist Party. This maneuver, known to Trotskyists as a "French turn" because the Fourth Internationalists in France had already done the same thing, was sought by Cannon (at first in a minority) as a means of reaching the dynamic left wing of the Socialists before the layer of youthful militants was lost to Stalinist or reformist pressures. On a July 3, 1935, James Burnham, Hook's collaborator on the AWP-CLA merger and NYU colleague, now a leading Trotskyist, wrote him, "You will be able to do a great deal with the SP business—and it may be that you and I should work out a few plans along those lines in confidence." Keep the merger proposal secret, Burnham warned Hook, but sound out the views of the Socialist leadership. Late in life Hook would often aver, as with his subsequent recollections of the AWP-CLA merger of 1934, that he had been tricked by the Trotskyists; they had promised him, he alleged, not to form a faction in the Socialist Party if he helped them gain entry. Yet in a July 15, 1935, letter Burnham unabashedly told Hook that the Trotskyist aim was to "build and strengthen something of a real left nucleus within the SP." Burnham proposed that the two of them form an action team to bring about the unification, with Hook working on the SP and its youth affiliate—the Young People's So-

---

5 Hook, "Revolutionary Mythology," review of *Introduction to Marxism* by August Thalheimer, *The Nation* 142 (4 March 1936): 288–90. On Thalheimer, see Robert Alexander, *The Right Opposition* (Westport, Conn.: Greenwood, 1981), 135–55.

cialist League (YPSL)—while Burnham built support for the move within the WP-US. Hook was a shrewd choice for the task. Although critical of the Socialist Party throughout the decade, he had been on cordial terms with Norman Thomas since 1931, when he had sent the perennial Socialist presidential candidate one of his articles on Marx. Hook had also received admiring letters from the Socialist Party's Pennsylvania state organizer in 1932 and its national labor secretary, Paul Porter, in 1934. His independence from organizational attachments, moreover, meant that he could serve as a credible bridge from the Trotskyists to the Socialists.[6]

In the end, Hook proved crucial to the Trotskyists' ambition. He wrote to Thomas urging that the Socialist Party admit members of the WP-US as equal members. The Communist Party's "social patriotism" would hasten the drive to war if it took control of the labor movement, and only a merger would stop the SP from being swamped organizationally and ideologically by the CP. The SP would also benefit from having a new range of WP-US sympathizers to draw upon, including Louis Hacker, Max Eastman, John Dos Passos, Lionel Abel, and Lionel Trilling. Hook next invited Thomas and Cannon to his apartment on Barrow Street in Greenwich Village, where they laid the foundation for the final fusion. The Trotskyists agreed to suspend publication of *The Militant* and the *New International* and to enter the SP as individuals, rather than in the form of a group merger. In March 1936 the great majority at the national convention of the WP-US voted to disband and entered the Socialist Party.[7]

[6] Burnham-Hook collaboration: Burnham to SH, 8 June 1935 (Hook Papers, box 132); Burnham to SH, 3 and 15 July 1935 (Hook Papers, box 8); Rorty to SH, 6 July 1936 (Hook Papers, box 132). For later on allegations of Trotskyist bad faith, see Hook, *Out of Step*, 224; SH to Alan Wald, 23 September 1988 (Wald Collection). Socialist Party contacts: Paul Porter to SH, 14 November 1934 (Hook Papers, box 159); Arthur G. McDonnell to SH, 12 February 1932 (Hook Papers, box 40, folder 13).
[7] The resistance came from two small groups: the first, around Hugo Oehler, was expelled from the WP-US in October 1935; the second, including A. J. Muste, Albert Glotzer, and Martin Abern, went along with the entry. Norman Thomas's biographers affirm Hook's crucial role but also imply, erroneously, that Hook was a member of the Trotskyist organization at the time. Bernard K. Johnpoll, *Pacifist's Progress: Norman Thomas and the Decline of American Socialism* (1970; Westport, Conn.: Greenwood, 1987), 180, writes that there were "continual negotiations between Norman Thomas and the Trotskyite leaders, chief among them Sidney Hook, a professor of philosophy at New York University, Max Shachtman, and James P. Cannon. Hook acted as an intermediary between Cannon and Thomas." W. A. Swanberg, *Norman Thomas* (New York: Scribner, 1976), 192, writes that "the entry of some 300 Trotskyites into the Socialist Party was effected early in 1936 through the mediation of Sidney Hook, professor of philosophy at New York University, one of their number." Hook was indeed the intermediary, but he was neither a member of the WP-US nor a Trotskyist in the complete ideological sense, given his philosophical differences with Trotsky. Hook was, to be precise, a WP-US sympathizer whose revolutionary Marxism and opposition to Stalinism placed him closer to Trotskyism than to any other organized current. On his letter to Thomas and final merger agreement, see M. S. Venkataramani, "Leon Trotsky's Adventure in American Radical Politics, 1935–37," *International Review of Social History* 9 (1964): 10.

The unification inadvertently brought about a welcome reconvergence with John Dewey. Dewey's political hopes of the late 1920s and early 1930s had been invested in a radically democratic middle-class liberalism expressed in independent groups such as the Farmer-Labor Party of Minnesota. When no national campaign congealed out of such coalitions in 1936, he endorsed Socialist candidate Norman Thomas. Though arriving by different routes, Hook and Dewey both supported the stated aims of the SP and endorsed its 1936 presidential campaign. Mentor and student appeared closer in politics than ever before.[8]

With an enthusiasm unmatched since the days of the League of Professional Groups for Foster and Ford, Hook threw himself behind Thomas. He did not join the SP, but in his writing he extolled the instrument of the revolutionary party. In the October 1936 issue of the Socialist Party's theoretical journal, the *American Socialist Monthly,* Hook underscored the crucial function of the "political party in educating, organizing and leading the masses, and in supplying a principle of continuity in the vicissitudes of struggle." In another article written late that year Hook stated, "One of the conditions which must be fulfilled before socialism can be realized is the presence of a political group with an appropriate program and will to action." Whatever his own personal reasons for holding back from joining the Socialist Party, his ardor for the importance of socialist organization, expressed in shades of Lenin, was undiminished.[9]

Hook devoted such energy to the presidential campaign that fall that Thomas wrote him a personal note of thanks for "immensely valuable help" in arranging a New York dinner on the candidate's behalf. Among other services, Hook pulled together "an organization of artists, thinkers and intellectuals for Thomas and Nelson," as he put it in a letter to V. F. Calverton. The pamphlet issued by the Thomas and Nelson Independent Committee, *Socialism in Our Time: A Challenge to Professionals and Intellectuals* (1936), was a call for professionals to commit themselves to revolutionary action, one remarkably consistent with that made by *Culture and the Crisis* four years before, except that in this instance the Socialist rather than the Communist Party was the standard-bearer of revolutionary hope. "The basic issue of our time," declared the pamphlet, "to which all other political and social issues are subordinate, is the issue of capitalism against socialism, the issue of the class struggle of the workers against their exploiters, for power and the achievement of socialism." Democratic Party reformism could not meliorate American capitalism in the long run, and

8   Robert Westbrook, *John Dewey and American Democracy* (Ithaca: Cornell University Press, 1991), 450–51.
9   Hook, "The Scope of Marxian Theory," *American Socialist Monthly* 5 (October 1936): 28–33; Hook, "Marxism and Values," *Marxist Quarterly* 1 (January–March 1937): 40–41.

"what social reform cannot do, social revolution must." The Popular Front was wholly ineffectual as a remedy for fascism, because "reliance on capitalist democracy, in place of a positive struggle for Socialism, far from being a bulwark against Fascism, in the end permits or even leads to Fascism." *Socialism in Our Time* excoriated the Communist Party for its erratic politics, cult of infallibility, suppression of dissent, and dogma in the arts and sciences, and called for wresting state power from the capitalists and replacing them with democratically elected councils of workers.[10]

That was a program and rationale quite unusual in the Socialist Party's history after its 1919 split, harking back to the wartime politics of class struggle in the era of Eugene V. Debs and Hook's high school days. Hook's accord with Dewey and support for Thomas in the campaign of November 1936, in short, should not be misconstrued as an embrace of social democracy. *Socialism in Our Time* was avowedly revolutionary. Even though Dewey continued to place a greater faith in the middle class than did Hook, he too was unquestionably radical at the time, calling for the socialization of the commanding heights of the economy and criticizing the New Deal for its collaboration with big business. Some Socialists, including Norman Thomas, were social democrats pushed leftward by the atmosphere of the Depression, but many who backed his campaign in 1936—including the Thomas and Nelson Independent Committee—were genuinely revolutionary.

In the early 1930s Hook and other revolutionaries had criticized the SP for its milk-and-cookies gradualism. By 1936, however, the Socialist Party appeared quite different. It stood substantially to the left of the piecemeal New Deal; its right-wing Old Guard had split away to form the Social-Democratic Federation in early 1936 after a young layer known as "the Militants" had forced more radical planks in the SP's domestic program. The party's left wing had been further strengthened by the entry of the Trotskyists in March. The Thomas and Nelson Independent Committee included some holdovers from Thomas's 1932 campaign, among them Dewey, Reinhold Niebuhr, Robert Morss Lovett, and Freda Kirchwey. But it also included three—Sidney Hook, James Rorty, and Meyer Schapiro—whose names had appeared on the pro-Communist *Culture and the Crisis* in 1932, plus many revolutionary Marxist intellectuals: John Wheelwright, George Novack, Sherry Mangan, James T. Farrell, V. F. Calverton, Max

---

[10]   Hook received both the generic letter sent out to all key supporters and a personal note from Thomas: Norman Thomas to SH, 4 November 1936 (Hook Papers, box 26); SH to V. F. Calverton (V. F. Calverton Papers, New York Public Library, Hook Correspondence). *Socialism in Our Time: A Challenge to Professionals and Intellectuals* (New York: Thomas and Nelson Independent Committee, 1936) may have been written by Hook, but the authorship was anonymous.

Eastman, James Burnham. Meanwhile, the Communist Party, ultrarevolutionary in the early 1930s, had begun to forge Popular Fronts between Communists and liberals against fascism and war. This about-face from hypermilitance to accommodation with liberalism meant that the Socialist Party, once scorned by Communists as cowardly and reformist, was left virtually alone on the radical scene in 1936 in arguing uncompromisingly for class struggle against capitalism and socialist revolution as the only permanent solution to fascism and imperialist war. Although it retained a noticeable social democratic layer, especially at the leadership level, the Socialist Party also contained the strongest concentration of revolutionary socialist forces in the United States.

The Trotsky Defense Committee, 1936–37

In August 1936 a political trial opened in Moscow which, in combination with the three trials that followed in the next two years, would stun the world. In the docks of the accused stood almost every one of the surviving luminaries of the October Revolution, charged with betraying the struggle they had led. Grigori Zinoviev, Lev Kamenev, and many second-tier Bolshevik leaders were accused of industrial sabotage, counterrevolutionary espionage, and assassination plots against loyal Soviet officials. Leon Trotsky, although he was not present at the trials and had not even been in the Soviet Union during the period when the crimes were allegedly perpetrated, was charged in absentia with organizing and directing the campaign of anti-Soviet terrorism through a secret alliance with Nazi Germany and with the aid of his son in Western Europe. None of the defendants mounted any protest against the charges; rather, they confessed fully and called for the direst punishment possible. Ghastly at the time, the trials appear even more ghastly now, when they are known to have been merely the most visible aspect of a society-wide purge in which millions of people were arrested and executed by administrative decree.[11]

It is therefore difficult to fathom how the Moscow trials could have been widely defended by liberal intellectuals in the United States. Although the apologists were in all cases sympathetic to the Soviet Union, few were Communist partisans. Most were liberals enamored of the technological and economic achievements of the USSR during a decade of global economic collapse. Above all, they apologized for the show trials because of their fear

[11]   On the Moscow trials, see Alan Wald, *The New York Intellectuals: The Rise and Decline of the Anti-Stalinist Left from the 1930s to the 1980s* (Chapel Hill: University of North Carlinia Press, 1987), 128; A. Y. Vyshinsky, *Trotskyism: In the Service of Fascism against Socialism and Peace* (New York: Workers Library, 1936); Robert C. Tucker and Stephen F. Cohen, eds., *The Great Purge Trial* (New York: Grosset & Dunlap, 1965).

John Dewey as chairman of the Commission of Inquiry, Mexico, April 1937. (Courtesy Special Collections, Morris Library, Southern Illinois University.)

Leon Trotsky and Diego Rivera at the Dewey Commission hearings, Mexico, April 1937. (Courtesy Special Collections, Morris Library, Southern Illinois University.)

that fascism was ascendant. Fascism, they believed, could most readily be defeated by the kind of broad strategic alliances of Communists and liberals exemplified by the Spanish and French Popular Fronts, and questioning the Moscow trials would risk destroying the singularly important coalition. Socialist novelist Upton Sinclair, for example, answered Hook's objections to his defense of the Moscow trials with the declaration that "fascism is the enemy of our time and Russia is one of the principal allies we have to depend upon." Sinclair rejected the proposition that "several score trained revolutionaries could be induced by any method whatsoever to go into court and admit actions which they had not committed."[12]

For dissident socialists, the trials brought sharply into focus the consequences of Stalin's reign for the character of the Soviet Union. James T. Farrell, a novelist who began in this period to reconsider his favorable disposition toward the Communist Party, later recalled their momentous character: "If the official version of the trials were true, then the co-workers of Lenin and leaders of the Bolshevik Revolution must be considered as one of the worst gangs of scoundrels in history; if the Trials were a frame-up, then the leaders of Soviet Russia were perpetuating one of the most monstrous frameups in all history." Frame-up it was. To Trotsky, the idealization of and compromise with Stalin's rule by fellow-traveling middle-class liberals in the capitalist democracies was merely a confirmation of the Soviet bureaucracy's antirevolutionary character; the more conservative the bureaucratic stratum in the Soviet Union became in defense of its privilege, the more enamored of it bourgeois intellectuals became.[13]

Because of his longstanding opposition to the Stalin bureaucracy, Sidney Hook was predisposed to skepticism when the Moscow trials opened. He had already been approached earlier that year by Trotskyist acquaintances—first Felix Morrow, then Herbert Solow—and had agreed to assist in whatever way he could the newly established American Committee for the Defense of Leon Trotsky. Early in its life the committee was committed primarily to securing the right of safe asylum for the exiled revolutionary leader, who had been hounded mercilessly from country to country since his expulsion from the Soviet Union in 1929. Hook's most important mission for the committee was his solicitation of John Dewey's endorsement. There is no doubt that Hook was crucial to securing Dewey's participation, because even on such a decisive issue and even for his favorite student, Dewey dragged his feet. On April 4 he wrote to Hook, "If the request had come from anyone else I would have refused at once—I am more than dis-

[12] Upton Sinclair to SH, 22 and 30 March 1938 (Hook Papers, box 27). See also Wald, *The New York Intellectuals*, 129.
[13] James T. Farrell, "Dewey in Mexico," in *John Dewey*, ed. Sidney Hook (New York: Dial, 1950), 358.

tracted, I am irritated by the no. of things I've got into—I'm caught in the many-toothed jaw. Can you have mercy on my soul?" No mercy was forthcoming, and Hook soon persuaded Dewey to endorse the right of political asylum for Trotsky as well as the call for the embattled Marxist dissident's right to a fair hearing to respond to the charges leveled against him in Moscow.[14]

Dewey's affiliation was vital to the Trotsky defense effort. In an era when most liberal intellectuals saw the Soviet Union as either an advanced form of civilization worthy of admiration or a crucial partner in the overriding antifascist struggle of the moment, Dewey's name gave the campaign credibility that it would not otherwise have had. The central administrative figures of the committee, George Novack and Felix Morrow, were committed to Trotsky's political program, but in order to appeal to a wider audience, the committee needed a steering directorate comprising independent intellectuals of considerable stature. Hook, who had agreed to serve on the executive committee, again played an indispensable role as go-between. His friendship with Dewey guaranteed him a friendly ear, and his political history as a dissident revolutionary socialist gave him a ready empathy for Trotsky.[15]

After winning Dewey's endorsement, Hook had to reassure his mentor repeatedly of the legitimacy of the project. On November 16, 1936, Dewey wrote to Hook that his patience was wearing thin with the Trotskyists, for in his view they were blurring the distinction between defending Trotsky's right to a fair hearing and defending his politics:

> I was willing to sign the statement about Trotsky's right to a public hearing, although I have no sympathy with what seems to me to be his abstract ideological fanaticism—But I do not think it fair to me as a signer that the headquarters of the Trotsky faction in this country should circulate that letter in connection with an attack upon the entire Moscow Trial. I certainly would not have put my signature to a document containing some statements that

[14] JD to SH, 4 April, n.y. (Hook Papers, box 174). In *Out of Step,* 224–25, Hook mentions discussions also with Morrow and Solow. No correspondence survives, but his recollection is in accord with the formation of the committee as reconstructed by Wald in *The New York Intellectuals,* 130—except for his recollection that he was responsible for convincing Norman Thomas to join the committee. Wald reports that James Burnham, Max Shachtman, and George Novack were assigned by the Trotskyists to confer with SP leaders Thomas and Devere Allen. Also, Hook recalls that Thomas was hesitant to commit to the effort because of the "deceptive factional practices of the Trotskyists," but the faction fight that led to the split between the Trotskyists and the SP did not really erupt until the following summer.
[15] Max Shachtman, who credited Hook with securing Dewey's involvement, explained that Hook "was rather friendly to us at the time": "The Reminiscences of Max Shachtman," 1963 (Columbia University Oral History Research Office), 291.

are made in the *Nation* article. I should certainly have not signed the statement if I had anticipated the use to be made of it. I am not writing you this because I hold you responsible for this use, but because I signed in response to your letter & I don't know who else to write.

In a subsequent letter Dewey expressed further doubts. He had attended a dinner party. When the conversation turned to a discussion of the Trotsky case, some of the other guests criticized the committee's name. "Of course," Dewey wrote, "Defense Committee is the usual name for all Committees that are trying to enable a fair defense. . . . But in this case, they are insisting that the name means that we are engaged in the defense of Trotsky in a way that assumes his innocence—it is probable that aside from those who want to discredit the Com. this appearance has caused misunderstanding among those who are otherwise fairminded."[16]

In the end Hook persuaded Dewey to shelve his second thoughts. Not only did Dewey's name remain on the letterhead of the American Committee for the Defense of Leon Trotsky, but in early 1937 Dewey agreed to head the Provisional Commission of Inquiry into the Charges Made against Leon Trotsky in the Moscow Trials. The Preliminary Commission, a special international subgroup of the Provisional Commission, made plans to hold hearings in Mexico, where Trotsky had obtained asylum in January 1937, so that the whole body could compare his testimony with the charges lodged against him by the defendants' confessions in Moscow.

Not all were as willing to endorse the inquiry as Dewey. Albert Einstein, whose endorsement of the defense effort Hook solicited in February 1937, chose a route—evasion of responsibility—more typical of those asked to lend their names to the call for a fair hearing. Einstein agreed that "every accused," including Trotsky, deserved "the opportunity to prove his innocence." But he was concerned about the paucity of competent jurists, and he refused to endorse the commission's effort on the grounds that the hearing would merely serve as a grandstand for Trotsky: "The question is raised because Trotsky is an extremely active and adroit politician, who might well search for an effective platform for the presentation and promulgation of his political goals in the public sphere . . . . I'm afraid that the only result would be Trotsky's own self-promotion without the possibility of a well-grounded judgment." Hook's further appeals to Einstein—including a personal visit to him in Princeton—fell on deaf ears, even though

[16] JD to SH, 16 November 1936 (Hook Papers, box 174); JD to SH, 12 March 1937 (Hook-Dewey Collection, box 1, folder 2). Hook's written responses, if any, do not survive; it is possible that he resolved Dewey's doubts in conversation.

the physicist privately told Max Eastman in June that the "confessions" in the Moscow trials were obviously bogus.[17]

Einstein's response represented one of many ways that prominent intellectuals of the time—even many of those who were confused or dismayed by the spectacle of defendants confessing to outlandish, far-fetched wrecking campaigns without a word of denial—declined to protest the fate of the Moscow victims. Those who did speak out were subjected to intense pressure. On February 16, 1937, for example, a letter appeared in the *New Masses,* the chief Communist literary journal, warning liberals on the Trotsky defense committee that they were being used; among the fifty signers were such leading writers and intellectuals as Lillian Wald, Heywood Broun, Max Lerner, Louis Fischer, Corliss Lamont, Robert S. Lynd, Theodore Dreiser, and Lillian Hellman. Committees members began to run into considerable flak. Corliss Lamont sent them articles from mass circulation magazines which corroborated the official version of the Moscow trials. Often, however, such tactics backfired. Louis Adamic, for example, had had doubts similar to those Dewey had raised about the dual meaning of "defense" in the committee's title and had resolved to resign from it—only to experience such a deluge of pressure from Stalinists and anti-Trotskyists to quit that he decided to stick it out. Mary McCarthy, after experiencing an identical wave of criticism, had an identical reaction.[18]

Most who signed up for the defense committee found their conscience pricked in the more conventional way: by concern for fairness, justice, and civil liberties. Hook expended a great deal of energy trying to rouse intellectuals' sense of responsibility. He even traveled to Connecticut to try, without success, to win over his old associate Matthew Josephson, a well-known Communist sympathizer. He wrote to Bertrand Russell, whose wife replied that he "agrees warmly with every word of the admirable statement about Trotsky which you enclosed" and promised that Russell would join the English committee. With this rash of activity and the broiling political atmosphere, Mary McCarthy recalled, the joke among New

[17] Albert Einstein to SH, 23 February 1937, trans. Joseph Fracchia (Hook Papers, box 12); SH to Einstein, 22 February and 10 March 1937 (Hook Papers, box 12); *Out of Step,* 462–66; Max Eastman, *Great Companions* (New York: Farrar, Straus & Cudahy, 1959), 33.

[18] Louis Adamic, *My America, 1928–1938* (New York: Harper, 1938), 82: "I seriously objected to the defense part of the name of the Trotsky Committee. Why did he need anybody's defense? Mine, for instance? Possessor of great literary ability, he was fully capable of writing a defense of himself. And so on." Adamic decided to remain a supporter despite his misgivings, in large part because of the harassment he had received. For the *New Masses* letter, see Alan Wald, *James T. Farrell* (New York: New York University Press, 1978), 64–67; on Mary McCarthy, Terry A. Cooney, *The Rise of the New York Intellectuals: Partisan Review and Its Circle* (Madison: University of Wisconsin Press, 1986), 102–3; see also Corliss Lamont to SH, 31 December 1937 (Hook Papers, box 18).

York intellectuals was that Hook "looked under the bed every night before retiring."[19]

But it was not Hook who convinced Dewey to serve as chairman of the Provisional Commission of Inquiry into the Charges Made against Leon Trotsky in the Moscow Trials. That was Dewey's own doing. Hook's recollection was that he offered Dewey no opinion on the matter, believing that the seventy-eight-year-old philosopher was best left to make the difficult decision on his own. He was sure to be subject to vilification and harassment, and his children vociferously opposed his participation in an undertaking that they considered dubious and dangerous. Furthermore, it would requie a much greater commitment on Dewey's part than had the American defense committee. Dewey would have to read voluminously, from both the Moscow trial records and Trotsky's writings, and that task, combined with the necessary journey to Mexico, was bound to be time-consuming and draining, forcing him to interrupt his work-in-progress, *Logic*, which he considered the culmination of his philosophical thought. Hook's acute knowledge of these complicating factors prevented Hook from unequivocally recommending that Dewey serve on the Provisional Commission. When Dewey asked Hook what he thought he should do, though, Hook conspicuously did not tell him *not* to serve, and many assumed that Hook was responsible when, in the end, Dewey agreed to take on the project. Dewey's son Fred, who had urged his father not to involve himself in the affair, was so furious that he pulled Hook aside one day and called him a "son of a bitch."[20]

The Commission of Inquiry, 1937

The mood was tense when the Preliminary Commission of Inquiry into the Charges Made against Leon Trotsky in the Moscow Trials—the Dewey Commission—convened in an outlying district of Mexico City in April 1937. The hearings were held in Trotsky's study at the villa of Diego Rivera, the Mexican muralist who had declared his allegiance to Trotsky's ideas. Since the charges of treason orchestrated by Stalin against Trotsky

[19] Matthew Josephson, *Infidel in the Temple* (New York: Knopf, 1967), 167–68; P. H. Russell to SH, 1 March 1937 (Leon Trotsky Papers, Harvard University); Mary McCarthy, *Intellectual Memoirs: New York, 1936–1938* (New York: Harcourt Brace Jovanovich, 1992), 41.
[20] A legend lingers in some quarters that James P. Cannon persuaded Dewey to serve; it is highly suspect, though Dewey did meet with Cannon once to hear his appeal. James T. Farrell, reported in his diary that Philip Rahv, a *Partisan Review* editor, saw Cannon drunk at a dinner party and bragging that he had won Dewey over by telling him it was his "moral duty" to serve on the commission (Wald, *James T. Farrell*, 68). But Hook (*Out of Step*, 227–28) recalls, plausibly, that Cannon's obsequious attempt to ingratiate himself with Dewey "almost scuttled the matter" and Cannon makes no mention of the episode in his semi-autobiographical *History of American Trotskyism* (New York: Pathfinder, 1972).

amounted essentially to a death sentence, anxiety ran high. Arriving travelers were enlisted to help carry and stack bricks to barricade the villa's windows. Trotsky's political associates served as bodyguards, their weapons in plain view during the proceedings. For a full week, in thirteen lengthy hearings, the assembled panel of intellectuals led by Dewey cross-examined Trotsky. Most of the questions—asked mainly by Albert Goldman, Trotsky's attorney, and Commission of Inquiry members Otto Ruehle, Benjamin Stolberg, Suzanne La Follette, and Carlton Beals—centered on Trotsky's written opinions regarding political terrorism and the nature of his proposal for political revolution in the Soviet Union. Trotsky presented evidence of his and his son's whereabouts and activities for the prior decade so as to demonstrate that neither one of them could have been at the meetings they were supposed to have held in Western Europe with German agents and the Moscow defendants. Neither Soviet lawyers nor representatives of the American or Mexican Communist Parties were in attendance, despite having been invited. Nonetheless, the hearings amounted to a virtual countertrial, permitting Trotsky to defend his innocence and rebut the allegations of Soviet prosecutors before a tribunal of independent minds.[21]

Dewey conducted his chairmanship duties with characteristic seriousness of mind. He opened the hearings with a condemnation of those nations that had denied asylum to Trotsky and a salute to Mexico for its courage and courtesy. He presided over the subsequent hearings alertly, occasionally interjecting searching questions. The novelist James T. Farrell, who accompanied Dewey on the train trip to the hearings, recalled years later, "All the way to Mexico he worked. He read completely through the documents. He went to Mexico more or less thinking that Stalin rather than Trotsky was right. On the basis of the evidence that Trotsky presented, plus what Dewey read on the Moscow trials, he came to the conclusion that Trotsky and the other defendants were right. However, he did not agree with Trotsky's political views." Other accounts suggest that before arriving in Mexico, Dewey had decided that the Moscow trials did not establish Trotsky's guilt but that neither could he be certain of Trotsky's innocence. In either case, Dewey was at first skeptical but by the end of the hearings had been persuaded of Trotsky's innocence. The rest of the commission agreed, although it did not release its first massive report until late in the year.[22]

[21] Rich accounts of the hearings may be found in Isaac Deutscher, *The Prophet Outcast* (New York: Oxford University Press, 1970), 371–82; Wald, *The New York Intellectuals*, 132–39; and Wald, *James T. Farrell*, 60–75. See also Preliminary Commission of Inquiry, *The Case of Leon Trotsky* (New York: Harper, 1937); and Commission of Inquiry, *Not Guilty* (New York: Harper, 1938).

[22] For Farrell's remarks, see Corliss Lamont, ed., *Dialogue on John Dewey* (New York: Horizon Press, 1959), 69.

To avoid even the appearance of impropriety, Dewey avoided any personal contact with Trotsky outside the hearing sessions for the duration of his stay in Mexico. This scrupulous, self-imposed code of conduct prevented him from exploring philosophical issues with Trotsky as fully as he would have liked, since the criminal charges at hand did not provide much latitude for debate over epistemology and metaphysics. "I should have liked to have a talk with Trotsky along the line of some of my questions," Dewey wrote to Hook that summer. "I saw he was not getting the drift as my questions were not strictly relevant to the hearings and [as] time was getting short, I didn't press them." Still, Dewey was just as impressed as Hook by Trotsky's brilliance: "You are right about Trotsky's summation. It was and is, I think, literature of high order."[23]

The admiration was mutual. Trotsky, in his summation, referred to Dewey as "the personification of genuine American idealism" and "a man of unshakable moral authority."[24] This reciprocal respect was sincere, not gushing. Neither man had suffered amnesia about their important political and philosophical differences. Their meeting stimulated both of them to reflect more deeply on the distinctions each made between Marxism and pragmatism. Within a year their differences would occasion a debate between them in the pages of the *New International*, the American Trotskyist journal. But Dewey's help in clearing Trotsky's name before the world entailed a limited rapprochement between the two figures that Hook both welcomed and sought to shield from attack. During 1937, Hook turned his political acumen to the task of defending the commission's verdict: "Not Guilty."

Even before its findings were declared, the Dewey Commission began to draw fire in the United States from both Communists and liberals sympathetic to Stalin's Soviet Union. In April 1937, as the commission began its work in Mexico, *New Republic* editor Malcolm Cowley reviewed G. L. Piatakov's *The Case of the Anti-Soviet Trotskyite Center*, a summary of the Soviet prosecution's allegations in the Moscow trials. Cowley, arguably the most sophisticated of fellow-traveling liberals, declared Trotsky guilty as charged, resting his judgment upon the confessions obtained in the Moscow trials. Hook replied in a searing letter printed two months later. In addition to noting that no material evidence supported the confessions of the accused, he blasted Cowley's assertion that Trotsky could be presumed guilty because he had called for a political revolution against the Stalinist bureaucracy. Hook suggested that there was a parallel between such specious attacks on Trotsky and right-wing anti-communism: "Since

[23] JD to SH, 14 August [1937?] (Hook-Dewey Collection, box 1, folder 2).
[24] Leon Trotsky, "Why and Wherefore These Trials?" in *The Case of Leon Trotsky*, by Preliminary Commission of Inquiry (New York: Harper, 1937), 585.

when does it follow that because an individual desires to overthrow a government, he therefore is guilty of arson, sabotage, espionage in the service of the enemy, and assassination? It is these crimes of which Trotsky has been accused and not of being opposed to the Stalin regime. On Mr. Cowley's view, it would be quite justified for an American patriot to charge members of the Communist Party with all sorts of crimes from arson to assassination merely because they desire to overthrow the government. This is precisely what Red-baiters do here, and what Hitler does in Germany."[25]

The rift between American intellectuals over the Moscow trials grew wider in late May when Dewey, who had been associated with the *New Republic* since its founding as the flagship journal of liberal opinion more than twenty years before, grew so despondent over its editorial campaign against a public hearing for Trotsky that he sent a letter of repudiation to editor Bruce Bliven. Dewey noted a contradiction in the *New Republic*'s approach to the Moscow trials: on one hand, it asserted that the trials were "not the affairs of American liberals"; on the other, it printed a disproportionate amount of material alleging the guilt of those tried. "I cannot understand how the Journal which identified liberalism with the spirit of full and free discussion could take the attitude of belittling in advance the attempt to give Mr Trotsky a full opportunity for a hearing," he wrote, adding that the magazine had "unconsciously if not deliberately" repeated "the familiar attitude of the CP in saying that some members of the Inquiry are Trotskyites. Unless believing that Trotsky has a right to a hearing is proof of being a Trotskyite no member of the Inquiry, including the five men on the French sub-commission, is or ever has been a Trotskyite." In protest, Dewey refused to write for the *New Republic* ever again.[26]

On behalf of the *New Republic*, Cowley responded with a personal letter expressing hope that Dewey would continue to contribute. He tried to impress Dewey with the disruptive character of Trotsky's supporters. Ever since the Trotskyists forced the dissolution of the League of Professional Groups, he alleged, they had promoted the malicious thesis "that because I didn't like Trotsky (which is certainly true) I was also a slave of Stalin and the Comintern (which certainly has very little to do with what I have written)." Cowley appealed to Dewey on the grounds that "estimates of one country or of one man should [not] be allowed to divide people who agree on so many other subjects." Yet somewhat contradictorily, he underscored his belief that Trotsky was "touched with paranoia, with delu-

[25] Malcolm Cowley, review of *The Case of the Anti-Soviet Trotskyite Center*, by G. L. Piatakov, *New Republic* 70 (7 April 1937): 267–70; Hook, "Both Their Houses," *New Republic* 91 (2 June 1937): 104.
[26] JD to Bruce Bliven, 26 May 1937 (Hook-Dewey Collection).

sions of persecution and grandeur." Though phrased with literary delicacy, Cowley's essential contention was that any criticism of the Soviet Union or Stalin was divisive and detrimental to the progressive movement. Dewey replied that his aim was to discern the truth, wherever it lay, especially given the monumental significance of the dispute: "As far as I personally am concerned, if it were merely a matter of Trotsky as an individual while I should have felt that he had a right to a hearing I shouldn't have engaged in the enterprise of an inquiry. I have plenty of other things to do. But with Russia and Soviet methods so constantly held up to us as a model for America, I think it is necessary for the clarification of American political thought and action that an honest effort be made to get at the truth."[27]

Another argument against Trotsky by a fellow-traveling liberal was advanced in the *Southern Review* that summer. Frederick Schuman, like many intellectuals favorably disposed toward Stalin, made a point of emphasizing his formal independence in order to lay claim to dispassionate assessment of the trials. "As a political scientist and a liberal," he assured his readers, "the writer abjures both Stalinism and Trotskyism and abhors dictatorship and terrorism in all their forms." Nonetheless, Schuman in the end defended an alliance with Stalin's USSR as a necessary bulwark against fascism, insisting that "the democratic West must, for its own security, dry its tears for fallen heroes and accept Moscow's hand." Like Cowley, Schuman argued that Trotsky's call for political revolution and justification of terror implied that he was probably guilty as charged. Schuman further maintained that the dispute was a factional division within Marxism which could not be decided from the vantage point of liberalism: "Moral judgments are here futile, even when made by liberal philosophers. Both Stalinism and Trotskyism, along with fascism, stand outside the ethics of liberalism. To make moral choices, to condemn either Trotsky or Stalin as unethical, is pointless. Both are Machiavellian."[28]

A series of comments and replies followed. Malcolm Cowley agreed that the issues raised by the Moscow trials were "political rather than moral" and that "liberals who get mixed up in the controversy on moral grounds are stooges and suckers." Carleton Beals, an expert on Latin America, had served on the Dewey Commission until its eleventh hearing, then quit and returned to the United States to denounce the hearings as a sham, creating suspicion among commission members that he had planned to do so all along in order to discredit the effort. In his comments on Schuman he

[27] Malcolm Cowley to JD, 4 June 1937, and JD to Cowley, 2 June 1937 (Hook-Dewey Collection, box 1, folder 2). Despite their dates, the second of these obviously followed the first.
[28] Frederick Schuman, "Leon Trotsky: Martyr or Renegade?" *Southern Review* 3 (Summer 1937): 51–74.

claimed that he had been "predisposed to Trotsky's favor before I went to Mexico" but was now convinced that the Moscow "confessions were not torture or drug confessions; that even if pressure were used, the confessions were bona fide and real." Others gave Schuman's performance a poorer rating. Max Eastman decried the "pretense to be a detached liberal" as "one of the everyday tricks of the Stalin propaganda." Eastman identified a long series of factual mistakes made by Schuman, amounting to a grossly erroneous portrayal of Trotsky, and objected to what he characterized as Schuman's effort to make Trotsky into a "rank extremist," noting that in *The Revolution Betrayed* (1937) Trotsky explained that he had been for a considerable time committed to "a policy of *reform within the party,* not revolution against it." James T. Farrell likewise cited "inaccuracy, prejudice, misinformation and misrepresentation on every page" and observed that Schuman had failed to recognize an elementary distinction in Trotsky's thought: Trotsky was an advocate of mass revolutionary action, which almost certainly would require force and violence, but he was also a severe critic of the kind of individual terrorism alleged in the Moscow trials.[29]

Hook entered the *Southern Review* fray with "Liberalism and the Case of Leon Trotsky," which dealt more thoroughly than had either Eastman or Farrell with the philosophical supposition of Schuman and Cowley that liberals could not make moral judgments regarding a dispute within Marxism or between Soviet leaders. "If we made no moral judgments," Hook responded, "we could only *describe* political affairs, we could never *rationally act* upon them. Those who say they have no use for moral judgments are really concealing their actual moral judgment: *viz.,* whatever is, is right." In support of Farrell's contention that Trotsky had never advocated the kind of terrorism with which he had been charged at the Moscow trials, Hook observed that Trotsky's pamphlet *In Defense of Terrorism* defended the Russian Revolution, not conspiratorial violence. Its title, Hook explained, was a play upon Karl Kautsky's *Terrorism and Communism,* the social democratic critique of revolutionary socialism to which Trotsky was responding. Hook also replied swiftly to Schuman's suggestion that Trotsky's strategic political defeats proved him wrong. Was not Hitler, asked Hook, a model of political shrewdness? In drawing this implicit comparison between Hitler and Stalin, Hook for the first time opened up a line of inquiry that would eventually become a major theme for him. He noted that even a spokesman for the French Foreign Office, a Popular Front socialist who approved of the Franco-Soviet pact, had called the Russian regime a "quasi-

---

[29] See Malcolm Cowley, Max Eastman, John Dewey, Carleton Beals, and James T. Farrell, "Correspondence," *Southern Review* 3 (Summer 1937): 199–208. Dewey's contribution was minimal; he simply stated that to do the piece justice he would have to draft a full-length article, not write a few comments.

Fascist state." "If this is true," Hook asked, "how can American liberals who are not indifferent to Fascism in Germany, Italy and Spain be indifferent to events in Russia?" At this germinal stage Hook did not equate Nazi Germany and the Soviet Union as manifestations of the same ideology or political system. He merely emphasized the striking similarity of their tactical methods—something Trotsky, too, had done in his testimony before the Dewey Commission.[30]

The liberal values of political liberty and open inquiry, which he thought were threatened by capitalism in a time of crisis, had always informed Hook's Marxism. That revolutionary theme was somewhat muted in his *Southern Review* intervention, however, and to depict the type of socialism he opposed he had begun to use the term "totalitarian," which would later be crucial in steering his politics in a rightward direction. "I do not pretend, like Mr. Schuman, to have no social opinions," wrote Hook in a cover letter accompanying his manuscript to the editors of *Southern Review.* "As far as doctrine is concerned I am a 'democratic, as distinct from a totalitarian, socialist.' If liberalism be defined as a wholehearted acceptance of the methods of scientific inquiry in all problems of social life, then I am a liberal in this sense and in no other."[31]

Marxism contra Stalinism, 1937

Because Hook's entire corpus argued that the values of democracy and scientific inquiry were perfectly compatible with revolutionary socialism, there was no reason to think that his criticism of the Moscow trials would precipitate a reconsideration of Marxism. From the first word of the Moscow trials in 1936 until early 1938, Hook kept up his involvement in Marxist intellectual projects. He was present at both the founding of the *Marxist Quarterly* and the reestablishment of *Partisan Review,* the best independent Marxist journals of the decade. He was an attentive observer of and participant in—albeit from the margin—developments within revolutionary socialist organizations. Even as the crackdown in the USSR became ever more grotesque and barbaric, Hook's objections to Stalinism re-

[30] Hook, "Liberalism and the Case of Leon Trotsky," *Southern Review* 3 (Autumn 1937): 267–82. That fall Hook also became involved in defending the Dewey Commission against the allegations of Carleton Beals, the defecting commissioner, who, Hook said, had not been reluctant to serve but had tried to "wreck and discredit" the hearings from the beginning. Hook, Beals replied, was "a fanatical Trotsky zealot" trying to use Dewey for "narrow factional purposes," whereas he (Beals) "truly" admired Dewey. Hook coolly shot back that Beals was "following the time-worn practice of attorneys who, having no case, can do nothing else but abuse the plaintiff." See untitled exchange among Hook, Beals, Schuman, and Farrell, *Southern Review* 3 (August 1937): 406–15.
[31] SH to Erskine, 12 August 1937 (Southern Review Papers, Yale University, Beinecke Rare Book and Manuscript Library).

mained thoroughly grounded in revolutionary Marxism, and in this respect his political standpoint in 1936–38 was Trotskyesque, if not Trotskyist.

Hook was never a doctrinal adherent of Trotskyism in the complete sense of the word, nor was he a member of any of the successive Trotskyist organizations of the late 1930s. But he was closer to that socialist tendency than to any other, both in the main contours of his thought and in his political activity. Hook lent his name and connections not only to Trotsky's legal defense but to the dissemination of Trotsky's political views. In a letter of late summer 1937 to *Southern Review*'s editors, Hook enclosed a rebuttal to Schuman that Trotsky had drafted, with a casual note that "some of Mr. Trotsky's friends" had asked him to forward it. "I have been told by some of Mr. Trotsky's friends," Hook repeated in his next letter to the *Southern Review* editors, "that he has some very fresh and striking material, as yet unpublished, on a variety of subjects, ranging from Pushkin whose centenary was just celebrated to the recent developments in the Red Army. And of course on Russia to-day and the Moscow trials. It ought not be difficult to get something from him particularly in view of the fair-mindedness you have shown in respect to the controversy about him."[32]

Hook's continuing proximity to Trotsky and his American followers was also evident that summer when a controversy that had brewed for some time within the Socialist Party came to a boil. Once inside the SP the Trotskyists had begun to use the *Socialist Appeal,* published by Albert Goldman in Chicago, to make their views known. They operated as the "Appeal" caucus and won to their perspective a majority of the Young People's Socialist League, including leaders Ernest Erber and Hal Draper. The key issues of debate, apart from the greater importance the Trotskyists placed upon defending Trotsky's life and refuting the Moscow trials' allegations, were twofold. First, the Socialist Party's official position on the Spanish Civil War—in which a fascist insurrection was battling a diverse array of forces, including a Republican government—was to support the Popular Front, whereas the Appeal group wanted instead to advocate a united front of all workers' parties and organizations, with the aim of workers' control. Second, the Appeal group joined forces with a "Clarity" caucus led by Herbert Zam and Gus Tyler to oppose SP endorsement of American Labor Party candidates in the New York city council races, favoring instead an authentic break from the Democratic Party and the building of a party committed to independent political action and a working-class program.[33]

[32] SH to Erskine, 16 and 26 August 1937 (Southern Review Papers, Yale University, Beinecke Rare Book and Manuscript Library).
[33] The American Labor Party, despite its title, was essentially a vehicle for running Democratic candidates on a ticket that could attract the votes of citizens who refused to support the Democratic machine. It was a primary vehicle of CP Popular Front activity.

In an effort to clamp down on this growing threat to its hegemony, the Socialist leadership moved at the party's convention in March 1937 to prohibit all internal organs and restrict the decision-making capacities of branches. The accusation of the leadership was that Trotskyist activity had been disruptive and undisciplined; the Trotskyists maintained that their democratic rights to express their views within the organization were being denied. In June 1937 the national committee of the Trotskyist caucus met in New York and decided to publish its resolutions in defiance of the leadership's decree. In retaliation, SP leaders in July 1937 suspended from membership several of the most prominent dissidents in New York—including Hook's NYU colleague James Burnham, who had been an outspoken critic of Jack Altman, executive secretary of the New York local. Other Trotskyist members appealed the expulsions and called for a referendum and a special convention of the Socialist Party to resolve the controversy democratically. But on August 9, 1937, with the blessing of Norman Thomas, the New York local's leadership voted to expel fifty-four members of the Trotskyist caucus.[34]

Hook, though not a Socialist Party member, came down clearly in favor of the rights of the Trotskyists in the internal dispute. In the *Saturday Review* for August 28, 1937, just as the struggle reached its high pitch, Hook examined *American Socialism* by Harry W. Laidler, executive director of the League for Industrial Democracy and one of the most important SP leaders. Although Hook faulted the pedestrian style and tinge of nationalism reflected in the book's title, his review praised Laidler for distinguishing between the New Deal and "genuine socialism," as well as between socialism and "what passes for communism in Stalin's Russia." Socialism's future, Hook observed, depended upon effective criticism of Stalinism: "As the recent bloody events in Russia have demonstrated, it is essential that socialists be more clearly aware of what they wish to substitute for capitalism if the consequences of their rule are not to lead to the betrayal of their ideals." The problem was strategic, not just moral, "for no large group of the American people, least of all American workers, can be won for socialism so long as they identify it in any way with the one-party totalitarian Russian dictatorship." Because *American Socialism* was "devoted to the aims and practical program of American socialism," Hook wrote, it should have provided an "extended discussion of the past, present and future of the American Socialist Party." In particular, Hook worried, "Is the Socialist Party to remain faithful to the old socialist principle: 'freedom in thought and

---

[34] See Cannon, *History of American Trotskyism*, 247–50; interview with George Breitman in *The Founding of the Socialist Workers Party: Minutes and Resolutions, 1938–39*, ed. George Breitman (New York: Monad, 1982), 17–36; and Venkataramani, "Leon Trotsky's Adventure in American Radical Politics," 1–46.

unity in action'? . . . [Or] is it to capitulate to the Communist Party demand that Socialist Party members who share some of the views of Trotsky, from whom by the way Dr. Laidler is not afraid to quote, be excluded?"[35]

These rhetorical questions demonstrated Hook's sympathy for the democratic rights of the embattled Trostkyist bloc inside the Socialist Party. That alone placed him for all practical purposes in the Trotskyist camp. One did not have to be a Trotskyist proper to be a target of the social democratic leaders. That was illustrated on Labor Day, when the national executive committee decided to expel any Socialist connected with the Appeal caucus who would not repudiate it by October 1. Immediately prior to this stern announcement Hook appealed to Laidler directly, in a personal letter. Concerned above all with preserving a strong countervailing force to the CP, Hook warned that the Socialist leadership's battle against the Trotskyists might lead the Communists to seek an alliance, if not fusion, with the SP, on the grounds that the enemy of their enemy might well be wooed. Laidler responded that the expulsions were made necessary by the Appeal group's failure to abide by decisions and other breaches of discipline. "As for our embracing Stalinism," he wrote, "I don't think that there need to be any fear on that score. In our fight against the Trotskyites, we made it plain that we were after a militant Socialist party, not a Trotskyist or Stalinist or Communist party." As a final overture, Laidler invited Hook to join the Socialist Party—an offer Hook declined.[36]

Another of Hook's revolutionary projects suffered fragmentation at the same time. Hook had helped to plan the new *Marxist Quarterly,* which published its first issue in January 1937 and brought together, briefly, some of the most talented Marxist thinkers in the United States. At their center was Lewis Corey, who (under his given name of Louis Fraina) had been a leading Communist in the early 1920s. Resurfacing as Corey in the 1930s, he wrote several impressive works of Marxian political economy and sociology, including *The Decline of American Capitalism* (1934) and *The Crisis of the Middle Class* (1935). Corey had been offered the inaugural editorial position at *Science & Society,* a semi-independent scholarly journal within the orbit of the Communist Party, launched in 1936. But when Corey's conditions were refused by the scholars planning *Science & Society,* he decided to initiate the *Marxist Quarterly.* Like Hook's earlier bringing together of such disparate figures as Muste, Thomas, and Cannon, the *Marxist Quarterly* was an unusual collaboration of divergent and competing strains within Marxism. In 1936 Corey won financial backing from Corliss Lamont, a Communist Party sympathizer, and brought together a colorful

35 Hook, "Socialism for a Democracy," *Saturday Review* 16 (28 August 1937): 20.
36 Harry W. Laidler to SH, 18 August 1937 (Hook Papers, box 132). Hook's initial letter to Laidler does not survive, but its message can be inferred from Laidler's response.

editorial board composed of James Burnham and George Novack, Trotskyists; Will Herberg and Bertram D. Wolfe, Lovestoneites; Herbert Zam, a former Lovestoneite who had defected in the mid-1930s to the Socialist Party; and several independent radicals, including Hook, historian Louis Hacker, and art historian Meyer Schapiro. Corey himself was a member of the Lovestone group between 1937 and 1939, though he kept his membership so secret that it was unknown to Hook at the time.[37]

The first issue of the *Marxist Quarterly* carried an editorial calling for fresh and compelling Marxist writing "rooted in American history, conditions and problems," and, indeed, the fledgling publication drew essays of impressive quality and breadth. Delmore Schwartz and Meyer Schapiro squared off over abstract art. Corliss Lamont depicted John Dewey. Corey explored the nature of social class in the United States. There were historical excavations of the railroad strike of 1877 and the Civil War. Karl Korsch contributed an essay titled "Leading Principles of Marxism." But after this promising flash the journal rapidly disintegrated in a bitter battle over a subject only tangentially related to the American conditions it had pledged to concentrate upon: the Moscow trials, the paramount cause for dispute within the American left in 1937. When Lamont, Wolfe, and Herberg defended the initial trial, Burnham, Novack, and Zam resigned from the board. Then, when Stalin's prosecutor turned the proceedings against Nikolai Bukharin, to whom the Lovestoneites were loyal, Wolfe and Herberg became critical of the trials—prompting Lamont to withdraw his monetary support on grounds that the magazine was becoming "anti-Soviet." By its second issue the *Marxist Quarterly*'s editorial roster was only half what it had been, its chief financial backer among those who had quit. Over the summer of 1937 Hook and Schapiro tried to secure alternative sources of funding, but their efforts were to no avail. The magazine collapsed by year's end, drawing the curtain on the short life of a publication Irving Howe later called "probably the most distinguished Marxist journal ever published in this country."[38]

---

[37] On the history of the *Marxist Quarterly*, see Lewis Corey to Bertram D. Wolfe, 1 March 1952 (Hook Papers, box 132); SH to Paul Berman, 24 April 1973 (Hook Papers, box 112); Meyer Schapiro to SH, 7 June 1937 (Hook Papers, box 26). Published accounts include Michael Harrington, Introduction to *Marxist Quarterly* (New York: Greenwood Reprint, 1968); Wald, *The New York Intellectuals*, 152–54; and Christopher Phelps, "*Science & Society* and the *Marxist Quarterly*," *Science & Society* 57 (Fall 1993): 359–62. On Corey and the Lovestone group, see SH to Howard Brick, 1 March 1982 (Brick Collection). See also Paul M. Buhle, *A Dreamer's Paradise Lost: Louis C. Fraina/Lewis Corey (1892–1953) and the Decline of Intellectual Radicalism in the United States* (New Jersey: Humanities, 1995).

[38] Howe, "The New York Intellectuals," 219, was mistaken when he ascribed the dissolution of the magazine to "differences among its founders, some like James Burnham holding to a revolutionary Marxist line and others like Sidney Hook and Lewis Corey moving toward versions of liberalism and social democracy." Hook and Corey remained staunchly revolutionary; the Moscow trials were the cause of the dispute.

As summer waned in 1937, Hook could only have been ambivalent about the prospects for his politics. The Moscow trials had damaged the Soviet Union's moral claim to have fulfilled the socialist ideal. The establishment of the Dewey Commission in the face of slander and harassment was a signal achievement. But the ranks of the American Communist Party continued to swell, especially in New York, largely because of the Popular Front against fascism and war. And the dissident left seemed incapable of cohering: the Socialist Party was in the process of kicking out the Trotskyists, and the fissure of the *Marxist Quarterly* did not bode well for independent Marxist scholarship. The situation was even bleaker than it had been earlier that year, when Hook had written to the Austrian socialist Max Adler that "American publishers are too commercial minded to bring out philosophical books on subjects like Marxism and the American radical political movement is too weak and not sufficiently interested in philosophy to do so. In addition the American radical political movements are too sectarian to be interested in any thinker who is not a *Partei-philosoph,* that is to say, no philosopher at all." If Hook found hope anywhere in the early fall of 1937, it was in the circle of New York intellectuals forming around the newly reorganized *Partisan Review,* the reconstitution of which was announced in the *Marxist Quarterly*'s fated final issue.[39]

Like Hook four years earlier, painfully discovering the costs of the Communist Party's insistence upon uniformity in philosophy, a new contingent of writers and critics was beginning to chafe against the Party's heavy-handed strictures in the realm of culture. Despite their initial attraction to Communism, they were finding the CP crude and clumsy—not because it was Marxist but because its ideas increasingly lacked the intellectual grace and power that had drawn them to Marxism in the first place. Prominent among the newly discontented were William Phillips and Philip Rahv, editors of the Party-affiliated literary journal *Partisan Review,* launched in 1934 as the organ of the John Reed Clubs. By 1936 Phillips and Rahv had grown profoundly discontented with a Party line that had first upheld "proletarian" literature and then, with the political turn toward the Popular Front in 1935, promoted a "popular" literature evocative of national culture. After some faltering efforts to finance the magazine under the auspices of the Socialist Party, they were finally able in mid-1937 to relaunch *Partisan Review* as a cultural review independent of any political party. The first clear indication that the editors were to make a decisive break with Communism came at the Second Writers' Congress in New York City in June 1937, where, from the floor at a session on literary criticism, they accused the speakers of hackneyed aesthetics and corrupt politics. Just as the

---

[39] SH to Max Adler, 11 January 1937 (Hook Papers, box 5).

Dewey Commission had demonstrated that opposition to Stalinism could be carried out responsibly by a coalition of the dissident left, so the re-creation of *Partisan Review* as an independent forum for culture was a significant milestone in the development of New York anti-Stalinist radicalism.[40]

The new *Partisan Review* rejected any attempt to measure art with a political yardstick and espoused a modernist aesthetics of the avant-garde—upholding the poetry of T. S. Eliot and Ezra Pound, the novels of James Joyce and Franz Kafka—combined, somewhat paradoxically, with a deeply social and historical sensibility. In its initial years the reconstituted quarterly was proudly attached to Marxism and revolutionary socialism, with a focus on arts and letters. Art, literature, drama, and poetry were never foremost in Hook's mind, certainly not in the way they were for other New York intellectuals. (He once told Saul Bellow that William Faulkner was an excellent writer whose books would be greatly improved by dynamic ideas. "I'll be glad to give him some," Hook said. "It would make a tremendous difference. Do you know him?")[41] But Hook was friends with many who became alienated from the Communist Party as much for its cultural as for its political offenses. His old Columbia classmate Meyer Schapiro, who had collaborated with Hook on the *Marxist Quarterly* and would soon begin contributing to *Partisan Review*, wrote to Hook with hilarity in June 1937 about the literary criticism session at the Second Writers' Congress. The Popular Front's literary representatives, Schapiro reported, had delivered "the usual appeal for the resurrection of Longfellow as an anti-fascist (the argument was like this: Freiligrath praised Longfellow; Marx praised Freiligrath; therefore we as Marxists ought to praise and preserve Longfellow; and as a verification,—the Village Blacksmith is about a worker!)."[42]

40 On *Partisan Review*, see Cooney, *The Rise of the New York Intellectuals;* James Burkhart Gilbert, *Writers and Partisans: A History of Literary Radicalism in America* (New York: John Wiley, 1968); and Wald, *The New York Intellectuals.* The classic intellectual history of the Communist literary left is Daniel Aaron, *Writers on the Left* (1961; New York: Columbia University Press, 1992).

41 Saul Bellow, "Writers, Intellectuals, Politics," *National Interest* 31 (Spring 1993): 128.

42 Meyer Schapiro to SH, 7 June 1937 (Hook Papers, box 26). See also Alan Wallach, "Schapiro, Meyer," in *The Encyclopedia of the American Left*, ed. Mary Jo Buhle, Paul Buhle and Dan Georgakas (Urbana: University of Illinois Press, 1992), 677–78; and Alan Wallach, "Marxist Art Historian: Meyer Schapiro, 1904–1996," *Against the Current* 62 (May–June 1996), 52. What defined the aesthetics of *Partisan Review* was a set of predilictions formed by a generational encounter with Marxism and modernism more than a fully articulated theory. Its stance was well described in *Making It* (New York: Random House, 1967), 115–16, by Norman Podhoretz, the second-generation New York intellectual who would subsequently be a pioneer of neoconservatism: "The elements were these: out of the experience of the break with Stalinism, independence of mind—meaning a mind dictated to by nothing but its own sense of reality, and highly skeptical, even suspicious, of other senses of reality; out of the schooling in Marxism, a tendency to view all phenomena, including the arts, in their historical and social context; *but,* out of the schooling in modernism, a simultaneous belief in the irreducible status and freedom of a work of art; out of the schooling in modernism, too, a

Partisan Review's turn toward Trotskyism was welcomed warmly by the beleaguered anti-Stalinist left. Coming as it did at a moment when official Communism was moving to decimate the ranks of the original revolutionaries of 1917 on trumped-up charges in the Soviet Union, to suppress militant experiments in self-organization by anarchist and revolutionary socialist workers in Barcelona, and to adapt to bourgeois democracy in the advanced capitalist countries, the defection of a significant group of Communist intellectuals to the camp of revolutionary Marxism was highly significant. But standard histories of *Partisan Review* accord the journal somewhat too much importance in the particular case of Hook, for they tend to credit the journal with the generation of American intellectual anti-Stalinism and only weakly situate it as a culmination of earlier developments. In the typical tale, Hook appears drawn to the review and is then propelled, along with the rest of its writers and editors, into the postwar limelight. Hook's involvement, however, was not the personal political breakthrough that it was for so many others. When the *Partisan Review* departed from the Communist Party and crossed the Rubicon in 1937, Hook was already waiting on the opposite bank.

Indeed, Hook probably exerted more of an influence on the *Partisan Review* circle, which was appreciative of his authoritative knowledge of Marxism, than *PR* exerted upon him. Eager to redeem and reclaim revolutionary socialism from the Communists, whose Popular Front strategy represented a return to reformism and class collaboration, Rahv, Phillips, and others looked to anti-Stalinist Marxism to help them regain their intellectual bearings, and few were as familiar with that terrain as Hook. Delmore Schwartz, a brilliant if erratic young writer in the *Partisan Review* milieu, enrolled in Hook's classes and told his friend William Barrett that Hook was an "incomparable teacher." Hook's sway was particularly forceful over William Phillips, who had taken his classes at NYU in the early 1930s, including a graduate seminar. Hook had tried to persuade Phillips to sever his ties to the Communist Party, and when that at last took place in 1937, Phillips generally looked to his former teacher for political advice, though not always did they see eye to eye. The *Partisan Review* editors and Hook were part of a current whose gravitational center was Trotskyism. In 1938 *PR* printed two articles by Trotsky—one defending surreal-

passionate interest in the great masters of that movement and a contemptuous distaste for their 'middlebrow' enemies and for the 'philistine' critical rhetoric typically employed by such; out of the feeling of beleaguered isolation shared with the masters of the modernist movement themselves, elitism—the conviction that *others* were not worth taking into consideration except to attack, and need not be addressed in one's writing; out of that feeling as well, a sense of hopelessness as to the fate of American culture at large and the correlative conviction that integrity and standards were only possible among 'us.' The style, then, was characteristically hypercritical, learned, allusive."

ism, another proclaiming the need for revolutionary art to be free from control by cultural commissars. In 1939 editor Dwight Macdonald joined the Socialist Workers Party, the Trotskyist organization formed on New Year's Day 1938 by the dissidents who had been expelled from the Socialist Party in 1937. For Hook, therefore, the *Partisan Review* offered some new ears to bend and a new forum for his writings, but his political and philosophical thought required no transformation. His relationship with *PR* merely fit his pattern of several years: expounding a revolutionary Marxism critical of Stalinism, and collaborating by association with the Trotskyist movement without fully endorsing Trotskyism or taking on the responsibilities and programatic commitments that membership in a socialist organization entailed.[43]

When the first issue of the new *Partisan Review* appeared in December 1937, it featured Hooks's review of Kenneth Burke's *Attitudes toward History*. The choice of book and reviewer appropriately joined the cultural emphases of the periodical with Hook's philosophical and political expertise. Burke, a literary theorist sympathetic to the Communist Party and its cultural progam, had taken up problems of theory that fell within Hook's range. In his scathing assessment, "The Technique of Mystification," Hook faulted Burke for his cloudy style and logical incoherence. (He was not unique in finding Burke muddled. William Phillips later recalled that when Burke raised the chant "We Write for the Working Class" in a May Day parade one year, the writers around him burst into laughter, because even they—serious intellectuals all—found Burke's writing incomprehensible.) Hook blasted Burke for rejecting on "organic" grounds any criticism of Russia or the Communist Party. "The ideological homogeneity he so warmly embraces," he wrote, "will induce a creeping paralysis of the creative centers which means death to the craftsman." Here Hook was finally getting in a jab at a view that he had first encountered in a letter from Burke four years before, in which Burke had written, no doubt maddening Hook, "Concerning the matter of my 'orthodoxy': having heard so much about the many difficulties which many sincere and enterprising men have met with, I made peace with myself by the following formula: I would think of myself simply as anti-capitalist and pro-communist, and let all the rest go hang. Insofar as the various warring groups will accept me as an ally, I am with them. I fully respect the impulse to conformity which

[43] In letters to Alan Wald, Hook claimed to have been instrumental in persuading Rahv and Phillips to break with the CP: Hook to Wald, 1 August 1974 and 17 July 1982 (Wald Collection). That is not Phillips's recollection: William Phillips to author, 19 October 1993. On Hook and *Partisan Review*, see William Barrett, *The Truants: Adventures among the Intellectuals* (Garden City, N.Y.: Anchor, 1982), 214; William Phillips, *A Partisan View: Five Decades of the Literary Life* (New York: Stein & Day, 1983), 45.

the 'official' group has manifested, but I heartily agree with you in thinking very little of the ways in which this impulse has often been manifested."[44]

In a reply to Hook's review, Burke held that Hook had ignored the anti-capitalist character of *Attitudes toward History:* "Is it not noteworthy that never once, not even to answer in the negative, does Hook ask whether there is one single ingredient in my book that might be used (either as it is, or after such-and-such improvement) for anti-capitalist diagnosis and exhortation?" This omission, Burke argued, meant that "it is a misnomer for him to designate himself a partisan of the Left at all." Hook apparently had lost interest in "the analysis of capitalist dilemmas and the ways of surmounting them," Burke contended, and thus also his claim to radicalism. "A strange complaint!" Hook exclaimed. "When Burke attacks socialist critics of Stalinism, does he call attention to their anti-capitalism? He does not! Or when he criticizes Trotsky, Dewey or Farrell? He does not! But just as soon as his own position is probed, he makes loud outcry that he is not being given credit for his socialist intentions. . . . I refuse to give him credit for his 'socialism'—*until I know what kind of socialism he believes in!*" Hook held that his own socialist views were well established, quite known to Burke, and hardly demanded recapitulation in every review, particularly in a socialist publication such as *Partisan Review.* To Burke's doubts about whether he was really a socialist, Hook replied with a question of his own: "Is Burke really serious?"[45]

Like the *Partisan Review* circle, at the outset of 1938 Hook was still close to Trotskyism. Unlike Macdonald, he did not join the Socialist Workers Party. But many of Hook's old AWP comrades, including James Burnham, were members of the new organization, which was named to emphasize its roots in both the Socialist Party and the Workers Party of the United States. Hook had shown solidarity with both those groups, and the SWP's leaders viewed him as an ally. In a March 24, 1938, conversation on the topic of independent intellectuals, Max Shachtman reported to Trotsky that Hook "nine times out of ten agrees with the party." Compared with many other intellectuals, Shachtman said, Hook was quite friendly: "His differences with us are on the philosophic field; in the [Dewey] committee Hook defended us. It is interesting that even in some details where he did not agree with us he defended us." After hearing Shachtman's report, Trotsky—who was often suspicious of intellectuals because of their capacity to alienate workers and

---

[44]   The copy of the letter retained in Hook's files has a large exclamation point beside the text: Burke to SH, 27 December 1933 (Hook Papers, box 8). See also Hook, "The Technique of Mystification," review of *Attitudes toward History* by Kenneth Burke, *Partisan Review* 4 (December 1937): 57–62; William Phillips, *A Partisan View*, 59.

[45]   Kenneth Burke, "Is Mr. Hook a Socialist?" and Hook, "Is Mr. Burke Serious?" *Partisan Review* 4 (January 1938): 40–44, 44–47.

dominate working-class parties—advised his American lieutenant to let the sympathizers, including the *Partisan Review* group, remain independent.[46]

Hook was often understood by others to be a Trotskyist, though he resisted the designation. When Crane Brinton, the British historian of ideas and revolutions, referred to Hook as a "Trotzkyist" in *Saturday Review,* he was forced to answer a letter of objection from Hook. "My point," wrote Brinton, "is that such terms—and in the French Revolution, for instance, terms like Hébertiste and Dantoniste—have definite and precise meanings only for insiders . . . I meant merely that you were solidly against Stalin; and for John Jones—and even for the subscribers of *Saturday Review*—the best way of saying that a man is against Stalin is to say that he is for Trotzky." Much of the confusion in such cases derived from the narrow condition of organizational membership Hook gave to the term "Trotskyist" and the wider political and intellectual meaning of the term as others understood it. In 1949 Hook remonstrated with Irving Howe for calling him an "ex-Trotskyist" in a private exchange. Howe, far more informed on the contours of Trotskyism than Brinton, gave an instructive response: "By using the phrase, ex-Trotskyist (which I distinctly recall your employing) I was not, in any case, trying to say you had a party card. But you can hardly deny a general agreement with the Trotskyist position during the mid-'30s. One doesn't have to belong to an organization to be a Marxist, a Leninist, a Trotskyist, or, for that matter, a Social Democrat."[47]

Means and Ends, 1937–38

One great paradox in the late 1930s was that even as the Stalinist regime's blunders and atrocities stripped away the illusions of many of its American sympathizers, the same horrors contributed to the disorientation and fragmentation of the anti-Stalinist left. From the beginning of the Moscow trials in 1936 through the Nazi-Soviet pact of 1939, many saw clearly for the first time that the bureaucratic consolidation of power in the Soviet Union contradicted the most elementary egalitarian and internationalist precepts of socialism. Far from building "socialism in one country," as Stalin had announced in the early 1920s, a bureaucratic ruling class was presiding over the expansion of a repressive, gargantuan state whose

---

[46] Interview with George Breitman in Breitman, *The Founding of the Socialist Workers Party,* 32; Leon Trotsky, "Defense Organization and Attitude toward Intellectuals," in *Writings of Leon Trotsky (1937–38),* ed. Naomi Allen and George Breitman (New York: Pathfinder, 1976), 294–99.

[47] Crane Brinton to SH, 27 September 1937 (Hook Papers, box 7); Irving Howe to SH, 5 April 1949 (Hook Papers, box 15). Brinton (1898–1968) would soon publish his best-known work, *The Anatomy of Revolution* (1938). Howe (1920–93), a Shachtmanite in 1949, subsequently founded the social democratic magazine *Dissent.*

monstrous proportions and methods could no longer be disguised. Yet the results of the advanced degeneration of the USSR—show trials, mass executions, forced collectivization of agriculture, compromise with the fascist bloc, and increasingly dictatorial rule over all aspects of social and cultural life—amounted to such a twisted perversion of the socialist ideal that even anti-Stalinist intellectuals, whose analysis had been essentially right all along, were compelled to ask themselves, once again, "What went wrong?" Many no longer found the old answers adequate. One after another, though not all, of the anti-Stalinist intellectuals, concluded that Stalinism had its seeds in the doctrines of Lenin and put aside the aim of socialist revolution as a wishful, dangerous pursuit. Some, including Max Eastman and James Burnham, would eventually go so far as to hold Marx himself amoral and socialism itself responsible for Stalinism.

Though he would go partway down that path, Hook remained unshaken in his revolutionary convictions through the first blasts from the Moscow trials. He and others, turning toward an investigation of the moral question of ends and means, reached the conclusion that revolutionary Marxism, far from being "amoral," had at its core a defensible moral theory. To the premier issue of the *Marxist Quarterly* Hook contributed "Marxism and Values," an exposition of the first order demonstrating the maturity of his pragmatist Marxism. Marxism, he wrote, was distinguished from other forms of socialist thought in that its partisans do not merely desire socialism: "For the Marxist, the affirmation of the socialist ideal is made in the context of a scientific study of society, its productive possibilities, and the social and human costs involved in its realization." Marxism thus was critical of other varieties of socialism not because they upheld ideals or morality but because of the *abstract character* of their morality. Other socialisms were premised upon ahistorical moral ideals: the Kantian categorical imperative, the social principles of Christianity, or assertions of the eternally good, true, and beautiful. Each of these strategies was flawed by its distance from actual human experience. Marxism, Hook wrote, instead "relates the socialist ideal to the historic facts at hand, to the needs of the working masses and the probable outcome of the pursuit of alternative ideals." The Marxist alternative to abstract moralism and philosophical absolutism, he explained, is a historical and therefore empirical moral theory: "For Marxists, morals like any other part of culture, say law, art, educational theory and practice, is a function of a complex of material factors, of varied weight, e.g., geography, mode of production, class interests, etc." Not by logic alone could one deduce from Marxist historical analysis the proper course of action to be pursued at any given time, but Marxist judgments of value were not therefore arbitrary or irrational: "For the *method* by which they are reached bestows upon them the character of rationality even though they are rooted in human needs, preferences and interests. This method is critical, historical and experimental."[48]

Marxist method, in a word, was *pragmatic*. Marxists made moral judgments after inquiring into specific psychological and social needs, historical conditions and their possibilities, and potential paths of action and their likely consequences. The rising idea that Marxism and fascism were totalitarian twins, equally "amoral," was thus without foundation. Under fascist rule, Hook observed, "the scientific method of analyzing and testing judgments of value is ruled out at the very start as irrelevant." Fascism's problem was not amorality but rather its moral absolutism, its insistence upon imposing its own prejudices uniformly and universally. Fascism mobilized honor, dignity, order, egoism, and unity as shallow, insincere "symbols of persuasion." Of course, scientific method did not require one to approach every situation with a blank slate of a mind, free of preconceived moral precepts; people necessarily enter into experiences with a range of assumptions, and Hook was quick to admit that "in every moral situation we have as part of the given data an entire set of values taken over from tradition, habit and the outcome of previous moral situations." His point was to insist that those moral propositions be *"reaffirmed* in the process of critical, scientific inquiry." If not borne out, they ought to be rejected or revised. Marxism could not assert absolute moral laws, therefore, but it could arrive at *ultimate preferences* influenced by relevant knowledge of the world, related to the means necessary to give them effect, and tested over a period of time—thus permitting reevaluation. "The morality of Marxist socialism," Hook concluded, "is an historical morality which admits of ultimate values, but not of final or eternal ones." Ultimate values were guideposts for action to be treated with flexibility and tested in practice; final values claimed eternal verity and had no dialectical connection to experience. This useful distinction between future goals was a signal theoretical attainment for Hook's pragmatist Marxism.[49]

Could a socialist revolution be conducted in a manner consistent with this moral method? "Socialism, democracy and scientific method," Hook maintained, "are indissolubly connected. Neither one can fully come into its own without the other." But Hook was no social democrat making obeisance to bourgeois electoral and legal norms as the exclusively democratic road to socialism. Even when there was no social consensus about values, he argued, Marxists should act decisively: "Marxists assert that their values

---

[48] Hook, "Marxism and Values," *Marxist Quarterly* 1 (January–March 1937): 39, 40, 43.
[49] Ibid., 44, 45.

are 'valid' in virtue of the scientific study of the interests at the basis of these values and the possibilities of gratifying, by social change and the frustration of *some* of the interests of those who oppose socialism, the interests of progressively wider groups of the population including those who are now opposed to socialism."[50]

Nearly a year later, when Hook amplified this case for a pragmatist and revolutionary morality, a new tone of doubt pervaded his writing, and his position came perilously close to the moral absolutism he had condemned. Nontheless, he remained persuaded that a moral theory of socialist revolution was possible. In reviewing British writer Aldous Huxley's book *Ends and Means* for *The Nation,* Hook saluted Huxley for demonstrating that "the end justifies the means" is not ample justification in cases where the means are "bound to achieve their precise opposite." But Huxley's writing, Hook contented, had "less cogency and persuasiveness" when he offered his own moral proposals, which were "metaphysical speculation." Even if "the end justifies the means" was an inadequate basis for establishing revolutionary justice, Hook insisted upon a plan spelling out the instruments necessary to achieve a classless society, not mere moral platitudes. *Ends and Means* was "marred by an ethical absolutism," Hook complained, and Huxley had no way of explaining "how, even from a long-term point of view, the strategic posts of influence, so necessary for social change, can be won in the face of indifference or active opposition." This lucid restatement of his critique of gradualist and legal reform recalled Hook's earliest writings as an undergraduate against pacifist "non-resistance." He condemned Huxley for relying upon "questionable non-resistant techniques of social change," a reliance "inconsistent with his emphasis upon the importance of intelligence or awareness in ethical analysis." In Huxley's world, Hook wrote, "only the most necessary social reforms will be undertaken and never against widespread opposition and violence." Despite these political and historical criticisms, he saluted Huxley for "unerring insight" in addressing the topic of means and ends, "the basic moral problem of our times," and concluded with the subdued observation that history warrants "caution when fire is to be met with fire and violence with violence."[51]

Hook continued to defend revolutionary applications of force, since the odds were against a peaceful, easy transition to socialism, whatever its level of popular support. But his thought on the question was unstable and uneasy. In praising Huxley's contention that ends *never* justify some means, Hook inadvertently risked moral absolutism. That danger was manifest

[50] Ibid.
[51] Hook, "Means and Ends," review of *Ends and Means* by Aldous Huxley, *The Nation* 145 (11 December 1937): 656, 658.

when he expounded favorably upon Huxley's point with illustrations taken from Stalinist policy:

> Against those who would save democracy by waging a war against fascism, he points out that this involves "inevitably the transformation of democracy into fascism." Against those who would further the ultimate truth with immediate lies, counterpose to the uncritical worship of a leader an even more uncritical worship of a bigger leader, combat fascism with the methods of fascism—all on the ground that the end justifies the means—Huxley replies: "The end cannot justify the means for the simple and obvious reason that the means employed determine the nature of the end produced."

A few months before, Hook had written similarly that because "means cannot be dissociated from ends," so "love cannot be evoked by fear and terror, and . . . truth cannot be served by lies—even by well intentioned ones." In such formulations he came dangerously close to sneaking Kant's categorical imperative in through the back door. Suggesting that violence, lies, and force are never justified, no matter what the end, seemed to conflate two discrete propositions—that *any* means is justified by an intended good end, and that *certain* means are justified by the particular ends they bring about—either of which can be implied by the vague assertion that "the end justifies the means." While Hook openly declared himself against moral rigidity, below the surface his philosophy was risking contradiction. He did not seem willing to permit the methods that had historically been necessary to the successful conduct of class struggle and revolution. If violence was absolutely forbidden, for example, how could a democratically elected socialist government ever expropriate property if the ruling class organized a military rebellion? Were striking workers obliged to watch passively as scabs took their places in the shop? If lies were never permissible, how could the underground resistance to Nazi rule possibly function? How, indeed, could workers under Stalinism organize? The sea of official lies and blood in the Soviet Union proved that honesty and respect for human life had to be foremost in the array of socialist values. Presumption had to rest with truth and persuasion. But could the use of undesirable means be ruled out in every instance?[52]

That was the question the entire left was groping to answer. The following month Hook took a step toward clearing up the confusion he had left in his own writings on the subject by contributing to a controversy in *Common Sense,* advocate of a leftish middle-class populism. In 1938 *Common*

---

[52] Hook, "Means and Ends," 656; Hook, untitled contribution to symposium on "The Bearing of Education," *Social Research* 4 (September 1937): 401–4.

Sense sponsored a symposium on Marxism and violence initiated by its editor, Selden Rodman, who declared that "Trotskyism and Stalinism stem from the same absolutist philosophy." Whether Lenin or Trotsky or Stalin occupied the Kremlin would make no difference, Rodman argued; each man was philosophically given to violence and disregard of democratic methods. The resultant debate revealed the degree to which moral confusion and doubt had taken a toll on the confidence of the independent and revolutionary left.[53]

In their introduction to the collected responses to Rodman's article, the editors of *Common Sense* stated that they opposed any lies or violence, although they admitted that that, too, might be a kind of absolutism. The bulk of the contributors shared the editors' opposition to violent revolution and the Bolshevik heritage without, however, admitting to any attendant complications. "I am sure," Aldous Huxley confidently asserted, "that you cannot use large scale violence without producing the all too familiar results of large scale violence—in more general terms, that means determine ends." Liberal journalist Eugene Lyons—whose *Assignment in Utopia* (1937) told of his disillusionment with the Russian regime—called Stalin's rule "the fruit of the Machiavellism planted in Russia by Lenin and his associates." John Dewey, while upholding the judgment of the Commission of Inquiry that Trotsky was not involved in the specific crimes for which he was charged, nonetheless expressed agreement with Rodman that "American radicals (and I would add the American people generally) must resort to quite other tactics and philosophy than that of violent Marxist-Leninist class struggle, and must also study what has gone on and is still going on in the U.S.S.R., in connection with that philosophy."

Both Max Eastman and Benjamin Stolberg held the Russian Revolution *indirectly* responsible for Stalin but refused to conflate Stalin with Lenin. Eastman restated his old position that Stalin, Trotsky, Lenin, and Marx were all guilty of philosophical absolutism carried over from Hegel, but he cautioned that this did not make them all guilty of the same crimes. Stolberg, even while insisting that it was wrong to see Lenin and Stalin as part of a continuous line of descent, wrote in a somewhat fatalistic vein: "The question is why is a Lenin followed by a Stalin? Why do revolutions have Thermidors? Thus I profoundly believe the early Christianity had in it the seeds which led to the Inquisition. But I equally profoundly believe that it makes no sense whatever to identify St. Paul with Torquemada."[54]

[53] Selden Rodman, "Trotsky in the Kremlin: An Interview," *Common Sense* 6 (December 1937): 17–20.
[54] "Violence, For and Against: A Symposium on Marx, Stalin and Trotsky," *Common Sense* 7 (January 1938): 19–23.

Only Hook unequivocally defended the heritage of the October Revolution. Harold Loeb did call attention to the American Revolution as an example of how a violent revolution might be just. "It seems to me," wrote Loeb, "that a philosophy of change which denies the possibility of good ever coming out of evil, of end ever justifying means, is a denial of one of the fructifying factors in human history."[55] But since Loeb left his remarks at that, his position was an admission of historical paradox more than a moral philosophy of revolution. The task of articulating such a view was left to Hook, who in high polemical form blasted *Common Sense* editor Rodman for trying "to reduce the momentous moral issue of the Moscow trials to the relatively unimportant question whether one gangster was justified in bumping off another." Three great issues, Hook asserted, were at stake: Was Trotsky innocent or guilty, and what conclusion should be drawn from his innocence or guilt? Would Trotsky or Lenin have done what Stalin did, had either one of them stayed in power? Were Stalin's actions the consequence of Marxism?[56]

Trotsky's innocence, Hook maintained, had been established with finality by the Dewey Commission; even Rodman had conceded it. In saying that Trotsky was innocent of the crimes for which he had been assailed but was nevertheless philosophically equivalent to Stalin, Hook alleged, Rodman was akin to reactionaries who asserted that Sacco and Vanzetti were innocent but that they *could* have done what they were accused of doing. The logical conclusion to be drawn from Trotsky's innocence, Hook argued, was not that Trotsky was amoral but rather that the Stalin regime and its supporters around the world "will stop at nothing to frame and destroy *all* who follow the light of their own reason and refuse to be terrorized into silence." Stalinism had demonstrated *its* willingness to use any means to achieve its ends, which were themselves despotic. Trotsky, by contrast, stood absolved.

But if he had won the power struggle within the Soviet leadership, would Trotsky have acted like Stalin? Hook's approach complemented that of Trotsky, who had written in August 1937, "It is not a question of a match between Stalin and Trotsky, but of an antagonism between the bureaucracy and the proletariat." In accord with the empirical theory of value that he had articulated in "Marxism and Values," Hook proposed that the question be resolved through a historical investigation of Trotsky's actions when he *was* in power. Did the judicial system in the early Soviet Union function according to due process? What were Trotsky's actions during the

[55] Ibid.
[56] All quotations from Hook through the end of this section are taken from his contribution to the symposium, "As a (Marxist) Professor Sees It," *Common Sense* 7 (January 1938): 22–23.

civil war? Revolutionaries could disagree with Lenin's and Trotsky's handling of certain problems, Hook acknowledged; a negotiated peace might have sufficed to quell the rebellion at Kronstadt, for example, where an armed uprising of sailors in the early Soviet period was suppressed by the Red Army under Trotsky's direction. In the late 1930s the specter of Kronstadt was often held up to substantiate the claim that Trotsky was identical to Stalin, but Hook abjured such a judgment: "Lenin and Trotsky were indisputably guilty of harshness and brutality—as were the leaders of civil war and revolution in every country of the world. (Cromwell, Sherman, etc.) This is important in evaluating the validity of revolutions and the nature of revolutionary process. But it is a far cry from this to the crimes of which Stalin has been guilty." Lenin and Trotsky made errors, but only someone who opposed violent revolution on principle could extrapolate from such mistakes a condemnation of the Soviet revolution in its entirety:

> Only those who are opposed to any use of violence at any time by any side—like genuine Christians and Tolstoyans—have a right to blanket condemnation of Lenin and Trotsky. As revolutionists they were committed to the use of revolutionary means. It is rather late in the day to discover that they were revolutionists. It is impermissible to use that discovery to insinuate that they were therefore committed to employ the same means which Stalin, who is *not* fighting civil war, is now using in Russia.

In fact, Hook wrote, during the period of their rule Lenin and Trotsky had declined to use any and all available means to defeat their political enemies. In direct contrast to the Moscow trials, Hook recounted, stood the July 1922 trial of several members of the Social Revolutionary Party. Even though the trials were conducted after repeated SR assassinations of Bolshevik leaders and attempts on the lives of Trotsky and Lenin, no frame-up was employed to secure conviction; the Social Revolutionaries did not recant their views; they were permitted foreign counsel; and even when found guilty, they were not executed.[57]

Could the actions of Stalin be traced to the writings of Marx? Hook set himself apart from most of the other contributors to the *Common Sense* forum by refuting any implication that Stalinism was the logical outcome of classical Marxism. "The fact that Stalin calls himself a Marxist," Hook retorted, "does not prove this, any more than the fact that those who were responsible for the death of Sacco-Vanzetti called themselves liberals and democrats proves that their judicial crime flowed from the philosophy of

[57] *Writings of Leon Trotsky, 1936–37*, ed. Naomi Allen and George Breitman (New York: Pathfinder, 1978), 429.

democratic liberalism. Torquemada called himself a follower of Christ and so does Franco." In a terse recapitulation of his Marxist critique of Stalinism, Hook wrote, "Only those who have *not* read Marx can assert that he believed (a) the end justifies any means, (b) in a dictatorship of a minority political party over the proletariat, (c) in the dictatorship of a secretariat or a beloved disciple over the party, proletariat or population at large."

Hook's article concluded with a short digest of his political principles. Topping the list was an assertion of the enduring soundness of Marxist economic analysis and "historical materialism *methodologically* interpreted." To this Hook added that neither Lenin nor Trotsky was responsible for "the degeneration of the Russian Revolution under Stalin and his bureaucracy." Hook also offered some more surprising positions, however, distancing himself from Trotsky and his American followers with a subtle, critical, yet still revolutionary assessment of Soviet history. "Both Lenin and Trotsky were indirectly responsible for a set of institutions, practices and habits of thought which made it *easier* for men like Stalin and his clique to emerge to power," Hook wrote. "The former made capital political errors; the latter are guilty of, and morally responsible for, the worst set of crimes in the history of the socialist movement. The fundamental error of Lenin and Trotsky was the underestimation of the importance of *democratic processes* even in the period of revolution and civil war." The seeds of degeneration were not in revolution itself, as Stolberg's fatalism implied. Nor was it in Bolshevism, as Lyons's anti-Leninist answer had suggested; the October Revolution had been warranted. But Hook now argued that the leading figures of the Russian Revolution had committed a series of terrible errors by devoting insufficient attention to fostering democracy, leaving their revolution vulnerable to bureaucratic degeneration. The key to avoiding such mistakes in future revolutions, Hook concluded, was that Marxism "must assimilate in its present day formulation, particularly in the American here and now, the experimental philosophy as expressed in the major works of John Dewey."

Their Morals and Ours, 1938

Hook's intervention in the *Common Sense* symposium was one of his last moments as a frankly revolutionary intellectual. The precariousness of his emprise, combining pragmatism with Marxism, was apparent even in the pages of *Common Sense*. His defense of Marxist theory and the basic accomplishments of the Soviet revolution had come with a caveat that Marxism required a supplemental dose of Deweyan pragmatism. In the very same issue of the very same magazine, however, Dewey himself was urging radicals to adopt tactics "other than that of violent Marxist-Leninist class struggle." Moreover, even as Hook defended the Bolshevik revolution, he offered for the first time substantive criticisms of Lenin and Trotsky for having neglected democratic processes, marking a newly critical disposition toward the Bolshevik legacy. These intellectual tensions did not require the abandonment of Marxism—indeed, they might have been the seed of a new and higher revolutionary understanding—but from that time onward Hook began to back away from radicalism.[58]

For some time Hook had been attempting to work more or less within the parameters set by Trotsky on one side and Dewey on the other, even if he never agreed completely with either. His retreat, therefore, undoubtedly owed something to the increasingly open antagonism between Trotsky and Dewey in the last years of the 1930s. As late as his January 1938 *Partisan Review* reply to Kenneth Burke, Hook could in the same breath quite casually group Trotsky, Dewey, and Farrell as anti-Stalinists and anti-capitalists. But the association masked underlying divisions: Trotsky and Farrell advocated revolutionary socialism; Dewey represented a form of democratic politics that was neither revolutionary nor connected organically to the working class. By the end of 1938 their philosophical and political differences were the focus of a sharp public debate between Trotsky and Dewey. Faced with this division, Hook leaned toward Dewey and eventually placed his revolutionary aims on the back burner, where they cooled.

It would be an error, however, to ascribe Hook's political transformation in 1938 simply to personal loyalty. His shift in views was complicated and uneven, and he did not express his reasoning in a discrete moment conveniently accessible to the historian. Above all, his thinking must be situated in the volatile social and political climate of 1938. As the historian and cultural critic Mike Davis notes, after the second slump of the Great Depression in 1937 "the crucial integrative props of Rooseveltian Democracy—economic restoration, social reformism, and suspension of state repression—were openly in crisis, and seemingly propitious conditions again existed for the further growth of local labor or farmer-labor movements and their eventual national coalescence." The following year, writes Davis, was "the most advantageous opportunity for revolutionary politics in the twentieth century"—but instead, 1938 was a disaster for the left. The working-class movement split into a virtual civil war as the AFL and CIO fought it out, with the AFL promoting a renewed conservative trade unionism and a withdrawal from all labor party formations, causing independent

58   Hook's line of thought here, had he developed it further, might have anticipated Samuel Farber's nuanced recent work, *Before Stalinism: The Rise and Fall of Soviet Democracy* (New York: Verso, 1990), which upholds the October Revolution but is highly critical of mainstream Bolshevism for its failure to deepen and expand workers' democracy.

political prospects to deflate despite the excellent opportunity created by the New Deal's crisis. The Communist Party, heavily implanted in the CIO, had at the same time become bound to the Democratic Party, and although it continued to expand numerically, its character as a working-class formation was diluting (between 1935 and 1941 the non-blue-collar component jumped from just 5 percent of Communist Party membership to almost 45 percent). The Socialists had declined numerically to a point of insignificance, and the Trotskyist movement would suffer a debilitating split in 1940, minimizing its potential to challenge CP hegemony on the left. Labor historian David Montgomery confirms Davis's estimation of a missed chance: "In the crisis of the New Deal following the economic slump of 1937, the labor movement, for all its new-found strength and militancy, offered no political alternative to the moribund capitalist system and its two parties."[59]

This lost opportunity for working-class politics, combined with a deep crisis of socialist organization, created a climate in which it was extraordinarily difficult for most American intellectuals to sustain their Marxism—which, at least in classical form, hinged upon a practical and active connection to the working-class movement. Yet this conjuncture, though extremely important, was not the only factor relevant to Hook's change of mind. Something as general as the balance of class forces rarely impresses itself in immediately identifiable ways upon individual consciousness. The fissure of radical working-class politics was one condition (and not a cause, in any unilinear sense) of the political impasse which was the moment of Hook's retreat from revolution.

A more immediate factor was the spiraling crisis of confidence on the anti-Stalinist left, especially as anxiety mounted over questions of ends and means. The whole of the anti-Stalinist intelligentsia was ensnared in moral quandaries with potentially disorienting and debilitating psychological effects. Despite Hook's earlier affirmation that Marxism had a plausible and laudable moral theory, he began to suffer the doubts that plagued all independent Marxists faced as the Moscow trials dragged on: How could Marxism be redeemed from its association with Stalinism? Did Marxism really have the moral resources to resist the new barbarism in Russia? "We were not prepared for defeat," wrote *Partisan Review* editor Philip Rahv in a melancholy April 1938 essay on the Moscow trials. "The future had our confidence, which we granted freely, sustained by the tradition of Marxism. In that tradition we saw the marriage of science and humanism. But now, amidst all these ferocious surprises, who has the strength to re-affirm

59   Mike Davis, *Prisoners of the American Dream: Politics and Economy in the History of the US Working Class* (New York: Verso, 1986), 67–69; David Montgomery, *Workers' Control in America* (Cambridge: Cambridge University Press, 1979), 169.

his beliefs, to transcend the feeling that we had been duped? One is afraid of one's fear. Will it soon become so precise as to exclude hope?"[60]

Rahv's essay, though filled with a tragic sensibility, ended by arguing that classical Marxism and revolutionary politics remained valid. Others in Hook's circle of acquaintances were having deeper doubts. In December 1937, Columbia University literature professor Lionel Trilling wrote to Hook, "The superbly single-minded commitment of the intellectual to an ethics of power is really quite a spectacle to watch. And that goes, it seems, not only for literary Stalinists but for our intelligent Trotskyist friends as well." John Anderson, an Australian philosopher who had written on Marxism and ethics, went even further:

> It now seems to me that criticism of Stalinism is totally inadequate unless it carries with it criticism of Bolshevism from its inception, particularly of its gross errors in regard to democracy in the October revolution and in the whole of its party history; and I think also that these errors (sectarianism, tyranny, detachment of the "professional revolutionist" alike from cultural and proletarian life) are bound up with the belief in "dialectic"—are characteristic of the fanatic who believes he is fulfilling a "historic mission." But it seems to me demonstrable that Marx suffered from the same errors and that he believed all nature to be "dialectical."

Likewise, Socialist Party leader Norman Thomas, with whom Hook's correspondence had lapsed after the SP's mid-1937 expulsion of the Trotskyists, wrote in March 1938 to thank Hook for an article he had sent him on the pro-Soviet activities of Corliss Lamont, adding, "I am more and more of the opinion . . . that the great Lenin himself was partly responsible for the situation by reason of his doctrine of the monolithic party headed by one leader and the doctrine that the end justifies any means."[61]

During the spring of 1938 Hook became more and more of that very opinion His doubts about Leninism gave rise to three departures from his prior philosophy: increasing criticism of the Leninist theory of the relationship of the party to the working class and to socialist revolution; a repudiation of Trotsky's conviction that the Soviet Union was a workers' state, however deformed; and a revisitation of the question of ends and means, this time in the aftermath of the clash between Trotsky and Dewey. In none of these areas did Hook undergo a sudden, obvious conversion of mind; some of his doubts and recasting had begun somewhat earlier. But as he considered these issues in

[60]   Philip Rahv, "Trials of the Mind," *Partisan Review* 4 (April 1938): 3–11.
[61]   Lionel Trilling to SH, 10 December 1937 (Hook Papers, box 26); John Anderson to SH, 1 March 1938 (Hook Papers, box 5); Norman Thomas to SH, 29 March 1938 (Hook Papers, box 28).

combination and in the midst of the international and domestic political chaos of 1938, Hook came unevenly to abandon his revolutionary commitment, a departure culminating in a decisive essay completed in that summer.

As his *Common Sense* article had revealed, Hook was moving toward a less charitable view of the conduct of Lenin and Trotsky during the first years of the Soviet revolution. He still believed that a political party was necessary to organize revolutionary activity, that conditions sometimes required the use of revolutionary force, and that the October Revolution had been justified. Since the mid-1930s he had been convinced that any political party which hoped to establish workers' democracy had to adhere to democratic norms by building majority support in the population, respecting the rights of other parties to exist, and fostering democratic participation internally. But even in his sharpest-tongued moments, as when he criticized American Trotskyist leader Max Shachtman in his 1934 article "On Workers' Democracy," Hook had upheld workers' democracy as the essence of the Leninism and Bolshevism. It was one thing to chastise a particular formulation by a political comrade with whom one shared broad agreement, moreover, and another to paint entire political tendencies with a broad brush. Increasingly, Hook associated Leninism and communism, of no matter what variety, with violation of democratic norms. In an April 1937 symposium sponsored by the New School for Social Research and later published in *Social Research*, Hook criticized dictatorial actions by a minority party over the whole of the working class:

> If I were to mention any one doctrine which has led to the fateful consequences described, it would be the dogma, accepted by all orthodox communists, that a workers' democracy must be achieved by a minority one-party dictatorship which presumably knows what are the real interests of the workers better than the workers themselves, and which feels justified by such presumed knowledge to *compel* them to accept the policies of the Communist Party by the use of the school, radio, press, and ultimately the bayonet. This is a far cry from Marx's own conception of the workers' state.

The ambiguous phrase "all orthodox communists" was sufficiently sweeping that it might be taken to include all those, like the Trotskyists, who would lay claim to the communist mantle, even though they were on record as opponents of single-party dictatorship. At this stage, however, Hook was still speaking of "the degeneration of the Russian state from a workers' democracy (the real meaning of Marx's phrase, 'the dictatorship of the proletariat') to a dictatorship of a party *over* the proletariat," indicating that he remained a defender of soviet democracy.[62]

62 Hook, untitled contribution to "The Bearing of Education," 401–4.

Nor did Hook yet disavow all appropriate uses of violence in social revolution. In February 1938, in response to a letter of protest from a University of Chicago professor, Hook clarified that he did not profess "the *necessity* of a certain amount of liquidating," but that if a socialist government came to power by democratic means, began to nationalize industry, "and a minority group pulled another Fort Sumter, then if I couldn't buy them off, or head them off by negotiation, I'd fight them." As with his uncertain stance on ends and means in his review of Huxley's book, however, Hook was ambivalent. If he insisted upon majority support in all instances, it was only a matter of time before he would reconsider the Bolshevik revolution itself. (Although the Bolsheviks were in the lead of a majority of the urban working class in October 1917, workers were not the whole of the Russian population, which was preponderantly peasant. As a rule, moreover, the memberships of individual political parties, no matter how popular, are *always* social minorities.)[63]

At the same time, Hook began to reconsider Trotsky's theory that the Soviet Union was a workers' state. Analysis of the Soviet state would prove one of the most vexing issues for the small and marginal movement of dissenting Marxists, debated time and again, always with ferocity, because so much hung in the balance. In the mid-1930s Hook had agreed with Trotsky that the Soviet Union, deformed by bureaucratic degeneration under Stalin, was worthy of critical defense against threats from imperialism. Trotsky believed that it warranted such defense because of the revolutionary displacement of the capitalist ruling class, the establishment of state control over basic industries, and the presence of economic planning, though he also believed that the Soviet Union would require a political revolution against the parasitical bureaucratic caste to restore workers' democracy. Some in the Trotskyist movement—notably Joseph Carter, Manny Geltman, and James Burnham (Hook's former AWP comrade and NYU colleague who had expressed doubts about "workers' state" terminology as early as August 1936)—began in the late 1930s to argue against Trotsky's analysis, positing instead that the Soviet state had degenerated into so privileged a regime that it could no longer claim to represent, even in a faint and distorted manner, the interests of workers. For consideration at the founding convention of the Socialist Workers Party in early 1938, Burnham and Carter wrote a strong argument against the proposition that the USSR remained a workers' state.[64]

[63] SH to Frank Knight, 22 February 1938 (Hook Papers, box 17).
[64] The theory that the USSR under Stalin had passed beyond the degeneration of a workers' state to a wholly distinct regime, controlled by a new bureaucratic class, neither bourgeois nor proletarian, had been suggested as early as 1929 by Christian Rakovsky, a member of the Left Opposition in Russia. Joseph Carter appears to have been the first to raise the is-

In an April 1938 *Partisan Review* article, "Some Social Uses and Abuses of Semantics," Hook followed the lead of Burnham and Carter, arguing that the term "workers' state" was meaningless unless it applied to a state run by the workers themselves. "If by a workers' state we mean that the decisions and administrative bodies are democratically controlled by the working population," he wrote, "then only a knave or a fool can assert that Stalinist Russia is a workers' state, no matter how we characterize its economy." In another article that spring—written, significantly, for the Socialist Party's theoretical journal, *Socialist Review,* a publication to which Hook had not contributed since the mid-1937 expulsion of the Trotskyists—Hook held that a country which had sold goods to Nazi Germany, oil to Japan for use in invading China, various raw materials to Italy during its Ethiopian campaign, and sundry supplies to Franco's Spain via Italian ports did not deserve the name "workers' state."[65]

Again, principled rejection of single-party dictatorship and jettisoning of the theory of the Soviet Union as a workers' state need not have entailed an abandonment of revolutionary Marxism, despite protests of dogmatists now and then to the contrary. The conclusions to which Hook was coming were perfectly consistent with the later formulations of "socialism from be-

---

sue within the SWP. The concept of a new class society was given the name "bureaucratic collectivism" by the semi-fascist Bruno Rizzi, whose idiosyncratic *The Bureaucratization of the World* (1939) viewed the development as progressive. James Burnham's *The Managerial Revolution* (1941), written immediately after his break from Marxism, saw the New Deal, Nazism, and Stalinism as equal manifestations of a managerial revolution that threatened to extinguish world freedom. Max Shachtman was the U.S. revolutionary socialist leader most responsible for the popularization of the theory of a new class, which he helped recast in 1940 as "bureaucratic collectivism," although his version of the theory was incompatible with both Rizzi's and Burnham's, remaining rooted in revolutionary Marxism and a politics of workers' power. Dissident socialist philosophers in Eastern Europe in the 1950s and 1960s, apparently independently, created varieties of this "new class" theory. A related though dissimilar theory (with its own variations) has held the Soviet regime to be "state capitalist." For the orthodox Trotskyist position on behalf of the USSR as a degenerated workers' state, see Leon Trotsky, *In Defense of Marxism* (New York: Pathfinder, 1973); and James P. Cannon, *The Struggle for a Proletarian Party* (New York: Pathfinder, 1972). For general treatments of the debates within Trotskyism, see Breitman, *The Founding of the Socialist Workers Party;* A. Belden Fields, *Trotskyism and Maoism* (New York: Autonomedia, 1988); Richard Gombin, *The Origins of Modern Leftism* (London: Penguin, 1975); and Paul Bellis, *Marxism and the USSR* (New Jersey: Humanities, 1979). On theories of a bureaucratic new class, see Peter Drucker, *Max Shachtman and His Left* (New Jersey: Humanities, 1994); Max Shachtman, *The Bureaucratic Revolution* (New York: Donald, 1962); Bruno Rizzi, *The Bureaucratization of the World* (New York: Free Press, 1985); James Burnham, *The Managerial Revolution* (New York: John Day, 1941); Milovan Djilas, *The New Class* (New York: Praeger, 1957); Jack Trautman, ed., *Bureaucratic Collectivism: The Stalinist Social System* (Detroit: Sun Press, 1974); and Ernest E. Haberkern and Arthur Lipow, eds., *Neither Capitalism nor Socialism: Theories of Bureaucratic Collectivism* (New Jersey: Humanities, 1996).
[65] Trotsky, *In Defense of Marxism;* Hook, "Some Social Uses and Abuses of Semantics," *Partisan Review* 4 (April 1938): 14–28; Hook, "Thoughts in Season," *Socialist Review* 6 (May–June 1938): 6–7, 16.

low" by Hal Draper, for example, who remained a revolutionary and international socialist for his entire life.[66] In the context of American socialism in 1938, however, Hook's new conclusions did effectively constrict his horizon of action, for no credible current of organized socialism outside the Socialist Workers Party combined a thoroughgoing anti-Stalinism with revolutionary politics—and the SWP's official position upheld Trotsky's analysis of the Soviet Union and the Bolshevik revolution. Trotsky, from Mexican exile, insisted that the Soviet bureaucracy was a ruling *caste,* not class, because the privileges and property of bureaucrats were not hereditary, and a majority of the SWP affirmed his analysis. Hook could have allied himself with the Burnham-Carter minority, which would shortly win a powerful ally in Max Shachtman, but the effort to change the SWP would be a long, thankless struggle fought against Trotsky, who was bound to have the advantage. Moreover, Hook appeared to be in the process of rejecting "orthodox communism" altogether. The Right Opposition was not a live option for him, because he had always had profound political and philosophical disagreements with the Lovestone group, which was much closer in its main line of thought to the Communist Party. The Lovestoneites were, in any case, in disarray as a result of the trial of Bukharin and their adaptation to the trade union bureaucracy; by 1941 their group would dissolve. Social democracy was the only organized current available if Hook was not to abandon socialism altogether—but that was not an obvious choice either, for despite the rigidities of Trotskyism circa 1938, no socialist current was democratically pure. The social democratic leaders of the Socialist Party with whom Hook would ally by year's end had purged dissident revolutionaries from their group a year before, a move that Hook had protested at the time. They were only one generation removed from the orthodox and compromised classical German Social Democracy that Hook had opposed throughout his political life.

The Socialist Workers Party was, in many respects, a more attractive organization. At its formation it had a fairly large, seasoned trade union membership, with significant fractions in major unions. Its intellectual periphery and membership, grouped around *Partisan Review,* was impressive. It had won over the majority of the Socialist Party's youth group. But this potential was dampened by the anti-intellectual prejudices of James P. Cannon and a related overreliance for theoretical development upon Trotsky, whose relocation to Mexico had enhanced his already considerable influence over the American movement.[67] The resulting intellectual insularity

---

[66] See, e.g., Hal Draper, *Socialism from Below,* ed. Ernest Haberkern (New Jersey: Humanities, 1992).

[67] Despite the distortions caused by what even its author now calls its "tendentious factionalism," Tim Wohlforth, *The Struggle for Marxism in the United States: A History of American Trot-*

of American Trotskyism was a factor in Hook's retreat from revolution. The right to the expression of minority views and the formation of dissenting tendencies still existed in the SWP, in marked contrast to the Communist Party, but his old comrade Burnham was increasingly restless. As editor of the SWP's theoretical journal, *New International*, Burnham worked with Hook in the summer of 1938 to persuade Dewey to respond to Trotsky's article "Their Morals and Ours," which had appeared in the February issue. Burnham wrote to Hook of his eagerness "to encourage the publication of 'discussion' articles outside of and even against 'Trotskyism.' As you know, this is counter to the customary practice of the past." There was limited enthusiasm for such an open-ended editorial stance within the revolutionary movement, however, and Burnham confessed a desire to talk with Hook about his growing uneasiness concerning "the general problem of Bolshevism: If it is the case that without the revolution civilization perishes; and that only under the leadership of the Bolsheviks can the revolution succeed; but that the present ideology and practice of Bolshevism carries the seeds of totalitarianism; (all three of which premises seem most plausible); then what to do for a longer term perspective than month by month? I feel that both of us are wasting energies and too much scattering fire."[68] Burnham's pessimism would culminate in his renunciation of Marxism and his gloomy prospectus for Western civilization, *The Managerial Revolution* (1941), which would in turn take him far to the right: as an editor of William F. Buckley's *National Review* in the 1950s he advocated a military "rollback" of Communism.[69]

Hook's transformation, though not identical, would be no less dramatic, and all the more striking because Trotsky's essay "Their Morals and Ours" was closely akin in its moral propositions to Hook's own "Marxism and Values" of just one year before. Trotsky sought, as had Hook, to refute the growing claim that Leninism and Stalinism were one and the same. Philistines, Trotsky wrote, think that "Czarism and Bolshevism are twins. Twins are likewise discovered in fascism and communism." Trotsky noted the curious fact that the Stalinists, long occupied with exterminating and

skyism, 2d ed. (New York: Labor Publications, 1971), 37–65, makes many of these points fairly well. Needless to say, I challenge the book's imputation that the disproportionate imbalance between Cannon as organizer-builder and Trotsky as teacher was due to the corrupting influence of American pragmatism, a judgment Wohlforth seems to continue to uphold. See Tim Wohlforth, *The Prophet's Children: Travels on the American Left* (New Jersey: Humanities, 1994), 118. His 1971 remarks about the failure of the SWP to successfully integrate its intellectual members into organizational life, on the other hand, warrant further consideration.
[68] Burnham to SH, 12 June 1938 (Hook Papers, box 132).
[69] See John P. Diggins, *Up from Communism* (1975; New York: Columbia University Press, 1994); and Paul LeBlanc, "From Revolutionary Intellectual to Conservative Master-Thinker: The Anti-Democratic Odyssey of James Burnham," *left history* 3 (Spring–Summer 1995): 49–81.

persecuting Trotskyists, were now considered "essentially" one and the same as their victims—even by liberals who only a year before had been willing to accept the Stalinist account of the Moscow trials! Having thus ridiculed the amalgamation of divergent social systems under the rubric of "totalitarianism," Trotsky turned to the more profound question of Marxism and morality.[70]

The Jesuit phrase that "the end justifies the means," Trotsky contended, was never meant to imply that *any* end justifies *any* means; rather, it meant that "the means in itself can be a matter of indifference but that the moral justification or condemnation of the given means flows from the end." Shooting, Trotsky observed, is in itself a matter of indifference; shooting a mad dog at a baby's throat is a virtue; shooting with intent to murder is a crime. To allow that ends may justify means is not to excuse immorality or invite amorality. Nor, however, would it resolve the problem of morality, for it leaves unanswered the crucial question of what justifies the end. Universal moral precepts, including Kant's categorical imperative, are Olympian and vacuous, Trotsky argued. "Every science," he wrote in a remarkably pragmatic vein, "including also the 'science of revolution,' is verified by experience." Means had to be tested in practice, and their end had to be historically rooted: "From the Marxist point of view, which expresses the historical interests of the proletariat, the end is justified if it leads to increasing the power of man over nature and to the abolition of the power of man over man." Was *any* mean to those ends justified? Definitely not:

> Permissible and obligatory are those and only those means, we answer, which unite the revolutionary proletariat, fill their hearts with irreconcilable hostility to oppression, teach them contempt for official morality and its democratic echoers, imbue them with consciousness of their own historic mission, raise their courage and spirit of self-sacrifice in the struggle. Precisely from this it flows that *not* all means are permissible. When we say that the end justifies the means, then for us the conclusion follows that the great revolutionary end spurns those base means and ways which set one part of the working class against other parts, or attempt to make the masses happy without their participation; or lower the faith of the masses in themselves and their organization, replacing it by worship for the "leaders."

There were no automatic answers, wrote Trotsky: "The living experience of the movement under the clarification of theory provides the correct answer to these problems."[71]

[70] Leon Trotsky, "Their Morals and Ours" (February 1938), in *Their Morals and Ours* by Leon Trotsky, John Dewey, and George Novack (New York: Pathfinder, 1972), 10.
[71] Trotsky, "Their Morals and Ours," 13–14, 19, 36–37.

This historical and revolutionary method of moral judgment mandated criticism of conspiratorial terrorism (which seeks to replace mass movement with individual heroes) as well as Stalinism and social democracy (each of which claim to liberate the workers without the participation of the workers themselves). Trotsky's opposition to moral and philosophical absolutism, his argument on behalf of testing moral action in practice, his reference to "the living experience of the movement" as the arbiter of judgment, and his advocacy of the application of scientific and historical method to morality made his point of view perfectly reconcilable with Hook's in "Marxism and Values." But it was no longer clear that Hook agreed with his own article. After assisting Burnham in persuading Dewey to respond to Trotsky, he advised Dewey about how to revise his draft, and Dewey accepted many of Hook's suggestions.[72] Even before Dewey's response appeared, Trotsky had caught wind of Hook's hand in it. In a private letter to Raya Dunayevskaya, his former secretary, he spoke of having learned that his article on morals had "provoked great dissatisfaction in Dr. Dewey, Sidney Hook, and others, and that they intend to smash my bad philosophy. I am very glad to hear this." The united front established at the time of the Commission of Inquiry, wrote Trotsky, would benefit from honest mutual criticism: "An open polemic will reestablish things in their natural proportions and relations." Although he referred to Dewey and Hook as friends, Trotsky concluded that they belonged "to the camp of radical bourgeois democracy and not to the camp of the proletariat." In the case of Hook, Trotsky's judgment was unfair, but if (over)generously interpreted as a prediction, it would soon prove prescient.[73]

Dewey's "Means and Ends," published in July 1938, began by granting that Trotsky's essay had been enormously successful in demonstrating the hypocrisy of a number of his opponents who accused him of violence while themselves advocating violence in other instances. Dewey also rejected "absolutistic ethics based on the alleged deliverances of conscience, or a moral sense, or some brand of eternal truths" and agreed that "the end in the sense of consequences provides the only basis for moral ideas and action, and therefore provides the only justification that can be found for means employed." His sole point of criticism was that Trotsky did not consider all available means to bring about the liberation of humanity. Instead, Dewey alleged, Trotsky deduced the need for class struggle from an independent source—an interpretation of history—which posited that class

[72] See JD to SH, 4 and 5 June 1938 (Hook-Dewey Papers, box 1, folder 5). The drafts of the essay and Hook's comments do not survive, but Dewey's letters acknowledge Hook's critical role.
[73] Leon Trotsky, "For an Open Polemic with the Liberals," in *Writings of Leon Trotsky (1937–38)*, 370.

struggle is the sole suitable means to achieve human liberation. It appeared, Dewey argued, that Trotsky returned to "the position that the *end-in-view* (as distinct from objective consequences) justifies the use of any means in line with the class struggle and that it justifies the neglect of all other means." Dewey called instead for the widest exploration of possible means of social change. If consideration was not given to positions other than class struggle, Dewey stated, then Trotsky was bound to a new form of absolutism as strict as philosophical idealism and orthodox religion had ever been: "There appears to be a curious transfer among orthodox Marxists of allegiance from the ideals of socialism and the scientific methods of attaining them (scientific in the sense of being based on the objective relations of means and consequences) to the class struggle as the law of historical change."[74]

Trotsky never found the time to respond to Dewey before his life was cut short by a Soviet agent in 1940. He would not have had much trouble demonstrating the misleading implication of Dewey's suggestion that he would have to endorse "any means in line with the class struggle," since he had clearly specified that not "any means" were acceptable. His conviction that pragmatism was the expression of middle-class progressivism and incapable of extending beyond radical bourgeois democracy is well established. But a different sort of reply to Dewey could have been drawn from the earlier thought of Sidney Hook, which contained many resources for defending the plausibility of a pragmatism compatible with revolutionary Marxism: that the class struggle is not metaphysically deduced but historically demonstrable; that class struggle, far from being constrictive or absolutist, is historically variant, waged with a tremendous range of tactics and strategies, and therefore does not dictate *particular* courses of action in any given instance; that class struggle is impermanent, for it may be transcended by revolutionary transformation; that working-class organization is an effective instrument of revolution, as illustrated by the examples of the Paris Commune and the original soviets; and, finally, that gradualism and reformism, the implied alternative in Dewey's experimental model, had proved themselves strategically impotent in countless instances. In short, even on the experiential grounds advocated by Dewey, the case for Trotsky's revolutionary morality could have been established—despite Trotsky's own suspicion of pragmatism.[75]

[74] John Dewey, "Means and Ends" (July 1938), in Trotsky, Dewey, and Novack, *Their Morals and Ours*, 52, 54, 56.
[75] The dissident Russian revolutionary Victor Serge, in unpublished remarks, criticized Trotsky's position from a revolutionary Marxist perspective also potentially compatible with Hook's earlier views. See Steven Lukes, *Marxism and Morality* (Oxford: Oxford University Press, 1987), 123–24.

But Hook, already on the road to social democracy, had no interest in upholding revolutionary socialism. He had tended toward the reverse, in fact, by aiding Dewey in drafting his response. That summer his own extended critique of Trotsky in a review of *The Revolution Betrayed* marked the distance Hook had traveled toward social democracy. He himself understood that his "Reflections on the Russian Revolution" marked a turning-point. When he sent the article to the *Southern Review* editors in August 1938, he described it as

> a critique of the fundamental assumptions of Bolshevist theory and practice as held by Lenin, Stalin and Trotsky, from the standpoint of a democratic theory of social change. I regard it as one of the most important things I have written not merely because it has taken me more than a year to do but because its challenge is directed to myths and legends entertained by an ever growing number of people. The coming November marks the twenty first anniversary of the Russian Revolution—it is of age and must be evaluated not as an experiment but as a result.

In a subsequent letter, Hook wrote that he anticipated "a lively response from any or all groups who think they are in possession of the 'holy Grail.'" Although the *Southern Review* could not accommodate the article in its fall issue, as Hook had hoped, they promised to publish it that January. Hook considered the article so important that he suggested sending an announcement of the Winter 1939 issue to a select list of several hundred names: "This is the first time that I have ever made a suggestion of this kind to any of the numerous periodicals for which I have written. I do so in this case because I regard this article as very important as indicating my own position on basic issues concerning which many people have written me." When the editors agreed with his proposal, Hook supplied them with a list, stipulating that recipients not be informed of his involvement.[76]

In "Reflections on the Russian Revolution" Hook abandoned his *Common Sense* position that although the Bolshevik leaders had made some serious political errors, their revolution was a justified step toward workers' democracy and human liberation. As his point of departure he took up *The Revolution Betrayed* (1936), Trotsky's magnum opus. None of Trotsky's ideas, Hook argued, were adequate to explain the degeneration of the Russian Revolution into Stalinism. Trotsky had noted the failure of revolutions elsewhere to materialize; the decimation of the most committed so-

[76] SH to Pipkin, 6 August 1938; SH to Albert Erskine, 15 December 1938; Erskine to SH, 20 December 1938; SH to Erskine, 22 December 1938 (Southern Review Papers, Yale University, Beinecke Rare Book and Manuscript Library). The list of names does not survive, unfortunately.

cialist workers in the civil war; the psychological letdown after the revolution and the resultant demoralization and careerism; the sickness and death of Lenin, the most capable leader; and the failure to provide for the material well-being of the masses because of the backward and war-torn economy. These efforts to locate the cause of degeneration in historical processes, Hook claimed, were nothing but "a rationalization of defeat." Trotsky begged the question of the political actions and moral responsibility of the Bolsheviks themselves, because none of the factors he cited were within the control of the Bolshevik Party.[77]

Hook contended that Trotsky could not exempt his party from moral criticism, given his own moral and political excoriation of reformism, for which there was also historical and economic explanation. Trotsky's pronouncements against reformism, Hook argued, "only make sense on the assumption that 'productive forces'—the motor power of his social necessity—on some of the most crucial occasions of history, are not decisive, neither in the first nor in the last instance." Trotsky's mistake, Hook posited, derived from a philosophy of history in which "the dialectic process in *nature* and *society* guarantee the victory of socialism." This premise of "orthodox Marxism" was religious: "It is no accident that the belief in a *Natur-dialectic* is the foundation stone of the theology of dialectical materialism." Whether or not Hook had accurately characterized Trotsky's philosophy, this line of argument indicated a significant leap of thought for him. In his 1936 review of August Thalheimer's book, he had distinguished the monistic dialectical materialism of "orthodox" Marxism from the experimental dialectical materialism of Marx. Now he ruled out dialectical materialism of *any* kind, judging it a telltale sign of orthodoxy and a theology antithetical to Marx. In combination with his criticisms of Trotsky, this suggested that Hook was moving toward an abandonment of revolutionary politics altogether, for it was increasingly difficult to imagine any revolutionary Marxism that would not in his mind be guilty of orthodoxy, dogmatism, and the seeds of totalitarian rule.[78]

The objective factors contributing to bureaucratic degeneration, as identified by Trotsky, should be set aside, Hook argued. More important were the actions of the Bolshevik Party itself, which had been guilty of repeated violations of democratic practice:

Questions of causation are always tangled knots, but I think it can be established that, given the conditions in which the Russian Revolution was begun, the only controllable factor that led to the degeneration of the Russian Rev-

[77] Hook, "Reflections on the Russian Revolution," *Southern Review* 4 (Winter 1939): 440.
[78] Ibid., 437, 441.

olution and its Thermidorian regime was the abrogation of working-class and peasant democracy, signalized by the suppression of all other political parties and the concentration of all power in the hands of the Communist Party. . . . The more forcibly the Communist Party exercised its dictatorship over other working-class parties, the more pervasive became the dictatorship of the Secretariat within the Communist Party itself.

The defeat of democracy within the Party, Hook asserted, had also been responsible for the political defeat of Trotsky, for in every instance in which Trotsky lost ground the reason was the denial to him and his followers of equal rights of assembly, agitation, and publication, as well as the outright repression of his faction.[79]

Against Trotsky's thesis that the dictatorship of the party was not part of essential Bolshevik doctrine but a temporary defensive maneuver under conditions of civil war and economic collapse, Hook maintained that the Bolsheviks had long identified the dictatorship of their party with that of the class. Of Hook's examples, however, the only concrete one was taken from the Fourth Congress of the Comintern, a body that had no real bearing on the matter, since Trotsky too would have identified its declarations as indicative of the nascent degeneration. Hook overturned his own earlier estimation of the benevolence of the early Bolshevik government without indicating that only one year before he had given it credit for judicial due process and evenhanded treatment of political opponents. "For every act of violence against Bolshevik leaders," he now asserted, "there were hundreds committed against their political opponents"; though there was some democracy in the early years, the overwhelming tendency was in the direction of one-party rule, with all alternative working-class formations condemned as counterrevolutionary. This dictatorial proclivity, Hook wrote, had its roots in the theory of a "vanguard" party. Socialists worthy of the name, he maintained, must admit "that there is a heterogeneity of interests in the working class as such and that different political parties represent them," so that no particular party can claim to be "the" vanguard. Instead, parties should understand themselves to represent "that part of the working class which in the course of free discussion and experience, gives it its confidence." Political leadership, yes; political dictatorship, no.[80]

A substantial body of revolutionary socialist thought in the intervening fifty years has come to affirm many of the moral and political tenets Hook expressed in "Reflections on the Russian Revolution," including his call for

[79] Ibid., 450–51.
[80] Ibid., 455, 458.

multiparty democracy under socialism and his critique of the potential dangers of "vanguard" pretensions. These were not fatal missteps but perspicacious truths, an advance over the blanket endorsement, common to Trotskyists of the time, of every action of Lenin and the Bolsheviks. But Hook no longer argued from a consistent position in favor of the October Revolution, such as that articulated by Rosa Luxemburg, who supported the Soviet uprising and considered it a great advance for humanity despite her severe criticisms of certain practices of Lenin and his party. Unlike Luxemburg, in no instance did Hook declare his basic solidarity with the Soviet revolution. He even implied at one point that the bourgeois democracy of Kerensky might have offered a superior alternative to both czarism and Bolshevism. By deriding the economic, military, and personal exigencies that Trotsky had considered pertinent to the fate of the revolution, and by dismissing those factors as nothing more than "rationalizations of defeat," Hook withdrew his analysis from the empirical realm that his earlier moral theory had emphasized and held the Russian revolutionaries to an abstract model of democracy approaching moral absolutism.

That Hook was moving quickly toward a qualitatively different politics and philosophy was intimated in his analysis of Trotskyism and Stalinism. He still argued that there was a basic distinction between the enormous crimes of Stalin and the historical record of Trotsky, but he added a new judgment:

> There are other aspects of Stalinism, less ghastly in their immediate impact, but just as dangerous to the ideals of socialism as those already enumerated. These flow from the advocacy of a minority party dictatorship during the transition period—in reality, a period which never ends—from capitalism to socialism. To the extent that Trotsky takes this view, Trotskyism and Stalinism, despite their antipodal differences on "the permanent revolution" or "socialism in one country," are politically one and the same. Despite the cultivated ambiguity of Lenin on party dictatorship, this was his view, too. Today since Trotsky no longer defends party dictatorship in principle, and interprets his past adherence to it as an exigency of historical circumstances, the identification of Stalinism and Trotskyism is impermissible. But until he takes a more positive stand and attacks it in principle, there will always be some suspicion that after all, potentially, Trotskyism is capable of developing into Stalinism.[81]

By these carefully couched words Hook condemned Trotskyism and Stalinism equally as "politically one and the same" without actually identifying

[81] Ibid., 461.

one with the other. Within half a year he would throw reticence to the wind, equate Trotskyism and Stalinism, and begin writing for the leading organ of right-wing social democracy, the *New Leader,* which was sponsored by the Social Democratic Federation, American section of the Second International and organ of the right-wing social democrats who had split from the Socialist Party of the mid-1930s.

How far Hook had moved was apparent even to James Burnham, whose own privately expressed doubts had provided part of the context of Hook's rethinking. Burnham joined forces with Max Shachtman, the finest pen of the American revolutionary socialist movement, to answer Hook in a brilliant riposte to backsliding intellectual radicals. Burnham and Shachtman singled out Hook's *Southern Review* apostasy, arguing that the real issue was neither one-party dictatorship (which they showed from quotation that Lenin, Trotsky, the Bolsheviks, and contemporary revolutionary socialists all rejected as a political principle) nor "the apostrophes to Truth and Freedom by which Hook has lately taken to climaxing his essays," but rather "an attack on revolutionary Marxism, on Bolshevism, and a growing *rapprochement* with reformism of both social-democratic and bourgeois varieties." Hook's turnabout was not prompted by fresh data, they observed, but by a new political perspective. His account of the Soviet revolution, they polemicized with devastating effect, was highly selective:

> In arguing for his thesis, Hook includes not one word of mention of the negative evidence well known to him and not to the bulk of those who will read the article. Not a word of *State and Revolution,* Lenin's magnificent formulation of workers' democracy, written on the very eve of October in order to explain to the masses not merely of Russia but of the world and for the future (as a guide if the Bolsheviks should at that time fail in achieving their aims) the meaning of workers' democracy. Not a word of Lenin's constant struggle, from the first year of the revolution until his death, against the bureaucratization of the party and state apparatus. Not a word on the great discussions over Brest-Litovsk, the Polish campaign, trade union policy. Not a word to indicate to the reader that the Bolsheviks invited the Mensheviks and S.R.s to form the government jointly with them, and that the Mensheviks and right wing S.R.s, standing on the basis of the Constituent Assembly, declined of their own will. Not a word to recall that those of the left S.R.s who had not meanwhile fused with the Bolsheviks voluntarily and deliberately withdrew from the government because of their disagreement with the Brest-Litovsk Treaty, and publicly announced themselves against the Soviet state power. Not a word of the fact that in 1923 Trotsky began the struggle of the Opposition on the issue of workers' democracy nor of the continuous struggle of the Opposition against Stalin's anti-democracy from then onward.

Shachtman and Burnham charged that many anti-Stalinist intellectuals, Hook included, were devolving "from a revolutionary Marxist position, or one close to it, *towards* reformism, or a little beyond it to bourgeois liberalism (or, in some cases, scarcely concealed passivity)."[82]

Turnabout, 1938

Was pragmatism responsible for the abandonment of beliefs that Hook had adamantly defended for twenty years? Pragmatism carried an intellectual emphasis on action that gave Hook a predisposition to search for political and moral error. A pragmatist cast overlay his claim that the degeneration of the Soviet regime stemmed directly from the thought and actions of the Bolsheviks. But these are insufficient. Hook had been a pragmatist almost as long as he had been a revolutionary. Pragmatism does not in itself explain his transformation. He had previously drawn upon pragmatism to argue something quite different, defending the revolutionary socialist tradition of action, organization, and workers' control as superior to both social democratic and Stalinist varieties of fatalism. Never before had he ignored the emphasis on historical conditions integral to Marxism, as he appeared to do in his review of Trotsky's *The Revolution Betrayed*.

The sources of Hook's shift lay, rather, in the unsettling historical situation and the way he chose to meet it. It is impossible to overemphasize the disastrous political developments: the dramatic new horrors of the Stalin regime unveiled at the Moscow trials, the rising threat of fascism and war in Europe, and the unparalleled success of the American Communist Party in swaying middle-class intellectuals to its program. Radical sectors of the U.S. working class, despite the fissures of the New Deal, experienced political disarray and defeat in 1938, diminishing the grounds for revolutionary hope and action. Hook was also ensnared in potentially difficult philosophical quandaries, including the moral problem of means and ends which faced the whole of the anti-Stalinist left. The political projects to which he was committed had all but disintegrated in 1937, when the *Marxist Quarterly* imploded and the Trotskyists were expelled from the Socialist Party. Those setbacks were partially offset by the re-creation of *Partisan Review*, but the division of Trotskyism and social democracy into separate, implacably opposed blocs brought to an unhappy conclusion Hook's brief period of simultaneous solidarity with both revolutionary socialism and the radical wing of social democracy under the umbrella of the Socialist Party.

[82] James Burnham and Max Shachtman, "Intellectuals in Retreat," *New International* 5 (January 1939): 3–22; the lengthy extract is from p. 10. The article lost some of its force when Burnham followed suit, going on to embrace not merely reformism or liberalism but out-and-out McCarthyism during the Cold War.

Finally, when the public philosophical dispute between Dewey and Trotsky in 1938 brought to an end their limited common cause of 1936–37, it became much harder for Hook to sustain his anti-Stalinist Deweyan Marxism. Meanwhile, personal acquaintances who harbored increasing skepticism about the Trotskyist alternative were sharing their thoughts with Hook, and he simultaneously resumed writing for the Socialist Party's journal and communicating with Norman Thomas. Some forces tugged Hook toward social democracy; some pushed him away from revolutionary politics; none invited fence-sitting.

This constellation of developments affected Hook's options considerably. No one of them could wholly determine his path; even in the face of all of them together, he could conceivably have preserved his revolutionary Marxism, but it would have involved considerable loss and sacrifice. Hook's predicament was real. It cannot be understood adequately by way of the epithets that the left routinely heaps upon its wayward souls: renegade, apostate, sellout. Hook's disavowal of Trotskyism, on the other hand, should not be seen as purely principled and democratic, a move from ideology to democracy. By the end of 1938 Hook was writing for the sharply anti-communist *New Leader* and allying himself with the same Socialist Party leaders who only a year before had violated basic democratic norms by expelling all Trotskyists and their sympathizers. Although there were unquestionably sectarian and sclerotic aspects to the Socialist Workers Party, it is not as though Burnham alone in the SWP was testing the waters for a new variant of revolutionary socialism that would move beyond the confines of orthodox Trotskyism. Almost half the SWP membership under the leadership of Shachtman, Burnham, and others decided to attempt precisely that in 1939–40, discarding the theory of "workers' states" in order to oppose both Stalinism and capitalism equally in the interests of a Third Camp of the world's exploited and oppressed peoples. Hook thus had democratic revolutionary socialist options open to him. But the rightward direction of his emerging world view manifested itself most clearly in the theory of "totalitarianism," which he began to advocate forcefully in 1939, for that theory had at its core an idea that Hook had until then rejected: the postulation that communism and fascism were virtually one and the same.

CHAPTER FIVE

The Constraints of Cultural Freedom, 1938–73

On a purely formal plane, Hook's thought in the final years of the 1930s was consistent with his earlier radicalism. His commitments to socialism, scientific method, democracy, and anti-Stalinism were undiminished. But as his anti-communist perspective crystallized, he gave to these themes—gradually in some cases, abruptly in others—a vastly different content and meaning. Previously, his opposition to Stalinism had been founded on the proposition that the Soviet bureaucracy was the antithesis of genuine communism, a counterrevolutionary reversal of the original aims of the October Revolution of 1917. By 1940 Hook was hostile to all revolutionary politics—especially to the Soviet revolution and Leninism. Formerly, his commitment to scientific method had been imbued with the understanding that all social observation is political and that Marxism obliges its adherents to support liberation struggles of the oppressed and exploited by means consistent with revolutionary morality and appropriate to historical conditions. Now, scientific method became for Hook a circumscribing boundary that effectively ruled out revolutionary thought and class partisanship as dogmatic. From a radical conception of democracy which held that participatory self-governance and intellectual freedom could never be satisfactorily secured within capitalist society, Hook retreated to a defense of existing Western institutions as the realistic alternative to totalitarianism. All his intellectual talents and energies were set to the task of exposing and opposing Nazi Germany and the Soviet Union, states that he began to equate through the use of formulas he had previously ridiculed as grossly erroneous in their conflation of fundamentally distinct social systems.

Democracy and socialism contracted in Hook's thought, so subtly that not even he appeared conscious of it at first. He still called himself a democratic socialist, but he was in retreat from revolution and increasingly aligned with social democracy, barely distinguished from liberal reformism in the degree of compromise with capitalist institutions he was willing to accept. He preserved his call for an independent labor party, but in place of his once sharp criticism of capitalism for its inherent inequities and degradations, Hook for all practical purposes (the ones that matter to a pragmatist) came by the beginning of the Second World War to accept bourgeois society as a real democratic alternative to totalitarianism. Increasingly in his writing, socialism was a vague ambition to be deferred until after the battle against totalitarianism was won and a social consensus achieved. It was no longer rooted in actual struggles by workers for better conditions and a new society, and its baseline was not the democratic rule of society from below by the working class. It was little more than a soft, far-away idea: a combination of rationalism and humanism within an expansive version of the welfare state.

In contrast to radicals who withdrew from political activity once disenchantment set in, Hook, if anything, gave to his new-found anti-communist zeal a more focused and organized expression than he had given to revolutionary socialism, at least since the days of the American Workers Party. The energies he had once expended on behalf of left-wing socialism were now devoted to an organization that he created and dominated: the Committee for Cultural Freedom, which in its brief life before the Second World War occupied the vanguard of anti-communist liberalism and set the pattern for its Cold War successors: the Congress for Cultural Freedom and its American affiliate, the American Committee for Cultural Freedom. Hook threw himself into fierce struggle against his opponents—in many instances not diehard Stalinists and fellow-traveling liberals but his former comrades in the very revolutionary movement he had once supported. As always, he elaborated on these new judgments with a prodigious outpouring of philosophical scholarship. He prepared a book on John Dewey's thought in time to present it for his mentor's eightieth birthday in 1939, and he published a volume of political and philosophical essays: *Reason, Social Myths, and Democracy* (1940). Each manifested the shift from capitalism to "totalitarianism" as the primary object of Hook's politics.

Hook with son Ernie picnicking at summer home of philosopher and friend Ernest Nagel, 1938. (Courtesy Ernest Hook.)

Hook lighting candles for daughter Susan as son Ernie looks on, August 23, 1942. (Courtesy Ernest Hook.)

Hook reading, in overalls, at Vermont summer home with son Ernie, circa 1943. (Courtesy Ernest Hook.)

Late in 1938 Hook circulated a confidential manifesto for a newly planned League against Totalitarianism. Signed by Hook, John Dewey, and its primary author, the journalist Eugene Lyons, the document requested that other intellectuals add their names to the statement. "Under varying labels and colors," the manifesto declared, "but with an unwavering hatred for the free mind, the totalitarian ideal is already enthroned in Germany, Italy, Russia, Japan and Spain." It looked almost exclusively to the intellectual and creative sphere, defining as totalitarian those nations in which art, science, and pedagogy had been "forcibly turned into court clowns for a deified state, an infallible leader and prescribed articles of social faith." The LAT, the statement proclaimed, would be committed "to no particular social philosophy—but only to a fundamental criterion for evaluating all social philosophies today: Whether it permits the thinker and the artist to function independently of political, religious, or racial dogmas." The League against Totalitarianism hoped to give anti-communism the same respectability that the League against War and Fascism and the League of American Writers had given to Communist politics in the cultural sphere. By the spring of 1939, however, the group settled upon the alternative name of the Committee for Cultural Freedom, presumably because it would not risk confusion with any Popular Front organization and sounded less conspiratorial.[1]

None of those in the revolutionary socialist milieu from which Hook was departing would object to condemnation of intellectual suppression and political tyranny in the Soviet Union or Nazi Germany; Stalinism and fascism were their sworn enemies. Quickly, however, dispute arose over how best to understand the varying national regimes that the LAT statement grouped together as "totalitarian," as well as what alternative, socialist revolution or compromise with capitalist democracy, offered the best strategy. On December 8, 1938, for instance, Dwight Macdonald—the talented literary journalist who knew Hook through the *Partisan Review* and was moving closer to Trotskyism at the very time Hook was rejecting it—wrote to him that the manifesto made "totalitarianism appear like some blight or pestilence which is mysteriously sweeping over certain portions of the earth." Macdonald feared that the new organization would amount to the equivalent of a Popular Front consortium of bourgeois liberals and radicals, directed in this instance against an ill-defined totalitarianism rather

---

[1] Untitled confidential draft of LAT manifesto (Dwight Macdonald Papers, Yale University, Sterling Memorial Library). Hook's circulation of the manifesto is revealed in, e.g., SH to Jerome Frank, 26 April 1939 (Jerome Frank Papers, Yale University, Sterling Memorial Library).

than fascism: "Unless the concrete political and economic roots of totalitarianism are exposed, it seems to me, the LAT becomes one more emotional, witchburning, classless-middle-class outfit . . . with totalitarianism substituted for fascism as the bogeyman." Its program had so much in common with the anti-communist congressional investigating committee led by conservative Martin Dies, wrote Macdonald, that he considered it equally "empty and even potentially red-baiting." The new organization, he suggested, ought instead to set itself apart from such reactionary activity by straightforwardly expressing "that its sympathies are on the left, with the masses and against their exploiters."[2]

Many on the anti-Stalinist left were, like Macdonald, unwilling to accept the identification of incompatible social systems sheerly on the basis of certain shared political characteristics. They were critical of fascist Italy, Nazi Germany, and Stalin's Soviet Union for their shared repressive characteristics of concentration of power under a dictatorial leader, suppression of dissent, and single-party political monopoly, but they objected to a politics premised primarily upon opposition to an undifferentiated "totalitarianism."[3] Nonetheless, Hook and his anti-communist colleagues stuck to the new approach they had taken in the LAT manifesto, changing only a few phrases from the original draft to launch their new organization. On May 27, 1939, a statement announcing the formation of the Committee for Cultural Freedom appeared in *The Nation*, signed by ninety-seven prominent writers and intellectuals.[4]

Nation editor Freda Kirchwey condemned the CCF in the very same issue in which the founding manifesto appeared. Kirchwey, a left-liberal partial to the Popular Front, assailed what she viewed as an attempt "to create a clear division on the Left by relegating members of the Communist Party and the vague ranks of its sympathizers to outer totalitarian darkness." The "only important feature of the present manifesto is its emphasis on Russian totalitarianism," she argued, since that was the only aspect that would invite disagreement among liberals and radicals. Kirchwey agreed that the Communist Party "is a nuisance and a menace to all its opponents" but maintained that Communists nonetheless "perform necessary func-

[2] Dwight Macdonald to SH, 6 December 1938 (Dwight Macdonald Papers, Yale University, Sterling Memorial Library).
[3] In their remarks on the "League of Abandoned Hopes," as they redubbed it, James Burnham and Max Shachtman charged that "these anti-Stalinists are forming a typically Stalinist People's Front—without the Stalinists"; see their "Intellectuals in Retreat," *New International* 5 (January 1939): 18–19.
[4] "Manifesto," *The Nation* 148 (27 May 1939): 626. The CCF signers included Louis Adamic, V. F. Calverton, Rudolf Carnap, George S. Counts, Merle Curti, John Dewey, Max Eastman, Irwin Edman, Horace Kallen, Suzanne LaFollette, Arthur Lovejoy, H. A. Overstreet, John Dos Passos, James Rorty, George Schuyler, Benjamin Stolberg, Norman Thomas, and William Carlos Williams.

tions in the confused struggle of our time," helping to build organizations "which clearly serve the cause not of 'totalitarian doctrine' but of a more workable democracy." Although she was more candidly critical of the Communist Party than were most Popular Front supporters, Kirchwey's assertion of the need to suppress disagreements between liberals and radicals in order to preserve unity against fascism reflected the most debilitating and undemocratic aspect of the Popular Front: its refusal to tolerate criticism of Stalin's rule in the Soviet Union, a country it considered pivotal to any successful anti-fascist coalition. In a brief rejoinder, Hook easily pinpointed Kirchwey's confusion: "If the Communist Party is guilty of even some of the disgraceful and illiberal practices which she herself underscores, why, in heaven's name, should decent people not 'differentiate' themselves from it?" Kirchwey replied, weakly, "If Communists and non-Communists and even anti-Communists could forget their mutual recriminations and concentrate on the major task of our generation, there would be better hope of its successful accomplishment."[5]

The CCF came in for similar criticism from other anti-fascist liberals, notably the *New Republic* and a hastily convened "Committee of 400." Led by Corliss Lamont—Hook's Columbia classmate and *Marxist Quarterly* colleague who had parted ways with him over the issue of the Moscow trials in 1937, and who served as National Chairman of the American Friends of the Soviet Union—the Committee of 400 in August 1939 issued a counterstatement charging "fascists and their allies" with attempting to disrupt the unity of progressive forces "by sowing suspicion between the Soviet Union and other nations interested in maintaining peace." The statement—devoted in the main to the importance of "Soviet socialism" as as an obstacle to "totalitarian fascism," and suggesting that critics of Stalinism were akin to friends of fascism—was actually signed by 165 people (a greater number than the 97 public backers of the CCF statement, but a far cry from 400).[6]

Many of the signers were chagrined upon waking up one week later to discover in the morning paper that the Soviet Union and Nazi Germany had signed a nonaggression pact, carving up Poland and permitting Hitler

[5] Freda Kirchwey, "Red Totalitarianism," *The Nation* 148 (27 May 1939): 605–6; Hook, Letter to the Editor, and Kirchwey, reply to Hook, *The Nation* 148 (17 June 1939): 710–11.

[6] Besides Lamont, the ranks of the Committee of 400 included Newton Arvin, Waldo Frank, Dashiell Hammett, Granville Hicks, Leo Huberman, Meridel LeSeur, Robert Morss Lovett, F. O. Matthiessen, Carey McWilliams, S. J. Perelman, Frederick Schuman, George Seldes, James Thurber, and Richard Wright. William Carlos Williams, who had originally signed the CCF manifesto, crossed over to the Lamont group. *Nation* editors Max Lerner and I. F. Stone also signed the Commitee of 400 statement, though a majority of the board opposed it in an editorial. The full list of signators is printed in Eugene Lyons, *The Red Decade* (New York: Arlington House, 1971), 349–51. See also Hook, *Out of Step* (New York: Harper & Row, 1987), 266–69.

to annex neighboring territories. Since the Popular Front rested on the thesis that the Soviet Union, whatever its faults, was an implacable foe of war and fascism, the Stalin-Hitler pact caused substantial defections from the Communist Party. Among those who resigned, Granville Hicks later wrote that the timing of the publication of the Committee of 400 statement and the pact's announcement "made a lot of those of us who signed it feel silly—and worse than silly."[7]

The Nazi-Soviet pact did not automatically confirm the "totalitarianism" thesis, which equated the two states and societies by treating them as more similar than not. Some intellectuals contested both the Committee for Cultural Freedom and Popular Front liberalism, vowing uncompromising opposition to bureaucratic rule in the Soviet Union and undiminished opposition to capitalism, fascism, and imperialism. Their approach, contained in essence in Dwight Macdonald's 1938 letter to Hook, cohered in mid-1939 with the formation of the League for Cultural Freedom and Socialism, with members drawn primarily from *Partisan Review* writers and the Socialist Workers Party milieu—in other words, from more or less Trotskyist circles. Like the CCF, the League for Cultural Freedom and Socialism deplored the repressive features of Stalinism and fascism. Unlike the CCF, it argued that socialism was required before genuine cultural freedom could be established and that any attempt to secure cultural freedom without attention to the class struggle was likely to devolve into a conventional liberalism. "It goes without saying," the LCFS statement declared, "that we do not subscribe to the currently fashionable catchword: 'Neither communism nor fascism.' On the contrary, we recognize that the liberation of culture is inseparable from the liberation of the working classes and of all humanity."[8]

These Marxist intellectuals were soon divided, however, for a great debate erupted in 1939 over how to evaluate the European war and analyze the social system of Stalin's Soviet Union. Theoretical differences over such questions had existed in the Socialist Workers Party from its inception, but they were brought to a head by the Nazi-Soviet pact of August 1939, which was rapidly followed by the German invasion of Poland and the advance of the Red Army into Poland, Lithuania, Latvia, Estonia, and Finland. How

---

[7] Granville Hicks, *Where We Came Out* (New York: Viking, 1954), 58.

[8] The LCFS roster included Lionel Abel, James Burnham, V. F. Calverton, F. W. Dupee, James T. Farrell, Clement Greenberg, Melvin J. Lasky, Sherry Mangan, George Novack, Kenneth Patchen, William Phillips, Philip Rahv, Kenneth Rexroth, James Rorty, Harold Rosenberg, Meyer Schapiro, Delmore Schwartz, John Wheelwright, Bertram D. Wolfe, and William Carlos Williams (who apparently did not miss any opportunity to sign a statement in 1939). See League for Cultural Freedom and Socialism, "War Is the Issue!" *Partisan Review* 6 (Fall 1939): 125–27; Hook, *Out of Step*, 262.

was the traditional Trotskyist slogan "unconditional defense of the USSR" to be applied in this new situation, in which the influence of the Soviet bureaucracy was extending over new territories within a tacit accord with German imperialism? A majority of the SWP, led by James P. Cannon and supported from Mexico by Trotsky, called for defense of the Red Army's conquests on the grounds that the USSR was a degenerated workers' state: deformed, repressive, dominated by a bureaucratic caste deserving to be dislodged by a political revolution of the workers, but worthy of defense from imperialism because the socialized property forms brought about by the October Revolution represented a substantial advance beyond capitalism. A large minority led by Max Shachtman and James Burnham argued for revisiting that theory in light of recent history: the USSR, they held, had produced a historically unprecedented bureaucratic social formation antagonistic to the interests of the workers. Socialism, they argued, could not be imposed from above on Eastern Europe by the Red Army's bayonets.[9]

Despite these irreconcilable differences, neither side in the debate within revolutionary socialism proposed—as Hook, in effect, did—to rely upon bourgeois democracy as the alternative to Stalinism and fascism. Both Marxist tendencies called, as Hook previously had, for working-class revolutionary political action to establish egalitarian, participatory societies. Despite their analytical disagreement over European developments and the USSR, revolutionary socialists of both varieties continued to maintain that the differences between fascist and Communist regimes were as great as their apparent similarities. The brutal, dictatorial character of the political regime under fascism and Nazism, they argued, only strengthened the ruling class of finance capital. In the Soviet Union, by contrast, the rule of capital had been eliminated by the October Revolution of 1917, which abolished private property at the commanding heights of the economy. This crucial distinction in property forms distinguished Stalinism from fascism. Fascism, revolutionary socialists insisted, must be understood as the product of capitalism in crisis—not as a twin of Stalinism, which was the result of a quite different crisis, the bureaucratic deterioration of a workers' revolution. The struggle against Stalinism, they also held, had to be combined with the struggle against capitalism, since capitalist encirclement and the failure of revolutions to materialize abroad were the main causes

---

[9] In 1939–40 the theoretical lines were not drawn as neatly as the political lines. Only after April 1940, when approximately 40 percent of the SWP membership left to form the Workers Party, would Shachtman begin to use the term "bureaucratic collectivism." The Workers Party would call upon socialists to defend the interests of the "Third Camp" of the exploited and oppressed against both empires, Stalinist and capitalist, East and West. See Chapter 4, note 64, for a fuller analysis of the debate within Trotskyism over the Soviet state.

of the emergence of a bureaucratic stratum within the Soviet Union.

Hook had at first aligned himself with the dissident Trotskyists who denied that the Soviet Union was any longer a "workers' state" in any meaningful sense of the term, but he had traveled so far by 1939 that he could no longer identify with the minority within revolutionary socialism. Although he continued to call himself a socialist, he had nothing but disdain for the approach of the League for Cultural Freedom and Socialism, which he considered hopelessly sectarian. The LCFS included many of the figures with whom he had been closely associated on the anti-Stalinist left, but Hook now repudiated the analysis he had once articulated. Broad-based, unified opposition to totalitarianism, he was now arguing, could be built only by eschewing any particular analysis of its cause or nature. For Hook, the degree of civil liberties and cultural freedom under democratic capitalism was so superior to the odious conditions of totalitarianism that a call for socialism as the only guarantor of cultural freedom seemed ludicrous. But his new perspective was shaped less by a rejection of sectarianism than by a restricted definition of democracy. In "On Workers' Democracy," Hook had argued in 1934 that those who viewed the fundamental question of the age as democracy or dictatorship were guilty of "a profound error which flows from isolating the political phase of the socio-economic process, and considering it to be the chief independent causal factor moulding patterns of social thought and behavior." The central conflict, he wrote then, was "not democracy versus dictatorship but capitalism versus communism." Workers' democracy—not merely "the registration of consent" but "the actual power to control the conditions and direction of social life"—had always to be in the forefront, since from freedom of ownership flowed political, social, and cultural power. But in 1938, in his *Southern Review* article "Democracy as a Way of Life," he wrote, strikingly, "A democratic society is one where the government rests upon the consent of the governed." Hook's philosophical passage from radical democracy to liberal democracy (from *power* to *consent*) could not have been more evident.[10]

He defended his new anti-totalitarian program in an exchange with the radical writer Max Nomad in the fall of 1939. An opinion piece by Nomad in the *New Leader* had argued that full employment was the antidote to fascism, since only systemic reform would ease the disaffection that was the breeding ground for reaction: "Fascism can be fought only by attacking the present status quo in behalf of greater concessions to the underdog. It cannot be fought mainly in the name of 'liberty' and 'democracy.'" Hook, sign-

[10] Hook, "On Workers' Democracy," *Modern Monthly* 8 (October 1934): 529–30, 541; Hook, "Democracy as a Way of Life," *Southern Review* 4 (Summer 1938): 47.

ing his rebuttal as chairman of the CCF executive committee, admitted that workers who followed the Stalinists or fascists were looking for "a full dinner pail," but he also maintained that "what they must be made to see by education and organization and struggle is that where liberty and democracy are lost, there can be no genuine economic security." Fights for liberty and democracy, he argued, inevitably involved fights for "progressively higher living conditions." Nomad, in return, accused Hook of being "remote from reality" if he thought the fight for liberty was the same as the fight against economic desperation, and he accused Hook of reviving the program of old-time social democracy, which had failed to fend off fascism the first time around. The primary need of the moment, wrote Nomad, was primarily for mass action for radical social reforms to abolish poverty and unemployment. The Nomad-Hook exchange left the impression that the antagonists were talking past each other. It does not take much imagination to see that campaigns for economic justice and political democracy can be combined. Hook exaggerated their similarity by claiming that they were simply identical, but he was correct about their compatibility. What his debate with Nomad demonstrated was the increasingly one-sided quality of Hook's emphasis. His devotion to the CCF caused his vision of fundamental social transformation to recede and made anti-totalitarianism dominant, almost to the point of exclusivity, in his political thought and action.[11]

The Committee for Cultural Freedom boasted many notables in its top leadership—including John Dewey as honorary chairman and Ferdinand Lundberg as secretary—but Hook was its real driving force. Together with Frank N. Trager, a right-wing Socialist who had helped lead the social democratic purge of Trotskyists from the New York branch in 1937, Hook chaired the Committee on Plans and Organization, the backbone of the CCF. That committee—commissioned by a gathering in Columbia University's Seth Low Hall on May 16, 1939, of signers of the CCF manifesto—first met on June 16 at the home of John Dewey, where the chief topic of discussion was the pressure being applied from various liberal quarters upon CCF members to resign. Dewey and Hook agreed at a follow-up meeting on September 11 to draft a response to the Committee of 400 letter, a decision that was affirmed at the general membership meeting on October 1 at Columbia. Hook's leadership was also in evidence when he chaired the first public meeting sponsored by the CCF at Town Hall on Friday, October 13, 1939. There the subject "Cultural Freedom and the World Cri-

[11] Max Nomad, "Fight on Status Quo Best Weapon against Fascism," *New Leader* 22 (2 September 1939): 10; Hook, "Fight for Civil Liberties Can Balk 'Totalitarianites,'" *New Leader* 22 (7 October 1939): 5; Max Nomad, "Only 'Bread and Butter' Campaign Will Swing Masses against Fascists," *New Leader* 22 (9 October 1939): 5, 7.

sis" was addressed by a panel of prominent anti-communists, including General W. C. Krivitsky, a Soviet defector, and Harry D. Gideonse, president of Brooklyn College.[12]

The anti-totalitarian approach of the Committee for Cultural Freedom meant that an entire range of economic and social issues, which Hook had assured Nomad were implicit in any push for liberty, never actually rose to the fore in its publicity and discussions. The organization produced several detailed research reports, among them "Stalinist Outposts in the United States," a list of Communist "front" groups; and "Nazi Outposts in the United States," a similar treatment of proto-fascist formations. As their titles indicated, both reports treated domestic movements as little more than local offices of foreign powers. When the first edition of the CCF's *Bulletin* appeared on October 15, 1939, the implications of its theory of totalitarianism were on full display. Although the newsletter's articles were unsigned, the full-throated polemics on Stalinism carried hints of Hook's editorial pen, one piece referring, for example, to the "Stalinazi Pact" as proof "that all totalitarian dictators are brothers under the skin."[13]

Even the articles in the *Bulletin* that reflected the generally liberal hue of the Committee for Cultural Freedom illustrated the constrictions that the theory of totalitarianism was imposing upon those radicals and reformers who had embraced it. An unsigned editorial, "The Browder Case and Civil Liberties," decried the decision of Harvard University to deny Communist Party leader Earl Browder the opportunity to speak, yet it argued that no curtailment of civil liberties was at stake for no one had the right to speak on private grounds without invitation; the decision, it maintained, was not antithetical to liberty but *unwise*. Similarly, in "Mr. Dies—and 'Americanism'" the CCF attacked the House Un-American Activities Committee chair, but its chief objection was that Dies "plays into the hands of the American cohorts of Stalin and Hitler, just as they play into the hands of domestic reactionaries." This statement prefigured Hook's later Cold War argument that the problem with Senator Joseph McCarthy was not his

[12] This lineup prompted Corliss Lamont to tar the CCF as "your Dies-Krivitsky sub-committee" in a sour private letter to Hook. He thanked Hook for disparaging his book *You Might Like Socialism* at the Town Hall meeting, and expressed hope that the publicity would help sales and that "you are not becoming over-excited in these troublous times": Corliss Lamont to SH, 19 October 1939 (Hook Papers, box 18). See CCF Committee on Plans and Organization, Minutes, 16 May and 26 June 1939, 11 September and 1 October 1939 (ACCF Records, New York University, box 2, folder 8); CCF letterhead and Town Hall meeting flier (ACCF Records, NYU, Tamiment Library, box 2, folder 7); Hook speech to CCF meeting, 13 October 1939 (Hook Papers, box 43, folder 33).
[13] This argument, though rhetorically effective at the moment of the Nazi-Soviet pact, made it difficult for theorists of totalitarian identity to explain the Nazi turnabout in 1941, which brought the Soviets into the Allied camp. See CCF Report No. 2, CCF Report No. 3, and CCF *Bulletin*, 15 October 1939, 9 (ACCF Records, NYU, Tamiment Library, box 2, folder 9).

aims but his clumsy, counterproductive methods. In only one instance, African American writer George S. Schuyler's "Cultural Freedom and the American Negro" (June 1940), did the *Bulletin* sharply criticize any institutional aspect of American society in a manner that would call into question the contrast between "free" and "totalitarian" worlds. "A few, risen above the mired mass, have won honors and acclaim," wrote Schuyler of black Americans. "But it has been despite American 'freedom,' and not because of it. Although there has been a noticeable improvement in race relations since the first World War, we are so far from according Negroes equal opportunity, rights and privileges, that our criticism of the dictatorships is grimly laughable." Schuyler's uncompromising comments only cast a brighter light on the failure of other CCF members, including Hook, to put forward similar criticisms of American society consistently. Hook undoubtedly would have objected to segregation if asked about it, but the leading member of the Committee for Cultural Freedom at the same time considered American society, despite its flaws, a beacon of cultural democracy in need less of criticism than of intellectual defense against the totalitarian menace.[14]

The Constriction of Pragmatism and Marxism, 1939–40

On epistemology and method Sidney Hook and John Dewey had often been in agreement; in matters of politics, less often. Hook's efforts from the late 1920s to the mid-1930s to prod Dewey in a revolutionary direction had been largely futile, for although he was a socialist and radical democrat with occasional revolutionary impulses, Dewey in practice remained a reformist. Even as Hook began to adopt a liberalism more conventional than he had previously countenanced, he met resistance from Dewey. The elderly philospher consented to serve as honorary chairman of the CCF, a highly symbolic role, and to help refute the *New Republic*'s attacks on the organization, but he declined to exploit the occasion of his eightieth birthday for a public celebration of liberal democracy, as Hook wished. And when Hook sent him a draft reply to the Committee of 400 circular, Dewey recommended a response "of somewhat different tenor," one that would avoid a "severe and direct attack upon the CPs responsible for the letter" so as "not to imitate their tactics." Finally, the Nazi-Soviet nonaggression pact of August 1939 led Dewey to resign his position as honorary chairman of the CCF. Unlike Hook and others who were driven by

[14] "The Browder Case and Civil Liberties," and "Mr. Dies—and 'Americanism,'" both in CCF *Bulletin* 2:1 (n.d.): 11, 12; George S. Schuyler, "Cultural Freedom and the American Negro," CCF *Bulletin*, June 1940, 1.

the turn of events to an even more aggressive and hardline anti-communism, Dewey concluded pragmatically that with Stalinism so severely discredited, its disgrace afforded him an opportunity to place his energies elsewhere. "When I accepted," he wrote to Hook on November 16, 1939, "there was a certain crisis which seemed to me clearly to call for my doing what I did and I am not at all sorry. But the Stalinite action, now a matter of common knowledge, in connection with Hitler has, it seems to be, very much reduced if not destroyed that crisis as far as liberals in this country are concerned, so that emergency, which influenced me before, no longer applies to my action."[15]

Although Hook had had to tug a half-willing Dewey along on his new-found crusade against totalitarianism, he found on paper and in the realm of philosophy a more pliant Dewey. Hook had long argued that Deweyan pragmatism required revolutionary socialism for its fulfillment, since experimental reason and participatory democracy could never be wholly realized within class society. In a striking reversal carried out in his first full-length book since *From Hegel to Marx,* Hook now praised pragmatism as an eloquent restatement of social democracy in an American idiom. *John Dewey* (1939), written to mark Dewey's eightieth birthday, called him the "philosopher of American democracy" and his pragmatism a philosophy for the "plain man." Only a few years after his critique of abstract moralism from the perspective of pragmatism and historical materialism, Hook wrote that Dewey "speaks for those who wish to see the crucial problems and conflicts of our day settled by a voluntary consent obtained by persuasion, and not by terror and bloodshed." Although Dewey was not a pure pacifist in Hook's estimation (the conditions under which a departure from pacifism was warranted were not supplied), he did seek to make every effort for a peaceful and democratic transition to socialism. Dewey acknowledged class struggles, Hook wrote, but opposed incantations of "the class struggle" to justify forceful means. If Dewey and Marx were perhaps still compatible, Hook's new-found Marx was incompatible with Bolshevism. Previously, Hook had defended the Soviet revolution as less bloodthirsty and destructive than the imperialism it had overturned. Now he had no good word for any revolutionary current or idea, and he showed an unprecedented enthusiasm for Dewey's program of educational activity, gradual reform, and middle-class radicalism, instruments that he had previously

---

[15] On the same day, Dewey wrote to assure Frank N. Trager, that "the Committee is now so successfully launched" that it no longer required "such adventitious support as the use of my name may have given it at first." See JD to SH, 22 March, 9 April, 13 September, and 16 November 1939; JD to Frank Trager, 16, 18, and 22 November 1939 (all in Hook-Dewey Collection, box 1, folder 6).

considered potentially beneficiary but ultimately insufficient as means of social change.[16]

In "John Dewey at Eighty," a lengthy editorial for the *New Leader*, Hook revealed even more overtly his changed understanding of socialism and pragmatism. He criticized "those who look for infallible guidance to a dogma or a leader, whether it be to DeLeon or Lenin, Trotsky or Stalin." He recapitulated his familiar appreciation of Dewey's scientific method in a manner no different from his earlier formulations, but he came to a surprising conclusion: "Because he follows the lead of scientific method, Dewey refuses to be bound in his thinking by easy oppositions like capitalism *or* socialism, socialism *or* fascism, totalitarianism *or* democracy. Once these terms are given empirical content, we can see that their presence or absence is a matter of degree." In these sentences, which only a few years before Hook would have blasted as muddleheaded, he treated social systems and political ideologies in the same way that pragmatists treat philosophical dualisms. Historical conflicts between such incompatible modes of production as socialism and capitalism, and irreconcilable conflicts between such ideologies as socialism and fascism, he treated like the sort of conceptual opposition—such as existence and being—that pragmatism sought to transcend. Hook was dismissing conflicts of great *practical* force as if they were metaphysical antics. Given that he had thrown himself fully into the fight for "democracy" against "totalitarianism," it was odd that he included that pairing in his list of artificial oppositions, but his rationale soon became apparent. "At any definite time," wrote Hook, in a vivid example of how far his vision had contracted to a politics of gradual reform, "the choice is between greater or less freedom, greater or less security." What was true in such a statement was trite; what was missing was the strategy of revolutionary practice that Hook had once judged necessary to attain and secure genuine freedom and security. He still disparaged "inching along" when "sometimes it is necessary to take a yard," but he insisted upon "the use of means which are continuous with our end-in-view," an ambiguous phrase that seemed to require purity of the Kantian variety. Scientific method, always important to Hook's pragmatism, also took on a newly hardened and formal character when he wrote that adherence to scientific method as the means of settling disputes—not any concrete political issue, such as the war—was the chief gauge by which to judge whether socialists were true to their professed ideals.[17]

The degree to which Hook's Marxism had evaporated and his pragmatism become a pale shadow of its former self was also in view in *Reason, So-*

16 Hook, *John Dewey: An Intellectual Portrait* (New York: John Day, 1939), 238.
17 Hook, "John Dewey at Eighty," *New Leader* 22 (28 October 1939): 5.

cial Myths, and Democracy (1940), a collection and revision of the essays he had written over several years. Hook now suggested that it might be appropriate, even necessary, for people of good will to discard "Marxism" as a self-identifying term. The remaining virtue of socialism, he argued, was its argument against capitalism, a system incapable of permanently resolving its problems. The task for socialists, however, was to demonstrate that socialism would in fact be better, an assumption that could no longer be taken for granted. Rather than arguing that Stalinism was the antithesis of Marxism, Hook now suggested that Stalinism might have arisen from Marxism as a doctrine, without conceding the culpability of Marx himself. In a breathtaking reversal of his 1933 position in *Towards the Understanding of Karl Marx*, undertaken with the aid of highly selective textual evidence, Hook now asserted that Lenin was naive, wantonly murderous, and, above all, guilty of the modern debasement of Marx.

Not only Lenin but the whole of revolutionary socialism came in for excoriation. In a not-so-oblique reference to Trotskyism, Hook dismissed those who, "proud of their orthodoxy," are "compelled to say as they run from the brutal blows of reaction, that it is all happening according to the principles of Marxism. Win or lose, their doctrines are right. Every defeat is an additional confirmation." During the Moscow trials Hook had eloquently assailed this very theme by combating the Stalinist slander of Trotskyists as historical "losers" whose belief in their correctness was disproved by their political failure. Hook also now propounded some of the very ideas he had denounced in *Common Sense* in early 1938. To his "Reflections on the Russian Revolution," which in its *Southern Review* form had cautioned that "the identification of Stalinism and Trotskyism is impermissible," even while calling them similar, Hook added a new paragraph suggesting that Trotskyism and Stalinism were "socially identical twins fathered by Leninism." He offered no textual justification for this about-face, despite his many remonstrations about the need for scientific proof and method. "This suggests," he declared in a phrase that would become one of his favorites, repeated in countless articles and letters, "that Trotskyism is Stalinism *manqué*."[18]

Marxism, Hook concluded, had been above all a colossal moral failure because it had resulted in untold horrors in practice and obfuscation and dogma in theory. Historical materialism had amounted to nothing more than economic determinism, and Marx's rationalism and humanism had been abandoned, starting with Lenin. Hook's ever more strident condemnation of his erstwhile Marxist heroes was in piquant contrast to his own increasingly uncritical admiration of Dewey. The legacy of Marx, Hook as-

[18]   Hook, *Reason, Social Myths and Democracy* (New York: John Day, 1940), 106, 179.

serted, was to be found "not so much in contemporary Marxists or Marxist movements as in the thought of individuals who, identifying Marxism with Marx, naturally regard themselves as utterly opposed to him. The most outstanding figure in the world today in whom the best elements of Marx's thought are present is John Dewey." Criticism of Dewey had vanished along with Hook's revolutionary conviction. Dewey now appeared Marx incarnate. What was worthwhile in Marx was carried on in Dewey: rationalism and humanism. These admirable but abstract values, along with scientific method, were upheld by Hook as constituting the only way to resuscitate the socialist tradition. Rather than pursuing the distinction between "ultimate" and "final" values which he had creatively suggested in "Marxism and Values," Hook made scientific method and an ill-defined humanism into political litmus tests—final values, as it were. In form, he affirmed what he had always affirmed: a commitment to experimental flexibility. In substance, he no longer accepted any contemporary revolutionary activity as compatible with science, humanism, and rationalism. Hook had stripped from the philosophy of both Marx and Dewey their revolutionary implications. He had passed into a world quite different from that of *Towards the Understanding of Karl Marx*, where he had emphasized revolutionary practice as the essence of Marxism, and into a world equally removed from that of *From Hegel to Marx*, where he had recounted Marx's repudiation of abstractly ethical and rational socialisms and upheld Marx's conviction that socialism could mean nothing apart from the revolutionary activity of the working class. In *Reason, Social Myths, and Democracy* Hook was bent upon confronting revolution, not reformism; "totalitarianism," not capital.[19]

Democracy to Hook had come to mean principally civil liberties and fair elections. Those had always been valued by him, but gone was his analysis of bourgeois democracy as an inadequate, stunted form of democracy masking the social domination of a ruling class. Capitalist democracy now appeared the real alternative to Stalinism and fascism, a resource to be nurtured and appreciated against all totalitarian onslaughts. He warned that the "Trojan horse" of totalitarian treason, "no matter what protective coloration it wears—and it will usually be found wrapped up in counterfeit symbols of patriotism or in recently acquired vestments of the Bill of Rights—must be swiftly dealt with if democracy is to survive." By constricting anti-Stalinism to the defense of a fragile U.S. democracy, Hook had forgotten his own warning in "Communism without Dogmas" (1934) that "to take the rules of political democracy in a profit society . . . as the *fixed* limits within which to struggle for a truly human society, is to give a lease in

[19]   Ibid., 132.

perpetuity to the capitalist dictatorship upon the lives of the people." He likewise now considered fascism a system of a new type, totalitarianism, rather than an acutely reactionary form of bourgeois rule. He therefore chose to ally with the West against it, shedding as a result his belief that fascism could never be laid to rest permanently so long as capitalism, with its recurring crises, existed. Hook's fiercest barbs were aimed no longer at capitalism but at the left, including anti-Stalinist revolutionary socialism. Leninism, Stalinism, Trotskyism, even Catholicism: all were totalitarian, employing "*miracle, mystery* and *authority* —to order a society in behalf of a bureaucratic hierarchy." Hook held Trotsky to be more intelligent than Stalin but no different "in principle." Intellectual responsiblity for Hook now rested on a narrowly construed defense of "cultural freedom" against the perceived ideologists of totalitarianism. Marxism itself was suspect. No one who called himself a Marxist was in Hook's judgment as close in outlook to Marx as Dewey, a professed opponent of Marxism.[20]

Just as Hook was completing *Reason, Social Myths and Democracy*, Trotsky was murdered at Stalin's initiative. Hook dedicated his book, obliquely, "To the memory of a Great Adversary," but the revolutionary whom Hook so honored while accusing him of dogmatism and latent totalitarianism would doubtless have returned the favor with a characteristically sharp rebuke. Trotsky had expressed exasperation shortly before his death with the presumption of Dewey that "the decay and degeneration of the Soviet bureaucracy disqualifies communism and that the decay of democracy proves the vitality of liberalism." Trotsky referred sternly to "the unbridgeable gulf between Marxists and the conservative petty-bourgeois democrats who once a week recall that they are socialists." Only a few years before, Hook might have found Trotsky's polemic bracing. Now he had entered into the precise milieu that was its target.[21]

Failures of Nerve, 1940–45

Nowhere was the transvaluation of Hook's politics more dramatic than on the subject of war. Ever since his days as a high school agitator he had promoted working-class internationalism and opposed imperialist war. Throughout the 1930s he had been an acid critic of Communists and supporters of the Popular Front who advocated alliances with democratic im-

[20]   Ibid., 76, 179, 296; Hook, "Communism without Dogmas," in *The Meaning of Marx*, ed. Sidney Hook (New York: Farrar & Rinehart, 1934), 66.
[21]   Leon Trotsky, "Thomas's Letter and Dewey's Speech," and "Petty-Bourgeois Democracy and Moralizers," in *Writings of Leon Trotsky, Supplement (1934–40)*, ed. George Breitman (New York: Pathfinder, 1979), 752, 868. See also Hook, *Reason, Social Myths and Democracy*, flyleaf and 152 n. 3a.

perialism and bourgeois liberalism to guard against fascism. In addition to his philosophical objections to the ossified Marxism of the Comintern and his abhorrence of political dictatorship and repression in the Soviet Union, Hook had been a remorseless critic of the American Communist Party's call for a "democratic peace front" between liberals and radicals. He was equally unsympathetic to the Communists' international strategy of advocating a collective security alliance of France, Britain, the United States, and the Soviet Union to obstruct the fascist powers of Italy, Germany, and Japan, and he took pleasure in contrasting that policy to the revolutionary internationalism of the Bolsheviks. "I have an English translation of an article by Plekhanov written in 1918 (after the Bolsheviks took power) in which P. explains why he supported the war," Hook wrote to V. F. Calverton in 1936, offering to let him publish it. "His reasons sound like a take-off on the Stalinists today and to the *cognoscenti* the article is extremely funny."[22]

Even in early 1938, when he was backing away from many other revolutionary tenets, Hook resisted the mounting drive to war. The Soviet Union, Hook declared flatly, was an unreliable ally against fascism. He observed that it had sold oil to Japan which was being used in its war to seize China; shipped oil, coal tar, wheat, lumber, and coal to Italy during its Ethiopian campaign; and provided supplies to Franco by way of its shipments to Italy. It had even traded with Germany. Rather than representing an exemplary challenge to Nazi racialism, Hook noted, the Soviet Union was itself deeply anti-Semitic, having massacred more Jews than Hitler, according to some reports (this was prior to the Holocaust, of course). Hook argued even more vehemently against the notion that military preparation carried out in the name of "collective security" was the best strategy against fascism. Though people are motivated to fight wars for psychological, moral, and political reasons, he wrote, military conflicts have basically economic causes: "War is as natural *between* capitalist nations as strikes are *within* capitalist nations." Although no one wanted wars, like strikes they could not be avoided in the long run under a system driven by the pursuit of profits and riven with crises. "The only genuine alternative to war is socialism," he concluded, "and the only effective struggle in the long run against war is a struggle against the economic conditions which breed wars." Hook compared pro-war socialists in 1938 to the pro-war socialists of 1914, who betrayed the international solidarity of the working class for a false national identity. In this case the identity was based in the Soviet Union: "Mr. Browder is not for democracy but for a minority Communist Party dictatorship

[22]   SH to V. F. Calverton, n.d. but signed "Yours for Thomas and Nelson," thus assuring a 1936 date (V. F. Calverton Papers, New York Public Library, Hook Correspondence).

in the interest of the Russian democracy. He is not for peace but for a war in which capitalist America and Stalinist Russia will be allies, even if such a war brings fascism to America." How could the fascists be stymied? "They cannot be stopped by war on the part of *capitalist* powers. They can be stopped by internal opposition and by *socialist* powers."[23]

Memories of the futile carnage of the First World War—when millions had gone to their deaths in a "war to end all wars," a war to "make the world safe for democracy"—loomed large in the minds of all revolutionary socialists. Calls for collective security against Germany were not only fruitless, Hook warned, but positively dangerous, for they risked a new world slaughter. In late 1938, writing in the *New Leader,* he called the Communist Parties of the world "the leading war-mongers in their respective countries" because of their belief that if the "capitalist countries of Europe and America can be embroiled in a war with Germany, the USSR will be safe." The result, Hook concluded, would be panic in German ruling circles. The Communist call for a global breakoff of all trade and diplomacy with Germany was "a preparatory war measure that may lead to the extermination of every Jew in Germany." In another article Hook raised the fear, common on the left, that a war against German Nazism might only bring fascism to America, not by defeat at the hands of the European right but because of the measures taken to prosecute the war: the adoption of authoritarian state controls.[24]

For the early part of 1939, even after taking up a politics centered upon anti-totalitarianism, Hook refused to countenance any collaboration with bourgeois powers against either Nazi Germany or the Soviet Union. In the spring issue of *Partisan Review* he offered one of his most spirited attacks yet on collective security in "The Anatomy of the Popular Front." After characteristic criticisms of Lenin, Stalin, and "extremist sects which are important only as illustrative material for political psycho-pathology" (presumably a reference to the Trotskyist movement), Hook turned full force on that part of the left which supported Roosevelt, "a man and strategy publicly dedicated to the defense of capitalism, often used synonymously with democracy." Popular Front backing for the New Deal order, Hook maintained, prevented the emergence of a labor party dedicated to independent working-class action. Roosevelt's preparation for war—"the last resort of every capitalist statesman or politician who desires to stave off fun-

[23] Hook, "Thoughts in Season," *Socialist Review* 6 (May–June 1938): 6–7, 16; Hook, "Logic, Politics, and Plain Decency," *Social Frontier* 4 (March 1938): 192; Hook, "Promise without Dogma: A Social Philosophy for Jews," *Menorah Journal* 25 (October–December 1937): 273–88.
[24] Hook, untitled substitute column for Eugene Lyons, *New Leader* 21 (26 November 1938): 8; Hook, "Logic, Politics, and Plain Decency," 190–92.

damental social change"—would mean "fascism in full military dress." Thus, the Communist Party's Popular Front gambit was in reality likely to "stabilize capitalism," Hook maintained. It had confused itself with a united front: the collaboration around particular issues between parties of the same class.[25]

So firm an anti-capitalist position, a rare feature in Hook's writings by 1939, is explained primarily by his desire to strip the Communists of their radical mystique. No insult could deflate the Popular Front radicals more than the charge of accommodating capitalism. Yet Hook continued to oppose socialist support for military action by bourgeois powers against the fascist states even after the Nazi-Soviet pact of August 1939. In a collective letter published in *Partisan Review* and addressed to the League of American Writers, the main intellectual group of the Popular Front, Hook joined other radicals (many of them members of the competing League for Cultural Freedom and Socialism) to ask the LAW what it concluded from the pact and the consequent partition of Poland. The first set of questions asked by the letter's signers was revealing: "What is the character of the present war? Is it an imperialist war or a war of the democracies against Fascism?" The clear implication was that the war was imperialist, for the Hitler-Stalin pact was completely discordant with the LAW's familiar line that the Soviet Union was a great democratic ally against fascism.[26]

By the summer of 1940, however, Hook's views on imperialism had gone the way of his views on revolution. It was not as though Nazi expansion were new. Throughout the late 1930s, while Hook repeatedly denounced calls for collective security, Hitler had appropriated new territories one after the other: the Rhineland, 1936; Austria, 1938; Czechoslovakia, 1938–39; Poland, 1939. In 1940, however, as Belgium and France fell to the Germans and Italy joined the war on the Axis side, the reality of the prospect of German victory hit home more acutely in England and the United States. Britain appeared to stand alone, and the air battle over London in the summer of 1940, combined with the Nazi-Soviet non-aggression pact and his new political opposition to totalitarianism above all else, convinced Hook of the need for military support against the Nazi forces. "Democratic capitalism," he announced in the *New Leader,* "if it is preserved against the onslaughts of Fascism, gives at least the possibility of organized activity in behalf of socialism; the victory of Fascism carries with it the practical certainty of the total liquidation of the labor and socialist movement throughout the world."[27]

[25] Hook, "The Anatomy of the Popular Front," *Partisan Review* 6 (Spring 1939): 29–45.
[26] "A Letter to the L.A.W.," *Partisan Review* 6 (Fall 1939): 127–28. Signers included Dewey, Dupee, Farrell, Hacker, Lundberg, Lyons, Nomad, Phillips, Rahv, Schapiro, and Stolberg.
[27] Hook, "Socialism, Common Sense and the War," *New Leader* 23 (31 August 1940): 7.

Hook's turnaround took place within the severe crisis of American radicalism brought about by the Second World War. The Communist Party, although it recovered numerically between 1942 and 1945, never regained the level of public credibility as the vanguard of left-liberalism that it had enjoyed prior to the Nazi-Soviet pact. The anti-Stalinist left did not benefit from the CP's crisis, for it practically disintegrated with the division of the Socialist Workers Party into two small groups in 1940. The reluctance of both groups to embrace the war limited their recruitment in the wartime environment, but for all their marginality, both consequent organizations—Cannon's SWP and Shachtman's Workers Party—demonstrated courage in refusing to subordinate the independent interests of labor to the war cause. Though they suffered obscurity and persecution for their unpopular beliefs, they did preserve a perspective on both the war and American politics that permitted them to keep their principles intact in the postwar period. They raised traditional socialist arguments against the war as an interimperialist rivalry, without simply replaying arguments made against the First World War. They refused to call for American intervention, but once the United States did join the Allied war effort, they did not revive the slogan of "revolutionary defeatism" that radicals had raised along the Eastern Front in 1917–18, for they understood that the Second World War was distinct in character. Only with the end of hostilities did they raise the slogan "bring the troops home now," which would become the rallying cry of the anti-war movement of the 1960s.

Revolutionary socialists, in other words, sought the military defeat of Nazism but refused to extend political support to the imperialist powers as a reliable vehicle for that effort. They recognized the mortal threat posed by fascism to working-class organization, including trade unions, and supported the resistance movement in Nazi-occupied countries. In both the SWP and the WP conscripted members served in the armed forces, and neither group attempted to obstruct military operations directed against the fascist powers. Cannon, in particular, developed a creative war policy that demanded democratic control of the military with the election of officers by rank-and-file soldiers and sailors, and control of war industries and military training by working-class organizations, especially the CIO. Because they refused to subordinate the interests of working people to the Allied war effort or Soviet foreign policy, both organizations agitated against the "no-strike pledge" in the CIO unions. None of these activities had much practical effect, however, particularly since the leaders of the SWP were prosecuted under the anti-communist Smith Act and jailed in 1941 for "sedition."[28]

---

[28]   Cannon's defense in that trial was exceptionally lucid: James P. Cannon, *Socialism on Trial* (1942; New York: Pioneer, 1949). For other revolutionary positions on the war from that time, see James P. Cannon, *The Socialist Workers Party in World War II: Writings and Speeches,*

American entry into the Second World War meant not only the military defeat of Nazism and Italian and Japanese fascism but also strike repression, preservation of segregation, internment of Japanese Americans, the development and use of the atomic bomb, and tremendous carnage from incineration bombings. The outcome secured global postwar hegemony for the American empire as well as the lockhold of the Soviet Union over Eastern Europe, setting the stage for the Cold War. Radical criticism of the Second World War may in these respects have been far-sighted, not a purely bullheaded refusal to separate 1941 from 1914, even if throughout most of the war American socialist revolutionaries, like the entire world, did not know the true dimensions of the systematic extermination of Jews, gypsies, homosexuals, and mentally handicapped children under the Nazi regime.[29]

It is not useful to interpret Hook's about-face on the war as a craven sellout to imperialism, because his decision to advocate American entry into the war took place in the context of a dramatic, horrifying spread of Nazi forces across Europe. The specter of a Nazi Britain broke the anti-war

---

1940–43 (New York: Pathfinder, 1975); and C. L. R. James, George Breitman, Edgar Keemer, et al., *Fighting Racism in World War II* (New York: Monad, 1980). The best historical treatments of the revolutionary left's politics during the war are by Alan Wald in *The New York Intellectuals: The Rise and Decline of the Anti-Stalinist Left from the 1930s to the 1980s* (Chapel Hill: University of North Carolina Press, 1987); and his essay "The New York Intellectuals in Retreat," in *Socialist Perspectives*, ed. Phyllis and Julius Jacobson (Princeton: Karz-Cohl, 1983), 155–83. These sources are heavily focused on the SWP; the Workers Party's wartime experience is given fictional treatment in Harvey Swados, *Standing Fast* (New York: Ballantine, 1971).

[29] Ernest Mandel, who fought in the underground resistance against the Nazis in Belgium, argues that the war should be understood as a combination of five different kinds of struggles, which warranted different responses from revolutionaries: (1) an interimperialist war between plunderers, to be given no support at all; (2) a just war of self-defense by the USSR against Nazi imperial aggression; (3) a just war of resistance by semi-colonial China against Japanese imperial occupation; (4) just wars of national liberation by oppressed colonial peoples against their imperial overlords, such as the Ethiopians against Italy; and (5) a just war of resistance by workers and the oppressed in the occupied countries of Europe against the Nazis. These wars were interconnected in complex ways, and even the just struggles were often led by forces to which democratic revolutionary socialists could extend no political confidence, making the task of intelligent analysis and action extremely hard. But, Mandel underscores, "within the imperialist countries, any wrong characterization of the nature of the inter-imperialist war, any notion that because of the specific nature of Nazi, Italian or Japanese imperialism, there was an element of justice in the war of British, French, American, Belgian, or Dutch imperialism against the opposing imperialist camp, would lead only to systematic sacrifice of immediate working-class interests, to systematic class collaboration, and to the strangling of revolutionary possibilities at the end of the war." That was certainly the outcome for Hook. See Ernest Mandel, *Revolutionary Marxism Today* (London: New Left Books, 1979), 165; see also Mandel, *The Meaning of the Second World War* (London: Verso, 1986). Other historical assessments critical of the war are Gabriel Kolko, *The Politics of War* (New York: Random House, 1968); Studs Terkel, *"The Good War": An Oral History of World War Two* (New York: Ballantine, 1985); and Howard Zinn, *A People's History of the United States* (New York: Harper, 1980).

stance of many radicals. The tragedy of Hook's choice, however, was that it disarmed most of what remained of his critical perspective on capitalism and set him in opposition to the rest of the socialist movement, which saw the defeat of fascism as its foremost aim but would not condone a strategy reliant upon imperialist powers. Hook paid the price in "The New Failure of Nerve," a pair of *Partisan Review* essays in 1943. The first installment, accompanied by contributions from John Dewey and Ernest Nagel on naturalism, extended the long-established secular and anti-religious theme in Hook's philosophy. This time Hook took to task those Catholic and Protestant philosophers, including Reinhold Niebuhr and Jacques Maritain, who had used the tragedy of the war to proclaim religion the antidote to despair, and who criticized scientific method on theological grounds and held it responsible for the collapse of morality under totalitarianism. The loss of confidence in scientific method and the new popularity of transcendental metaphysics, Hook argued, was a flight from responsibility into religious dogma and subjectivism. Far from serving to safeguard democracy, religious moralism betrayed an ominous lack of respect for disbelief and was the result not of warranted argument but of multiple conditions—capitalist crisis, the rise of totalitarianism, the collapse of a rational socialist alternative—which gave rise to desires for comfort and consolation.

Hook's second essay was the real bombshell. It linked the Protestant and neo-Thomist flight from reality to a blistering attack on the socialist left—not so much on the Communist Party, to which his opposition was well known, but on all those who to one degree or another continued to oppose the war, a spectrum that included all his old allies in the new-born Workers Party, the Socialist Party, and the Socialist Workers Party, as well as independent anti-war activists of other persuasions. Hook condemned what he called the "utopianism" of Socialists, such as Norman Thomas, and of the Trotskyists, whom he cryptically called "Platonist" because, he charged, they were worshipers of an abstract system of Ideas having nothing to do with reality. Socialist opponents of the war, he alleged, were equally unscientific in method, for they too clung to comforting dogmas, obstinately refusing to understand that in a war between capitalist governments it made a difference that one was fascist and the other democratic: "If Hitler is defeated, it is by no means assured that democratic socialism has a future. But it at least has a chance! It is the failure to grasp this simple piece of wisdom which marks the political insanity of infantile leftism."[30]

Although Hook was in full assault against the rest of the left, he retained a radical patina. He continued to call for independent political action and

[30] Hook, "The Failure of the Left," *Partisan Review* 10 (March–April 1943): 168.

for a labor party outside the Democratic Party, and he rejected the claim of some socialists that the gradual expansion of government bureaucracy amounted to an expanding socialism. He recommended that organized labor demand to see *total* prosecution of the war, regardless of capitalist property relations, and that it insist on democratic conduct of the war by having representatives chosen by labor, not administration appointees, serve on war counsels. In Hook's judgment, his support for American entrance into the war did not entail political capitulation: "By preserving its independence, by giving critical political support to the war against Hitler without accepting entire political responsibility for its conduct, the labor movement will be in a much stronger position to influence its course, and to take the lead in domestic reconstruction when post-war reaction sets in." This bore remarkable similarity to Dewey's 1917 arguments for liberal support of the First World War, which as a boy Hook had adamantly opposed. His line of thought, like Dewey's, supported national unity for the war's duration—not the exercise of labor's prerogative to strike and organize on behalf of its distinct social interests. In this manner, Hook's wartime politics had converged with the Communist Party's wartime Popular Front, which under left-wing cover discouraged struggle for civil rights, strikes, and criticism of the internment of Japanese Americans—all in order to defend the Soviet Union. Hook's motivation, of course, was different: defense of political democracy. But he too was moving toward a reformism and total support for the Allied war effort which necessitated the suspension of struggles for social justice at home.[31]

The response was not long in issuing from revolutionary socialist quarters. In the *Fourth International* (as the Socialist Workers Party's theoretical journal was renamed in 1940 after the *New International* was taken over by the newly formed Workers Party), Albert Goldman, writing under the pseudonym M. Morrison, observed wryly that Hook's term "failure of nerve" hardly applied to those who had formulated a position on the war and stuck to it despite immense pressures to abandon it. Rather, he wrote archly, "one is tempted to say [Hook] is actually attempting to forestall the accusation that he himself has lost his nerve."[32]

Paritan Review published a more thorough rejoinder to Hook by his old friend Meyer Schapiro, who adopted the pseudonym David Merian because Columbia University, where he taught, was infamous for having fired anti-war faculty during the First World War. After objecting to Hook's identification of all critics of the war—even those whose method was historical, materialist and naturalist—with religious obscurantists under the single

---

[31] Ibid., 176.
[32] M. Morrison, "Sidney Hook's Attack on Trotskyism," *Fourth International*, July 1943, 212.

rubric of a "failure of nerve," Schapiro quipped, "This is one of the minor casualties of the war: Sidney Hook, wounded in the head while stumbling over his own barricade against the Trotskyists."[33] By accusing the revolutionary left of a "failure of nerve," Schapiro noted, Hook was giving a harder time to those socialists who had held to their unpopular views throughout the war than to those such as James Burnham who had abandoned socialism altogether. Hook, not the left, had changed, argued Schapiro. It was Hook who had abandoned his longstanding criticism of Popular Front nationalism and compromise with imperialism, and who had come to defend an interimperialist war against fascism as the best means for defense of Enlightenment values and the American Dream. "Yet those who have continued to believe what he believed in the spring of 1939," Schapiro wrote pointedly, "are Platonists, lunatics, bohemians, drunkards and metaphysicians."[34]

The problem with Hook's demand for "total democracy" in prosecuting the war, according to Schapiro, was that properly implementing it required a social revolution, an aim that Hook had abandoned. Hook's labor program, indeed, was an exact replica of the Popular Front, merely dressed up by an amorphous representation for labor in the management of the war. Hook mentioned nothing about the treatment of black Americans or the disproportionate financial burden of the war borne by working people. Ultimately, Schapiro wrote, a labor party of the type Hook advocated would have to choose between support for the war—which would demand full production in industry, without disruption—and the social demands of labor and black people, the fulfillment of which would probably require strikes and other uncompromising stances. Seen in that light, the democratic potential for a vigorously pro-war and yet truly "independent" labor party did not seem great.

Only because Hook had abandoned revolutionary Marxism in theory as well as in politics, Schapiro maintained, could he dare to link religion and Marxism as equal "failures of nerve." Hook's perspective did not admit that method is insufficient and cannot suffice without theory. After all, capitalism was perfectly capable of employing scientific method in industry and in politics, albeit for limited aims. Schapiro reminded Hook of his own earlier arguments that social science could not be a pure science in the same sense as natural science, since it inescapably involved a standpoint. This elementary distinction had recently been lost on Hook, who now held Marx-

[33] David Merian, "The Nerve of Sidney Hook," *Partisan Review* 10 (May–June 1943): 248. Hook recalled that he had advised Meyer Schapiro to take a pseudonym in the debate, but Schapiro could not remember Hook's doing so and was certain that the editors of *Partisan Review* were the first to recommend it: interview with Meyer Schapiro, 25 October 1993.
[34] David Merian, "The Nerve of Sidney Hook," 251.

ism responsible for what it could not avoid—taking sides in class conflict—without acknowledging that a class-divided society would never achieve consensus on socialism: "It is inconceivable that all investigators accept the findings on which the proposals for socialism are based. . . . The lambs have nothing to gain from such seminars with the wolves, but the wolves have every reason to encourage such hopes."[35]

In reply to Schapiro, Hook insisted that the war program he had outlined for labor was a united—not a popular—front, since it entailed the strict independence of labor. As Hook surely knew, this was misleading. The term "united front" had always been used within the revolutionary socialist movement to describe alliances between working-class organizations and parties around particular issues, whereas a "popular front" permitted alliances with other classes and social layers. By that standard, Hook's program—even if it should result in the creation of an independent labor party—was a popular front, for it called upon both labor and capital within the United States and Britain to prosecute the war against fascism to the fullest extent possible. Yet Hook blasted Schapiro for his obliviousness to the enormous danger of fascism and the lack of practical alternatives. He called his old friend's rejoinder a textbook case of "sickly failure of nerve, social irresponsibility, and absence of concrete political intelligence."[36]

The "failure of nerve" debate revealed the practical consequences of Hook's transformations. From a vigorous critic of imperialist war as incapable of resolving the systemic causes of fascism, he turned almost overnight into a partisan of Allied military efforts as the only real alternative to Nazism. From a defense of revolutionary working-class activity, he came to an embrace of collaboration between labor and capital on the "common" issue of the war. From condemning any socialist who claimed dogmatically that Marxism is a science, he came to call any socialist who was not scientific—according to his meaning of the term—a dogmatist. Most markedly, in contrast to his long and varied attempts to foster socialist unity, Hook began to direct his hottest fire at the left. Despite some critical remarks about the Roosevelt administration, his anti-totalitarianism led him to find his most mistaken opponents on the anti-war left. Phrases like "sickly failure of nerve," "humorless fanatic," and other epithets in his rebuttal to Schapiro demonstrated an exceptional level of invective, recalling, as Alan Wald has noted, the sort of abuse that Hook himself had received from Communist apparatchiks such as V. J. Jerome, Harry Wicks,

[35] Ibid., 256.
[36] Hook, "Politics of Wonderland," *Partisan Review* 10 (May–June 1943): 262. See also David Merian, "Socialism and the Failure of Nerve—The Controversy Continued," and Hook, "Faith, Hope, and Dialectic: Merian in Wonderland," both in *Partisan Review* 10 (September–October 1943): 473–76, 476–81.

and Earl Browder.[37] The use of psychological terms to tar his political opponents introduced ad hominem methods into the writing of a thinker who, while polemical, had never before relied upon name-calling to do his work. The logic of anti-totalitarianism had, in all these ominous ways, set the stage for Hook's role in the Cold War.[38]

From World War to Cold War, 1945–1973

Between 1939 and 1945, Sidney Hook had perfected the politics of liberal anti-communism, and this finely honed world view, well suited to the postwar moment, brought him new public prominence after 1945. When he announced in 1947 that he was dropping the term Marxism as a designation for his own world view, he positioned himself as the rebel for giving up the term. "It would appear," he wrote in *Partisan Review*, "that if I were justified in my interpretation of Marx's meaning, I would perhaps be the only true Marxist left in the world. This is too much for my sense of humor, and so I have decided to abandon the term as a descriptive epithet of my position—all the more willingly because I am interested in the validity of ideas rather than in their historical derivation." But he was merely relinquishing a label that had long lost its power to convince, especially since he had already called the term into doubt in *Reason, Social Myths, and Democracy* seven years before. It did not take much courage to sacrifice such an "epithet" in the year of loyalty oaths and containment, moreover. The reconciliation en masse of the New York intellectuals with liberalism and the West does more to explain Hook's final rejection of Marxism than any commitment to the "validity of ideas," a laudable abstraction that had never before prevented him from being a Marxist.[39]

In the same article, "The Future of Socialism," Hook claimed to have spent the "last twenty years" fighting both the "orthodox Marxism" of social democracy and "Leninism-Trotskyism-Stalinism." But that claim ob-

---

[37] Wald, *The New York Intellectuals*, 211.

[38] The Communist Party had never given up castigating Hook, even if it could not comprehend his political evolution. Sender Garlin, in the *Daily Worker*, December 12, 1942, wrote that the editors of New York University's student newspaper had become infected with "political hookworm, a disease contracted from too close association with Prof. Sidney Hook, the chief carrier of the Trotskyite bacilli at NYU." This would have surprised the Trotskyists whom Hook was routinely abusing, but it did raise the eyebrow of J. Edgar Hoover, who directed his New York agents to investigate Hook for "possible Trotskyite sympathies or connections." The FBI for some time followed and reported on Hook's activities, but in 1949, finally satisfied that Hook was no revolutionary threat, the New York Special Agent in Charge wrote Hoover that "this case is being considered closed by this office." J. Edgar Hoover to SAC, New York, 5 January 1945, and Edward Scheidt to J. Edgar Hoover, 7 April 1949 (FBI files made available to author through Freedom of Information Act request).

[39] Hook, "The Future of Socialism," *Partisan Review* 14 (January–February 1947): 23–36.

scured his past: he had spent the better part of those twenty years *defending* Leninism on the whole. He was within the Stalinist camp in the 1932 election, and he spent the next five years as a fellow traveler of Trotskyism. His own opposition to social democratic "orthodox Marxism" was in doubt. To be sure, he was a critic of fatalism and mechanism, but his recommendation that "a union of all democratic elements in the community" should "throw its full strength behind the slowly evolving pattern of British socialism, now shedding its rather mangy coat of imperialism, and against the Russian police state" showed how much he had come to identify the gradual expansion of the welfare state with socialism and confused decolonization with the dissolution of imperialism.[40]

In countless articles and forums Hook urged liberals and intellectuals of good will to recognize the perils of their epoch and rise to the defense of "democratic societies." The defunct Committee for Cultural Freedom was reincarnated in two successor organizations that Hook helped to create and lead in the late 1940s and early 1950s: the Congress for Cultural Freedom, global in scope, and its domestic affiliate, the American Committee for Cultural Freedom. Both sought to rally Atlantic intellectuals to the side of the United States, an activity ostensibly carried out in fulfillment of the critical responsibilities of independent minds, though both groups were so favorably viewed by the American political establishment that many of their activities were sponsored by the Central Intelligence Agency. That this compromising fact was disguised from most members should not obscure the coziness between the ACCF and an American empire that Hook had once opposed from the left. Despite his initial claims, Hook's adoption of a politics premised upon the equation of the USSR with Nazi Germany and his endorsement of American military aims during the Second World War had prefigured a postwar sacrifice of political and intellectual autonomy from ruling powers except in strictly formal matters.[41]

Hook was later both proud and sensitive about his conduct during the Cold War. In his memoir, written toward the very end of his life, he claimed in three separate places that he had opposed the politics of Senator Joseph McCarthy. He did call for a movement to retire McCarthy from public life a few months after the 1952 election, following the latter's absurd charge that the Voice of America was a hotbed of Communist infiltration. But that was three years after the Wisconsin senator first became a national sensation with charges that Communists were running the State Department.

[40]   Ibid.
[41]   On the new CCF, ACCF, and CIA, see Christopher Lasch, "The Cultural Cold War," in *The Agony of the American Left* (New York: Knopf, 1969), 63–114. Hook, *Out of Step*, 426, says that he suspected but had no actual personal knowledge of CIA funding.

Hook's criticism came much later than that of some others associated with the ACCF, such as Richard Rovere—and then only because he had concluded that McCarthy's crudities were ineffectual and counterproductive, not because he thought that anti-communism itself presented any inherent danger to civil liberties. Hook's principal identity in the late 1940s and early 1950s—indeed, for the remainder of his life—was as a resolute anti-communist. He became a virtual house writer for the *New York Times* on issues of Communism and education, and anti-communism was the largest single topic of his works. Rather than putting him in a position to thwart postwar reaction—as he had speculated it might when justifying his initial support for U.S. military action on the side of the Allies—his decision to promote the broadest possible alliance against "totalitarianism" had dulled his capacity to oppose reaction when it set in.[42]

Indeed, Hook was a leading figure in the creation of a repressive, censorious atmosphere within higher education, carried out, naturally, under the guise of cultural freedom. Hook's "Heresy, Yes—Conspiracy, No!"— first published in the *New York Times Magazine* in 1950, then distributed as a pamphlet by the ACCF, eventually incorporated into a book of the same title—became perhaps the most influential justification for firing Communists and suspected Communists from universities and schools in the early 1950s, when hundreds of instructors lost their jobs because of their left-wing backgrounds or their refusal to inform investigative committees of the names of radicals they had known.[43] Hook advanced the argument that heresy, the public expression of dissenting forms of thought, should be distinguished from conspiracy, secret plots carried out without respect for prevailing legal and political norms. With an appearance of even-handedness, he condemned both the "cultural vigilantism" of the extreme right, which wanted to stamp out both conspiracy *and* heresy, and Communists and their dupes who manipulated natural sympathies for heresy in order to carry out their malevolent conspiracies. The problem with the right wing, in Hook's reckoning, was its blundering methods, not its analysis of Communism. By assembling various disquieting excerpts from the writings of Lenin and Stalin, he sought to show that American Communists were not advocates of unpopular ideas, or heretics, but part of a conscious global conspiracy bent upon world domination. The USSR, he maintained, was a state dedicated to world revolution—not, as he once had held, a cautious

<hr>

42 Hook, "Mr. McCarthy Criticized," *New York Times*, 8 May 1953, 24.
43 See Hook, "Heresy Yes—but Conspiracy, No," *New York Times Magazine*, 9 July 1950, 12, 38–39; Hook, "To Counter the Big Lie—A Basic Strategy," *New York Times Magazine*, 11 March 1951, 9, 59–64; Hook, *Heresy, Yes—Conspiracy, No!* (New York: American Committee for Cultural Freedom, n.d.); Hook, *Heresy, Yes—Conspiracy, No!* (New York: John Day, 1953).

state with foreign policy concerns as conservative as any other because of its Stalinist degeneration. Ever since Lenin, he argued in 1952, Communism had not been "an open and honestly avowed heresy but an international conspiracy centered in the Kremlin, in a state of undeclared war against democratic institutions." Communists were agents of a subversive foreign power; by that disloyalty they disqualified themselves from the standard protections of dissent. Even though Hook objected to the intrusion of congressional investigative committees into campus affairs, he wanted an equivalent result: that higher education clean its own house of Communist Party members. On the basis of a few internal Party documents dating from the 1930s, he argued that the objective of Communist teachers was to indoctrinate their students; no Communist could therefore claim legitimate standing in the educational profession. He also defended the Smith Act—under which eighteen Trotskyists and many more Communists were imprisoned for merely *advocating* the overthrow of the government— as consistent with civil liberties and political democracy. Hook's arguments validated the Cold War conduct of liberal university administrators, whose internal purging by bureaucratic mechanism of suspect scholars was far more damaging to political freedom than the more vulgar antics of McCarthyist legislators.[44]

The most revealing reaction to Hook's new blend of politics and philosophy came not from the Communists (incapable by that time of saying anything more sophisticated than that pragmatism was the philosophy of imperialism) but from John Dewey, who proved just as unwilling to endorse Hook's Cold War enthusiasms as he had been to accompany Hook down his revolutionary road of the 1930s. Hook used a general characterization of Communism, namely, that it prevented its adherents from following evidence freely in the classroom by binding them to purvey Party dogma, as prima facie grounds for dismissal of individuals without concrete investigation of their particular actions in the classroom. Hook expressly urged this approach as a method for universities to cleanse themselves so as to prevent legislative committees from doing it for them. But Dewey viewed the matter as a question of "the pragmatic criterion of judgment vs. abstract principle as criterion." Empirical investigation of classroom practice

[44] See Hook, *Convictions* (Buffalo: Prometheus, 1990), 195. Hook's arguments against Leninism and the right of Communists to teach in the schools, as well as his defense of the Smith Act, were subjected to a long, devastating assessment by socialists Gordon Haskell and Julius Jacobson (writing under his mother's maiden name, Falk): Julius Falk and Gordon Haskell, "Civil Liberties and the Philosopher of the Cold War," *New International* 19 (July–August 1953): 184–227. They demonstrated in immaculate detail that Hook's quotations from Lenin were grossly abbreviated and shorn of context, amounting to a distortion just as great as the Stalinist "lies" and "deception" Hook was out to refute.

was, he maintained, the best indication of actual conduct. Even if the Communist Party mandated that its members pledge their loyalty, Dewey cautioned, "to assume without evidence that every teacher who had taken the pledge was *therefore* unfit to teach seemed—and still seems—to me to be entering on a dangerous policy." The emergent Cold War hysteria, in which burden of proof tended to rest on the individual teacher, troubled Dewey far more than Hook.[45]

The aging Dewey's defense of a democratic standard of judgment cannot help but bring to mind the earlier, and more democratic, Hook. Not all accounts of Hook's Cold War politics have taken that earlier moment seriously. Christopher Lasch argued in *The Agony of the American Left* (1969) that the Congress for Cultural Freedom's union of intellect and power, its casting of cultural freedom in a way that served the interests of U.S. elites, was the result of "the amazing persistence and tenacity of the Bolshevik habit of mind even among those who now rejected whatever was radical and liberating in Bolshevism." CCF organizers, Lasch wrote, "clung to the congenial view of intellectuals as the vanguard of history and to the crude and simplified dialectic . . . which passed for Marxism in left-wing circles of the thirties." It took "no special powers of discernment," he concluded, to see that Hook's "attack on communism in the fifties expressed itself in formulations that were themselves derived from the cruder sort of Marxist cant."[46] Something might be said for Lasch's postulation that those intellectuals who chose the West in the Cold War were not, ultimately, so unlike their ideological counterparts in the opposite camp, but in Hook's case at least, Lasch misrepresented 1930s Marxism. Throughout his Marxist years, including his period of admiration for Lenin and the October Revolution, Hook was committed to workers' control and socialism from below. Although he believed that organization and political leadership were indispensable to socialist politics, he was in no way elitist or theoretically crude. The Hook of 1936 and of 1956 were not inversions of each other; they were polar opposites. Hook's post-1939 politics were a renunciation, not reconfiguration, of his revolutionary commitments.[47]

Nor can it be sufficiently emphasized that Hook's rejection of Marxism and abdication of revolutionary aims did not come about as the result of

[45] JD to SH, 23 June and 21 July 1949 (Hook-Dewey Collection). See the excellent analysis in Robert Westbrook, *John Dewey and American Democracy* (Ithaca: Cornell University Press, 1991), 492–95.

[46] Lasch, *The Agony of the American Left*, 67–68.

[47] Lasch's point is revived, just as unadvisedly, in the claim that the New York intellectuals' "continuing vanguardism enabled them to complete the transition from radical to legitimist without too painful a sense of contradiction": Hugh Wilford, "An Oasis: The New York Intellectuals in the Late 1940s," *Journal of American Studies* 28 (August 1994): 223.

some inner logic of pragmatism (an allegation made more frequently by scholars on the left than Lasch's charge of an ingrained yet inverted Leninism). Hook's Cold War philosophy was bereft of the radically democratic edge of Deweyan pragmatism. Rather than insist, like Dewey, upon the radical conclusions that follow from the reverence for human dignity, justice, and capacity in liberal political philosophy, Hook's liberal realism of the 1950s was a pinched diatribe that often seemed to have the singular aim of uprooting communism. His energy was devoted not so much to the critical exploration of progressive possibilities as to the excoriation of what he had come to call the "ritualistic liberal, unable to distinguish between the heresy which a free society must tolerate and the conspiracy which it may not." Hook had once enjoined Dewey to recognize that class struggle and revolutionary engagement, not class collaboration, were the only viable way to realize pragmatism's social and philosophical aims. But by 1969 Hook disdained the notion that pragmatism legitimated activism: "To interpret the pragmatic principle that thought and action are related, as if the action necessarily had to be something practical or useful or convenient or progressive, is to convert it into a slogan of philistinism and social uplift."[48]

That sort of disdain for drawing active conclusions from pragmatist method, so different from Hook's early spirit, applied only to organized expressions of opposition to capitalism. In other political connections, Hook celebrated fusion of thought and action. In the famous symposium "Our Country and Our Culture," organized by *Partisan Review* in 1952, Hook, who seemed puzzled that any intellectual could be alienated or estranged from American culture, urged all intellectuals to put their brains in the service of the Cold War: "The democratic West will require the critical support, the dedicated energy and above all, the intelligence, of its intellectuals if it is to survive as a free culture." The obligation of socialist intellectuals to foster the creation of socialist democracies, East *and* West, had evaporated in Hook's understanding of culture and intellectual pursuits. His position of "critical support" for the United States in the *Partisan Review* symposium was so hard to distinguish from unconditional acceptance that Hook had ended up "preaching a 'pragmatism' that was the very antithesis of pragmatic, making a religion out of the defense of the 'free world,'" as Lasch wrote in *The New Radicalism in America* (1965). The left and the experimental disposition were better represented in "Our Country and Our Culture" by independent socialist Irving Howe, who neither made a fetish of estrangement nor called for Cold War loyalty: "Veering and tacking as history compels him, the socialist intellectual must try to de-

[48]   Hook, *Academic Freedom and Academic Anarchy* (New York: Delta, 1971), xvi.

fend democracy with some realism while maintaining his independence from and opposition to the status quo."[49]

Hook kept up a prolific rate of publication, but as he came to fixate on communism, his intellectual power and influence were not what they once had been. As William Barrett recalls, Phillips and Rahv, the editors of *Partisan Review*, in the end saw Hook as "a kind of Johnny One-note, clear and forceful but always monotonous in the one issue he was always pursuing." Russell Jacoby has observed that although Hook published dozens of books in the postwar period, almost all of them—even *The Quest for Being* (1961) and *Pragmatism and the Tragic Sense of Life* (1974), whose titles would seem to indicate sustained works of philosophy—are either compilations of his own magazine articles, book reviews, encyclopedia entries, and lectures or else compilations of others' work edited by him. Hook issued a steady stream of political polemic and commentary, but in the postwar years he made no lasting contribution to philosophical scholarship. Each and every book was sure to include the claim that democracy was under seige and that the threat of communism warranted the most vigorous measures of cultural defense. "Herein lies an old tale," writes Jacoby. "As a Marxist sympathizer he wrote thoughtful and philosophical books; as a sworn enemy of Marxism, he fell into a philosophical rut, endlessly recasting the same positions." Given this strange coexistence of keenness in argument with a "deposit of sterility, like rust on a beautiful machine," Irving Howe observed, "even his friends had to admit that something was missing in Hook, some imaginative flair or depth of sensibility that might complement his intellectual virtuosity."[50]

In the opening years of the 1960s, describing his evolution, Hook announced that his major transformation in thought had occurred when he came to recognize "that the chief issue of our time" was not a struggle "between socialism and capitalism, a nationally controlled versus a free enterprise economy," but rather "between democracy on the one hand, conceived not only politically but as a way of life, and totalitarianism on the other." Here was not only departure from but caricature of his own earlier ideas. By defining socialism as state ownership, a criterion that he would never have accepted when he was revolutionary, Hook had an easier time

---

[49] The impact of Lasch's criticism was deadened, however, because he mistakenly ascribed to Hook the belief that the Soviet Union was a "system of total error," whereas Hook had called it "a system of total terror": Christopher Lasch, *The New Radicalism in America* (New York: Knopf, 1965), 306–7. See also Sidney Hook, "Our Country and Our Culture," and Irving Howe, "Our Country and Our Culture," *Partisan Review* 14 (September–October 1952): 569–74, 577.
[50] William Barrett, *The Truants: Adventures among the Intellectuals* (Garden City, N.Y.: Anchor, 1982), 82; Russell Jacoby, *The Last Intellectuals* (New York: Basic, 1987), 104; Irving Howe, *A Margin of Hope* (San Diego: Harcourt Brace Jovanovich, 1982), 211.

making his progression appear transparently rational. The suppression of any mention of workers' control was compounded by his adoption of the phrase "free enterprise," the preferred euphemism for capitalism.[51]

On the verge of a New Left that would embrace many of the same liberatory ideals (though without, at first, socialist theory and class analysis) that he had so powerfully articulated in his youth, Hook's thought had petrified. His social criticism had receded into acquiescence. He considered the existing order basically democratic and opposed such organizations of the new radicalism as Students for a Democratic Society (SDS), whose early hallmark was the concept of participatory democracy. Despite Hook's own student days as a troublemaker and opponent of imperialist aggression during the First World War, he denounced the youthful radicalism of the 1960s as recrudescent barbarism, a dire threat to democratic liberties, and refused to countenance U.S. withdrawal from Vietnam unless it could be accompanied by reciprocal action from North Vietnam—a solution that reproduced U.S. officials' rationale for propping up the corrupt, authoritarian regime in the South. He predictably opposed all radical uprisings in the postwar capitalist world as "totalitarian"—condoning upheavals only when they erupted within the Soviet bloc. Hook, who had once hoped to generate a revolutionary American labor movement, the glimmers of which he saw in the great 1934 strikes at Toledo and Minneapolis, now alleged that student sit-ins against the Vietnam War were altogether different from the sit-down strikes of the 1930s because, he claimed, the labor movement "did not demand the abolition or restructuring of the entire industrial system in the way that SDS and its allies demand the revolutionary transformation or, more moderately, the restructuring of the university." Hook told a *New York Times* reporter in 1968, "There's a small group that is out to provoke and destroy the university," and his writings warned even more direly of a "Trojan horse in American higher education": not the student militants, whose threat was undisguised, but soft administrators and faculty who retreated "before the politics of confrontation."[52]

This helps to explain why an entire generation of radicals neglected, for the most part in ignorance, Hook's early work. Hook had become one of the "weary, know-it-all . . . old disillusioned radicals" that the New Left prophet C. Wright Mills had in mind when he castigated those intellectu-

51 Hook, introduction to Eduard Bernstein, *Evolutionary Socialism* (New York: Schocken, 1961), xx, xvi. See also Hook, "The Fallacies of Ritualistic Liberalism," in *Political Power and Personal Freedom* (New York: Collier, 1962).
52 John Leo, "Hook Favors Bigger Role for Faculty," *New York Times*, 29 September 1968; Hook, *Academic Freedom and Academic Anarchy*, 134, 242–43. See also "Dr. Hook Calls Freedom 'Not Absolute,'" *Temple University News*, 4 March 1965, in which, shortly after the Free Speech Movement, Hook says, "At present academic freedom needs to be defended especially against some university students."

als "who at least verbally cling to socialist kinds of ideals, but when you get down to it do not dare to get their hands dirty."[53] Whenever Hook's name rolled across a New Left mimeograph machine, it was on a list of sell-outs or renegades. In a New Left sociology journal, for instance, he was denounced as one of the "masters of apology" caught up in an "exercise in self-congratulation."[54]

The assumption prevailed on the New Left that Hook's earlier radicalism must have contained some fatal flaw or weakness that caused him to wind up as he did. Thus when Sidney Hook retired from NYU's Washington Square College in 1973 and took up residence at the Hoover Institution in Palo Alto, California, hardly anyone was capable of remembering that when he first began teaching some forty-five years earlier, his values and activities were not unlike those of the radical democrats and socialist revolutionaries he had spent the recent decades attacking.

---

53 C. Wright Mills, *Listen, Yankee* (New York: Ballantine, 1960), 149.
54 Joseph E. Hansen, "A Dialectical Critique of Empiricism," *Catalyst*, Summer 1967, 19.

E P I L O G U E

The Marxism of Sidney Hook

Altogether too many critical examinations of the early thought of Sidney Hook have succumbed to the temptation to fault Hook's early philosophy for his subsequent deterioration. In "The Marxism of Sidney Hook," which appeared in the theoretical journal *Telos* in 1972, Cristiano Camporesi denied that the Moscow trials were a real factor in Hook's transition. Rather, he maintained, the blame lay in Hook's pragmatism: "His failure to realize the importance of the theory of alienation within Marxism, his uncritical acceptance of the scientific method as a direct pipeline to truth, and the persistence of pragmatism as his broader philosophical framework all combined to propel Hook towards a politically reactionary and philosophically irrelevant position." The orthodox Trotskyist philosopher George Novack held to a similar position: "During the 1930s Hook paraded as a free-thinking philosopher of the extreme Left intent on combatting the twin perversions of Marxism by the reformist Social Democrats and the Stalinists. Despite his pretensions, he was actually engaged in trimming dialectical materialism to a pragmatist pattern that fitted the political opportunism that carried him away from the revolutionary struggle."[1]

[1] Cristiano Camporesi, "The Marxism of Sidney Hook," *Telos* 12 (Summer 1972): 128; George Novack, *Polemics in Marxist Philosophy* (New York: Pathfinder, 1978), 109. Further examples of this line of argument are cited in the introduction to this book.

Sidney Hook at Hoover Institution, 1984, standing in front of posters of John Dewey and Karl Marx. (Courtesy Victoria Rouse, © 1984. All Rights Reserved.)

As Marx understood, thought is not the exclusive determinant of action. Ideas usually cannot be explained simply in terms of antecedent thought. It is true, of course, that the development of many ideas can be explained in terms of the internal problems pursued, encountered, and resolved by a given method or body of thought. For individual thinkers like Hook, however, external influences—social and political history, political affiliations, comrades, teachers, colleagues, friends, family—are usually at least as important in shaping significant choices. At different moments, one or another influence may rise to the fore, but all act in general to give meaning and direction to intellectual activity.

The familiar philosophical thesis that Hook's later anti-communism was the simple result of his pragmatism is a poor substitute for biography and history. Precisely because of his pragmatist understanding, the young Hook was led to emphasize the *revolutionary* elements of action, experiment, and democracy in Marx. After finding the instrument of the Communist Party clumsy and bureaucratic, he helped to initiate a new experiment in action, the American Workers Party. With the constructive aid of pragmatism—perhaps not exclusively because of it but certainly not in spite of it—he had arrived at a revolutionary socialism opposed to capitalism and Stalinism alike. The assumption that Hook's pragmatism caused his break with Marxism in the late 1930s, therefore, gets the relationship backward. In the first instance, it ignores the kind of Marxism that Hook helped forge in the early 1930s, a Marxism deeply informed by pragmatism. One might argue plausibly that some other doctrine could have supplied him with a comparable sensibility, but it is inescapable that *pragmatism* was the crucial influence in Hook's case.

The standard radical thesis also fails to grasp that Hook's later opposition to revolutionary thought was not a simple abandonment of Marxism and embrace of an unalloyed pragmatism. That transition involved both a gradual abandonment of Marxism *and* a contraction of pragmatism as he had previously understood it. The pragmatist insistence on provisional truth and experimental method was in his later thought not extended to revolutionary thought, organization, and history. After 1940 Hook claimed still to be a pragmatist, sometimes even a Marxist, but he had more accurately adopted a liberal formalism characterized by a rigid and carefully circumscribed conception of democracy and scientific method. It is accurate to see this formalism as the transitional pivot point of Hook's thought but mistaken to assign responsibility for it to pragmatism, for it has little in common with the experimental and radically democratic thought of John Dewey.

Despite the stigma still attached to Hook's name in some circles, his Marxism of the 1920s and 1930s warrants closer examination. The impulse to identify some personal shortcoming or prior ideological error as the cause of his rightward turn is understandable, but it has resulted in the vilification and dismissal of an important contribution to Marxist philosophy. Hook's theoretical focus upon working-class emancipation and his parallel efforts at forging revolutionary socialist unity belie both the orthodox Trotskyist accusation that his pragmatism was a superficial "petty-bourgeois" deviation and the liberal interpretation that his early work, as William Barrett more cordially suggests, "assimilates Marxism to the philosophy of American pragmatism, and in spirit transforms it into a more militant form of the American progressivism of the earlier part of the century."[2] It was in method and procedure, not class orientation or general politics, that pragmatism seasoned Hook's Marxism. What socialists of some stripes discovered only in the wake of Eastern Europe's anti-bureaucratic revolutions of 1989, Sidney Hook understood in his critique of Stal-

[2] William Barrett, *The Truants: Adventures among the Intellectuals* (Garden City: Anchor, 1982), 215.

inism some sixty years earlier: that the claims of bureaucratic states to the legacy of communism were perverse and false. Marxist theory, moreover, has yet to absorb in full the lesson of socialist politics that Hook—following the lead of many socialist writers, beginning with Marx—comprehended well: that any socialism worthy of the name must incorporate an appreciation (not just toleration) of open debate and disagreement, of experimentation and the will to revise ideas in accord with the lessons of experience, and of the centrality of democracy within the revolutionary process. That these aspects of Hook's Marxism owed their genesis and peculiar formulation to the democratic radicalism and experimental naturalism of Deweyan pragmatism should discourage further attempts to mischaracterize his early thought by associating it with bourgeois liberalism.

A handful of Hook's later conservative, liberal, and social democratic admirers have tried to suggest that Hook was always inspired by the same ideals. Paul Kurtz, for example, writes that he was a "lifelong social democrat," a claim that can be made only if Hook's extensive criticism of social democracy over a twenty-year period is ignored. Kurtz's related assertion that "in the nineteen thirties he criticized the rise of fascism, communism, Leninism, Stalinism, and Trotskyism" is equally obfuscatory. Hook always opposed fascism; from 1933 onward he was a relentless critic of Stalinism; but for most of the 1930s he was a critical defender of communism, Leninism, and Trotskyism.[3]

Most of Hook's later conservative, liberal, and social democratic admirers have better understood the fundamental difference between his later and early thought. But though they acknowledge a sharp discontinuity between his early Marxism and his subsequent ideas, they have no real interest in Hook's Marxist days except as a foil for his mature reason. This sort of analysis usually collapses Hook's thought into two moments: Communist and anti-communist. Such a bifurcation does not explain his five years of revolutionary theory and practice after breaking decisively with the Communist Party. To Hook's later admirers, revolution and democracy, communism and freedom, are unavoidably antithetical. They simply cannot imagine the radically egalitarian and participatory society advocated by Hook in his mid-1930s writings on workers' democracy. They cannot conceive of a revolutionary anti-Stalinism opposed to capitalism and bureaucratic collectivism alike.

Sidney Hook is best understood as a casualty in the tragedy of the American left, not a villain or hero in its melodrama. His work of the 1920s and

[3]   Paul Kurtz, preface to *Sidney Hook: Philosopher of Democracy and Humanism* (Buffalo, N.Y.: Prometheus, 1983), x.

1930s is important not as an object lesson of the corrosive dangers of pragmatism or a passing youthful romanticism but as an eloquent elaboration
and defense of revolutionary socialism. His later thought was not the logical consequence of his early views but the antithesis of them. Indeed, the
early Sidney Hook often criticized in high polemical form the very ideas
that he subsequently came to embrace. In his later writings he abandoned
his belief that the working class could legitimately take its destiny into its
own hands despite the imperfectly, if not falsely, "democratic" laws established to protect the private privileges of ruling groups. Discarding his class
analysis of the bourgeois state, reverting to the reformism that he had refuted with care in *Towards the Understanding of Karl Marx,* he arrived at a
truncated, accommodationist vision of democracy that was at best a faint
echo of his earlier radicalism. Finally, Hook came to equate Communism
and fascism, elevating their superficial political similarities to demonstrate
their identity, denying any difference in their social structures and modes
of operation, collapsing both into a monolithic "totalitarianism." He had
inveighed against precisely such an analysis in "Communism without Dogmas," but the combined experience of the Moscow trials, fascist advances,
and looming war led him to forget his earlier logic. Hook put the struggle
for socialism on the back burner, holding an abstractly defined and essentially liberal notion of "freedom" to be the decisive and, for all *practical* purposes, only question of the day. From his admirable refusal to compromise
with Stalinism, Hook made the misguided (from a socialist standpoint)
leap to accepting capitalism as the best practical ally against fascism and
Stalinism. That strategy did not flow inevitably from either his anti-Stalinism or his pragmatism. Hook's early polemics against Stalinism, liberalism,
and social democracy provide all that is needed for a fruitful critique of his
own later position.

In his memoir, *Out of Step,* Hook held that his Marxism of the Great Depression did not foresee, and was therefore outmoded by, the long postwar
boom of capitalist expansion and the burgeoning welfare state. *Towards the
Understanding of Karl Marx,* he liked to say, was published when capitalism
appeared to have exhausted itself. It is true that the young Hook, like many
others of the early and middle 1930s, proclaimed from time to time that
the future involved a stark choice between fascism and communism. In
that he was mistaken. His Marxism, however, was not bound to any conjunctural aspect of his analysis of capitalist crisis. Hook himself had become a revolutionary socialist on the eve of the First World War, long
before the economic trauma of the 1930s. His vigilance against fatalism in
Marxism, including economic determinism, as well as his insistence that
creative and intelligent revolutionary action is the touchstone of Marxism,
were hardly dependent upon the Depression for their merit. One flawed

forecast, moreover, need not discredit Hook's framework, for one of his fundamental premises was that Marxism should revise its understanding in light of experience, which is to say in light of error. Furthermore, Hook's extensive examinations of Marxist intellectual history meant that his understanding of the doctrine's application and meaning was not tied to any particular moment. His Marxism was attuned to the social context of its day, but its theoretical propositions are not bound simplistically by such connections.

If Hook's early thought cannot be limited to the 1930s, neither can it be upheld as a Rosetta Stone for the contemporary crisis of Marxist theory and practice. There is little danger, to be sure, that a renewed appreciation of Hook's early writings might result in hagiography. Now, as it did throughout his career, Hook's work generates more respect than affection, more recognition than devotion. Nonetheless, it is appropriate to caution that his Marxism suffered from the deficiences of its epoch—offering almost nothing pertaining directly to the crucial issues of race and gender, or ecology, which have contributed so much to the enrichment of contemporary social theory. Furthermore, although his concentration on the active, purposive, and practical character of social life was an excellent and necessary corrective to the petrified Marxism of the degenerated Comintern, his emphasis on human agency left him exposed to the danger of moral formalism—a temptation to which he eventually succumbed in his *Southern Review* article on the Russian Revolution, in which he disregarded historical conditions and made the Bolshevik revolutionaries themselves entirely responsible for the Stalinist degeneration. Hook's theoretical weakness in political economy and historical theory left him vulnerable to the idealist assumption that all failings and inadequacies could be explained simply in terms of wrongheaded plans of action. Hook's Marxism need not have foundered upon the reef of moralism, but one ought not turn a blind eye toward its structural weaknesses.

The significance of Hook's revolutionary socialism may be gauged in part by assessing its place in the political and intellectual history of American radicalism. Hook was virtually the only Marxist academic philosopher in the late 1920s and early 1930s, and he was the foremost expert on Marx in a New York intellectual milieu that English historian Eric Hobsbawm calls the "most important Western group of non-Stalinist Marxist intellectuals."[4] Hook's leadership of the American Workers Party and his status as the favorite pupil of John Dewey —architect of what is often characterized as the distinctively American philosophy, pragmatism—make him an ex-

---

[4]   E. J. Hobsbawm, *Echoes of the Marseillaise* (New Brunswick, N.J.: Rutgers University Press, 1990), 135 n. 34.

emplary counterpoint to the Cold War myth that Marxism has never taken and can never take root in American culture. For various reasons, the "American approach" of the AWP did not thrive in its successor organizations, but Hook's thought in the mid-1930s was a refreshing expression of Marxism in the American vernacular which might aid socialists today who seek a radical politics appropriate to an American idiom.

Hook's exploration of Marxism and values, his interpretation of dialectical materialism as experimental naturalism, and his succinct recapitulation of Marx in his influential *Towards the Understanding of Karl Marx* all indicate that American Marxist theory is not as superficial as stereotypes would suggest. Derogation of American Marxism has occurred at the hands of Eurocentric Marxists, both in the United States and in Europe, but it has also issued from those who see American socialism as a failure because of the feebleness of its theory. In his important *Marxian Socialism in the United States* (1952), for example, the sociologist Daniel Bell sought to explain the failure of American revolutionary socialism in part by writing that "such ideas as cultural diversity, or the role of value systems in influencing political behavior, were alien to Marxist thought." Hook shared his generation's inattentiveness to "cultural diversity" in the contemporary multiculturalist association of the term, of course, but his entire early project stands in stark contradiction to Bell's meaning: that American Marxists had given no serious consideration to the relationship between values and political activity.[5]

Perry Anderson's brilliant overview of twentieth-century revolutionary theory, *Considerations on Western Marxism* (1979), offers a useful framework for further situating and evaluating Sidney Hook's early thought. Anderson argues that the defining temperament of Western Marxism, particularly in its mature period after the Second World War, was a deep pessimism brought about by the experience of fascism, the growth and stability of the advanced capitalist economies, and the consolidation of bureaucratic rule in Eastern Europe. Although his Marxism did not endure as long as that of the main figures of Western Marxism, Hook's work more than that of any other American Marxist of the 1920s or 1930s bore the characteristic traits of a Marxism whose primary locus was Italy, Germany, and France. Like the first generation of Western Marxists—including Georg Lukács, Karl Korsch, Antonio Gramsci, Walter Benjamin, Max Horkheimer, and Herbert Marcuse—Hook came of age as a radical during the First World War. Like Lukács, Korsch, and Gramsci, he first became interested in Marxist theory as a young revolutionary socialist activist. Like the Western Marx-

---

[5] Daniel Bell, *Marxian Socialism in the United States* (1952; Ithaca: Cornell University Press, 1996), xli.

ists as a whole, Hook sought to defeat determinism with the aid of a philosophy outside of Marxism—in his case, pragmatism. Like them, he became fixated on issues of philosophy (particularly method and epistemology), displayed considerable interest in the relationship of Hegel to Marx, and wrote little or no social and economic theory. And like most of the Western Marxists, Hook took an academic position that eventually played a part in his withdrawal from revolutionary activism.[6]

Yet the early Hook does not fully fit the characteristic pattern of Western Marxism outlined by Anderson. His ongoing work in researching, translating, and explicating Marx corresponds more to the project of recovering Marx which was undertaken in Europe by an earlier "second" generation of Marxists, notably Kautsky and Plekhanov, the major theorists of German and Russian Social Democracy. Further, Hook displayed a greater level of theoretical internationalism than did most of the Western Marxists, borrowing from and criticizing Lukács and Korsch, traveling to Germany and the Soviet Union and taking up the problems of Nazism and Stalinism in his writings. Hook also differed from Western Marxism stylistically, striving for a crystalline clarity in his prose and adopting an urgency in tone rather than a studied loftiness. Moreover, because of his Deweyan emphasis on radical democracy and his Leninist commitment to revolutionary action, during his Marxist period he never completely severed his ties to organized socialism and was consistently involved in political activity of one sort or another; therefore, he never neglected political theory—as evidenced by his sophisticated writings on workers' democracy and forms of dictatorship—and he did not become consumed by issues of aesthetics and culture, as did the Western Marxists.

Finally, the main line of Hook's political trajectory set him apart from the main current of Western Marxism. According to Anderson, the centrality of Communism on the European left meant that the Western Marxists took two routes: some enrolled in a Communist Party and accepted its political discipline in return for its tolerance of their relatively abstruse theoretical deviations; others remained apart from Communist organization entirely, which freed them from political dictation but also sacrificed their anchorage in the social class to which Marxism was supposedly bound. The American Communist Party was not willing to accord Hook theoretical latitude, and it was unlikely in any case that he would have willingly suppressed his political criticisms in exchange. Nor did he take the second route, however, for his role first as a leader of the AWP and then as a fellow traveler with the Workers Party of the United States and the Socialist Party gave him a practical connection to labor radicalism. This was a frag-

6   See Perry Anderson, *Considerations on Western Marxism* (London: Verso, 1979).

ile link to the working class, however, and he lacked a secure mooring at the time of the labor movement's setbacks in 1938, defeats that occurred as the anti-Stalinist left entered great moral and psychological crisis caused by the Moscow trials. Hook was subject to the same "dialectic of defeat" that shaped the thought of the Western Marxists, but his response took on a different character because of his ingrained commitment to anti-Stalinism, his pragmatist outlook, and his personal disposition to action. Hook was temperamentally unable to develop a detached, gloomy, cultural philosophy like that of the Frankfurt School. Instead, he shifted allegiances and eventually dropped Marxism altogether, turning from anti-Communist radicalism to anti-communist liberalism.[7]

The early Marxism of Sidney Hook therefore falls more in the line of descent of the classical Marxist tradition of Marx, Lenin, and Trotsky than within the Western Marxism developed by his European contemporaries. In contrast to the dominant trend of Western Marxism, for roughly twenty years Hook sustained a connection between theoretical work and revolutionary practice. Furthermore, his emphasis on democracy and experimental flexibility led him to an explicit anti-Stalinism, whereas the Western Marxists, because of the dominance of the Communist Parties in their countries, saw official Communism as the lodestone of all relevant politics and—either through compromise with the Communist Party or by rejecting it and building nothing else in its place—drifted away from political practice. Hook's major themes were not pessimistic ones of isolation, defeat, and despair but affirmative ones of vigorous action, democratic capacity, and revolutionary possibility. He was not a mindless optimist, of course, and he did confront the travesties of fascism and Stalinism directly in his writings. Like Marx, Lenin, and Trotsky, though, Hook always held out the hope of purposive activity and sought historical engagement. Unlike the classical Marxists, however, he was relatively inattentive to historical, economic, and social theory. This meant that his pragmatist philosophy of action was subject to separation from the experience that it claimed to understand. When it encountered historical defeat in the combination of fascism, Stalinism, and war, Hook's Marxism was unable to sustain its radical bearings.

The American left is once again in need of hope to carry it through hard times. The questions that Sidney Hook considered in his writings on revolution and democracy remain vital, and many of the solutions he put forward years ago have remarkable resonance today. A continuation of the habit of bitter denunciation would make it more difficult than ever for rad-

[7] The phrase "dialectic of defeat" was coined by Russell Jacoby; see his *Dialectic of Defeat: Contours of Western Marxism* (Cambridge: Cambridge University Press, 1981).

icals today to absorb the lessons of Hook's experience and appreciate his revolutionary accomplishments. Like a classical tragedy, Hook's story should be experienced as a warning. The greatest strength of his early thought—his insistence on the ability of working people and their allies through democratic and participatory activity to change the world and control their own lives—was twisted, paradoxically, into a flaw when the key concept of democracy in his writings became an abstract standard, stripped of class analysis, with almost exclusively moralistic meaning.

What is living and what is dead in the Marxism of Sidney Hook? The dead we may leave to those, right and left, who have already buried the young Hook on many occasions. The living will be discovered only in action, by testing in further practice the ideas he prematurely abandoned.

Appendix on Sources

Manuscript Collections

Brooklyn College, Archives
　　Harry Slochower Papers
Columbia University, Butler Rare Book and Manuscript Library
　　Imre Kovacs Collection
　　W. W. Norton Collection
　　E. R. A. Seligman Collection
　　Lincoln Steffens Collection
Columbia University, Oral History Research Office
　　"The Reminiscences of Max Shachtman," 1963
Emory University, Robert W. Woodruff Library, Special Collections
　　Theodore Draper Papers
Harvard University, Houghton Library
　　Leon Trotsky Papers
Hoover Institution on War, Revolution, and Peace, Archives, Palo Alto
　　James Burnham Papers
　　Christopher Emmet Papers
　　Sidney Hook Papers
　　Boris Nicolaevsky Collection
　　Karl Popper Papers
　　Herbert Solow Papers
　　Freda Utley Papers
　　Bertram Wolfe Papers

Lilly Library, Indiana University, Bloomington, Indiana
  Arthur Bentley Manuscripts
  Max Eastman Manuscripts
  Leon Harris Manuscripts
  Upton Sinclair Manuscripts
New York Public Library, Rare Books and Manuscripts Divisions
  V. F. Calverton Papers (Astor, Lenox and Tilden Foundations)
New York University, Tamiment Library
  American Committee for Cultural Freedom (ACCF) Records
  Max Shachtman Papers
Southern Illinois University at Carbondale, Morris Library, Special Collections
  John Dewey Papers
  Open Court Publishing Company Records
  Sidney Hook Collection of John Dewey
State Historical Society of Wisconsin
  Socialist Workers Party Papers
University of Massachusetts at Amherst, Special Collections and Archives
  W. E. B. Du Bois Collection
University of Minnesota Library, Manuscripts Division
  George Perrigo Conger Papers
University of Oregon Library, Special Collections
  Robert Cantwell Papers
  James Hancock Rorty Papers
Yale University, Beinecke Rare Book and Manuscript Library, Yale Collection of
    American Literature
  Southern Review Papers
Yale University, Sterling Memorial Library, Manuscripts and Archives Department
  Alan Barth Papers
  Jerome Frank Papers
  Dwight Macdonald Papers

Governmental Files

Federal Bureau of Investigation
  Sidney Hook Files
City Clerk of New York
  Brooklyn Office, Vital Statistics

Personal Collections

Howard Brick, Professor, History Department, Washington University, St. Louis
  Correspondence and interview with Sidney Hook
Alan Wald, Professor, Department of English Literature and Language, University
    of Michigan
  Correspondence with Sidney Hook
Robert Westbrook, Professor, History Department, University of Rochester
  Correspondence with Sidney Hook

Author's Interviews

Abel, Lionel, 14 November, 1996
Garlin, Sender, 9 and 10 May 1992
Hook, Ann, 28 August 1993
Hook, Ernest B., 10 August 1996
Hook, John B., 23 August 1993
Paine, Freddy, 11 July 1996
Poulos, Eric, 12 September 1993
Schapiro, Meyer, 25 October 1993
Sharron, Mark, 28 August 1993
Widick, B. J., 23 March 1992

Index

All books and articles by Sidney Hook, except those listed under other authors' names.

Congress for Cultural Freedom (CCF), 199, 226, 229
Congress of Industrial Organizations (CIO), 180–81, 219
Cooney, Terry, 154n18, 167n40
Cope, Elmer, 110
Cope, Esther, 110
Corey, Lewis, 69, 72, 75; biographical sketch, 164
Cornforth, Maurice, 7n13
Counts, George, 110, 203n4
Cowley, Malcolm, 60, 69, 72, 75–77, 157–60
Crichton, Kyle, 69, 76
Cromwell, Oliver, 178
Crossman, Richard, 59n9
Cullen, Countee, 69
Curti, Merle, 203n4
Czechoslovakia, 218

Darwin, Charles, 125
Davis, Mike, 180–81
Debs, Eugene V., 20, 147
Decter, Midge, 2
De Leon, Daniel, 116, 212
Democracy, 8, 98, 100, 207, 243; bourgeois theories of, 103, 135; revolutionary or workers' theories of, 102–3, 115–22, 147, 173–74, 183
Democratic Party, 146, 162, 180–81, 222
Deutscher, Isaac, 156n21
Dewey, Fred, 155
Dewey, John, 6–7, 45, 54, 60, 72, 82, 92, 97, 99, 138, 146–47, 160n29, 179–80, 199, 202, 203n4, 208, 210–15, 221, 228–29, 239; views of Marx, 55–59; respect for Hook, 28–29; Hook's Marxist criticism of, 103–04; contrast with Cohen, 24–25, 28; relations with Communist Party, 84, 86; views and relations with Trotsky, 157–58, 176, 189–90, 197; action surrounding Moscow Trials, 151–53, 155–59; *Reconstruction in Philosophy* (1920), 27–28; *Liberalism and Social Action* (1935), 132–33; photo, 149. *See also* Pragmatism
Dialectical materialism, 36–38, 42–44, 49, 71, 81–86, 96, 100, 106–7, 124–27, 137, 143–44; Hook's rejection of after 1938, 192
Dictatorship of the proletariat, 107–8, 116–21, 183
Dies, Martin, 203, 209
Dietzgen, Joseph, 53
Diggins, John P., 11, 27n16, 39n36
Djilas, Milovan, 185n64

Don, Sam, 84–85, 86n51, 88
Dos Passos, John, 69, 93, 145, 203n4
Draper, Hal, 162, 186
Draper, Theodore, 32, 50, 67n21
Dreiser, Theodore, 69, 154
Drucker, Peter, 185n64
Du Bois, W. E. B., 72
Dupee, F. W., 205n8
Dunayevskaya, Raya, 189

Eastman, Max, 11n19, 38–44, 64–65, 80n41, 85, 92, 95, 96–100, 107, 145, 147–48, 154, 160, 172, 176, 203n4
Edman, Irwin, 203n4
Education, 57, 172. *See also* Hook, Sidney: teaching career
Einstein, Albert, 125, 153–54
Electric Autolite Company, 112–13
Eliot, T. S., 167
Encyclopedia of the Social Sciences, 53
Engels, Frederick, 35, 53n1, 84, 104; Hook's opinion of, 80
Epistemology, 36–38, 69, 84–85
Erber, Ernest, 162
Espionage, 46, 88n57
Ethics, 134–37, 159–61, 172–79, 181–90, 192–94, 211–12, 239
Ethiopia, 216

Farber, Samuel, 116n39, 180n58
Farmer-Labor Party, 146
Farrell, James T., 13, 147, 151, 155n20, 156, 160, 180, 205n8
Fascism, 45–46, 76–78, 102–3, 106, 125, 147, 151, 159–61, 173, 206, 209, 217–19, 238
Faulkner, William, 167
Federal Bureau of Investigation, 225n38
Feeley, Dianne, 111n31
Feuer, Lewis, 4n6
Feuerbach, Ludwig, 36, 83, 134, 137–38
Field, B. J., 93
Fields, A. Belden, 185n64
Fischer, Louis, 154
Fisk, Milton, 8n14
Foner, Philip S., 116n39
Ford, James W., 69; photo, 70
Foster, William Z., 69, 73–74; photo, 70
Fourth International, 61n12, 92, 114, 119–20. *See also* Trotskyism
Fourth International, 222
France, 136, 216, 218
Franco, Francisco, 216
Frank, Waldo, 69, 71, 77, 204n6

International Communist Opposition, 61n12
Internment of Japanese Americans, 220, 222
Isserman, Maurice, 11n19, 109n28
Italy, 202–3, 216, 218

Jacobson, Julius, 6, 61n12, 141n1, 228n44
Jacoby, Russell, 11, 231
James, C. L. R., 116n39, 220n28
Japan, 202, 216, 220
Jaspars, Karl, 45
Jerome, V. J., 84–86, 90, 123, 224
Jews and Jewishness, 18–20, 23, 33–34, 60, 63, 135, 216–17, 220. See also Anti-Semitism
Johanningsmeier, Edward P., 74n30, 75n31
John Dewey (1939), 211–12
Johnpoll, Bernard K., 145n7
John Reed Clubs, 50, 62, 166
Johnson, Arnold, 110, 122
Johnson, Aurelia Ricci, 110
Johnston, Mary Ann, 110
Josephson, Matthew, 9, 69, 72, 74, 154
Joyce, James, 167

Kafka, Franz, 167
Kaiser, Daniel, 116n39
Kallen, Horace, 203n4
Kamenev, Lev, 148
Kant, Immanuel, 134, 172, 175, 188
Kanter, Emmanuel, 67–68
Katz, Carrie. See Hook, Carrie Katz
Kautsky, Karl, 65, 79, 241; *Terrorism and Communism* (1918), 160
Kazin, Alfred, 19, 100
Keemer, Edgar, 220n28
Kellner, Douglas, 57
Kerr, Charles H., publisher, 68n23
Kirchwey, Freda, 147, 203–4
Kirkpatrick, Jeane, 2
Kissinger, Henry, 2
Klehr, Harvey, 74n30, 75n32, 86n51, 87n55, 114n37
Kloppenberg, James, 7n13, 27n16
Knight, Frank, 184
Kolko, Gabriel, 220n29
Korsch, Karl, 47, 79, 165, 240–41
Kristol, Irving, 2
Krivitsky, W. C., 209
Kronstadt, 178
Kuhn, Celia, 68–69
Kunitz, Joshua, 60

Kurtz, Paul, 4, 237
Kvitko, David, 31, 48, 51, 69

Labor movement, 109–13, 122, 180–81, 186, 219, 221–24, 232
La Follette, Suzanne, 156, 203n4
Laidler, Harry W., 163–64
Lamont, Corliss, 32, 66, 67n21, 87, 154, 164–65, 182, 204, 209n12
Landy, Avram, 84
Lasch, Christopher, 40, 116n39, 229–31
Laski, Harold, 61, 82
Lasky, Melvin J., 205n8
Law, 102, 172, 177–79
Lawson, John Howard, 141–42
League against Totalitarianism, 202
League against War and Fascism, 202
League for Cultural Freedom and Socialism, 205–7, 218
League for Industrial Democracy, 163
League of American Writers, 91, 202, 218
League of Professional Groups, 72–77, 90–91, 110, 128n57, 158; *Culture and the Crisis* (1932), 72–74, 146–48
Le Blanc, Paul, 116n39, 187n69
Left Opposition. See Trotskyism
Lenin, V. I., 37–38, 54, 64, 80–81, 87, 104, 111, 176–79, 191, 212–13, 228, 242; *Materialism and Empirio-Criticism* (1908), 31, 36–37, 51, 81, 89; *The State and Revolution* (1917), 22, 195; *What is to Be Done?* (1902), 65, 71–72, 81, 89
Leninism, 115–17, 191–96, 237; distinguished from or connected to Stalinism, 115–16n39, 171–72, 182; Hook's reconsideration and repudiation of, 182–86. See also Soviet Union
Lerner, Max, 60, 154, 204n6
LeSeuer, Meridel, 204n6
Lewin, Moshe, 116n39
Liberalism, 8, 101–4, 133, 159–61, 230
"Liberalism and the Case of Leon Trotsky" (1937), 160–61
Lipow, Arthur, 185n64
Literature, 167–68. See also Aesthetics
Lobkowicz, Nicholas, 57
Loeb, Harold, 177
London, Jack, 20
Longfellow, Henry, 167
Lore, Ludwig, 110, 113
Lovejoy, Arthur, 203n4
Lovestone, Jay, 61, 112, 186. See also Right Opposition
Lovett, Robert Morss, 147, 204n6

Oehler, Hugo, 145n7
O'Neill, William, 39n36, 99n11
"On Workers' Democracy" (1934), 117–18, 183, 207
"Our Country and Our Culture" (1952), 230
Out of Step (1987), 5, 12, 93n3, 96n7, 115, 238
Overstreet, Harry, 25, 87, 203n4

Pacifism, 178, 211
Paine, Freddy Drake, 127n56, 128
Parenti, Michael, 6
Partisan Review, 161, 166–71, 186, 196, 202, 205, 218, 221–25, 230–31
Pass, Joseph, 76, 84
Patchen, Kenneth, 205n8
Patriotism, 214
Patterson, William, 73
Paul, Saint, 53, 176
Pells, Richard, 39n36
Perelman, S. J., 204n6
Phenomenology, 45, 53
Phillips, William, 10–13, 166, 168, 169n43, 205n8, 231
"A Philosophical Dialogue" (1922), 25
Philosophy. *See* Aesthetics; Dialectical materialism; Epistemology; Ethics; Historical materialism; Marxism; Pragmatism
"The Philosophy of Dialectical Material-ism" (1928), 35–38
"The Philosophy of Non-Resistance" (1922), 25
"The Philosophy of Technics in the USSR" (1934), 123–27
Piatakov, G. L., 157–58
Piven, Frances Fox, 111n31
Plekhanov, Georgi, 83, 216, 241
Podhoretz, Norman, 14, 167–68n42
Pokrovsky, M. N., 62–63
Poland, 205, 218
Pollack, Sam, 112
Popular Front, 122, 147, 151, 162, 166–68, 202–5, 215–18, 222–24; distin-guished from united front, 224
Porter, Paul, 145
Pound, Ezra, 167
Pragmatism, 26–27, 29–30; Cohen's objec-tions to, 24; compatibility with Marxism, 6–9, 36–44, 54–59, 67–68, 82–89, 97–100, 103–4, 138–39, 172–74, 179, 186–87n67, 196–97, 211–15, 228–30, 234–37

Pragmatism and the Tragic Sense of Life (1974), 231
Preis, Art, 112, 127n56
Preliminary Commission of Inquiry into the Charges Made against Leon Trotsky in the Moscow Trials, 153, 155
Proletarian Party, 68n23
Provisional Commission of Inquiry into the Charges Made against Leon Trotsky in the Moscow Trials, 153, 155
Psychology, 40. *See also* Freud, Sigmund

The Quest for Being (1961), 231

Rahv, Philip, 11–12, 155n20, 166, 168, 169n43, 181–82, 205n8, 231
Rakovsky, Christian, 184n64
Ramuglia, Anthony, 110, 122
Ratner, Joseph, 48
Reagan, Ronald, 1–3
Reason, Social Myths and Democracy (1940), 199, 212–15, 225
Reed, John, 116n39
"Reflections on the Russian Revolution" (1939), 191–95, 213
Reich, Wilhelm, 40
Religion, 126, 134–35, 137–38, 221. *See also* Christianity; Jews and Jewishness
Revolution, 175. *See also* Marx, Karl; Lenin, V.I.; Soviet Union; Trotsky, Leon
Rexroth, Kenneth, 205n8
Rhineland, 218
Riazanov, David, 47–48
Right Opposition, 61, 64–65, 112, 165, 186
Rivera, Diego, 93, 155; photo, 150
Rizzi, Bruno, 185n64
Robinson, Jo Ann, 109n28
Rodman, Selden, 176–77
Roosevelt, Franklin Delano, 78, 180, 217, 224. *See also* New Deal
Rorty, James, 5, 44–45, 69, 72–73, 77, 90–91, 110, 127, 147, 205n8, 203n4
Rorty, Richard, 8n13, 26n16
Rosenberg, Harold, 12, 205n8
Rovere, Richard, 227
Rudas, Lásló, 106–7
Ruehle, Otto, 156
Ruge, Arnold, 134–35
Russell, Bertrand, 22–23, 61, 92, 100–104, 154
Russia. *See* Soviet Union

Sacco, Nicola, 31, 177–78
Saturday Review, 163, 171